Early Praise for *From Objects to Functions*

Rather than a reference about how to write a pure functional web application, this book is more about interesting ideas gathered from the author's field experience that an intermediate/experienced developer can analyze and re-use.

➤ **Simone Bordet**
   Lead, Eclipse Jetty

Uberto has amazingly managed to distill his extensive knowledge of real-world Kotlin into 400 clear, concise, and engaging pages. It's definitely not a book for the faint of heart—those who dare should prepare for a fascinating ride as he covers a wide range of concepts both new and established!

➤ **David Denton**
   Co-creator, http4k

This book is a concentration of good programming practices embedded in the functional paradigm. It helps you to rethink your API design as an algebra using functional patterns, highlighting all the benefits of functional programming as referential transparency, immutability, composition, reusability, and simplicity. It also gives you hints and references to good practices—starting from capturing requirements in User Stories to thinking from the start about how to deploy the software, creating a walking skeleton—and it shows that Kotlin helps with writing not only object-oriented code but also functional code.

➤ **Riccardo Fallico**
   Technology Service Specialist, Aviva Italia Servizi Scarl

This is a nice approach for practical application of functional programming; the book shows that it is not the theoretical and academic gibberish most people think it is. The focus is on functional programming, but you can learn some nice tricks about Kotlin on the way, even for those who are not experts on the language.

➤ **Carlos García Ibáñez**
   Engineering Manager, Telefonica Digital

Reading this book is like coding alongside Uberto. You come to learn what the fuss is about functional programming, and you leave with a blueprint and a bunch of techniques that you will use to build backend services for the next ten years.

➤ **Gabriele Lana**
   Software Craftsman, CleanCode

This is not an easy book, but it is an important book. Unlike most works on the topic it doesn't reject objects, but instead shows how objects and functions can be combined in a coherent way. It rewards rereading with more insights—I will be keeping it handy to return to as my understanding grows.

➤ **Duncan McGregor**
   Co-author, *Java to Kotlin: A Refactoring Guidebook*

This book is packed with practices learned from applying functional programming in real-world, business-critical, Kotlin projects. It deserves, and rewards, detailed study.

➤ **Nat Pryce**
   Co-author, *Java to Kotlin: A Refactoring Guidebook*

An amazing introduction and walkthrough of the functional paradigms and coding techniques required when using functional programming. This book is a must read for all developers who want to begin their journey and a good refresher for those experts on some of the more complex topics.

➤ **Jayesh Shavdia**
   Managing Director, Barclays

From Objects to Functions offers a comprehensive guide to functional programming, seamlessly blending theory and practice. By exploring the practical applications of the functional paradigm and building a real-world application using http4k, PostgreSQL, and Exposed, readers will gain a deep understanding of the power and potential of functional programming.

➤ **Simon Vergauwen**
   Maintainer, Arrow-kt.io

From Objects to Functions

Build Your Software Faster and Safer
with Functional Programming and Kotlin

Uberto Barbini

The Pragmatic Bookshelf

Dallas, Texas

For our complete catalog of hands-on, practical, and Pragmatic content for software developers, please visit *https://pragprog.com*.

The team that produced this book includes:

CEO: Dave Rankin
COO: Janet Furlow
Managing Editor: Tammy Coron
Development Editor: Adaobi Obi Tulton
Copy Editor: Karen Galle
Indexing: Potomac Indexing, LLC
Layout: Gilson Graphics
Founders: Andy Hunt and Dave Thomas

For sales, volume licensing, and support, please contact *support@pragprog.com*.

For international rights, please contact *rights@pragprog.com*.

ISBN-13: 978-1-68050-845-1
Book version: P1.0—September 2023

Contents

Acknowledgments ix

Preface xi

Introduction: Why Functional Programming? xvii

1. Preparing a New Application 1
   Defining the Sample Application   1
   Zettai: An Innovative To-Do List Application   3
   Letting Tests Guide Development   8
   Setting Up the Project   12
   Making Unit Tests Functional   13
   Recap   17
   Exercises   18

2. Handling HTTP Using Functions 21
   Kicking Off the Project   21
   Serving HTML Pages Functionally   23
   Starting Zettai   28
   Designing with Arrows   33
   Serving Lists from a Map   37
   Recap   40
   Exercises   40

3. Defining the Domain and Testing It 43
   Improving the Acceptance Tests   43
   Using Higher-Order Functions   51
   Separating the Domain from the Infrastructure   53
   Driving the Tests from the Domain   57
   Converting DDT to Pesticide   60
   Recap   68
   Exercises   69

4.   **Modeling the Domain and the Adapters** **73**

     Starting a New Story to Modify a List   73

     Using Functional Dependency Injection   82

     Debugging Functional Code   90

     Functional Domain Modeling   92

     Recap   102

     Exercises   103

5.   **Using Events to Modify the State** **107**

     Creating and Displaying To-Do Lists   107

     Storing the State Changes   112

     Unleashing the Power of Recursion   116

     Folding Events   121

     Discovering the Monoid   125

     Recap   126

     Exercises   127

6.   **Executing Commands to Generate Events** **131**

     Creating a New List   131

     Using Commands to Change the State   135

     Modeling the Domain with States and Events   136

     Writing Functional State Machines   144

     Connecting the Hub   149

     Understanding Commands and Events Better   153

     Recap   155

     Exercises   155

7.   **Handling Errors Functionally** **157**

     Handling Errors Better   157

     Learning Functors and Categories   163

     Using Functors to Handle Errors   171

     Working with Outcomes   173

     Recap   181

     Exercises   181

8.   **Using Functors to Project Events** **185**

     Projecting Our Events   185

     Running Queries on Functors   193

     Thinking in Terms of Functors   197

     Command and Query Responsibility Segregation (CQRS)   200

Recap 201
Exercises 201

9. **Using Monads to Persist Data Safely** 205
Persisting Safely 205
Connecting to the Database with Kotlin 210
Accessing Remote Data in a Functional Way 221
Exploring the Power of Monads 225
Recap 234
Exercises 235

10. **Reading Context to Handle Commands** 237
Accessing the Database with Monads 237
Handling Commands with Context Reader 245
Querying Projections from Database 250
Modeling the Domain with Event Sourcing 258
Recap 259
Exercises 259

11. **Validating Data with Applicatives** 263
Renaming a List 263
Transforming Functions with Two Parameters 273
Validating with Validations 276
Combining Applicative Functors 283
Improving the User Interface 293
Recap 299
Exercises 299

12. **Monitoring and Functional JSON** 301
Monitoring Our Application 301
Structured Logging 314
Making JSON Functional 318
Meeting Profunctors 323
Logging Database Calls 327
Recap 329
Exercises 329

13. **Designing a Functional Architecture** 331
Chasing Simplicity 331
Designing a Whole System 339
Translating to Code 343

Final Considerations   347
Exercises   348

A1. **What Is Functional Programming?** **349**
The Origins   349
Achieving Referential Transparency   355
Think in Morphisms   360
Recap   368

A2. **About Functional Kotlin** **371**
Setting Up Kotlin   371
Kotlin 101   374
Exploring the Kotlin Type System   387

A3. **A Pinch of Theory** **391**
Category Theory   391
It's All About Morphisms   400
Types over Types   403
Functors Are Mappers   406
The Mysterious Monad   410
Connecting Everything with Yoneda   412
Conclusion   415

A4. **Additional Resources** **417**
Programming   417
Category Theory   418

Bibliography **421**
Index **423**

Acknowledgments

Writing a book during a world pandemic and then a relocation to the other side of the world hasn't been without its challenges. This book wouldn't have been possible without the unwavering patience, support, and love of my wife Ayumi.

I am immensely grateful to my daughter Marina for reminding me often that there are more important things in life than writing books, such as building a dollhouse under her strict supervision.

I also wish to extend my thanks to my friends and colleagues: Asad Manji for his patience and insightful early review of each chapter, and in no particular order Nat Pryce, Duncan McGregor, David Denton, Ivan Sanchez, Dmitry Kandalov, Luca Minudel, Marco Heimeshoff, and Kirk Pepperdine for engaging in fruitful discussions and sharing their valuable knowledge. A special thanks goes to the beta-reader, Yonatan Karp-Rudin, who verified all the exercises and checked for inconsistencies between the code and the text.

The book's reviewers also deserve recognition for their significant contributions. Without their feedback, the book would have been much less impactful. I'd like to express my special appreciation to Jayesh Shavdia, Gabriele Lana, Simone Bordet, Giovanni Asproni, Mani Sarkar, Riccardo Fallico, Carlos García Ibáñez, Juan Pablo Santos Rodríguez, Arialdo Martini, and Matteo Vaccari for their praises and constructive criticism. Furthermore, I am indebted to Alberto Brandolini for teaching me about Event Storming and the DDD approach.

A special thanks to Ted Neward and J. B. Rainsberger for their invaluable support and encouragement during the initial phase of my book project. Their insights about the publishing industry were instrumental in helping me turn my idea into a reality.

Finally, thanks to Dave Rankin and Erica Sadun from Pragmatic Programmers for their help and enthusiasm on this project, and extra special thanks to Adaobi Obi Tulton for brushing up my unconnected phrases into fluent English and guiding me through the publishing process.

Preface

Functional programming makes my job more pleasant every day, even if it drives me crazy sometimes.

Learning about the functional style has profoundly changed how I design my applications; not only that, but it also made programming fun again. So my aim here is to write the book that I wished I'd read when I started learning functional programming.

I ended up as a developer by chance; I learned programming by writing video games in BASIC, and then I started writing small programs as a part-time job when studying philosophy at my university. At that time, I was writing a lot of (horrible) code and having a lot of fun. I didn't know anything about object-oriented principles, design patterns, and other such things. Still, my code worked, which was magic enough for me.

Around the year 2000, I started working on bigger projects and discovered automatic tests. This was a revelation for me, and it pushed me to study computer science more seriously. Once I learned more, my programs became more maintainable but also more complicated. I struggled more with writing code. This somehow removed the fun out of my job, but I told myself that I was a more "professional" programmer.

Then at some point, I decided to pursue simplicity and productivity over abstract principles, and started having fun again. With this book, I want to show how it's possible to use a functional design style and still have fun writing applications. In other words, this is a book written by a developer writing code every day for the benefit of other people like him.

As an industry, I think we need to improve the quality of the software we write. Functional programming isn't a silver bullet,[1] but it can help reduce the amount of work needed to deliver value to the business.

---

1. https://en.wikipedia.org/wiki/No_Silver_Bullet

Still, quality alone can't give us good velocity, but it can provide us with speed. To transform it into velocity, we also need direction. Without direction, we may build the perfect software only to find that it was not what our business needed.

About This Book

The main goal isn't to present original ideas or novel techniques but to show an easy way to learn and use functional thinking in your day-to-day work. I hope that the diagrams and explanations in this book will help you understand how it's possible to effectively eliminate mutable state and side effects by relying on functional programming constructs.

However, I don't think that functional programming itself is the ultimate goal. Rather, the goal is to quickly construct robust and adaptable software, and I believe functional programming, together with tests and domain exploration, is the best tool to accomplish this. Nevertheless, I'm not interested in functional programming just for the sake of it. If a partially functional solution performs better than a purely functional one, I wouldn't hesitate to suggest the former.

That being said, this book isn't exclusively about functional programming. As one of the reviewers accurately put it, this is a book on how to write better software using functional programming and other best practices, as per my personal experience in coding for over two decades. You may have different ideas about some of the code presented here; I think this is perfectly fine. I hope to pass on the idea of how to design software in a functional way, not to dictate the exact patterns that you should follow.

To me, this book is like a journey, and much like any adventure, there are many side quests that the hero (that will be you) needs to complete before advancing with the main mission.

For this reason, in this book, we'll also cover how to transform user stories into high-level tests to verify them. We'll look at other good practices for delivering a successful project. Even if they may not seem related to functional programming at first, they are part of the whole functional approach to writing applications, of which writing code is only a part.

I am aware of the possibility of covering too many topics without diving deeply enough into each one, making everybody unhappy. Nonetheless, I believe it's important to explore all the aspects of software development to show how to build software in a functional way. While I may not succeed in every area, it won't be for a lack of effort.

Who Should Read This Book

This is a book aimed at intermediate and expert programmers. I'll try to introduce each new concept, but this book takes many things for granted. But it should be possible to read this book without knowing Kotlin—it should be enough to know Java, C#, or a similar language.

When writing this book, I kept three categories of readers in mind:

- Seasoned developers with a solid background in object-oriented programming that are interested in knowing more about functional programming and its benefits

- Beginners to functional programming who struggle to translate the classic textbook example into a full application

- Programmers proficient in functional programming in other languages, such as Scala or F#, who are interested in Kotlin

However, a word of caution: I don't expect that you can fully understand the concepts behind this book without studying the code and undertaking at least some of the exercises. You might manage it, but personally, I know I wouldn't be able to.

How to Read This Book

In an effort to keep this book light and concise while maintaining clarity, some detailed explanations and interesting topics had to be left out. If you find yourself unsure about how something works, please refer to the included code.

In any case, for feedback or clarifications, you can always contact me through social media:

Twitter: https://twitter.com/ramtop

Medium: https://medium.com/@ramtop

LinkedIn: https://www.linkedin.com/in/uberto/

Mastodon: https://mastodon.online/@ramtop

Here are some suggestions to get the most out of this book.

The introduction aims to address the question of why using functional programming can be a good idea. However, if you are new to functional programming, it's recommended that you start by reading Appendix 1, What Is Functional Programming?, on page 349, first. This appendix provides a brief history of functional programming and presents practical examples of its principles to give you a clearer understanding of what functional programming is all about.

If you don't know (much) about Kotlin, you can refer at any moment to Appendix 2, About Functional Kotlin, on page 371, to better understand Kotlin syntax, comparing it with Java. It concentrates on Kotlin's functional idioms used in the rest of the book. Please remember that this book isn't a complete tutorial on Kotlin or the JVM. If you want a more complete—and fun-to-read—introduction to the Kotlin language from the ground up, I suggest *Programming Kotlin* by Venkat Subramaniam.

Chapters 1 through 12 are the core of the book, and they'll show how we can progressively build an application following functional design. They start gradually, but as our application progresses, we'll cover advanced concepts like monads, applicatives, and profunctors.

The idea is that reading the chapters in order will help you understand the process of building a complete application. For this reason you'll find the code from the book repository split into different steps that align with the progression of the chapters.

Steps 1 to 5 contain the code of the application as it appears every two chapters, from Chapter 2 to Chapter 10. Step 6 corresponds to Chapter 11, and step 7 corresponds to Chapter 12.

Still, if you aren't interested in some parts, it should be possible to skip to the next chapter. Each chapter starts with an explanation of what we'll focus on and ends with a recap of what we've discussed.

Each chapter in this book concludes with exercises designed to help you understand functional principles and verify your functional insight. Based on my experiences as both a teacher and a student, I believe the mastery of functional programming truly comes with a lot of practice. These exercises are especially beneficial when you find something hard to grasp. Writing and playing with code until it fully clicks is the best way to master any new concept. In the book's repository, you'll also find solutions for all exercises. You can compare your solutions with mine, keeping in mind that my approach isn't necessarily the best one.

The final chapter, Chapter 13, Designing a Functional Architecture, on page 331, is about how to design and build a complete software architecture spanning multiple services using a functional approach. It can be read independently from the previous chapters, and it has a higher-level perspective than they do.

Finally, if you are interested in understanding more about the theory behind functional programming, Appendix 3, A Pinch of Theory, on page 391, has an introduction to category theory. Appendix 4, Additional Resources, on page 417, contains some suggestions on where to find material to study this fascinating field further and help you better understand it.

Dear reader, if reading this book makes you smile and learn new things, just like I did while writing it, then I'll consider it a success.

There is no secret ingredient.
       Kung Fu Panda

Introduction: Why Functional Programming?

If you are a programmer used to object-oriented or procedural style, learning functional programming is nothing short of rewiring your brain. It's a daunting task with an exceptional reward: you'll be able to write better code with less effort.

But I don't want to scare you! When I was a kid, my grandma used to show me how to do origami. It was like magic. I couldn't believe that you could create such a beautiful crane out of a sheet of paper without a pair of scissors or any glue. But once you learn, creating origami isn't that difficult.

Functional programming is like doing origami—you start with something plain and then apply transformation over transformation until you get the shape you were looking for. There is even an operation called fold!

Before starting, we should ask ourselves why we want to learn about functional programming. Is it only a passing hype or a curiosity? There is nothing wrong with curiosity. On its own it's a good reason to learn something new, but I think functional programming is much more than that. Adopting the functional paradigm in our way of coding can really improve productivity and make us better programmers, for almost any definition of better.

What using functional programming gives us is the ability to break the logic of our code into simple computation elements—the pure functions we'll discuss soon—and then be able to combine them as if they were mathematical operations to obtain our goals. This is very different from how we write procedural code or do object-oriented programming.

The proof of the pudding is in the eating, as they say, and the proof of functional programming is in the coding. This book will teach you an approach that will allow you to solve business problems in less time by writing better code, meaning code that's easier to change and understand. In my own experience, writing functional code significantly increased my productivity while also being more fun.

Once you start thinking in a functional way, you won't look at any code in the same way as before. Even when not strictly using functional programming, learning it will give you powerful abstraction concepts to combine your data and your functions as if they were algebra.

But don't be afraid if you never liked algebra in school—as in my case—this is nothing like solving torturous and boring expressions. It's a journey to discover a new way of thinking, and your journey starts here.

We'll start introducing functional concepts gradually and as we use them we can progress with more advanced concepts. What we really care about is learning a new, effective way to code, that is, to bring value to our business. We'll mention some math theory, but we'll concentrate on things that can effectively help us in our day-to-day work.

Why Kotlin?

Eric Normand, expert software developer, teacher, and advocate of functional programming, says the key to doing functional programming is recognizing it as a paradigm and not as a set of features:[1]

> When people say they are doing functional programming what they mean is that they sprinkle reduce and map around and they use some pure functions. There's a lot of value in that. But otherwise their code is procedural. They have not learned the paradigm, only the features.

This book is about learning functional paradigm and using it in your daily work. While examples in Lisp or Haskell could have made this book much shorter, there are two compelling reasons against it:

- If the goal is to introduce functional programming to developers who are unfamiliar with it, a purely functional language would be a poor choice for didactic reasons. They would have to learn a new language first, and then become fluent enough in it to be able to apply the same principles to their main language. As much as I love learning new languages, I think that converting some procedural code to a functional version of the same is a more effective method. If you want to learn more, I highly recommend the study of a pure functional language, or even better, more than one.

---

1.   https://lispcast.com/fp-in-my-language/

- I am not convinced that a language that forces you to always use a completely functional paradigm is the optimal solution for every problem. I believe that using a mixed paradigm language is a better and more pragmatic option for most day-to-day programming tasks.

So why choose Kotlin out of all possible mixed-paradigm languages? Well, nothing is perfect in this world, but Kotlin is kind of a "Goldilocks language" that allows us to get most of the benefits of both functional and object-oriented programming. It has a smoother learning curve than Scala or Clojure and an easier integration with Java libraries. In addition, its type system is more functional friendly than Java's, and a few other nice features make it quite productive.

Finally, at least for me, Kotlin is a really fun language to work with. It's a language that naturally helps you where you need assistance and gets out of the way when you just want to write things down.

Joe asks:
Should I Know Kotlin Before Reading This Book?

You don't need to be proficient in Kotlin, but there is a lot of code in this book, so if you don't know it yet, you may want to learn it while advancing through this book. If you already know Java or a similar language—like C#—it shouldn't be too hard.

You can also look at Appendix 2 on page 371 to learn how to set up a Kotlin environment and for comparison between Kotlin code and the corresponding Java one.

In this book, we won't use existing functional programming libraries for Kotlin. Instead, we'll build our own library as the book progresses. In this way, we can progressively adopt a functional approach in the course of the book, going along with the grain of the language.[2]

What Functional Programming Is Really About

Since it has become a mainstream concept, functional programming means different things for different people. You'll find that definitions of what functional programming is are a dime a dozen, but, at the end of the day, the only thing that matters is *referential transparency*.

Referential transparency is a very simple but powerful concept: if within the code you're looking at you can replace any expression with its corresponding

---

2. https://wiki.c2.com/?GrainOfTheLanguage

value without changing the program behavior, then that code is referentially transparent and, consequently, functional.

If you can write code in this way, then you are a functional programmer, no matter the language or the libraries you use. We haven't defined what "expression" and "program behavior" are, yet. We'll do it later, but what is important here is to keep in mind that there is a very simple way to determine if some code is functional or not; you don't even need to fully understand how it works. If you can replace all the expressions with their values, then the code is functional; if not, it's not.

All the other things you may have heard of, like functors, higher-order functions, monads, and applicatives, are just tools—useful tools, but only tools. We'll cover them in this book, but using them won't make your code more functional and you can write functional code without using them.

So why do we need them at all? As we'll see, it can be challenging to keep most of our code functional—much to the joy of the publishing industry, given the multitude of books on this subject—and they are extremely useful tools.

We'll learn how to use them in the course of this book.

Is Re-Use Really Overrated?

Adopting functional programming will give us a code base with many small functions and data structures, each with a clear intent and without hidden side effects. This way, it would be possible to re-use the same functions in different places and combine them together to generate new behaviors rather than writing new code every time.

Code re-use is notoriously difficult. Some people even consider it overrated,[3] but as much as I agree on many points that Matteo Vaccari makes, I think code re-use (when done right) can make us more effective.

I'm not talking about something like, "Let's create a huge framework with all possible features and let's use it everywhere." Actually I'm advocating for the opposite: let's write simple, well-defined functions that can be re-used with no strings attached. Functional programming, with its emphasis on pure functions and immutable types, makes this much easier.

> I think the lack of reusability comes in object-oriented languages, not functional languages. Because the problem with object-oriented languages is they've got all

---

3.　http://matteo.vaccari.name/blog/archives/151

this implicit environment that they carry around with them. You wanted a banana but what you got was a gorilla holding the banana and the entire jungle.

—Joe Armstrong, creator of the Erlang language

This is arguably the main productivity boost that functional programming can give you: code that's easy to write, easy to read, and easy to re-use.

Unlearning Object-Oriented Programming

Often the hardest part of learning a new thing is to unlearn our old habits. There is nothing wrong with object-oriented programming in itself, but functional programming is a different paradigm that requires a different eye to look at things.

The goal isn't to forget object-oriented programming, but you need to put it aside when learning a new paradigm. It's easy to fall into the trap of writing code the same way; moreover, at the beginning, some things may feel strange or wrong.

Here are some examples of such differences.

Focus on Data Transformations Instead of Subjects and Actions

In designing object-oriented programs, it's natural to design a system looking at the names and verbs we use to describe it. For example, we can think of a series of actions of type: when X then A does Y. We're concentrating on what A can do and how we can call A; a good guess would be to start writing a class A with a method Y, and so on.

If we want to use functional programming, it's more important to look at our data—that is, the inputs and outputs of the whole system—and how it changes during the process. Identifying each transformation will provide the first guess at the functions and data structures we need.

Create Objects without Methods

Using a hybrid language like Kotlin, we'll write and use objects—in the sense of class instances—even when writing code in functional programming style. It's also natural to write methods instead of stand-alone functions to make the code easier to read. But it's not a problem if they don't have any.

Contrastingly, in object-oriented programming, having many classes with all public fields without any methods—that is, they have state but not behavior—is usually considered a bad smell, the so-called *anemic objects* antipattern.

In functional programming, this is quite normal. Since the objects are immutable and their fields are public, they don't need a behavior; any function can directly read what it needs from them.

What we should avoid are classes with a mutable state, using var properties or classes that can be changed by inheritance; we won't use any open classes (see Classes, on page 380) in this book.

Avoid Unnecessary Interfaces

In object-oriented languages—particularly in statically typed ones—it's common to define an interface to allow objects to collaborate with each other without relying on the concrete class implementations. Interfaces serve as contracts that govern interactions between classes. Although interfaces are preferable to direct class-to-class knowledge, there remains an element of dependency.

In functional programming, it's preferable to avoid declaring an interface at all, and instead let classes depend only on the signatures of the functions they need. In this way, any function with the same signature would work—it can be a class method or a lambda—without forcing us to implement an interface.

We'll still use interfaces when two objects need to collaborate following some kind of protocol made by multiple calls; in this case, interfaces would allow us to abstract on the protocol itself.

Don't Be Afraid of Complicated Generic Types

Languages that use generic types—like Java and C#—usually only apply one or two simple type parameters. The functional practice of using types created with many generic parameters is often seen as a sign of excessive complexity.

As we'll see in Generics Are Type Builders, on page 168, we should instead start thinking of generics as type builders. A List<T> isn't a type in itself, but it's something that allows us to generate all the specialized types we need. From this point of view, having four or five different generic variables in our definition isn't a big issue, as it's generally acceptable to have a constructor with four or five parameters.

On the other hand, if we finish having defined twenty or so parameters, then we should probably have done something different.

Recap

In this introduction, we presented the main actors of this book, Kotlin and functional programming. We considered which benefits they can bring us, and we looked at the biggest differences between functional and object-oriented code.

To better understand what functional programming really is, we'll explore the topic more in depth in the first appendix with some reference to the history of programming.

If you prefer to start writing code before reading the theory, in the next chapter, we'll start building a full application, putting all these principles to use with a concrete example to understand how they work together and support each other.

"Everything will turn out right, the world is built on that."
> *Mikhail Bulgakov, The Master and Margarita*

CHAPTER 1

Preparing a New Application

This book will show that the functional approach isn't limited to how we write code. To see it working from a broader perspective, we'll write a complete application from scratch to discover how the functional approach starts at the requirements collection phase and guides us safely to the final delivery.

Why is this? Can't I just teach you about functional programming without all the other stuff? Well, there are other books that already do that, and probably better than I could possibly do. My goal with this book isn't to explain functional programming in itself. I want to show you how to write a complete application step-by-step using the functional approach and, in all honesty, I don't know how to do that without writing a full application.

In this chapter, we begin building our application by gathering just enough requirements to start coding it. Defining the behavior as inputs and outputs will make it easier later to check that we have accomplished what we intended.

We'll also look at how tests can guide our design and start laying down the foundation of automatic testing for our project. Even if it may seem unnecessary, it's better to start it at the beginning; otherwise, when our application becomes more complicated, it will be difficult to adopt a test-driven style.

Regarding Kotlin code, every time we introduce a new language feature, a reference will point to the explanation of its specific syntax and use in Appendix 2, About Functional Kotlin, on page 371.

Defining the Sample Application

> The biggest cause of failure in software-intensive systems isn't technical failure; it's building the wrong thing.
>
> —*Implementing Lean Software Development: From Concept to Cash [PP06]*

We introduced the principles of functional programming and why they are important in the introduction. It's now time to leave the realm of pure theory and get our hands dirty. We want to build a complete application, but we can't start typing code right now. We first need to define what our application will do.

What kind of application should we build? It should be a not-too-big, kind of realistic application, something you would typically be asked to write for a company. All in all, a web application would work very well.

It's certainly possible to use the functional approach to write, say, mobile or desktop applications, but web applications are better suited for learning the new paradigm. They are very widely understood and are a perfect fit for functional programming since, ultimately, they are based on transforming a request into a response.

But you don't need to worry! Once you've learned the principles of functional programming, you'll be able to put them into practice on any kind of application: mobile, desktop, video games, and so on.

Imagining a New Product

I'm a very easily distracted person, so to improve my productivity and keep focus, I often write down to-do lists on a scrap of paper before starting something. Writing things down helps me stay focused on what the next steps are.

I've also tried to use applications to manage my to-do lists. It usually goes like this:

1. I write down a list of things.
2. While I'm progressing on that list, I start writing other lists.
3. After a while I have too many lists, and I can't see what's urgent and what's not, so I write urgent items down on a scrap of paper...

It would be useful to see all the items that are due soon from all the lists.

Another common issue is that I'm blocked from completing some items because I'm waiting for something—for example, a quote from a plumber. I'd like a way to know all the items that are pending for more than a given time, so I can recheck them.

Finally, I'd like to be able to see the whole history of a list: when I changed something and what exactly I changed.

So let's try to write a to-do list application that can help me, and people like me, stay focused!

Zettai: An Innovative To-Do List Application

Now, let's pick a name for our application. We'll call it Zettai (pronounced zet-TAHY) because it sounds nice, and it means "for sure" in Japanese, as in "I would do it for sure."

In the spirit of the Lean approach,[1] we'll define our requirements at the last possible moment, collect feedback, and learn from our implementation before proceeding with the next one.

What does this mean? Instead of writing a comprehensive list of requirements beforehand, we'll focus on the minimum set of features that will allow us to deliver some value. In the context of Zettai, that value will enable us to solve at least one of the problems previously listed.

The goal is to define the minimum set of features that would allow us to engage with the user and learn what our product should look like. We can specify these features by writing down some user stories.

Defining Our User Stories

User stories are very useful tools in Agile software development. They are a way to capture the description of a software feature from the user perspective. In the words of Rachel Davies:

> A user story starts out as an idea, like an egg. The idea hatches a conversation, through which the idea grows and changes shape, like a caterpillar. The conversation converges into specific test cases, like the formation of a chrysalis. These test cases contain what the software needs to do, and the software takes shape, enclosed by the story tests. Finally, working software emerges, like a beautiful butterfly. The cycle comes full circle after the software generates user feedback and new ideas.
>
> —*Agile Coaching [DS09]*

---

1.   http://theleanstartup.com/principles

In our case, since we're both the customer and the developer, we'll try to keep the roles separate.

A story must include the who, what, and why of the feature. It usually includes one or more scenarios describing possible outcomes of the same feature. For example, what happens if the to-do list doesn't exist or if the user wants to modify a list already "closed," and so on?

It also has to present a clear definition of when it can be considered finished and how we can verify it. But it shouldn't contain details of the interface or technical details; the story should stay concentrated on what the user wants to do, not on the technology.

Any to-do list software must allow users to write down and modify their lists. At the very minimum, users should be able to do the following:

1. See a single list
2. Create a new list with a name and a description
3. See all their lists
4. Add an item to a list with description and optional due date
5. Modify the name or the description of a list
6. Mark an item as "done" or "in progress," and edit the description
7. Archive a list when it's completed

On top of these basic features, we need some more stories to specifically address our customer's needs and make our application special. We want our customer to be able to do the following:

1. See items from all the open lists that are due soon
2. See all the items that are in a "pending" state
3. Put a list on temporary hold and specify a reason
4. See the entire history of a list

For each story, we need to declare how we can verify that the feature is working, or in other words, what are its acceptance criteria? When writing our user stories, we must remember that we don't need to capture all the details; the purpose is to use them as a reference to the discussions we had with business people and stakeholders.

For the same reason, we don't want to write stories for features that aren't relevant right now. For example, we'll need some kind of authentication, and perhaps reports, but we'll work on that later, so we don't need to discuss those stories now.

We can write them down on paper and append them to a physical board or use a software equivalent. If we use paper, we can write the acceptance criteria for each scenario on the back.

After having defined our stories, we can validate the whole idea of our application using event storming.

Validating Our Stories with Event Storming

Event storming is a very useful practice for collecting and sharing ideas about a new project we're going to build.[2] Its inventor, Alberto Brandolini, is fond of saying that writing software is, first of all, a learning process. Event storming allows us to learn from our application before writing it.

It's useful for sharing knowledge across teams. When we're in a big team with many stakeholders from different parts of the company, putting everyone all together in front of an empty wall that has to be filled with sticky notes helps a lot in terms of sharing a common vision for the project and comparing different perspectives.

Interestingly enough, event storming is also useful when working in a team of one, and we need to validate our stories and verify there are no (obvious) gaps in our understanding. Since we're a team of one, we'll use it to define our product.

It's beyond the scope of this book to explain how to successfully organize an event-storming workshop, but the quick version that you can do alone is pretty simple to try.

You start by writing down on a sticky note all the "things" that can happen relevant to your (future) application. They can be either something external to the application (for example, you just finished something you had to do) or something internal (for example, you checked the next thing to do). All these will be your events; try to describe them in the past tense to avoid ambiguities. For example:

1. I wrote a list of documents to collect to get the mortgage from the bank.
2. I created a new to-do list on the application.
3. I checked an item as done.
4. I read on the application all the stuff I have to do today.
5. I forgot something and need to reschedule it.
6. I added some notes to a task to do.

---

2.   https://www.eventstorming.com/

Then, arrange all the sticky notes on a blank surface—a wall for example—loosely ordered by their timing, from left to right. Also, try to group together events that are related to each other. Then, using notes of a different color, we can write down the actions that caused the events, if any. It should look a bit like this:

Finally, you must identify what actually triggered the events, either an inter-action with your application (for example, pressing a button) or an external event (for example, the end of the month). In this way, we can double check if our application will actually help us solve the original problem and which functionality it really needs to have.

The event-storming approach works very well with the functional way of working. Everything is described as a series of immutable events and flows that can be composed. As we'll see, event-driven systems are a natural fit for functional programming.

Preparing the Mock-Ups

The last bit of preparation is to make some mock-ups of what our application pages will look like. We don't want to put too many details into them, since they may change as we continue to learn what we need. Still, our mock-ups will help us develop the user interface for our application and we can use them as guides to write the HTML.

To identify the pages, we can use the previous event-storming exercise out-come. If we follow the list of events, that is, the sticky notes we attached to the wall, starting from the left, we can imagine what information we need to continue the journey. We particularly want to clarify any potential rabbit holes, comparing the user interface with the domain events that may happen for each possible state.

Reading the first events, it's clear that we need a page with all the lists the current user created. We can imagine something like this:

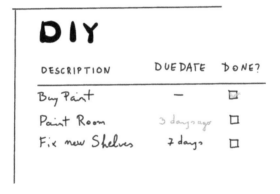

Then, proceeding with the events, we need a new page with the details of a specific to-do list:

Finally, we need a page with a general view of what the most urgent to-do items are across all lists:

These are only my sketches and you may have different ideas. It's also possible that when we implement these ideas, it will make sense to change them or to combine two of these views into a single HTML page. Graphic details are not important. What's important is to include in the sketches all the information we need to display to the user.

The simplest and most productive approach is to draw mock-ups after defining the user stories related to them but before writing the code. This lets us focus on what's really needed while developing the features, leaving the decorative touches for later.

Writing Requirements as Code

A possible objection to the use of lightweight techniques like user stories and event storming is that they don't leave behind much documentation once they have been completed. As developers, we love to have all the code we're working on completely and correctly documented. Or at least I'd love it, as long as the docs are always up-to-date and I don't have to write them myself.

Unfortunately, traditional documentation suffers from a number of potential problems: it's expensive to produce, it can become obsolete very quickly, and it's often incomplete or unclear. If we transform our requirements into something we can compile against our application, then it will be written together with the code and we can make sure it's updated at every commit. We'll also have some indication of its completeness by measuring how much of our code is covered by it.

So we need to document our application in a way that can't be ignored or forgotten by developers and stakeholders. We want something that will tell us if the application isn't doing what's documented, so we can either change the behavior or the documents. Is this asking too much? Fortunately for us, the answer exists, and it's called test-driven development.

Letting Tests Guide Development

Kent Beck introduced the idea to write the test before you write the implementation.[3] He called it "TestFirst" but now this technique is widely known by the more catchy term, *Test Driven Development* (TDD). It may seem counterintuitive at first. What's the point of writing the test if we haven't written the functionality yet? Surely you want to test something after you've created it. Yet, this practice is really effective. In this book, we'll concentrate on the characteristics that functional programming brings to TDD.

---

3.   http://wiki.c2.com/?CodeUnitTestFirst

Writing code in TDD means we start with a failing test, then we write the code to make it pass, and finally, we clean up our code until we're happy enough to switch to a new test. Due to the fact that green tests are marked in green and failing tests are marked in red in the reports, this is called the *red-green-refactor* cycle.

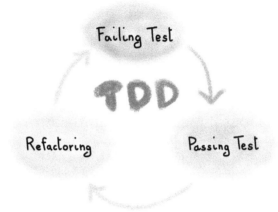

The main benefit of TDD is that it forces us to define our *success criteria*—what would represent a success for our code—before we start coding a tentative concrete solution. In other words, we're forced to think about what would be a solution to our problem before trying to solve it. This step is often overlooked, with the risk that we finish solving the wrong problem.

Writing tests forces us to clarify what the goals are that we want to achieve and what the prerequisites are that we want to start from. This is particularly useful for macro tests that operate on complex systems.

Thinking at a Sustainable Pace

Another important benefit of TDD is that it allows us to think at a sustainable pace and frees us from the need to keep everything in our mind. Once we put the tests in place, we know that we have defined the problem. So, we can interrupt our progress at any moment without the risk of forgetting something.

When we continue with our task, we can quickly get to where we left off, because we just need to look at the tests. This will alleviate the pressure to have to write the code very quickly, "because finally I have it all in my mind." Working with TDD will give us better code and fewer frustrations.

This is also related to the refactoring step of the TDD cycle; once we have verified the code behavior with testing, we can "switch" our brain from the "solve the problem" mentality to the "clean up the code" attitude.

Guiding the Design

A common feeling among TDD practitioners is that if a piece of software is easy to test, it's also easy to maintain and improve. In a word, the quality of code that's easy to test is higher than the quality of code that's hard to test. It's hard to write code that's easily testable. The best way to ensure easily testable code is to write tests from the beginning.

Tests will also help us keep the design simple for our application. Listening to our tests will often suggest better ways to improve our code. This is equally true for both object-oriented and functional paradigms.

 Joe asks:
What Does It Mean to Listen to Our Tests?

They won't speak to us, for sure!

But, if every time we make a design decision, we put some effort into choosing the direction that keeps everything easy to test, we can say that the tests did guide our design. Keep in mind that they are whispering rather than shouting.

Ensure Correctness

The last benefit is the most commonly overrated and misunderstood. Tests give us confidence that the system is working the way we understand it should work. This doesn't mean that a system written in TDD will have fewer bugs in it, but the bugs will be much faster to fix. This is because most of the defects are caused by conditions that the developer who wrote the code did not anticipate. Tests allow us to find bugs much quicker than using manual debugging on the whole application.

Since tests can be run automatically and relatively fast, we can also re-use them to revalidate our expectations in different environments.

Different Kinds of Tests

There are many kind of automatic tests; let's consider the most important ones:

- Unit Tests: tests that work on a unit of behavior—the smallest possible thing that you can effectively test. For example, a method of a class, a pure function, or a few closely related functions. They must be very fast to run, and they shouldn't interact with external systems.

- Integration Tests: tests to integrate with other systems. Their goal is to test the correct integration of two separate parts, for example, the application and the database, or the application and an external service. They can also be used to verify the interactions between parts of our systems. They are usually slower to run than unit tests.

- Acceptance Tests: tests that capture the acceptance criteria of our stories. They have an even bigger level of granularity than other tests. They test our full application end-to-end to ensure that a story or scenario works as expected. They usually simulate user interactions with our system and detect how the system reacted to verify that our system is still correct. They are slow to run, but they are the most important ones.

In addition to these three types of automatic tests, there are other tests that focus on specific aspects of our application, such as security, resilience, and load testing.

We'll look at a novel way to write acceptance tests later, in Driving the Tests from the Domain, on page 57.

The Two Schools of Testing

When starting a new application, in proper TDD fashion, we'll have two starting places: either we'll start writing small unit tests to model our core domain and then build the application layer after layer "inside-out," or we can write the acceptance tests first, and then complete the application "outside-in," finishing with the core domain.

The main advantage of the outside-in approach is that we're guided by the external constraints of the story we want to complete. If we start from the core domain itself, there is a risk we'll implement some functionality in a way that doesn't fit into our story, and we'll have to change the code again when we arrive to implement the external layer.

On the other hand, if we think that modeling the domain is the critical part of our application, and the external API can be decided later, then the inside-out approach might be better.

Another big difference is that if we write an acceptance test ahead of the implementation, we won't be able to make the test pass until the story scenario is completed, which can take hours or days. But we can't leave failing tests within the build, so we need to disable it or somehow mark it as work-in-progress.

The risks are that the broken acceptance tests stay broken forever, get forgotten about, or the feature itself gets deprioritized. Choosing the outside-in approach will require a certain discipline in keeping acceptance tests under control.

So at the end, either we start from the inside and we accept the risk of implementing the feature in a way that won't match what we need, or we start from the outside and accept the risk of keeping the acceptance test broken for a period of time.

In my opinion, the first risk is bigger than the second, and since this is a book and you (as reader) don't have any voice in this, I'll make the decision and we'll adopt an "outside-in" approach.

Setting Up the Project

Before we start working on the real application, we'll practice writing tests in Kotlin. The first step is to set up a new project.

We need to create a new zettai directory where we'll put the new project. We'll use Gradle as a build tool,[4] so we need to create the Gradle build file and then put everything in a Git repository.[5]

You can find all the code in the PragProg website page for this book.[6]

Test Libraries

Choosing the right dependencies for our projects is a very delicate task, and there is a fair possibility that we may regret any choice in the future. It's important to try to choose libraries that won't get in the way of our future developments, or at the very least, select the ones that impose the least constraints.

There are many libraries to help with automatic tests in the JVM and in Kotlin in particular. It's a choice that depends on personal taste and your writing style. These are what we need for this project:

- JUnit is the veteran of all unit-test libraries.[7] It has been rewritten multiple times. The latest major version is 5.x, and it introduced some useful new features like soft assertions and dynamic tests.

---

4. https://gradle.org/
5. https://git-scm.com/
6. https://pragprog.com/titles/uboop
7. https://junit.org/junit5/

- Strikt is an assertion library with a very nice and composable DSL that's easy to remember and auto-completion friendly.[8] It supports new JUnit5 soft assertions, allowing us to assert more than one property independently. There are other great assertion libraries, but I particularly like how well Strikt works with IDE suggestions.

Once done, we can import the Gradle file, and we should be able to open the project in our IDE. For more explanation about setting up Kotlin, see Setting Up Kotlin, on page 371.

Making Unit Tests Functional

As we saw, the smallest and most common test is the unit test. It's always a good idea to write a test before trying to solve a problem in code. But what does writing tests mean in practice? And how does functional programming differ from the traditional style?

One of the most-used templates for writing unit tests is called Given-When-Then (another name for it is Arrange-Act-Assert).[9] It works by splitting each test into three steps:

1. Given some conditions,
2. When something happens,
3. Then a testable result is expected.

We can apply it to functional programming as well: "Given 2 and 3, when I sum them, then I get 5 as result."

Even if it seems similar to the functional approach, in practice, it leans toward setting the state of an object and triggering a behavior. This is because the relation between Given, When, and Then is, on purpose, very weak. This is absolutely correct for testing an object-oriented module, where we want to test some behavior triggered by some conditions.

When we're testing pure functions, on the other hand, we only want to think about which properties are preserved by our functions and which aren't.

Our ideal test should focus on a function, or a chain of functions, that transforms an input type A to a different one B, and allows us to check that they work as expected; in other words, that we produce the correct B for each A.

We have two ways to test this. The first way is to provide a set of examples of instances of A with a corresponding set of expected B. Then, run it on each

---

8. https://strikt.io/
9. https://martinfowler.com/bliki/GivenWhenThen.html

A and verify the expected B is identical to the result. This approach is called test-by-example and it's useful when the possible values are limited or we want to reproduce some specific data from our production system.

The second way is to define some properties, which must be valid for any possible transformation A -> B, then try the function with a random selection of values for type A, and then verify that the property is maintained for all produced results. This approach is called *property testing* and it's great because it allows us to define how our software should work in general, rather than for some particular cases.

Our First Unit Test

To get a taste of functional testing, let's have a bit of fun and try to validate the addition operation in Kotlin.

We start by creating a new class, AdditionTest, in the test directory, with a simple test inside. We can start writing down some examples:

```
❶ class AdditionTest {

❷     @Test
❸     fun `add two numbers`() {
❹         expectThat(5 + 6).isEqualTo(11)
           expectThat(7 + 42).isEqualTo(49)
           expectThat(9999 + 1).isEqualTo(10000)
       }
   }
```

❶ This is the class grouping all the tests about addition.

❷ To mark a method as a test, we need to add the annotation Test.

❸ For the name of the method, we can use backticks to allow spaces for better readability.

❹ Strikt assertion DSL makes it easy to specify what we expect.

All IDEs allow us to run single tests easily. In IntelliJ, we can click on the green-red sign near the test name to run it and see the result in the test windows as shown in the screenshot on page 15.

This is an atypical test because it passed right away—after all, the addition operation is working fine in Kotlin—but we're focused on learning how to test pure functions, not on the function itself. But to be sure, you can add some wrong assertions, like expectThat(1 + 1).isEqualTo(3) to see the test fail. But there will be a lot of opportunities to see tests fail in the rest of the book.

```
Run:      AdditionTest
  ▶  ✓  ⊘  ↓↑  ↓⊤  ⊼  ÷   ↑  ↓  ⊕  ⬉  ⬈  ⚙    ✓ Tests passed: 1 of 1 test – 44 ms
  ✓  ✓ Test Results                    44 ms   /home/ubertobarbini/.sdkman/candidates/j
  ⟳     ✓ AdditionTest                  44 ms
  🔧        ✓ add two numbers()         44 ms   Process finished with exit code 0
```

We tested three additions chosen randomly; are they enough? How many
results would be enough to be confident? 100? 1000? We can see this approach
won't bring us very far. We can't verify all possible additions in this way.

What we can do instead is test the properties of the addition operation, using
random values as input. In this way, what we're testing is that the addition
works as expected, rather than testing its result directly. Don't worry if this
is confusing; we'll return to it later in Property Testing, on page 96.

From school, we remember three properties for addition; we can test them
like this:

❶ `fun randomNatural() = Random.nextInt(from = 1, until = 100_000_000)`

```
@Test
```
❷ `fun ` `zero identity`() {
❸   `repeat(100) {`
        `val x = randomNatural()`

        `expectThat(x + 0).isEqualTo(x)`
    `}`
`}`

```
@Test
```
❹ `fun ` `commutative property`() {
    `repeat(100) {`
        `val x = randomNatural()`
        `val y = randomNatural()`

        `expectThat(x + y).isEqualTo(y + x)`
    `}`
`}`

```
   @Test
⑤  fun `associative property`() {
       repeat(100) {
           val x = randomNatural()
           val y = randomNatural()
           val z = randomNatural()

⑥         expect {
               that((x + y) + z).isEqualTo(x + (y + z))
               that((y + z) + x).isEqualTo(y + (z + x))
               that((z + x) + y).isEqualTo(z + (x + y))
           }

       }
   }
```

❶ We first define a function that returns a random integer in the range we want to test. (We're happy with only positive numbers for this test.)

❷ The first property we test is that the result of any number added to zero is equal to the number itself.

❸ We repeat the test multiple times with random numbers to get more confidence.

❹ The second property we test is that the sum of two numbers doesn't change if we change the order in which we sum them.

❺ The third property we test is that the sum of three numbers doesn't change regardless of how we group them.

❻ Soft assertions allow us to run multiple assertions together; even if some are failing, we'll get all the results.

Even in this small example, we see how testing the properties of functions works differently from testing using an example data set. Finding the right properties to test can be tricky, while in traditional TDD, it's usually easy to identify the examples we want to test.

On the other hand, property testing can give us more confidence, and it often helps to discover problems with our code in a completely unexpected way.

Please Don't Mock Me

A consequence of focusing on testing functions is that we don't have much use for mocks or stubs.[10] In particular, we don't need a specialized library for creating mocks for our tests.

---

10. https://martinfowler.com/articles/mocksArentStubs.html

> ⸜/ ⸝   **Joe asks:**
> ஃ   **What About JUnit Parameterized Tests?**
>
> JUnit 5 allows us to run tests with different parameters that can be generated by a function.
>
> It's a great feature that generates a test for each input dynamically, so you can see them independently on the IDE.
>
> At first, parameterized tests seem like a good fit for our property tests, but in reality, they don't work very well when we run hundreds or thousands of tests, which are quite common for property testing.
>
> So, for the moment, it's easier to just repeat the test with random values many times.

In the object-oriented world, we often need to test the interaction between objects with a hidden mutable state. Since it's very hard to test two opaque objects together, we create a fake version of the collaborators of our class; those can be mocks or stubs, depending on how much detail we need to test.

Mocks are useful because we can simulate complex behavior and then verify the correct interactions at the end of our test. Stubs are simpler; we can use them to return an object with a specific state. Mocks and stubs are very powerful but also complex to use and make tests harder to maintain.

When writing tests for functional code, we can simply provide some input and test the expected results, or even better, test that our functions maintain their properties with any inputs. In any case, we don't have to look at the internal state or at the order of object calls.

Moreover, in many cases we can avoid using stubs or mocks, even when testing interactions with other components, by relying solely on simple functions, rather than interfaces. Later on (Add an Item in the Hub, on page 84), we'll delve into how much simpler it is to use ad hoc functions inside tests rather than setting up mock expectations and then verifying them.

Having said that, there will be a few cases where creating a stub implementation is still the simplest way to test our functional code; there's nothing wrong with that!

Recap

In this chapter, we defined the project that will accompany us for most of the book. We also saw how to define a minimum set of requirements for validating our product idea and how to transform them into stories that are easy to pick up and implement.

We also learned about automatic testing, the various kind of tests, and how we can test the properties of a function, without using hand-picked examples. Finally, we set up our project and wrote our first test in Kotlin!

Even if we didn't progress much in functional programming itself, this chapter laid the foundations for future chapters.

In the next chapter, we'll start writing our application. And we'll start learning how we can write down the stories as tests that the computer can automatically verify, and then, create the skeleton of a web service application that will develop in the following chapters.

Exercises

The exercises in this chapter will focus on user stories and property testing.

Here is your friendly reminder that nobody can learn functional programming by just reading code, and the best way to learn is by practicing. You can refer to the exercises folder in the book code repository for the starting point and some hints.

Exercise 1.1: Grocery Event Storming

For this exercise, you need to think about describing the typical experience at a grocery store in terms of events.

Try to write down on post-its all the things that can happen while trying to buy food in a small shop—things like "customer entered," "customer asked for something," and so on. Then try to reorder them in a rough timeline, and group together related ones. Can you identify what triggers them? How would you design an application for self checkout?

Exercise 1.2: Discounts in TDD

For this exercise, you need to write the logic for a cash register in strict TDD style.

You need to create a class, CashRegister, which receives the prices and the list of promotions of the day in the constructor.

Prices are a map of the name of the food with the price, for example, [milk: 1.5, bread: 0.9]. Each promotion has a food item and a discount attached, for example: [milk: "3x2", eggs: "8x6"]. We only have one kind of promotion: "MxN" where you pay for N items but you'll receive M.

The goal of the exercise is to implement the checkout method on the CashRegister that will calculate the price of a list of items, that is, ["milk","milk","milk"] tot price = 3.0.

Try to use random value generators instead of fixed values for your test.

Exercise 1.3: Addition Plus One Test

For this exercise, you need to add a new test to our suite of tests for the addition operation.

We want to test that if we have two random integer numbers inside a given range, if we take the smallest and we add 1 multiple times, at some point we'll get the bigger number.

Not all those who wander are lost.

> J.R.R. Tolkien, The Fellowship of the Ring

CHAPTER 2

Handling HTTP Using Functions

In the previous chapter, we decided what our application will be, and we defined a few stories and mock-ups that will help us to focus while implementing it. We saw how to lay the foundations of a new application. We also discussed automatic testing.

In this chapter, we'll continue the journey to look at how to build this application following a functional style and how this would be different from a more traditional approach.

We'll start converting one user story at a time into tests. This will help us focus our efforts on delivering the most important features quickly and then refine and integrate them in the following iterations.

We'll also consider the benefits of using functional design and how it can guide us effectively to a working implementation that's easy to maintain and understand, because it's made exclusively from composing small and simple functions.

Kicking Off the Project

From our list of Defining Our User Stories, on page 3, the first story is "See a single list," but before we start coding it, we should write a test. More precisely, we should write an *acceptance test*,[1] which is a test that can decide if our software would meet the customer's acceptance criteria.

But there is a problem; we still don't have a clear idea of how our application will look, so we risk spending time writing the wrong test. This is a common problem at the beginning of every project. In the words of Steve Freeman and Nat Pryce:

---

1. https://wiki.c2.com/?AcceptanceTest

> The quandary in writing and passing the first acceptance test is that it's hard to build both the tooling and the feature it's testing at the same time. (...) We can cut through this "first-feature paradox" by splitting it into two smaller problems. First, work out how to build, deploy, and test a "walking skeleton," then use that infrastructure to write the acceptance tests for the first meaningful feature. After that, everything will be in place for test-driven development of the rest of the system.
>
> —*Growing Object-Oriented Software, Guided by Tests [FP09]*

Walking Skeleton

So, we'll first write a *walking skeleton*, then we'll write the first test, and only after that will we implement the actual feature. Note that for the following stories we'll only need the test and the implementation, because we'll know how to test our application at that point.

But what's a walking skeleton exactly?

> A Walking Skeleton is a tiny implementation of the system that performs a small end-to-end function. It need not use the final architecture, but it should link together the main architectural components. The architecture and the functionality can then evolve in parallel.[2]
>
> —Alistair Cockburn

In other words, we need to prepare the infrastructure of our application and be ready to deploy it in production before starting to work on the actual business logic. The thought is that it's much easier to fix any issue when the application is an almost empty shell (a skeleton) than when it has all its logic and dependencies attached.

Once we're confident we can deploy it in our environments, we can start building the actual logic and adding the dependencies. Working on the logic first can lead to big problems when we want to deploy for the first time and discover that our assumptions about the environments were wrong.

It also helps us to keep migrations, tests, and deployment scripts updated and working from the beginning, rather than having to implement them on an already quite fat application once we decide to go live.

How to build a continuous integration/delivery pipeline, and how to use cloud services to deploy your application in different environments is beyond the scope of this book, but they are very important tasks that need to be done correctly to deploy our application.

---

2. http://alistair.cockburn.us/index.php/Walking_skeleton

In a real project, this is the step where we start building our deployment infrastructure and automating it. The goal is to show our first web page on the same infrastructure that we'll ultimately use in production; in other words, to make our skeleton walk!

Michael Nygard's *Release It! [Nyg07]* is a treasure trove of wisdom and advice on how to take care of these fundamental aspects of your system.

Serving HTML Pages Functionally

We know we need to implement an application to manage to-do lists; where should we start? In the previous chapter, we defined the user story we want to implement first. So, how do we proceed? We can start writing down the list of things we know for sure:

- The user's browser will send us an HTTP request.
- The browser is expecting a response containing an HTML page with the to-do list, or, if something went wrong, some information about the error.

In essence, we need to build a web service.

Surprisingly enough, the functional approach can help us even at this stage. Instead of looking at our application as a bunch of black boxes interacting, we'll focus on the inputs and desired outputs of each element. Moreover, looking at the transformations of our data, and considering which properties our system should preserve or ignore, will give us a comprehensive functional approach for the whole application life cycle. This covers the initial design through requirement gathering and the complete implementation of the system.

Using functional programming only for modeling our domain or to help our object react to changes would do a poor service to its potential. Functional programming can give us much more. We'll now look concretely at how to work in this way.

Web Server as a Function

If we look at the problem with a "functional eye," our application works as an "engine" that transforms inputs into outputs. We only need to consider what the specific inputs and outputs are. Reasoning in this way, we can describe any web service as a single function. As illustrated in the diagram on page 24, an 'HttpHandler' is a function that transforms a request into a response.

This is the fundamental rule of how to design functional programs: we examine what we have (inputs) and what we want (the outputs) to figure out the function that we need.

$$\underline{Http\ Handler}$$

$$Request \rightarrow Response$$

In Kotlin, we can express the type of the HttpHandler very clearly using Function Types, on page 376: (Request) -> Response.

Incidentally, there is a famous paper called "Your Server as a Function," by Marius Eriksen, which explains the functional approach they followed at Twitter to develop web servers:[3]

> Systems boundaries are represented by asynchronous functions called services. They provide a symmetric and uniform API: the same abstraction represents both clients and servers. Application-agnostic concerns (e.g., timeouts, retries, authentication) are encapsulated by filters which compose to build services from multiple independent modules.
>
> —Marius Eriksen

The core concept is the same as what we just stumbled upon: consider each web server as a function that transforms an HTTP request into an HTTP response. He calls this particular function a *service* (our HttpHandler). In the same way, a *filter* is a function that takes a service and returns another service.

This interesting paper explains the advantages that a functional approach brought to the humongous Twitter infrastructure in terms of simplicity, safety, and robustness. This approach will bring benefits to our project, regardless of the size, as we'll soon see.

At this point, you'll probably start having some ideas about how to design a web service in a functional way. What we need now is a ready-to-use web server to serve HTTP requests. Ideally, it would be great to have a Kotlin library that allows us to define a web server as a function, similar to what we've done in our examples so far.

Luckily for us, it already exists.

3.　https://monkey.org/~marius/funsrv.pdf

Introducing Http4k

Http4k is an HTTP library written in Kotlin that enables the serving and consuming of HTTP services in a functional way.[4] We'll soon see how easy it is to transform simple Kotlin functions into a running web server.

Under the hood, Http4k works as a wrapper around an HTTP server and HTTP client libraries. For the moment, we need only the server part. There are many options available for us to choose from. For Zettai, we're choosing Jetty as the backend, because it's fast and rock solid, but keep in mind that there are other possibilities.[5]

Jetty itself isn't written in a functional way, so does it matter if the internal web service isn't functional? As a matter of fact, not much. We don't care if the underlying implementation is functional or not, as long as its external interface is functional and allows us to compose over it in a functional way.

> At the end of the day, we aren't in search of some theoretical "mathematical purity"; we're using functional programming as a way to make our life easier, leveraging the power of functional composition.
>
> So far, as the functions of our library respect the functional rules, meaning they are referentially transparent, we don't care in which style they are written. If we dig deep enough, everything is compiled to machine code, which is absolutely nonfunctional, after all.

When choosing a library, it's really important to be sure that using it won't create problems with our existing code, and that it won't force us to change the architecture of our application in ways we don't like. Keeping this in mind, we can see why functional libraries are usually easier to use and integrate than object-oriented ones; remember the gorilla and the bananas mentioned in the introduction. Not having to worry about side effects and objects with mutable state is a big benefit when adopting a third-party library.

A Spike: Our First Web Page

Every time we consider using a new library, it's good practice to gain confidence with it by making a "spike," that is, what's the simplest thing we can do that will convince us this thing will work? The term comes from Ward Cunningham, who likened it to quickly driving a spike through a board.[6]

---

4. https://www.http4k.org/
5. https://www.eclipse.org/jetty/
6. https://twitter.com/WardCunningham/status/1223134450327752704

In this case, we should ask ourselves, "What's the simplest thing we can do with Http4k that will convince us it's the right tool for our job?" Let's look at what it takes to write a web page returning a greeting using Http4k. More precisely, we need to:

- Define an HTML greetings string.
- Write the main function returning our HTML unconditionally.
- Start Http4k with our function.

Once we add the reference to Http4k modules to the dependencies section of the Gradle build file (the details with all the code are on the book repository), we can write our main function (see Hello World, on page 372).

Apart from the HTML itself, we only need to write two lines of code!

```kotlin
val htmlPage = """
<html>
    <body>
        <h1 style="text-align:center; font-size:3em;" >
Hello Functional World!
        </h1>
    </body>
</html>"""
```
❶
```kotlin
val handler: HttpHandler = { Response(Status.OK).body(htmlPage) }

fun main() {
    handler.asServer(Jetty(8080)).start()
}
```
❷

❶ Here, we define a new function of type HttpHandler that returns our HTML page wrapped in a response, and we assign it to the variable handler.

❷ To start a web server, we use the extension function, asServer, of Http4k. This starts the web server, in this case Jetty, listening on port 8080, and it will use our handler to process the requests.

Not only is the code quite compact, it also reveals its intentions very clearly. If we launch it, we can see our "Hello Functional World!" on a browser.

Http4k Domain-Specific Language

You may wonder where the Response type comes from. It's part of Http4k together with the corresponding Request type. These two data classes present roughly the same data of HttpServletRequest and HttpServletResponse of the Java standard library but in a immutable and functional-friendly way.

As a matter of fact, many of the existing libraries we need to use are based on mutable types. Rather than handling directly mutable data structures in our functional code, it's better to wrap them inside immutable, concise, functional types, and use the Adapter design pattern[7] to use them instead of their mutable equivalents.

This is a very handy technique we can use when we need to introduce new functional design in an existing codebase or when we need to use an object-oriented library from our functional code.

Http4k also gives us a domain-specific language that allows us to quickly define our routes in a way that's easy to read and write. It requires us to bind each route to an HTTP verb and a function of type HttpHandler.

We can use Lambda Variables, on page 377, for each route, or we can pass Functions, on page 375.

```
val app: HttpHandler = routes(
    "/greetings" bind GET to ::greetings,
    "/data" bind POST to ::receiveData,
)

fun greetings(req: Request): Response = Response(OK).body(htmlPage)

fun receiveData(req: Request): Response = Response(CREATED)
    .body("Received: ${req.bodyString()}")

fun main() {
    app.asServer(Jetty(8080)).start()
}
```

❶ Here, we define a new route associated with path /greetings and the verb GET that executes function greetings.

❷ This is another route associated with path /data and the verb POST that executes function receiveData.

❸ Here, we print the same greetings as in the previous example.

❹ This is how we can read the content of the body of the POST request.

---

7. https://en.wikipedia.org/wiki/Adapter_pattern

Http4k will take care of returning a "404 Not Found Error" in case of a missing route and a "500 Internal Server Error" in case any exception got thrown, so we don't have to worry about these things.

Overall, the code is even more readable than our little example. We'll learn more about Http4k and its features—how to pass parameters, for example—in the next chapters. Now that we're satisfied with our spike, it's time to return to our application.

Handle the Risk

Both the walking skeleton and the spike are practices that may seem like a waste of time, but they help us manage the risk when building software.

The walking skeleton gives us the confidence that we can deploy our system correctly when it's still very easy to change—since it doesn't have any business logic in it.

The spike gives us the confidence that a certain technical solution is sound, and that it will serve our needs before we start using it inside our application. It allows us to write all the examples we need in a quick and dirty way without affecting our production code. Later, we can throw them away or use them as guidelines to integrate the solution in our application.

Starting Zettai

Now we can throw away the spike code and start to write the real main function. Since we decided that a list is owned by a user, it makes sense to encode this relationship inside the URL of our application to make it more user friendly, for example, like this:

```
http://localhost:8080/todo/user/listname
```

Once we start the application—from the command line or from the IDE—calling this URL will show the to-do list named "listname" of the user "user."

Let's put this route into our main function as we did previously with the spike:

```
fun main() {
    val app: HttpHandler = routes(
❶      "/todo/{user}/{list}" bind Method.GET to ::showList
    )
    app.asServer(Jetty(8080)).start()
}
❷ fun showList(req: Request): Response  {
```

```
❸      val user: String? = req.path("user")
       val list: String? = req.path("list")
       val htmlPage = """
<html>
    <body>
        <h1>Zettai</h1>
        <p>Here is the list <b>$list</b> of user <b>$user</b></p>
    </body>
❹ </html>"""
❺      return Response(OK).body(htmlPage)
   }
```

❶ We use curly brackets in the route to define where the user and the list name are specified inside the path.

❷ As expected, the showList() function has a Request as input and a Response as result.

❸ To extract the user and the list from request, we use the path() method that returns a nullable string.

❹ We produce some HTML with the parameters encoded inside.

❺ Finally, we return a Response with the HTML and the success code.

To test it, we can use a browser to call localhost:8080/todo/uberto/book with the application running:

Note that user and list names are taken from the URL path.

We can see the little question mark after the string type on the declaration of user and list; is it because we're unsure? Well, almost.

The question mark denotes a nullable type (Nullable Types, on page 387) and means that the function can return a String when the request has a valid path or null if it can't match it. We'll further explore how the way Kotlin handles nullability is beneficial to functional programming later, in The Problem with Null, on page 95.

As mentioned before, in a real project we should not be satisfied with the application running on our machine, but we also must include the deployment process and scripts in the walking skeleton. But, for the scope of this book, we can now call our walking skeleton done.

The First Acceptance Test

It's nice to be able to see our application deployed and running in the browser, but it isn't enough: we want to check it automatically from our tests, so every time we change our code, we can verify automatically everything is still working.

To do this, we need an HTTP client in our application as well, so we add the corresponding Http4k module to our Gradle configuration:

```
testImplementation "org.http4k:http4k-client-jetty:${http4kVersion}"
```

Then, we can start writing an acceptance test to retrieve a list:

```
❶ class SeeATodoListAT {

    @Test
❷   fun `List owners can see their lists`() {
        val user = "frank"
        val listName = "shopping"
        val foodToBuy = listOf("carrots", "apples", "milk")

❸       startTheApplication(user, listName, foodToBuy)

❹       val list = getToDoList(user, listName)

❺       expectThat(list.name).isEqualTo(listName)
        expectThat(list.items).isEqualTo(foodToBuy)

    }
}

❻ fun getToDoList(user: String, listName: String): ToDoList {
    val client = JettyClient()
    val request = Request(GET,
                "http://localhost:8081/todo/$user/$listName")

    val response = client(request)

    return if (response.status == Status.OK)
        parseResponse(response)
    else
        fail(response.toMessage())
}

fun parseResponse(html: String): ToDoList = TODO("parse the response")

fun startTheApplication(
❼       user: String, listName: String, items: List<String>) {

    val server = Zettai().asServer(Jetty(8081)) //a random port

    // todo setup user and list
}
```

❶ We start the acceptance test like a normal JUnit test.

❷ The test method name reflects a user story or part of a story.

❸ We need to start the application and set it up with some fixture data, in this case a user and a list.

❹ This is the core of our test; we simulate a user getting a list from the application. We haven't defined ToDoList type yet, so this won't compile.

❺ Here, we verify the list name is identical to the one we expected.

❻ This is how we interrogate our server. Note: as in Http4k, the HTTP client and server implement the same functional interface: HttpHandler. We leave the HTML parsing for later.

❼ This is how we want to start our server; we plan to extract the logic currently in the main function into Zettai type.

OK, we wrote the test, but it doesn't even compile! How can this help us? Well, this is the "magic" of TDD: just writing the test gives us a good direction for our application design. But it's not really possible to fully appreciate this while only reading a book; you have to try it for yourself.

So, how does the test we just wrote guide us? First, it tells us which classes to write to make the test compile, and some of their methods. We start with the Zettai class:

```
class Zettai(): HttpHandler{

    val routes = routes(
        "/todo/{user}/{list}" bind GET to ::showList
    )

    override fun invoke(req: Request): Response = routes(req)

    private fun showList(req: Request): Response  {
        val user = req.path("user").orEmtpy()
        val list = req.path("list").orEmtpy()
        val htmlPage = """
<html>
    <body>
        <h1>Zettai</h1>
        <p>Here is the list <b>$list</b> of user <b>$user</b></p>
    </body>
</html>"""
        return Response(Status.OK).body(htmlPage)
    }

}
```

❶ Our Zettai is an HTTP handler.

❷ We copied the routes from the previous main function using the knowledge learned in our Http4k spike.

❸ When a request comes, we'll use the routes to dispatch it. We'll discuss more about invoke in the next chapter.

❹ Also, this method is from our previous main function. We'll change it soon.

Now for the next step: we need to define the types, starting with the ToDoList that's preventing our test from compiling. But, we need to be careful about our language.

Ubiquitous Language

> Ubiquitous Language is the term Eric Evans uses in Domain Driven Design for the practice of building up a common, rigorous language between developers and users.
>
> —Martin Fowler

Now we can start defining the data structures and functions that directly represent the concept of our business. We want to use terms that would allow anyone who knows about the business, without being a programmer, to recognize what the code is trying to do.

Since we're working on software to manage to-do lists, we can start from the ToDoList:

```
data class ToDoList(val listName: ListName, val items: List<ToDoItem>)
data class ListName(val name: String)
```

Kotlin's data class syntax allows us to concisely define immutable types, particularly useful in functional programming. You can learn more in the appendix about Kotlin language, Data Classes, on page 381.

Our ToDoList is composed of a name and a list of ToDoItem elements. It may seem surprising to create a specific type for the list name, instead of using a common string, but using specific types makes our tasks easier when using functional programming (see the appendix section Define Your Types Precisely, on page 363).

In this particular case, we'll limit the possible valid name for our lists; for example, we don't want to have list names too long, or use special characters. Having a specific type will make all these checks easier.

It's also useful to be able to distinguish, in a type-safe way, the functions that work only on ListName from the functions that work for any possible string. For the same reason, we'll define a type to keep the name of our user:

```
data class User(val name: String)
```

Finally, we need to define the single item of a to-do list.

```
data class ToDoItem(val description: String)
enum class ToDoStatus { Todo, InProgress, Done, Blocked }
```

The description will be the description of the task to do, and it can be any text, so keeping it as String does make sense. We'll define very minimal types for the moment, because we only need to write the tests. We'll add more details to the items when we need them in the next chapters.

Run the Acceptance Test

With the classes in place, we can finally compile the acceptance test. We only need to slightly change the assertions in the test:

```
expectThat(list.listName.name).isEqualTo(listName)
expectThat(list.items.map { it.description }).isEqualTo(foodToBuy)
```

Now it's compiling, but the test still fails with this error:

```
"An operation is not implemented: parse the response"
```

This means we're on the right track. We have verified that our application is actually starting and communicating with the tests.

The failure itself isn't an issue; on the contrary, the acceptance test must continue to fail until we consider the story completed. It would be pointless to try to parse the response now, since we haven't finalized the correct response yet.

If we launch the test from the IDE in debug mode, we can also use it to debug the application step-by-step. With the acceptance test in place, we can now start to define the business model for our application.

Designing with Arrows

The function getToDoList() of the Zettai class currently doesn't do much. It's time we implement the core logic.

Can we write a function that takes a request and returns a response right away? Yes, we might be able to, but before proceeding, we should keep in mind an important principle of functional design: rather than having a big fat function, it's better to split each functionality into many small functions, and then compose them together.

To discover which small functions we need, let's try now to better define the functionality we need to implement:

1. It must get the user and the list name from the HTTP request.
2. It must fetch the list content.
3. It must render it into HTML.
4. Finally, it must return a Response with the HTML.

If any of these steps fail, it must return a generic error page. We'll see in later chapters how to handle errors in a more precise way.

The next step is to translate this list of steps into a diagram with arrows, where each arrow is a pure function, as discussed in the appendix about functional programming (see Keep Your Functions Pure, on page 355).

Here is the diagram:

Request $\xrightarrow{1}$ {User, ListName}
$\downarrow^2$
$\longrightarrow$ToDoList$\xrightarrow{3}$Html$\xrightarrow{4}$Response

The numbers refer to the functions mentioned in the preceding list. The meaning of the arrows is discussed in the following section.

> As you continue to progress through this book, you'll encounter numerous diagrams resembling the one shown previously. These diagrams serve as a visual aid to help illustrate the concepts discussed in the text, and aren't intended to follow a precise notation.
>
> These diagrams focus on the arrows and how they are interconnected. These arrows represent functions that receive the left term as input and generate the right term as output. At times, functions may have other functions as inputs or outputs, and in those cases, the function is drawn starting or terminating vertically, so it connects to the middle of the other function. This can be seen in second function of the previous diagram.
>
> Although colors and other visual cues are utilized, they don't carry any specific meaning. Rather, they are chosen to help in clarifying the concepts presented within the diagrams.

> The small Earth symbolizes that the task of "retrieving the list content" differs from the other functions. Instead of solely transforming the input parameters, it requires accessing external information. Therefore, it's equivalent to returning a function that performs an impure operation to calculate its result. We'll delve more deeply into this topic in the next chapter.

We can see how the four steps we mentioned earlier have been transformed into four functions working together to produce the expected result. To keep things simple, we're ignoring the possible errors for the moment. We'll discuss how to handle those errors later; see Null as an Error, on page 94.

The next step is to model the types our functions will use. We already defined User, ListName, and ToDoList; for our HTML, we only need to create a wrapper for the raw HTML string using a Kotlin data class (Data Classes, on page 381):

```
data class HtmlPage( val raw: String )
```

Combining Functions Together

Now that we have defined the functions and the types, we have all the ingredients we need to start writing our functions, at last! We can just follow the diagram, and create the simple functions one after the other. Let's start with the signature of the four functions.

As for the implementation, we'll leave it for later. So, we'll use the very convenient TODO() function that always throws a NotImplementedError; in this way, we're reminded that we must come back and finish it.

Note how the input and output types used by each function are enough to guess its intent, even without looking at the function name:

```
❶ fun extractListData(request: Request): Pair<User, ListName> = TODO()
❷ fun fetchListContent(listId: Pair<User, ListName>): ToDoList = TODO()
❸ fun renderHtml(list: ToDoList): HtmlPage = TODO()
❹ fun createResponse(html: HtmlPage): Response = TODO()
```

❶ This function extracts the user name and list name from the request.

❷ Here, we fetch the actual list data from our repository using the user name and the list name as key.

❸ This function has the responsibility to transform the list into an HTML page with all the content of the list.

❹ Finally, here we create an HTTP response with the generated HTML page as the body.

We're now taking advantage of one of the great joys of functional programming: once we define the signature of our functions—their input and output types—we can verify that we can compose the functions together as we wanted, even before writing their implementation! Complex behavior will naturally emerge from combining them together. In the end, it will be easy to implement and test them without all the problems caused by sharing state and side effects.

The main function must call our functions in a cascade:

```kotlin
fun getToDoList(request: Request): Response =
    createResponse(
        renderHtml(
            fetchListContent(
                extractListData(
                    request
                )
            )
        )
    )
```

This is the typical way we chain together function calls, but it's not very readable; sometimes it's called "Christmas tree indentation," for obvious reasons. Also, the order of the functions is reversed: the first function to be called (extractListData) must be in the innermost position.

Kotlin's let function lets us call a function over some data (Scope Functions, on page 379). Using it, we can chain a series of function calls where each one takes as input the output of the previous function to make the code much more readable. The code that follows is equivalent to the "Christmas tree" one but easier to read and closer to our design diagram:

```kotlin
fun getToDoList(request: Request): Response =
    request
        .let(::extractListData)
        .let(::fetchListContent)
        .let(::renderHtml)
        .let(::createResponse)
```

Note that the order of the functions is the opposite of the previous example.

The let function using a function reference works a bit like the | operator in the Linux shell and the |> in JavaScript and F#.

Here, the chaining works because all functions have a single input parameter. We'll see how functions with a single parameter are easier to compose. For this reason, we used a Pair as input parameter for fetchListContent instead of using a function with two parameters.

This example provided our first experience of how important it is to think in terms of function composition and immutable data types to effectively design in a functional way.

Note also that we don't care about implementation at the moment, we're just breaking the problem into simpler functions, which will be easier to implement (and to test).

Serving Lists from a Map

We can now put these four functions into our Zettai class and implement them there.

But first, we need to have some lists to show. For the moment, let's take the simplest possible approach and put them in an immutable map, injected in the constructor of Zettai, which contains the lists of each user of our system:

❶
```
data class Zettai(val lists: Map<User, List<ToDoList>>): HttpHandler{

    //routes functions are not changed...
```
❷
```
    private fun showList(request: Request): Response =
        request.let(::extractListData)
            .let(::fetchListContent)
            .let(::renderHtml)
            .let(::createResponse)
```
❸
```
    fun extractListData(request: Request): Pair<User, ListName> {
        val user = request.path("user").orEmpty()
        val list = request.path("list").orEmpty()
        return User(user) to ListName(list)
    }
```
❹
```
    fun fetchListContent(listId: Pair<User, ListName>): ToDoList =
        lists[listId.first]
        ?.firstOrNull { it.listName == listId.second }
        ?: error("List unknown")
```
❺
```
    fun renderHtml(todoList: ToDoList): HtmlPage =
        HtmlPage("""
        <html>
            <body>
                <h1>Zettai</h1>
                <h2>${todoList.listName.name}</h2>
                <table>
                    <tbody>${renderItems(todoList.items)}</tbody>
                </table>
            </body>
        </html>
        """.trimIndent()
        )
```

```
fun renderItems(items: List<ToDoItem>) =
    items.map {
        """<tr><td>${it.description}</td></tr>""".trimIndent()
    }.joinToString("")

fun createResponse(html: HtmlPage): Response =
    Response(Status.OK).body(html.raw)
}
```

❶ We added the map with users and lists in the constructor.

❷ This function is identical to our initial diagram.

❸ We extract the user and the list name from the request path.

❹ We return the correct list of the user from the map.

❺ Here, we create a simple HTML with the list data inside.

❻ Finally, we put the HTML page as the body in the successful response.

Note that in fetchListContent we're throwing an error if the list doesn't exist. This isn't very functional, because it goes against the principle of totality (see Consider All the Possible Inputs, on page 359), and what's more important, we would return an ugly error 500 to the user instead of a nice error page. We will see later how to handle errors better in Null as an Error, on page 94.

Parse the Response

Now that we have a complete implementation of our Zettai class, we can go back to our acceptance test and finish it. We also need to plug in some lists when we start the application. The data we're using as an example when running the test is called the *test fixture*:

```
private fun startTheApplication(
    user: String,
    listName: String,
    items: List<String>
) {
    val toDoList = ToDoList(ListName(listName), items.map(::ToDoItem))
    val lists = mapOf(User(user) to listOf(toDoList) )
    val server = Zettai(lists).asServer(Jetty(8081)) //different from main
    server.start()
}
```

We can now properly parse the response. We'll do something better later, but for the moment, we can make it pass using some regular expressions to extract the names from the HTML:

```
private fun parseResponse(html: String): ToDoList {
    val nameRegex = "<h2>.*<".toRegex()
    val listName = ListName(extractListName(nameRegex, html))
    val itemsRegex = "<td>.*?<".toRegex()
    val items = itemsRegex.findAll(html)
        .map { ToDoItem(extractItemDesc(it)) }.toList()
    return ToDoList(listName,items)
}

private fun extractListName(nameRegex: Regex, html: String): String =
    nameRegex.find(html)?.value
        ?.substringAfter("<h2>")
        ?.dropLast(1)
        .orEmpty()

private fun extractItemDesc(matchResult: MatchResult): String =
    matchResult.value.substringAfter("<td>").dropLast(1)
```

And now, finally, our first acceptance test is passing, proving that Zettai can display a to-do list!

Finish the Story

The final touch to finish our story is using the Zettai class in the main as well:

```
fun main() {
    val items = listOf("write chapter", "insert code", "draw diagrams")
    val toDoList = ToDoList(ListName("book"), items.map(::ToDoItem))
    val lists = mapOf(User("uberto") to listOf(toDoList) )

    val app: HttpHandler = Zettai(lists)
    app.asServer(Jetty(8080)).start() //starting the server

    println("Server started at http://localhost:8080/todo/uberto/book")
}
```

So, we can start our application and see the result in a browser:

Currently Zettai can only display the lists we had hard-coded in the main function. This isn't very useful, but it's a first step. We'll build on that in the next chapters.

Recap

In this chapter, we did a lot of work. First, we learned how a web server is just a function transforming HTTP requests into HTTP responses.

Then, we saw how to create our own functional web server using Http4k, showing a predefined set of to-do lists to the users.

We also started using tests to drive our design, and we wrote an acceptance test to clarify our requirements.

In the next chapter, we'll look at how to keep business domain functions separated by infrastructure and how to improve our acceptance tests in a way that will keep the focus on the business domain.

Exercises

The exercises in this chapter will focus on combining functions together.

Here is your friendly reminder that nobody can learn functional programming by just reading code, and the best way to learn is by practicing. You can refer to the exercises folder in the book code repository for the starting point and some hints.

Exercise 2.1: Chain Functions

In this exercise, we want to improve the readability of a chain of functions. At the beginning of this chapter we had the following code:

```
request
    .let(::extractListData)
    .let(::fetchListContent)
    .let(::renderHtml)
    .let(::createResponse)
```

Using Kotlin infix (see Infix Functions, on page 388) format we can transform it to a more declarative style like this:

```
val processFun = ::extractListData andThen
                 ::fetchListContent andThen
                 ::renderHtml andThen
                 ::createResponse

fun fetchList(request: Request): Response = processFun(request)
```

In other words, f andThen g is equivalent to g(f()). To define the type of our function it is convenient to use a type alias in this way:

```
typealias FUN<A, B> = (A) -> B

infix fun <A, B, C> FUN<A, B>.andThen(other: FUN<B, C>): FUN<A, C>
  = TODO()
```

To solve the exercise, you need to replace the TODO() call with the implementation of the function.

Exercise 2.2: A Functional Stack

For this exercise, we'll write a stack, which is a data type that allows us to push objects inside and pull them out in the last-in-first-out order, like a stack of plates.

Following functional principles, the stack must be immutable. This means that pushing an element will return a new stack and popping it will return a tuple with the element and a new stack instance. Here, you can find some example code that should work fine with your implementation of FunStack.

```
@Test
fun `push into the stack`(){
    val stack1 = FunStack<Char>()
    val stack2 = stack1.push('A')

    expectThat(stack1.size()).isEqualTo(0)
    expectThat(stack2.size()).isEqualTo(1)
}

@Test
fun `push push pop`(){
    val (b, stack) = FunStack<Char>()
        .push('A')
        .push('B')
        .pop()

    expectThat(stack.size()).isEqualTo(1)
    expectThat(b).isEqualTo('B')
}
```

Exercise 2.3: An RPN Calculator

This exercise consists of writing a Reverse Polish Notation calculator. RPN is a mathematical notation in which operators follow operands, instead of being in the middle and using parentheses. Reverse Polish Notation was independently reinvented by Friedrich L. Bauer and Edsger W. Dijkstra in the early 1960s to reduce the amount of computer memory needed to evaluate expressions. Let's see some examples:

```
val res = calc("4 5 +") //9.0
val res = calc("6 2 /") //3.0
val res = calc("5 6 2 1 + / *") //10.0
val res = calc("2 5 * 4 + 3 2 * 1 + /") //2.0
```

The algorithm works like this: you start with a list of numbers (operand) and operations and an empty stack. Then, starting from the left, you pick an element. If it's a number, you put it in the stack. If it's an operation, you pop up two operands from the stack and apply the operation to them. Finally, put the result on the stack again. A good starting point to solve this exercise is the functional stack code from the previous one.

Surprises are foolish things. The pleasure is not enhanced, and
the inconvenience is often considerable.

> Jane Austen, Emma

CHAPTER 3

Defining the Domain and Testing It

In the previous chapter, we wrote the first version of our application. It can show lists based on the preloaded data. We also wrote an acceptance test for it.

We learned how to combine functions together to obtain complex behavior from simple pure functions and how to treat HTTP calls as functions. In this chapter, we'll progress further, learning how to use higher-order functions.

We'll also look at the ports and adapters architecture and the benefits it can bring us. This will allow us to improve acceptance tests to make them easier to read, translating our features directly into code using domain concepts from an end-user perspective. The result will be our domain-driven tests, which will guide us through the book until we finish the application.

Improving the Acceptance Tests

Can we improve our acceptance tests? Even in small tests there are some issues, which will be much more evident when we work on more complicated use-cases.

Ideally:

- Our acceptance tests should only use domain terms, and they should avoid mentioning technical details, like the UI elements ("click on X button") or the transmission protocol ("assert that header Y is present").

- Each test should represent a use-case scenario; all tests in a file will form a user-story.

- Tests should focus on the use-case actors and their interactions.

- Assertions should be represented by methods with clear domain names, leaving the actual implementation out of the test itself, since they can be quite complicated to read.

Let's see how, following these principles, we can write better acceptance tests.

Testing the Negative Case

We should consider whether a single acceptance test is enough to cover our first story of viewing a single list. It's probably not.

We're testing only a single user with a single list, and we aren't testing that users can't see other users' lists. Therefore, we can now write a second test for the negative case:

```
@Test
fun `Only owners can see their lists`() {
    val listName = "shopping"

    startTheApplication("frank", listName, emptyList())

    expectThrows<AssertionFailedError> {
        getToDoList("bob", listName)
    }
}
```

What we're doing here is starting the application with a list created by the user frank and then trying to access it with the user bob. This shouldn't be possible, and we should expect that the method will throw an exception.

Luckily for us, this test is already passing. The standard testing cycle starts with a failing test, but sometimes we may want to add a test for a case that isn't covered, even if it's already working by chance, because it could break in the future.

Scenario Actors

First, we want to remove unnecessary details from the test itself. And since we want to focus more on the user interactions (the last two points of our list), we can start extracting an abstraction for the *actor* of the scenario. So, we can define the methods to call the application and the assertions on the expected results in the actor class:

```
❶ interface ScenarioActor{
    val name: String
}


class ToDoListOwner(override val name: String): ScenarioActor {

❷    fun canSeeTheList(listName: String, items: List<String>) {

❸        val expectedList = createList(listName, items)

❹        val list = getToDoList(name, listName)
```

```
⑤          expectThat(list).isEqualTo(expectedList)
       }

       private fun getToDoList(user: String, listName: String): ToDoList {
         //moved from the test to the actor
       }
}

private fun createList(listName: String, items: List<String>) =
    ToDoList(ListName(listName), items.map(::ToDoItem))
```

❶ We define a generic interface for actors, containing their name.

❷ The first method for our ToDoListOwner actor is a check that there is a list with name and items as expected. This will replace assertions in the test.

❸ From the method parameters we create the expected list, using a small utility function.

❹ We call the getToDoList method that was in the test before to get the list from the application.

❺ Finally, we compare the expected list with the one retrieved from the application.

When we rewrite the test using the actor, the result is already a bit clearer with respect to what's going on:

```
@Test
fun `List owners can see their lists`() {
    val listName = "shopping"
    val foodToBuy = listOf("carrots", "apples", "milk")
    val frank = ToDoListOwner("Frank")

    startTheApplication(frank.name, createList(listName, foodToBuy))

    frank.canSeeTheList(listName, foodToBuy)
}
```

Moving on to the next step, let's use our functional eye: the previous code relies heavily on the side effects (as discussed in Keep Your Functions Pure, on page 355) of the startTheApplication method. In other words, startTheApplication doesn't return its main "effect"—that is, the started application—as a result, and instead, the actor just assumes that the application will indeed start.

Note that this isn't just a problem because of some kind of theoretical purity or functional pride. What we want is that the test won't compile if the actor method is called from outside the context of an application, and we want to be sure the actor is calling the right methods on it.

To do that, let's extract a class to work as an abstraction for the application. In this way, we can pass it to the actor, and the actor will be able to use it directly.

 Joe asks:
Does This Make the Test Pure?

When testing (and using) the application, we can't avoid using impure functions, but we can make the dependency of the actor on the application as explicit as possible, reducing the impure part at the bare minimum and keeping it at the borders.

In this way, we can keep the actor and most of the test code pure. This will bring many advantages, as we'll see in the continuation of the book.

Application Facade

The Facade is a design pattern in which an object stands as a facade or proxy for a complex system, hiding the more complex innards and making it easy to interact with.[1] Here, we want to use it to extract information and give commands to our application without cluttering the test with technical details.

Our goal is to create an interface that abstracts the interactions with our application, allowing both querying its state and changing it. You may wonder about the benefits of this approach and why we can't continue to use our application directly as we have done so far. The main advantage of this facade is that it works as a contract that outlines all possible user actions on our application. As a result, it isn't possible for tests to "cheat" and directly call private methods. We will look at other advantages later (see Protocols, on page 58).

Let's start creating a class called ApplicationForAT, and let's move the getToDoList method and the parsing methods of the acceptance test there:

```
class ApplicationForAT {
    fun getToDoList(user: String, listName: String): ToDoList {
        //moved from the test...
    }

    //other private methods moved from the test...
}
```

---

1. https://en.wikipedia.org/wiki/Facade_pattern

For the moment, we can keep this class in the same file as the acceptance test, but once it's finished, we'll move it to its own file.

The next question is, how we can use the methods of our facade (getToDoList) from inside the actor? One possibility is to pass the ApplicationForAT to the actor's methods as a parameter, in this way:

```
class ToDoListOwner(override val name: String) : ScenarioActor {

    fun canSeeTheList(listName: String,
                      items: List<String>,
❶                    app: ApplicationForAT) {

        val expectedList = createList(listName, items)

        val list = app.getToDoList(name, listName)

        expectThat(list).isEqualTo(expectedList)

    }

    fun cannotSeeTheList(listName: String,
❷                        app: ApplicationForAT) {

        expectThrows<AssertionFailedError> {
            app.getToDoList(name, listName)
        }
    }

}
```

❶ We added the application facade as a new parameter.

❷ We did the same here.

If we try to run both tests now, we would find another problem: since we don't stop the server after the first test, the second test will fail because the HTTP port is still in use.

Looking at the problem in a more general way, we want to run the scenario in a controlled way, without leaking resources. So, rather than creating a web server and a web client inside our ApplicationForAT, let's pass them from outside in the constructor, and let's close the server after running the scenario.

For this we'll define a runScenario method that will take the steps as a block with Unit as result (see Unit, on page 376). In other words, each step only uses side effects to modify the system and they'll raise an error rather than returning a result. This is acceptable here because it's a test and the only result we expect is the absence of errors.

```
① class ApplicationForAT(val client: HttpHandler, val server: AutoCloseable) {
②     fun getToDoList(user: String, listName: String): ToDoList {
③         val response = client(Request(Method.GET, "/todo/$user/$listName"))
④         return if (response.status == Status.OK)
                parseResponse(response.bodyString())
            else
                fail(response.toMessage())
        }
⑤     fun runScenario(steps: (ApplicationForAT)->Unit) {
            server.use {
                steps(this)
            }
        }
// rest of methods
    }
```

❶ We pass the server and the client in the constructor.

❷ This method will call the server with the user and list name, parse the response, and return the list.

❸ Note that the client doesn't need to know the hostname, because it's already configured.

❹ We check the response status; if it's OK we parse the response, otherwise, we fail with an error.

❺ To run the whole scenario, we start the server here, then execute the steps on it, and at the end the server will close itself, since it's an Auto-Closeable.

And this is how the start method looks now. Note how we set the base Uri for the client to match the server. In this way, we can make sure the client is using the same port of the server and, in the future, we can even change this code to use a server deployed elsewhere:

```
fun startTheApplication(lists: Map<User, List<ToDoList>>): ApplicationForAT {
    val port = 8081 //different from main
    val server = Zettai(lists).asServer(Jetty(port))
    server.start()

    val client = ClientFilters
        .SetBaseUriFrom(Uri.of("http://localhost:$port/"))
        .then(JettyClient())
    return ApplicationForAT(client, server)
}
```

Going back to our acceptance test, let's see how it is now:

```
class SeeATodoListAT {
    val frank = ToDoListOwner("Frank")
    val shoppingItems = listOf("carrots", "apples", "milk")
    val frankList = createList("shopping", shoppingItems)

    val bob = ToDoListOwner("Bob")
    val gardenItems = listOf("fix the fence", "mowing the lawn")
    val bobList = createList("gardening", gardenItems)

    val lists = mapOf(
        frank.asUser() to listOf(frankList),
        bob.asUser() to listOf(bobList)
    )

    fun ToDoListOwner.asUser(): User = User(name)

    @Test
    fun `List owners can see their lists`() {

        val app = startTheApplication(lists)
        app.runScenario {
            frank.canSeeTheList("shopping", shoppingItems, it)

            bob.canSeeTheList("gardening", gardenItems, it)

        }
    }

    @Test
    fun `Only owners can see their lists`() {

        val app = startTheApplication(lists)
        app.runScenario {
            frank.cannotSeeTheList("gardening", it)

            bob.cannotSeeTheList("shopping", it)

        }
    }
}
```

This is starting to look good! It's now clear what the user actions are and that they need an application facade to run.

What's next? We can get rid of the it at the end of the actor's methods, the reference to the application facade, since it's a bit of an eyesore.

The best way to do it is to treat the step function as if it was data!

Step as a Function

Instead of having a method that takes a parameter, we can create a new function that requires that parameter and returns the function, without the need to explicitly pass the parameter.

Confusing? Let's see how it works in practice.

First, let's extract an interface with all the possible actions that an actor can use, which is only getToDoList for the moment:

```kotlin
interface Actions{
    fun getToDoList(user: String, listName: String): ToDoList?
}
```

Note that the interface will return a nullable ToDoList (as indicated by the question mark after the type). We'll discuss nullability in more depth later in The Problem with Null, on page 95.

We also make sure that ApplicationForAT implements Actions now.

Then, we define a type alias (see Type Alias, on page 383) for the function type, since it's long. Type aliases are a convenient Kotlin feature that allows us to keep our code easy to read and write, even when using complex types:

```kotlin
typealias Step = Actions.() -> Unit
```

This means that Step is the type of a function that takes an Action as receiver (see Extension Functions, on page 378) and returns Unit. We're using an extension function instead of a normal function, because it makes it easier to call methods on the Actions from inside the steps.

Then, we should change the method runScenario of the Actions interface to take a variable number of steps. Now, the implementation in ApplicationForAT looks like this:

```kotlin
fun runScenario(vararg steps: Step) {
    server.use {
        steps.onEach { step -> step(this) }
    }
}
```

In this way, we can execute each step, passing it the Actions interface as a parameter.

Going back to the actor, let's see how we can return a step as new function:

```kotlin
fun cannotSeeTheList(listName: String): Step = {
    expectThrows<AssertionFailedError> {
        getToDoList(name, listName)
    }
}
```

Note that the Step type alias is declared as an extension function, so getToDoList() is called on the returned function. For details about the syntax, see Return New Functions, on page 379.

Finally, this is how the tests look now, without the it (which was needed to reference the Actions interface) and passing a list of steps, instead of a block, to create the scenario:

```
@Test
fun `List owners can see their lists`() {
    val app = startTheApplication(lists)
    app.runScenario(
        frank.canSeeTheList("shopping", shoppingItems),
        bob.canSeeTheList("gardening", gardenItems)
    )
}

@Test
fun `Only owners can see their lists`() {
    val app = startTheApplication(lists)
    app.runScenario(
        frank.cannotSeeTheList("gardening"),
        bob.cannotSeeTheList("shopping")
    )
}
```

This looks pretty good, but what exactly did we just do? All those function references can be confusing!

Using Higher-Order Functions

It may be surprising to use other functions as inputs and outputs, but this is one of the most useful techniques in functional programming, so it's very important to understand it well.

Functions that operate on other functions as input or outputs are called higher-order functions. Any function has a type; they can be used as data, and we can create a new function and return it as a result of another function. Don't be afraid if all this seems complicated—it can be a bit mind bending at first, but with practice, it will soon become very natural.

A visual diagram, as shown on page 52, can help us understand how steps work. Here, actors are creating steps for the scenario to run.

Pure Higher-Order Function

A legitimate question at this point would be, "Can a higher-order function be pure? And what does it mean exactly?"

The answer is yes, and what it means is that the higher-order function must preserve referential transparency when given a pure function as an input.

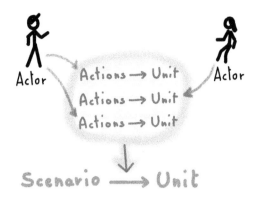

On the other hand, if we pass an impure computation as a parameter, the global result will be impure. However, despite this, the higher-order function itself will still maintain its purity.

For example, let's say we have a function that sums two numbers and logs the result. Something like this:

```
fun sumAndLog(a:Int, b:Int, log: (Int) -> Unit): Int =
    (a + b).also(log)
```

We can verify that it's a pure function by passing a pure function that doesn't do anything as log parameter:

```
val tot = sumAndLog(5, 6){}
```

In this case, sumAndLog is still completely referentially transparent.

As an example of impure computation, we can take the println function instead—its return type is Unit, but it prints on the console as a side effect. Now, if we pass println to our sumAndLog, it will produce a side effect—outputting the result on the standard output:

```
val tot = sumAndLog(5, 6, ::println)
```

However, `sumAndLog` itself still remains a pure function. It's important to understand the difference, because it will become more and more relevant as we proceed.

Another way to describe it is that invoking the `log` function constitutes a *functional effect* of our `sumAndLog` since its signature makes clear that it will call the logging function. Unlike side effects that occur unexpectedly, the act of calling the log function isn't concealed in any way.

Later in the book, in Learning Functors and Categories, on page 163, we will use data structures that will make the functional effects explicit in the type-system.

 We can also say that functional programming is the art of minimizing the code depending on side effects and keeping it at the outer edge of your programs.

Before we proceed with a new story, we need to discuss one more thing.

Separating the Domain from the Infrastructure

One of the general principles of good software design is that each module of our system should have only one reason to change. For this reason, we want to keep separate the logic that forms the business domain model from the technical implementation. We also want to keep our domain completely pure and without side effects, so we can easily test it and safely re-use its functions everywhere we need to.

An interesting question is how to distinguish what is business logic from what isn't? The main difference is at language level: business logic is something you can discuss with the business people, without using any technical terms such as serialization formats, network protocols, and so on. This can be hard if your business model is something technical, for example, if the product you are developing is a cloud platform.

On an even more general level, you can look at what you want to decouple in the design of your application. For example, do you really want to mix HTTP routing with JSON parsing and reporting logic? Probably not. Keeping all these aspects separate is the foundation of a clean design.

The Hub

So how can we keep the domain pure and separated from the rest? We'll use an interface to wrap all the domain logic and keep it separated from the external adapter. This approach is called Port and Adapter. It has been pro-posed by Alistair Cockburn,[2] and even if it's based on the object-oriented paradigm, it also works very well with functional programming.

The Port and Adapter Pattern

 Also known as Hexagonal Architecture, it's a software architecture pattern that aims to create software systems that are flexible, maintainable, and adaptable to change. The primary goal of this pattern is to create a separation between the core business logic of a system and the external dependencies it relies on, such as databases, web services, and user interfaces.

The idea is to introduce a layer of abstraction between the core logic and its external dependencies, known as ports and adapters. Ports define the interfaces through which the core logic communi-cates with the external dependencies, while adapters implement those interfaces and provide the actual communication with the external dependencies.

Overall, the Port and Adapter pattern is a powerful tool for creating maintainable and adaptable software systems, particularly in complex domains where external dependencies are numerous and subject to change.

You may wonder, why do we need yet another abstraction? Isn't it simpler if we just connect our domain functions to the HTTP layer?

Edsger W. Dijkstra said, "Being abstract is something profoundly different from being vague...The purpose of abstraction is not to be vague but to create a new semantic level in which one can be absolutely precise."

It may be simple to connect domain functions to the HTTP layer directly, but after a while, it will become very hard to separate one from the other. Intro-ducing an interface to separate the domain from the adapters will allow us to keep the separation precise.

This domain-wrapping interface works like a *hub*, since it stays in the center of our application, and it's connected to the external by many functions that work like the spokes of a wheel.

The hub defines and abstracts upon the boundaries between the domain and the technical layer—in a very precise and oddly satisfying way. The domain stays inside the hub and only communicates with the rest of the application

---

2.   https://alistaircockburn.com/Component%20plus%20strategy.pdf

using specific functions. I learned this approach while working with Nat Pryce. It also makes it easier to test each component separately.[3]

So far, we have only implemented a single story, but for the sake of explanation, let's consider a domain that has to connect with two databases, a message queue, an email server, and the HTTP routes. Here is a diagram to illustrate our implementation of ports and adapter architecture with hub and spokes:

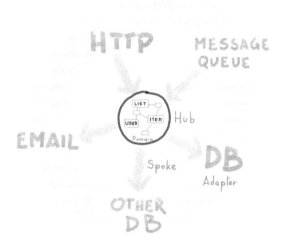

In this conceptual diagram, anything inside the hub is domain related, functionally pure, and can communicate with external components only using its "spokes"—the arrows around it. In this way, the business logic can change without any change on the technical layers, like our HTTP functions. At the same time, if we need to change a technical detail, we don't have to touch the business logic at all.

Note that some arrows are pointing inward and some pointing outward from the hub; in the diagram, the arrows follow the direction of the call. Inward arrows are mapped on methods of the hub that can be called by the outer adapters. Outward arrows represent the dependency methods that the domain logic inside the hub needs to call.

Plug the Hub into Zettai

Going back to our application, we said that we should put our business logic inside the hub; what does this mean in concrete terms? We defined four

---

3.   http://www.natpryce.com/articles/000772.html

functions in the previous chapter. Which ones are part of the domain in Zettai?

We can list them here with their signature:

Function Name	Function Type	Hub/Spoke
extractListData	(Request)-> Pair<User, ListName>	spoke
fetchListContent	(Pair<User, ListName>) -> ToDoList	hub
renderHtml	(ToDoList) -> HtmlPage	spoke
createResponse	(HtmlPage) -> Response	spoke

If we consider our types: User, ListName, and ToDoList are part of our domain model, while HtmlPage, Request, and Response are technical details of our implementation. If unsure, a simple test is to check which names can emerge if we describe our business to a nontechnical person.

The functions that have a domain type both as input and output are part of our domain; in our case, there is only one. The others are part of the spokes that connect the hub with the external world.

So, we create an equivalent to the fetchListContent function inside the hub. Let's start writing a test to see how we would like to use our hub:

```
@Test
fun `get list by user and name`() {
    val hub = ZettaiHub(listMap)

    val myList = hub.getList(user, list.listName)

    expectThat(myList).isEqualTo(list)
}
```

Let's proceed, defining our ZettaiHub interface. We need only one function from the inside of the hub to the external, the one to retrieve a ToDoList:

```
interface ZettaiHub {
    fun getList(user: User, listName: ListName): ToDoList?
}
```

When implementing the hub interface, it's important to keep in mind two things:

- The inside of the hub should stay functionally pure, without any side effects and external interactions.

- The hub needs external functions to complete the functionality, so we need to provide them from the outside.

\//   **Joe asks:**

ᔑᔑ   **Isn't It Premature to Create the Hub Interface Now?**

It may seem excessive to create an interface with a single method and a single implementation, but it's simpler and faster to enforce a clean design from the beginning rather than retrofit it later in a poorly designed application.

The key point here is that we aren't trying to guess future needs; that would be against the principles of lean development. What we're doing is defining and respecting a principle (namely the separation between domain and infrastructure) from the very beginning, in the simplest possible way.

Now we can implement the hub for the ToDoList. It gets the map of to-do lists and users in the constructor and implements our function:

```kotlin
class ToDoListHub(val lists: Map<User, List<ToDoList>>): ZettaiHub {

    override fun getList(user: User, listName: ListName): ToDoList? =
        lists[user]
        ?.firstOrNull { it.listName == listName }
}
```

Then we pass the hub to the Zettai class constructor, in lieu of the map of lists:

```kotlin
data class Zettai(val hub: ZettaiHub): HttpHandler{

    //rest of the methods...

    fun fetchListContent(listId: Pair<User, ListName>): ToDoList =
        hub.getList(listId.first, listId.second)
        ?: error("List unknown")
}
```

Note that the Actions interface of our acceptance tests has a method with exactly the same signature. This isn't a coincidence; if we're keeping our tests close to the domain, the actor's actions will be quite similar to the methods of the hub.

Now we have good acceptance tests and a clean design with the domain separated from the adapters. We can take advantage of this fact and add another tool to our toolkit.

Driving the Tests from the Domain

We did a good job so far, but how can we be sure that our acceptance tests will stay easy to read and maintain?

Unfortunately, as the application becomes more complicated, it's very easy to end up with acceptance tests that are very hard to understand and maintain. This is because what we really want to test will be hidden behind layers of nonessential details about the user interaction.

Nat Pryce, who is a big proponent of using acceptance testing to drive the design, came out with the idea of domain-driven tests (DDT) after getting tired of working with acceptance tests that were slow and hard to change because they were written in a kind of "click here and then click there" way.[4] The name comes from the concern that tests should be written using business domain terms. There is also a pun there since they are quite efficient in killing bugs (like the pesticide).

Protocols

So where is the innovation? It's the capability to write our end-to-end tests using only the language of the domain, independently from the adapters layer. In this way, we can run the tests several times using various methods of connecting to the domain, which I refer to as *protocols*.

For instance, we can run the tests quickly using only the in-memory implementation of the hub to verify the accuracy of the domain logic—the domain-only protocol. Then, we can run the tests again by starting the application locally and using HTTP calls to verify the complete functionality of the system—the local HTTP protocol. Finally, we can test it again in our stage environment, using deployed services to verify that the network and the deploying scripts are also correct—the remote HTTP protocol.

To accomplish this, we must adopt a single interface, which represents our actions, to abstract different implementations of our application (protocols). In this way, we're forced to define a common language in the test that stays independent of the specifics of each protocol.

Additionally, we aim to use the same terminology when conversing with business experts. Composing tests using domain-specific vocabulary allows for better communication between software developers and the rest of the business.

Overall, the goal of this approach is to describe our stories as interactions between human actors and the system domain. This technique simplifies the testing process and enhances communication in intricate software development projects. Here are some of its advantages:

---

4.   http://natpryce.com/articles/000819.html

- Fast failure feedback on the domain-only implementation
- End-to-end functionality testing on the HTTP implementation
- Verification that there is no business logic in the infrastructure layer
- Verification that there is no infrastructure dependency in the business layer

The first two points are quite evident, but the last two are less obvious. A common mistake is to let our domain model become dependent on technical details, for example, the value of an HTTP header. However, when creating a domain-only version of our DDT, we quickly realize that we don't have an HTTP header to pass, because we're not using HTTP. This scenario will force us to create a better domain abstraction that would capture the value of the header without depending on the technical details of the HTTP protocol.

Let's explore what all this means in practice.

Convert Acceptance Tests to DDT

To summarize, we want to run our test twice, once using only the hub and testing only the business logic, and then run it again against the real application.

It should look something like this:

```
@Test
fun `List owners can see their lists`() {

    val apps = listOf(
        startTheApplicationDomainOnly(lists)
        startTheApplicationHttp(lists),
    )

    apps.forEach{ app ->
        app.runScenario(
            frank.canSeeTheList("shopping", shoppingItems),
            bob.canSeeTheList("gardening", gardenItems)
        )
    }
}
```

There is some boilerplate code to write every time to launch the scenario, set up the applications, and so on.

Now, as it happens, I've used DDTs in several projects, and to avoid writing the boilerplate code every time, I have written an open source library that simplifies writing DDT in Kotlin, taking care of most of the repetitive tasks and using dynamic nested tests of JUnit5 to display each step as single test.

Converting DDT to Pesticide

My DDT library is called Pesticide (since DDT is a famous pesticide);[5] it's lightweight, with no external dependency apart from JUnit, and easy to customize to your needs.

Note that using Pesticide makes it easier to write DDTs, but you can write them using other libraries.

As a personal aside, I was first introduced to DDTs when I joined a team where Nat Pryce was the software architect. Even if I liked the idea from the start, I struggled to understand how to effectively write them. They seemed easy enough to write when pairing with Nat, but I couldn't write a decent one when I was alone.

The breakthrough moment for me was when I realized that they should describe the system from the point of view of its users, not from the point of view of the application software I was writing.

For this reason, as we'll see, in Pesticide you're forced to write the tests as a list of steps that originates from the scenario actor.

 Joe asks:
What about BDD and Cucumber?

Behavior Driven Design is a style of testing that also puts a lot of emphasis on the system behavior from the user's point of view, and Cucumber is a very popular library that makes it easy to use.

What DDTs introduce is forcing us to run the same tests on different protocols.

Speaking of libraries, it's definitely possible to write DDTs with Cucumber, but we would need some code anyway. Moreover, I think it's easier to write clean tests defining actors and actions as separate classes with their methods, rather than rely on text parsing like in Cucumber; at least this worked for us, but you may prefer another approach.

As ever, what's important is the principle, not the tools.

Scenario

Let's see how we can translate our acceptance tests into a DDT with Pesticide; it's quite simple because of all the work we did before.

---

5.   https://github.com/uberto/pesticide

Pesticide uses the same convention, with each test representing a *scenario* of a user story. This is what it looks like:

```
❶ typealias ZettaiDDT = DomainDrivenTest<ZettaiActions>

❷ fun allActions() = setOf(
       DomainOnlyActions(),
       HttpActions()
   )

❸ class SeeATodoListDDT : ZettaiDDT(allActions()) {

       @DDT
❹      fun `List owners can see their lists`() = ddtScenario {

           //here put the actors steps...

       }

   }
```

❶ This is a shortcut for the type for our DDT.

❷ Here, we define the set of actions we'll run our tests on. See the code later.

❸ Each test class has all the scenario to define a single user story. We need to inherit from the base DDT class and pass the list of actions.

❹ Each test method should be marked with @DDT and it'll consist of the result of the ddtScenario function. The name of the test should reflect the name of the scenario we're verifying.

It doesn't compile yet because we still need to create actions. This is easily remedied.

Actions and Protocols

We now need to define our actions in the Pesticide format. As we saw, the actions are working a bit like a translator between our application and the actors.

Porting the code from our acceptance test requires very few changes:

```
❶ interface ZettaiActions : DdtActions<DdtProtocol> {

       fun getToDoList(user: User, listName: ListName): ToDoList?
   }


❷ class DomainOnlyActions() : ZettaiActions {
❸     override val protocol: DdtProtocol = DomainOnly
❹     override fun prepare() = Ready

❺     private val lists: Map<User, List<ToDoList>> = emptyMap()

       private val hub = ToDoListHub(list)
```

```
⑥    override fun getToDoList(user: User, listName: ListName): ToDoList? =
         hub.getList(user, listName)

}

⑦ class HttpActions(val env: String = "local"): ZettaiActions {
     override val protocol: DdtProtocol = Http(env)
     override fun prepare(): DomainSetUp = TODO("launch the app")

     override fun getToDoList(user: User, listName: ListName): ToDoList =
         TODO("not implemented yet")

}
```

❶ This is the interface for our generic actions with the method we already defined. It has to inherit from DdtActions.

❷ Each of our concrete actions needs to inherit the ZettaiActions interface.

❸ Each implementation of DdtActions works on a different protocol. This is interacting only with the domain of our application.

❹ The prepare method of the actions is where we can do some setup work. Nothing is needed for the domain-only actions.

❺ For the moment, we'll use an empty map of lists for the hub; we'll see later how to fill them.

❻ We declare the hub and the method to get a list, as in the acceptance test.

❼ This is the implementation for the HTTP protocol. We can specify a deployment location; for the moment, local would be enough. We'll write the code later in the chapter.

Actors

As in our acceptance tests, we need one or more *actors*. They represent actual human users and will interact with the system.

In Pesticide, we need to inherit our actors from DdtActor; to represent the Zettai user that owns some to-do lists, we can create an actor called ToDoListOwner:

```
data class ToDoListOwner(override val name: String):
    DdtActor<ZettaiActions>()
```

The actor can only act on the application using the DDT actions. For this reason, we need to pass the ZettaiAction interface as a generic parameter to the actor.

Joe asks:
Why Do We Need Actors?

We could use the actions directly in the tests and do the assertions in the same place.

Our actors are representations of the real human beings that use our software. Their steps must represent the interactions they could have with our system. Hence, writing our tests as a list of actor steps nudges us toward writing in a way that's closer to the actual human interaction than the technical implementation.

Moreover, without the actors, we'll clutter the tests themselves with a lot of complicated assertions. For this reason, we want to keep all assertions inside the actors' methods, so tests will stay readable and clean.

Then, the actor will operate differently depending on the protocol of the actions. A visualization can make it clearer:

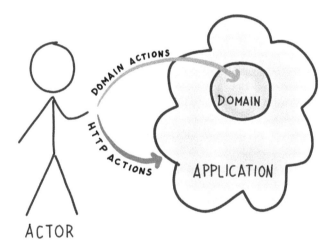

Steps

As we did in our acceptance test, we can now proceed to describe the user story as a list of steps. Each one is a method on an actor, and inside each step the actor interacts with the application using the current actions.

Writing the actor steps correctly is a very delicate task. We have two main concerns here: on one hand we want to keep the actor steps as close as possible to a real human interaction with the system, and on the other hand we want to keep all the assertions to verify the correctness of the system inside the actor steps. If the system behaves as expected, then we call the test a success; otherwise, it's a failure.

A good rule of thumb is to keep the actors' steps simple and clean—to keep separate the steps that query the application from the steps that operate a change in the application. In our case here, the step to add an item won't contain any assertions, and the step to verify the list won't change anything in the application.

It's also very important to keep all the assertions inside the steps, at least the assertions that we can express in domain terms. This means that the same verification must work for both HTTP and domain-only actions. If we need different assertions depending on the protocol, either we're testing some technical details or we have leaked some business logic into the technical adapters.

Convert to Pesticide DDT

We can now complete our first test using Pesticide. It's not very different from how we wrote the acceptance test, but there are some subtleties:

```
class SeeATodoListDDT : ZettaiDDT(allActions()) {

❶  val frank by NamedActor(::ToDoListOwner)

   val bob by NamedActor(::ToDoListOwner)

   val shoppingListName = "shopping"
   val shoppingItems = listOf("carrots", "apples", "milk")

   val gardenListName = "gardening"
   val gardenItems = listOf("fix the fence", "mowing the lawn")

   @DDT
   fun `List owners can see their lists`() = ddtScenario {
❷     setUp {
❸         frank.`starts with a list`(shoppingListName, shoppingItems)
           bob.`starts with a list`(gardenListName, gardenItems)
❹     }.thenPlay(
           frank.`can see #listname with #itemnames`(
                                 shoppingListName, shoppingItems),
❺         bob.`can see #listname with #itemnames`(
                                 gardenListName, gardenItems)
       )
   }
}
```

❶ Pesticide has a shorthand way to create actors using Kotlin delegation.

❷ In each scenario, there is an optional setup part where we can put the system in the correct state for the test to run.

❸ This action will associate the list with the user in the map inside the hub. It's a temporary hack, and we'll see a better solution in the next chapter.

❹ Here, we put the list of steps that constitutes the actual test.

❺ In the step name, the hashed words will be substituted in the test with the parameter value, to make them easier to read.

The test itself is easy to read and should sound like a natural language. Even nonprogrammers should be able read it to ensure that the requirements are met. Of course, they can't check the correctness of the actual code, but they should be able to spot errors in the logic of the interaction.

More generally speaking, it's not important if the test doesn't seem perfect on the first try. If we missed something—it can and does happen—we can always improve the test later. With time, our suite will become more and more reliable.

```kotlin
data class ToDoListOwner(override val name: String):
❶        DdtActor<ZettaiActions>() {
❷    val user = User(name)

    fun `can see #listname with #itemnames`(
                listName: String,
                expectedItems: List<String>) =
❸        step(listName, expectedItems) {
❹            val list = getToDoList(user, ListName(listName))
❺            expectThat(list)
                .isNotNull()
                .itemNames
                .containsExactlyInAnyOrder(expectedItems)
        }
    private val Assertion.Builder<ToDoList>.itemNames
        get() = get { items.map { it.description } }

}
```

❶ The actor should inherit from DdtActor and override the name property. The name will be added to all its actions when creating the step names.

❷ Since we use User multiple times, let's just define it as a field.

❸ Each method we use in our tests must be created with the step function. The hash signs in the method name will be substituted with the parameters we pass to the step function.

❹ For the first test, we added the getToDoList method on the actions and we called with the list name...

❺ ...so we can check that the items displayed are identical with those we were expecting.

Calling the Application

The last bit that's still missing in our conversion is defining the actions for the HTTP protocol. From there, we need to start the application, and we need to add an HTTP client to test it.

Let's visualize how HTTP actions should work:

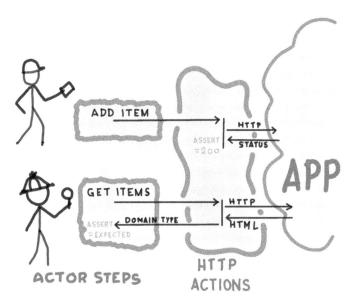

We use the prepare method of the actions to prepare the application and stop it at the end of the test:

❶
```
data class HttpActions(val env:String="local"): ZettaiActions {

    override val protocol: DdtProtocol = Http(env)

    val zettaiPort = 8000 //different from the one in main
```
❷
```
    val server = Zettai(hub).asServer(Jetty(zettaiPort))
```

```
③      val client = JettyClient()
④      override fun prepare(): DomainSetUp {
           server.start()
           return Ready
       }
⑤      override fun tearDown(): HttpActions =
           also { server.stop() }
       private fun callZettai(method: Method, path: String): Response =
           client( log( Request(
             method,
⑥            "http://localhost:$zettaiPort/$path")))
```

❶ We inherit from ZettaiActions and we put the protocol to HTTP. We store the environment name in the env field. Here, we only care about localhost, but we can run our tests in a remote environment as well.

❷ This is the local instance of Zettai server.

❸ This is the HTTP client that the action uses to talk with Zettai.

❹ Here, we start the local server before running the tests. We'll see later how to run DDTs against deployed environments.

❺ We stop the local server at the end of the test.

❻ This is the function to call Zettai. It will become more complex when we manage different environments.

The Final Test

We can now translate the second test from the acceptance to Pesticide in a similar way as the first. Let's look at the final result:

```
class SeeATodoListDDT : ZettaiDDT(allActions()) {

// declarations...

    @DDT
    fun `List owners can see their lists`() = ddtScenario {

        setUp {
            frank.`starts with a list`(shoppingListName, shoppingItems)
            bob.`starts with a list`(gardenListName, gardenItems)
        }.thenPlay(
            frank.`can see #listname with #itemnames`(
                                    shoppingListName, shoppingItems),
            bob.`can see #listname with #itemnames`(
                                    gardenListName, gardenItems)
        )
    }
```

```
@DDT
fun `Only owners can see their lists`() = ddtScenario {

    setUp {
        tom.`starts with a list`(shoppingListName, shoppingItems)
        adam.`starts with a list`(gardenListName, gardenItems)
    }.thenPlay(
        tom.`cannot see #listname`(gardenListName),
        adam.`cannot see #listname`(shoppingListName)
    )
}
}
```

This is how our first story, see a single list, has been translated into a DDT with Pesticide. It's a bit cleaner than our previous acceptance tests, and it now runs both on domain and HTTP protocol.

When running it from the IDE, this is what it looks like:

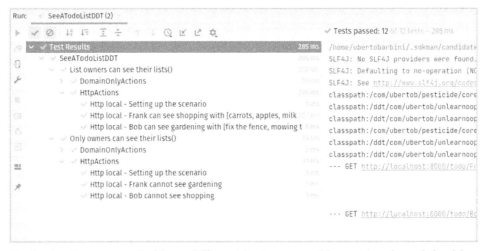

Each step is represented by a different test, grouped by protocol, and double-clicking on one will make the IDE jump directly to the code. Note also that the hashed names have been substituted with the actual list and item names.

Recap

In this chapter, we saw how to write down the stories as acceptance tests that the computer can automatically verify, and we discussed why it's important to do it before writing the actual code.

Then, we introduced one of the most important principles of good design: keep the domain logic separated from the infrastructure. We used the port and adapter pattern to do so, and we started operating on functions as data.

Last but not least, we looked at domain-driven tests and their advantages, and we rewrote the tests for our first story with the Pesticide library. We'll keep writing DDTs all across the book before implementing any new feature.

In the next chapter, we'll implement a new story and learn how to use higher-order functions to implement dependency injection in a functional way.

We'll also finish handling the requests and responses in the adapters.

Exercises

The exercises in this chapter will focus on DDT and higher-order functions.

Here is your friendly reminder that nobody can learn functional programming by just reading code, and the best way to learn is by practicing. You can refer to the exercises folder in the book code repository for the starting point and some hints.

Exercise 3.1: Cashier DDT

Looking at the instruction on the Pesticide website, try to create a DDT, DomainOnly. It has to be written from the perspective of a customer using a self-checkout machine, adding a single food item, and verifying the total.

Something like this:

```
enum class Item { carrot, milk }

interface CashierActions : DdtActions<DdtProtocol> {
    fun setupPrices(prices: Map<String, Double>)
    fun totalFor(actorName: String): Double
    fun addItem(actorName: String, qty: Int, item: Item)
}

class CashierDDT : DomainDrivenTest<CashierActions>(allActions) {

    val alice by NamedActor(::Customer)

    @DDT
    fun `customer can buy an item`() = ddtScenario {

        val prices = mapOf(carrot to 2.0, milk to 5.0)

        setUp {
            setupPrices(prices)
        }.thenPlay(
            alice.`can add #qty #item`(3, carrot),
            alice.`can add #qty #item`(1, milk),
            alice.`check total is #total`(11.0)
        )
    }
}
```

Exercise 3.2: Discounts DDT

For this exercise, add a new DDT test to verify the discount logic, define the promotions in the settings (for example, 3x2 on carrots), and add the steps to buy promoted items and verify the discounted price.

```
@DDT
fun `customer can benefit from 3x2 offer`() = ddtScenario {
    val prices = mapOf(carrot to 2.0, milk to 5.0)

    setUp {
        setupPrices(prices)
        setup3x2(milk)
    }.thenPlay(
        alice.`can add #qty #item`(3, carrot),
        alice.`can add #qty #item`(3, milk),
        alice.`check total is #total`(16.0)
    )
}
```

Exercise 3.3: Function as Result

For this exercise, write a function that takes a string as parameter and returns a new function that returns a specific character of the given string. You need to implement this function:

```
fun buildCharAtPos(s: String): (Int) -> Char = TODO()
```

...so that this test will pass:

```
val myCharAtPos = buildCharAtPos("Kotlin")
expectThat(myCharAtPos(0)).isEqualTo('K')
```

Exercise 3.4: Template Engine

For this exercise, you need to write a mini template engine. You need to implement these two functions, replacing the TODO() with the correct code:

```
data class StringTag(val text: String)

infix fun String.tag(value: String): Pair<String, StringTag> = TODO()

fun renderTemplate(template: String, data: Map<String, StringTag> ) = TODO()
```

...so that this test will pass:

```
val template = """
    Happy Birthday {name} {surname}!
    from {sender}.
""".trimIndent()
```

```
val data = mapOf("name" tag "Uberto",
                 "surname" tag "Barbini",
                 "sender" tag "PragProg")

val actual = renderTemplate(template, data)

val expected = """
    Happy Birthday Uberto Barbini!
    from PragProg.
""".trimIndent()

expectThat(actual).isEqualTo(expected)
```

If knowledge can create problems, it is not through ignorance
that we can solve them.

> Isaac Asimov

CHAPTER 4

Modeling the Domain and the Adapters

In the previous chapter, we learned about higher-order functions, the ports and adapters pattern, and domain-driven tests.

In this chapter, we'll implement a new story to add an item to a list, so we'll introduce mutability into our domain. We'll also see better how DDT can guide us, from defining the feature to code completion.

In the meanwhile, we'll focus on how to keep the domain model separated by technical adapters. And we'll improve both the adapters and the domain objects.

Starting a New Story to Modify a List

Let's consider the second story: adding an item to a list. Writing a DDT isn't difficult, but starting from scratch can be a bit daunting. The trick is to think in terms of a use-case scenario: how would we describe it using small actors' steps? To make the DDT compile we can add the steps as empty functions in the actor until we're satisfied with the scenario code.

```
class ModifyAToDoListDDT: ZettaiDDT(allActions()){

    val ann by NamedActor(::ToDoListOwner)

    @DDT
    fun `The list owner can add new items`() = ddtScenario {
        setup {
            ann.`starts with a list`("diy", emptyList())
        }.thenPlay(
            ann.`can add #item to #listname`("paint the shelf", "diy"),
            ann.`can add #item to #listname`("fix the gate", "diy"),
            ann.`can add #item to #listname`("change the lock", "diy"),
            ann.`can see #listname with #itemnames`("diy", listOf(
                "fix the gate", "paint the shelf", "change the lock"))
```

```
⑥        ).wip(LocalDate.of(2023,12,31), "Not implemented yet")
    }
}
```

❶ The name of the test class reflects the user story name.

❷ Each test represents a scenario of the story.

❸ We start with a list without items.

❹ Then, we call a new step to add an item three times.

❺ Finally, we check that the list has the three items.

❻ We mark the test as work-in-progress until it passes.

Note how we marked the new test with the wip method at the end. That's short for work-in-progress, since, as we said in the first chapter, our DDT won't pass until we finish the implementation at the end of this chapter.

)|/
ᵕ₰ᵕ **Joe asks:**

Why Do We Use Randomly Generated Values in the Unit Tests but Specific Examples in the DDTs?

This is a very good question. In the case of our unit tests, we want to make sure that we cover all corner cases and our functions are pure and total. For this reason, randomly generated values give us more confidence in the results, and since the tests are very fast, we can run them many times.

When it comes to tests that simulate actual usage scenarios, such as our DDTs, we're primarily interested in the cooperation between the development team and business stakeholders. Communication among different teams is simpler when discussing in terms of concrete examples, rather then in terms of logical relations, like the property tests assertions.

Work-in-Progress

In a normal unit test, we expect the test to fail for only a few minutes, and we'll definitely not commit it if it's not green. So, having a failing unit test isn't recommended.

Conversely, for DDTs and all end-to-end tests, it's acceptable for them to stay broken for days. They'll pass only when the story is completely finished.

We can see here a symmetrical principle: DDTs are the first tests we write and they'll be the last to pass. It's also a good practice to draft all the DDTs we need to complete the story when discussing with the business experts; in this way, we can quickly validate their utility and be sure not to forget important details. We can then proceed to implement and make them pass one by one, rechecking them often with the stakeholders.

To do this, we need a clear way to mark the tests we're working on, letting them run but ignoring the failure. We can also specify a tentative date to complete them, after which the test won't be ignored anymore. Then, if we forgot to fix them in time, they'll break the build, and it will remind us to complete them or to delete them if they aren't needed anymore.

Without the WIP notation, we have to remember which tests are supposed to fail and which aren't. This isn't a big issue right now since we have only two acceptance tests, but as soon as we start having many tests, the "accepted failures" would make the report very confusing.

Domain-Driven Test Process

The process of working with DDTs looks like a V:

1. We start with the Http version first so we can sort out the "plumbing" of our architecture.

2. When we arrive at the point where we need some domain logic, we switch to InMemory/DomainOnly DDTs and let them guide us in modeling the domain.

3. Then, we develop the needed components one by one, using unit tests.

4. After that, we fix the DomainOnly DDTs until they pass.

5. Finally, we return to the Http DDT and make sure the final infrastructure is working as expected.

In the following "V" diagram, we're now at phase one of the DDT to modify a list. We're going to add the new methods on the actors and the HTTP actions so we can make the test compile first.

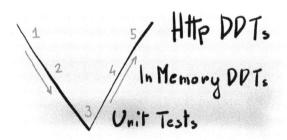

Joe asks:

Why Are We Starting from the HTTP and Not from the Hub?

As we discussed in the first chapter, writing functionalities starting from the external layers (the UI) and going to the internal ones is called "outside-in" style, whilst writing it from the internal domain and proceeding to the external layers is called "inside-out" style.

Which style should we use? There is no unique answer and it really depends on our constraints and acceptance criteria. DDTs are defined by the user actions on the external layer of the system; that's why starting from the HTTP layer makes sense.

On the other hand, if we wanted to develop a specific algorithm to solve a problem but we didn't care about the external layers, it would make more sense to use the inside-out style.

Actor Step

To make it compile we need to add a new step to the actor:

```
data class ToDoListOwner(override val name: String):
                                        DdtActor<ZettaiActions>() {

    val user = User(name)

    fun `can add #item to #listname`(itemName: String, listName: String) =
        step(itemName, listName) {
            val item = ToDoItem(itemName)
            addListItem(user, ListName(listName), item)
        }
    //rest of the methods
}
```

As we saw, the words starting with # in the method name will be replaced with the actual values when we run the test. Each step is defined inside the step method of the DdtActor. The step itself calls the addListItem on the actions with the correct parameters.

This is a general pattern. The actor steps only contain logic to call the actions, but they don't interact with the application directly. Here, we're sending a command to the application, so we don't have any result to verify. In case of steps that query the status of the application—like in the case of the can see #listname with #itemnames step—we would verify also that the result is what we expect.

HTTP Actions Call

To continue, we need to add the addListItem method to the ZettaiActions interface, so we can implement it in the HTTP and domain instance.

As we're in the first point of our "V" diagram, we'll leave the domain action with just a TODO in the implementation.

Instead, we'll start from the HTTP implementation. To simulate adding an item to a list, we need to submit an HTTP webform to the server with the item name and the item due date fields:

```
data class HttpActions(val env: String = "local"): ZettaiActions {

    override fun addListItem(user: User,
            listName: ListName, item: ToDoItem) {

        val response = submitToZettai(
            todoListUrl(user, listName),
            listOf( "itemname" to item.description,
                    "itemdue" to item.dueDate?.toString())
        )

        expectThat(response.status).isEqualTo(Status.SEE_OTHER)
    }

    private fun submitToZettai(path: String, webForm: Form): Response =
        client(log(
            Request(
                Method.POST,
                "http://localhost:$zettaiPort/$path")
            .body(webForm.toBody())))

//rest of methods...
}
```

Since the DDT now compiles, we can run it. This is how it looks in the IDE:

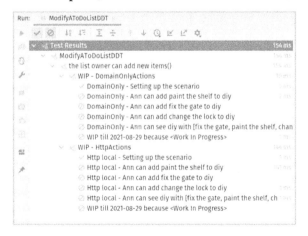

You can see that only the first step passes; the remaining steps are failing, but since the test is marked as work-in-progress, they are not failing the scenario.

Handle Different Pages

To progress on the implementation of our feature, we need a new HTTP endpoint to add a new item to a given list.

But, we have a new problem: so far we've created a function that returns an HTML page with a to-do list from a request, but this is only one among the many kinds of requests our web service will need to handle. How can we return different pages or API according to the details of the request?

We don't want to modify the function we already wrote; it's finished as it is and it shouldn't care about the other kinds of calls. We also don't want to write a function too specific with hardcoded values, because we couldn't reuse it. We want a generic reusable solution to this problem.

How can we combine together functions that handle different kinds of Request without changing our existing code? With another function, of course! More precisely, we need a function that takes a collection of functions as input and returns a new function.

In order to learn how to code it, let's leave our Zettai app for a moment, and let's have a spike on a minimal web service for operating on some data to learn how to define routes using higher-order functions.

CRUD Example

For this example, we need to Create, Read, Update, and Delete some resources. These are the basic four functions of persistent storage, called CRUD for short, and they are often associated with HTTP verbs in RESTful API. Let's say we already have four functions, from a Request to a Response, corresponding to each one and called (for lack of imagination) c, r, u, and d. How can we create a web server combining these four functions together? What we want is to be able to look at the Request and then process it with one of c, r, u, and d, according to the HTTP verb. Let's learn how to solve this problem using higher-order functions.

What we need now is another function, let's call it routes, that takes the list of our handler functions and returns a new handler that takes a Request and passes it to the correct "sub handler" (that is, one of c, r, u, or d) to produce a Response. This is the signature:

```
fun routes( c: HttpHandler, r: HttpHandler,
            u: HttpHandler, d: HttpHandler
): HttpHandler = TODO()
```

Let's use a diagram to visualize how the new routes function works:

From the Verb and Path we select which of the four functions (c,r,u,d) we're using on our Request.

How do we determine which is the correct HttpHandler to use for a given Request? We match the HTTP verb and the path of the Request with the expected API. When writing complex applications, we may need more sophisticated match rules that take into consideration the content type and other attributes of the Request—but the principle is the same. Here is our routes function:

```
fun routes(c: HttpHandler, r: HttpHandler,
           u: HttpHandler, d: HttpHandler
): HttpHandler = { request ->
    when ("${request.method} ${request.uri.path}") {
        "POST /data" -> c(request)
        "GET /data" -> r(request)
        "PUT /data" -> u(request)
        "DELETE /data" -> d(request)
        else -> Response(404, "NOT FOUND")
    }
}
```

❶ Here, we concatenate the HTTP verb and path to compare it against the cases we associated with the functions to call. For an explanation of the when keyword, see When, on page 384.

❷ If the Request does not match any of our cases, we create a new Response with HTTP error 404.

And now the good news: we don't have to implement our own routes function, because Http4k already did it for us! We met it when we did the Http4k spike, but now we understand better how it works.

Http4k uses a powerful Domain Specific Language to allow us to define all the routes in a declarative way, taking advantage of Kotlin capabilities. To learn more, see Infix Functions, on page 388.

A Route to Add an Item

After this mini spike, we can go back to Zettai, and add a new route to add a new item to a list:

```
class Zettai(val hub: ZettaiHub): HttpHandler {
    val httpHandler = routes(
        "/todo/{user}/{listname}" bind GET to ::getToDoList,
        "/todo/{user}/{listname}" bind POST to ::addNewItem
    )

    private fun addNewItem(request: Request): Response = TODO()

    //other methods...
}
```

❶ The function routes takes a list of routes as inputs and returns an HttpHandler.

❷ Each route is created by the bind infix function that takes a string representing the path and the union of an HTTP method and a function of type HttpHandler.

❸ We use the same path with a POST instead of a GET to add a new item to a list.

To implement the addNewItem function, we need to extract the relevant information from the HTTP path and the form and call a new method on the hub—which is our domain facade:

```
fun addNewItem(request: Request): Response {
    val user = request.path("user")
        ?.let(::User)
        ?: return Response(Status.BAD_REQUEST)
    val listName = request.path("listname")
        ?.let(::ListName)
        ?: return Response(Status.BAD_REQUEST)
    val item = request.form("itemname")
        ?.let(::ToDoItem(it))
        ?: return Response(Status.BAD_REQUEST)

    return hub.addItemToList(user, listName, item)
        ?.let { Response(Status.SEE_OTHER)
            .header("Location", "/todo/${user.name}/${listName.name}") }
        ?: Response(Status.NOT_FOUND)
}
```

```
class ToDoListHub(val fetcher: ToDoListUpdatableFetcher): ZettaiHub {

    override fun addItemToList(user: User,
        listName: ListName, item: ToDoItem): ToDoList? = TODO()
//...
}
```

❶ We extract user and list name from the request path, using the template defined in the route.

❷ We're using let to chain the functions if the result isn't null.

❸ We extract the item name from the HTML form.

❹ Once we have all three arguments, we call the hub method.

❺ In case of success, we redirect the browser to the list page, so the user can see the new item.

❻ In case of null, we return a 404 error status.

Note that the advantage of working in this way, from outside to inside, is that we can design our model API—the hub methods—as a perfect fit for the needs of our adapters—the HTTP routes in this case. Running the DDT now, we can see that our HTTP test is calling the hub, so the route handling is done correctly.

We're at point two on the "V" diagram, Domain-Driven Test Process, on page 75; we now need to switch to the domain-only DDT and try to make it pass.

The domain action must just delegate the call to the new method in the hub:

```
class DomainOnlyActions : ZettaiActions {
    override fun addListItem(user: User,
            listName: ListName, item: ToDoItem) {
        hub.addItemToList(user, listName, item)
    }
//...
}
```

We need to start working on the domain now and to implement the method on the hub that we left as TODO.

So far, our hub only used the model in read-only mode. We now need to modify the content of our model, but our hub must remain pure. This is a quite common problem and the easiest solution is to inject a dependency inside our hub that will handle the change.

We'll return to this problem with other solutions later, but now it's time to learn a new technique to add to the functional programmer's toolbox.

Using Functional Dependency Injection

Let's consider for a moment how the hub can delegate access to external resources—in other words, how we can inject functions inside the hub to allow the domain to communicate with the external services.

Dependency Injection

Dependency injection is an important principle of good design, not only in object-oriented programming, but also in functional programming. If our code needs to use some external dependencies, it should avoid creating them directly, and it should receive them from outside instead.

Keeping the creation of external dependencies separated from their usage allows us to keep our code more flexible and easier to test, as we can pass different implementations expecting different behaviors.

Comparison with Object-Oriented Dependency Injection

In the object-oriented world, dependency injection consists of passing the dependencies (objects) that an object needs from the external, rather than letting the object create them by itself. This can be done by passing them to the constructor or using some meta-programming technique like annotations or external configuration files.

In functional programming, functions are often preferred over objects—if this isn't clear now it will be as we progress with the book. As a result, we must pass dependencies as functions to the main function. How can we achieve this? We'll use another function (surprise, surprise!) that accepts dependencies as arguments and generates a new function with those dependencies embedded within. This can be quite confusing, so let's proceed with a concrete example.

Suppose we need a function that retrieves a particular list, given a User and a ListName. Let's start defining a type alias for this function, called ToDoListFetcher:

```
typealias ToDoListFetcher = (User, ListName) -> ToDoList?
```

But, to make it work we need to store the collection of all lists somewhere between calls, and we don't want break the functional purity accessing some external resource directly. What can we do?

We can solve this problem by adding a new parameter of type Map<User,Map<List-Name, ToDoList>> with the lists inside. We can visualize it in this way:

$$Map \langle User, Map \langle ListName, ToDoList \rangle \rangle$$

$$\{User, ListName\} \longrightarrow ToDoList$$

Let's call the new function mapFetcher:

```
typealias ToDoListMap = Map<User,Map<ListName, ToDoList>>

fun mapFetcher(map: ToDoListMap,
               user: User,
               list: ListName): ToDoList? =
    map[user]?.get(list)
```

Still, it'd be quite cumbersome to pass the map around every time we want to call the function. What we want instead is to create a new function from the map, which somehow can keep the map inside. Using this new function, we can extract the list from the map, passing only User and ListName.

Partial Application

We can visualize the injection of the map in this way:

$$Map$$

$$\{User, ListName\} \longrightarrow ToDoList$$

This technique is called a partial function application, and even if we didn't know the name, we already used the technique in the previous examples with the HttpHandler.

The main idea is quite simple. Let's say we have a function with a number of parameters, in our case, three. We want to associate it somehow with the first parameter and create a new function that only takes the remaining two parameters.

To proceed, let's define a function, called partial, which takes a function with three parameters and the first parameter as input and returns a new function with the rest of the parameters:

```
fun <A,B,C,R> partial(f: (A,B,C) -> R, a: A): (B,C) -> R = {
    b,c -> f(a,b,c)
}
```

So, in our case, provided we have a map of type ToDoListMap, we can create our fetcher function with only two parameters in this way:

```
val fetcher: ToDoListFetcher = partial(::mapFetcher, map)
```

If we want, we can extend the concept of partial application further, applying it again and again until we run out of function arguments.

In general, it's always possible to transform a function with any number of parameters in a chain of functions with only a single parameter each. This technique is usually called *currying*, from the name of the mathematician Haskell Curry (no relation with the delicious spicy dish).

 Joe asks:

Why Are There So Many Complicated Names in Functional Programming?

It's probably because mathematicians love to denote things precisely.

Partial application is so called because we partially apply the input parameters. But it's not that important to know all the names.

In mathematics, we have the commutative property of addition. We have probably forgotten the name, but the important part is to remember that 2 + 3 is equivalent to 3 + 2. Still, when talking about it, it's convenient to have a precise name.

I agree that mathematicians are sometimes terrible at naming things. Like programmers.

We can use this technique—a functional dependency injection—to pass some functions that will do the work to fetch and update our list to the database, a remote service, or a map in memory. Injecting external effects from our main function allows us to keep the hub pure and free from the details of the technical domain, because they stay at the margins, while the values read can be used by the main logic block.

Add an Item in the Hub

We're now at step three of the "V" diagram; everything is connected, but we need to implement the method on the hub.

So, let's add our external dependency on the hub to fetch the list. This is how ToDoListHub would look:

```
class ToDoListHub(val fetcher: ToDoListFetcher) : ZettaiHub {

    override fun getList(user: User, listName: ListName): ToDoList? =
        fetcher(user, listName)

    override fun addItemToList(user: User,
            listName: ListName, item: ToDoItem): ToDoList? = TODO()

}
```

Now that we have a rough idea of what we need, we can proceed with unit tests to guide our implementation:

```
class ToDoListHubTest {

    val fetcher = TODO("we need an implementation!")

    val hub = ToDoListHub(fetcher)

    //tests starts here
}
```

It's good practice to start the test with the simplest happy path of the element under test. In this way, we can gain useful feedback from the beginning.

Here, we want to test that we can get any list added to the fetcher using the correct user name and list name:

```
@Test
fun `get list by user and name`() {
    repeat(10) {
        val user = randomUser()
        val list = randomToDoList()

        // TODO ("assign the list to the user!")

        val myList = hub.getList(user, list.listName)

        expectThat(myList).isEqualTo(list)

    }
}
```

To progress, we need to define the fetcher function to read a list from some external source. In this way, we can set up data for our tests operating directly on the external source.

A possible solution is to use the partial higher-order function we saw before to associate the map to the fetcher function. But, there is another useful Kotlin feature that allows us to create partial functions in a more idiomatic way.

Functions as Invokable Classes

A surprising consequence of Kotlin's type system is that a class can inherit from a function type. This makes its implementations invokable, as if they were a function. Moreover, we can pass an instance of the invokable class wherever a function with the same signature is needed.

To declare a function type class, we only have to put the function type in the declaration where the superclass would have been, and then override the invoke method.

Using a class to implement a function offers us some advantages:

1. Any constructor parameter will be partially applied to the needed function.
2. Complex code can be neatly contained in private functions.
3. A state needed for an API can be stored between calls (for example, connections).

We're going to take advantage of this Kotlin feature to inject the necessary impure functions into our hub in a nice, clean way.

Storing Lists Outside the Hub

Since we want to change the map, we need to define a store using a mutable map of maps to fetch the list from:

```kotlin
typealias ToDoListStore = MutableMap<User, MutableMap<ListName, ToDoList>>

data class ToDoListFetcherFromMap(
    private val store: ToDoListStore
): ToDoListFetcher {

    override fun invoke(user: User, listName: ListName): ToDoList? =
        store[user]?.get(listName)

    fun assignListToUser(user: User, list: ToDoList): ToDoList? =
        store.compute(user) { _, value ->
            val listMap = value ?: mutableMapOf()
            listMap.apply { put(list.listName, list) }
        }?.let { list }
}
```

❶ We use a map of maps as our store.

❷ This is the functional interface. We return the ToDoList from the private map inside the store.

❸ To store a new list, we add it to the lists of the user, or we create the user with the list if it doesn't exist.

Putting it to work, our test is now complete:

```
class ToDoListHubTest {

    fun emptyStore(): ToDoListStore = mutableMapOf()

    val fetcher = ToDoListFetcherFromMap(emptyStore())

    val hub = ToDoListHub(fetcher)

    @Test
    fun `get list by user and name`() {
        repeat(10) {
            val user = randomUser()
            val list = randomToDoList()

            fetcher.assignListToUser(user, list)

            val myList = hub.getList(user, list.listName)

            expectThat(myList).isEqualTo(list)
        }
    }
}
```

You can see that pure functions are very simple to test, and they don't require special classes with special setups like stub or mocks. All our dependencies are just functions that we can implement as we want directly in the test.

Note that the ToDoListHub doesn't see the mutable map; its only dependency is on the fetcher.

At this point, the hub seems quite useless since we moved most of the logic to the fetcher, but it still works as a clear separation of the domain, and it will gain logic with the next use-cases.

Verify the Negative Case

We want to also test a negative case. Returning null means that our request can't be fulfilled. And, we want a test to verify that we can't retrieve a list if the user isn't correct:

```
@Test
fun `don't get list from other users`() {
    repeat(10) {
        val firstList = randomToDoList()
        val secondList = randomToDoList()
        val firstUser = randomUser()
        val secondUser = randomUser()

        fetcher.assignListToUser(firstUser, firstList)
        fetcher.assignListToUser(secondUser, secondList)
```

```
        expect {
            that(hub.getList(firstUser, secondList.listName)).isNull()
            that(hub.getList(secondUser, firstList.listName)).isNull()
        }
    }
}
```

Now, the hub finally works and all its tests are green. Note that we don't need any kind of persistence right now; we'll confront this problem later in Persisting Safely, on page 205. What we have now is a memory-only solution, but it will allow us to plug in a fully persistent layer later without having to change the existing code.

 Joe asks:

Is This the Best We Can Do with Functional Programming? Hiding External Effects in Apparently Pure Functions?

No, it isn't.

This is only the easiest way to separate pure from impure functions. We'll adopt a more powerful but also more complex way to keep external effects from creeping into our domain code in the chapter about functors and projections. Still, using invokable classes is easy, and it has its uses when the risk of mixing pure and impure code is relatively low.

Add an Item to the List

Now we're at the fourth step of the "V" diagram of DDT. We updated our model with unit tests, and we need to fix the hub so that the domain-only DDT will pass.

To implement the addItemToList method on the hub, we need a way to update the fetcher. Currently, our ToDoListFetcherFromMap has the addItemToList, but that isn't exposed on the ToDoListFetcher interface, so our hub can't use it.

We can dispense with the interface and declare our fetcher field of type ToDoListFetcherFromMap, but this would expose other implementation details that we don't want the hub to be aware of. A better way is to create a new interface with a new method to assign a list to a user:

```
interface ToDoListUpdatableFetcher: ToDoListFetcher{

    fun assignListToUser(user: User, list: ToDoList): ToDoList?

}
```

```
class ToDoListHub(val fetcher: ToDoListUpdatableFetcher): ZettaiHub {

    override fun getList(user: User, listName: ListName): ToDoList? =
        fetcher(user, listName)

    override fun addItemToList(user: User,
            listName: ListName, item: ToDoItem): ToDoList? =

        fetcher(user, listName)?.run {
            val newList = copy(items = items
                .filterNot{ it.description == item.description} + item)
            fetcher.assignListToUser (user, newList)
        }

}
```

Using ToDoListUpdatableFetcher, the hub can update the user list with the new item.

In this case we got lucky, because not only the domain-only DDTs are passing but also the HTTP ones. This is because we didn't change the way we render and parse the HTML response. Just keep in mind this isn't always the case.

Anyway, we fixed step four and step five of the "V" diagram together, and if we run our tests now, we can see that all the DDTs are passing. Actually, before running them, we have to remove the work-in-progress marker, otherwise they'll fail for an unexpected success!

Running them from the IDE will look like this:

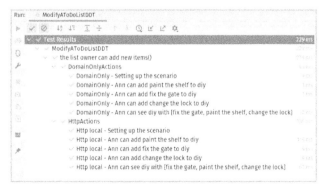

As we said at the start of the chapter, alternating in finishing implementation for DomainOnly and LocalHttp DDTs is very useful and helps us keep the focus on the feature. The advantage of finishing with the HTTP test is that once it's done, we know that the functionality is completely finished.

Debugging Functional Code

Before continuing with the next story, let's pause for a moment to consider the difficulties and the perks of a functional code base.

If you aren't convinced yet, you'll discover soon that writing and debugging higher-order functions and fully functional code can be difficult.

Trying to write all functions as a chain of type transformations, using a single expression and avoiding mutable variables, can make the code quite hard to write. It can be hard to understand how everything fits together and sometimes even why it's not compiling at all.

On the other hand, once it compiles correctly, we're usually pretty sure that there will be no surprises later. Once we're familiar with this style, it's also surprisingly easy to understand—there are no hidden dependencies, everything is declared.

The cost of taking into consideration all the cases upfront is amply counterbalanced by the benefit of not chasing corner cases later.

With practice, it's possible to write very elegant functional code, as the rest of this book will show, but still, there are a few tricks that can help.

As an example, let's consider the body of method addItemToList from the hub:

```
fetcher(user, listName)?.run {
    val newList = copy(items = items
        .filterNot { it.description == item.description } + item)
    fetcher.assignListToUser (user, newList)
}
```

We can rewrite it in a somewhat more verbose (but still perfectly functional) way, like this:

```
{
    val list: ToDoList? = fetcher(user, listName)
    return if (list == null) {
        null
    else {
        val oldItems = list.items.filterNot{
            it.description == item.description }
```

```
        val newItems = oldItems + item
        val newList = list.copy(items = newItems)
        fetcher.assignListToUser(user, newList)
    }
}
```

At the beginning, it can be useful to write code in this longer form, but after a while, having a long list of temporary variables can look redundant. Getting familiar with Kotlin's scope functions (Scope Functions, on page 379) can help us to simplify things.

Here, we can use run to remove the if and the return:

```
fetcher(user, listName)?.run {
    val oldItems = items.filterNot{
        it.description == item.description }
    val newItems = oldItems + item
    val newList = copy(items = newItems)
    fetcher.assignListToUser(user, newList)
}
```

Looking at the code, we need some temporary variables, because we need to replace an element of the to-do items. What we can do is extract a pure function with a clear name. Making it an extension function would keep the code terser:

```
fetcher(user, listName)?.run {
    val newList = copy(items = items.replaceItem(item))
    fetcher.assignListToUser(user, newList)
}

fun List<ToDoItem>.replaceItem(item: ToDoItem): List<ToDoItem> =
    filterNot { it.description == item.description } + item
```

 In general, extracting smaller functions can clarify the code for two reasons: their name can clarify their intent, and their type signature can help us if the code isn't compiling.

When in Doubt, Print It

Sometimes it's tempting to add a variable just because we want to print out its values for debugging purposes. Here's a more elegant way to define a generic extension function:

```
fun <T> T.printIt(prefix: String = ">"): T = also{ println("$prefix $this") }
```

...and then add it temporarily when we aren't sure what's going on:

```
fetcher(user, listName)?.run {
    val newList = copy(items = items.printIt("orig")
        .replaceItem(item).printIt("replaced"))
            .printIt("newList")
    fetcher.assignListToUser(user, newList)
}
```

Examining the console output produced by the test, we can see the list's contents before and after replacing an item. The main advantage of using printIt is that it requires minimal changes to our code. Since printIt returns the same value that it extends, adding it does not cause any code to break. Once we have resolved the issue at hand, we can remove the printIt call from our code.

Functional Domain Modeling

To improve as functional programmers, we need to learn how to model our domain in a functional way.

In object-oriented design, we start identifying the business entities that are involved in the business process. Business entities are real-world concepts, such as customers, orders, products, or invoices.

Once the relevant business entities have been identified, the next step is to map them to classes in our code and encapsulate the behavior of a particular concept. So, the aim is to create a software system that closely mirrors the real-world processes.

For example, we might create a Customer class that encapsulates data about a customer's name, contact information, and purchase history, as well as behavior such as placing an order or updating their profile.

Functional design, on the other hand, is based on transformations (arrows) of data types and their compositions.

So, when it comes to mapping a business process, we don't focus on the business entities but on the data that gets exchanged and its transformations. This means that we define functions that take in some data (say, the CustomerOrder), perform some computation (such as calculating the total cost of the order), and then return some other data as output (the final Invoice).

In a nutshell, the transition from object-oriented design to functional design is the transition from looking at your domain as entities collaborating with each other to looking at it as a network of transformations of immutable pieces of information. However, modeling a business domain in code is a very delicate operation, regardless of the paradigm we use.

Let's recap which principles we're following when defining good functional data structures. So far, we've already discussed two:

1. Immutability. Operating with immutable data structures allows us to use them inside pure functions. See Don't Trust Mutable Types, on page 357.

2. Naming. Denoting our types with precise names, as opposed to using primitives, is making the signature of our functions clearer and their intent simpler to understand. See Define Your Types Precisely, on page 363.

We now need to carefully consider a new quality for our types.

Low Cardinality

The cardinality of a type is defined as the number of all its possible values, for example:

Type	Cardinality	Example values
Boolean	2	true, false
Byte	256	00000000, 00000001, 00000010, …
Integer	2^{32}	MinInt .. MaxInt
String	~infinite	"", "a", "b", …

This is a way to look at types that may be surprising at first, but keeping cardinality as low as possible makes it impossible for our type to express values that don't have an actual meaning in our domain. This will make our global application state simpler to understand, and it will also reduce the checks we need to put in place.

It will also work as an anti-corruption layer, preventing invalid data from entering into our system by blocking them as close to the source as possible. In order to do that, we need specific constructors that verify our data from untrusted sources. To see what this means in practice, let's look again at ListName. We defined it in the previous chapter, but now we need to model it better and lower its cardinality.

A string can be millions of characters long, but this clearly doesn't make sense as a name for our to-do lists. We want to keep the length of the name reasonable, let's say between three and forty characters. We also decided to use ListName as part of our RESTful URLs, and to keep them easy to read in a browser, we want to restrict them to alphanumeric characters plus the hyphen sign without spaces.

Our goal is to limit the type's cardinality to only the relevant cases, instead of having to handle almost infinite possibilities. In this way, we have eliminated many potential sources of bugs by ensuring that only sensible list names are entered into our system.

Having said that, probably the main benefit of using precise types is that they restrict the ways we can manipulate their values to only those that actually make sense in the context of the application domain.

In other words, the ListName type represents the name of a to-do list. By assigning it a specific type, we can prevent errors, such as accidentally passing the list description instead of the name.

Null as an Error

A good pattern we can use here is to make the default constructor private, and instead, create two public static constructors, one to be used when we trust our source, and one for untrusted sources.

To define static constructors in Kotlin, see Objects and Companion Objects, on page 381.

```
data class ListName internal constructor(val name: String) {
    companion object {
        fun fromTrusted(name: String): ListName = ListName(name)
        fun fromUntrusted(name: String): ListName? = TODO("not defined yet")
    }
}
```

❶ The normal constructor is internal. To create a ListName, we need to choose one of the two companion object methods.

❷ When parsing the name from a source we trust, like our database, we can use this method, which will trust the input.

❸ When parsing the name from an external input like user input tests, we must use this method. If the name is correct, it will return ListName, otherwise, it will return null.

Please note, we created methods on the companion object, not as standalone functions, to ensure they reside in a specific namespace for easier discovery.

When reading the name from inside our domain or for tests, we can use the simpler trusting constructor, which will always return a new ListName. But every time we parse a name from outside our trusted sphere, for example, from the user input or an HTTP request, we must use the untrusting constructor.

We can see that fromUntrusted will return a ListName when the name is valid or null when the name isn't valid. In this case, the null represents the impossibility to create a new instance.

You may wonder if returning null is a good idea or not. But, what's the problem with null?

The Problem with Null

Null references were introduced for the first time by Tony Hoare in ALGOL, back in 1965, "simply because it was so easy to implement." He named this decision "my billion-dollar mistake."

To understand what the problem is with null, let's reflect on the fact that it allows our code to cheat! To see what I mean, in Java for example, we can have a method like this:

```
Customer getCustomer(String name) {
    if (name.isEmpty())
        return null;
    else
        return Customer(name);
}
```

Can you spot the (possible) bug? Our function expects a String as a parameter name, but it can instead receive a null. This poses a problem, as null is definitely not a String, and treating it as such would cause an exception.

Furthermore, while the function declares to return an instance of the Customer class, it could instead return null. In other words, our code declares one thing, but then it does another.

As a consequence, whoever is calling this method must also check if the result is null before using it. So, either we fill our code with checkpoints, or we risk a NullPointerException at runtime.

But note the problem isn't null per se. The problem is we expect an instance of a given type and instead we get null, which isn't. Edsger W. Dijkstra famously said all classes "will seem to be married polyamorously to the same person Null."

In Kotlin (and some other modern languages), we don't have this problem. Using the same example, we can return a nullable customer using a question mark, like this: Customer? This is a type defined by the union of Customer and null, so we can handle the two conditions explicitly. If we want to convert a Customer? to a Text, we need to consider both the valid case and the null case separately. For example, we can return an HTML page when we have a customer and an error message in case of null:

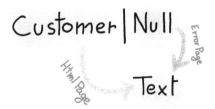

Kotlin's nullable types allow us to safely write total functions (see Consider All the Possible Inputs, on page 359), because the compiler will force us to handle both cases. Returning a null instead of an error is a very convenient pattern to handle failures when we don't care about the reason for the failure.

However, sometimes we actually do care about the reason for the failure. In such cases, we can consider a more nuanced (albeit complex) solution, which we'll explore later when discussing Handling Errors Better, on page 157.

Property Testing

As we saw in the first chapter, property testing can be useful to verify invariant properties of our functions. For example, here we want to test that we can't create a ListName with an invalid name using the ListName.fromUntrusted function.

To test this, we'll write the unit test for the fromUntrusted function as we learned in the first chapter in Our First Unit Test, on page 14.

So, instead of trying to figure out what would be valid examples, we'll define what the properties are that we want to verify. Using specific example values to test our functions, we can easily miss a critical corner case. Even more importantly, the test is hard to understand. Why these cases and not others? What are the rules exactly?

As we saw, the idea behind property testing is to generate many random values and verify that the properties we want to verify are still valid for any of the inputs. For this, we need to write a random string generator using Kotlin's generateSequence function. For a better understanding of sequences in Kotlin, see Sequences, on page 387.

```
fun stringsGenerator(charSet: String, minLen: Int, maxLen: Int)
  : Sequence<String> = generateSequence {
    randomString(charSet, minLen, maxLen)
}

fun randomString(charSet: String, minLen: Int, maxLen: Int) =
```

```
StringBuilder().run {
    repeat(Random.nextInt(maxLen - minLen) + minLen) {
        append(charSet.random())
    }
    toString()
}
```

Let's start testing the happy path—that is, the case without any error or exception. We want to validate all possible valid values for ListName. We can't test infinite cases, but with a string generator we can generate a number of random names (let's say 100) that should pass our test:

```
val validCharset = uppercase + lowercase + digits + "-"
val invalidCharset = " !@#$%^&*()_+={}[]|:;'<>,./?\u2202\u2203\u2204\u2205"

@Test
fun `Valid names are alphanum+hiphen between 3 and 40 chars length`() {

    stringsGenerator(validCharset, 3, 40)
        .take(100)
        .forEach {
            expectThat(ListName.fromUntrusted(it))
                .isEqualTo(ListName.fromTrusted(it))
        }
}
```

With this test in place, we can start implementing the fromUntrusted function. We can then continue adding tests for all the negative cases in the same way:

```
@Test
fun `Name cannot be empty`() {
    expectThat(ListName.fromUntrusted("")).isEqualTo(null)
}

@Test
fun `Names longer than 40 chars are not valid`() {

    stringsGenerator(validCharset, 41, 200)
        .take(100)
        .forEach {
            expectThat(ListName.fromUntrusted(it)).isEqualTo(null)
        }
}

@Test
fun `Invalid chars are not allowed in the name`() {

    stringsGenerator(validCharset, 1, 30)
        .map { substituteRandomChar(invalidCharset, it) }
        .take(1000).forEach {
            expectThat(ListName.fromUntrusted(it)).isEqualTo(null)
        }
}
```

One of the nice things about property testing is that we're forced to write different tests to test different properties of our functions. Guided by our tests, we finally write our function:

```
val validUrlPattern = Regex(pattern = "[A-Za-z0-9-]+")
fun fromUntrusted(name: String): ListName? =
    if (name.matches(validUrlPattern) && name.length in 1..40)
        fromTrusted(name)
    else
        null
```

And now we can verify that all our tests are passing:

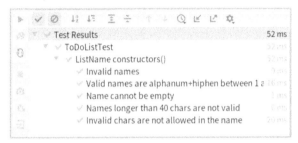

So, does property testing consist of just using randomly generated values? No, there is much more, as we'll see, but this is the first step. Having randomly generated values forces us to describe the test expectations in a more generic way and to start thinking about our domain in terms of its properties.

Our random generators are still dumb but it's possible to generate random examples in a more sophisticated way, for example, making sure to generate corner cases first. We also would like to not stop at the first failure but have a sample of failure cases. We'll see how to improve our property tests in the next chapter.

Nullable Fields in Types

The next types we want to improve are ToDoList and ToDoItem. These are clearly the main entities of our domain; we're writing a to-do list application after all. We should resist the temptation to add a lot of details to these types until we work on a story that requires them. For now, we define only the fields from the mockups that we discussed in Preparing the Mock-Ups, on page 6.

We just discussed Kotlin's nullable types. Should we make use of them in our domain modeling? Absolutely yes. The ToDoItem class has a nullable dueDate field, because we want to let the user be free to add or not a date to his items. As a general rule, nullable types are very convenient to map the optional attributes of the domain.

We also want to map all the possible states of the to-do item to an enum, using ToDoStatus.Todo as the default.

We can now start modifying the existing unit test to verify the possible values for the new fields, and then we can write our types:

```
data class ToDoList(val listName: ListName, val items: List<ToDoItem>)

data class ToDoItem(
    val description: String,
    val dueDate: LocalDate? = null,
    val status: ToDoStatus = ToDoStatus.Todo
)

enum class ToDoStatus { Todo, InProgress, Done, Blocked }
```

At this point, we want to refresh how we display the list to the user, including the status and the due date of items.

Better HTML

If we try using the application, we might note that the current HTML page is pretty poor. We can do a little better using Bootstrap style sheets.[1]

We only need to improve our renderPage function to transform a ToDoList into an HtmlPage. As the simplest possible solution, we'll just take advantage of Kotlin multiline String to define a very simple HTML page.

```
fun renderPage(todoList: ToDoList): HtmlPage =
    HtmlPage("""<html>…long and boring html template here…</html>""")
```

You can look at the actual HTML code in the source repository. This is how our list looks now:

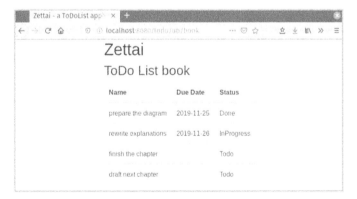

---

1.   https://getbootstrap.com/

Parsing the HTML

The only problem is that with the new HTML, our HTTP DDTs are failing, because the parsing function isn't working anymore.

Test the UI First

We could have followed a more systematic approach by interactively defining the new HTML in a browser, using a static file with an example list, iteratively modifying it until we were satisfied with the results. At that point, we'd change the unit tests and the DDTs to reflect the new HTML of the UI, and finally, adjust the code producing the HTML to match our tests.

However, in reality, I often prefer to experiment with the code directly, as it allows me to quickly adjust the UI until it meets my requirements, rather than modifying a static file.

Nonetheless, if there is a dedicated UI team in the organization, it may be better and safer to update the tests based on the new UI first.

Then, we need to rewrite the extractItemsFromPage function to our HttpActions method to parse the HTML and extract the items from it. For the actual parsing, we'll use Jsoup.[2] It's an easy-to-use library to extract data from any HTML:

```
private fun HtmlPage.parse(): Document = Jsoup.parse(raw)

fun extractItemsFromPage(html: HtmlPage): List<ToDoItem> =
    html.parse()
        .select("tr")
        .filter { it.select("td").size == 3 }
        .map {
            Triple(
                it.select("td")[0].text().orEmpty(),
                it.select("td")[1].text().toIsoLocalDate(),
                it.select("td")[2].text().orEmpty().toStatus()
            )
        }
        .map { (name, date, status) ->
            ToDoItem(name, date, status)
        }
```

---

2.   https://jsoup.org/

> \/ /   **Joe asks:**
> ‿ヾ
> # Why Do We Parse the HTML to Verify Our Code?
> # Doesn't It Risk Making Our Tests More Fragile?
>
> The risk definitely exists. We need to validate our story, and here, we care about the rendering to the HTML part, so we need to somehow verify the HTML page.
>
> Another approach is to instruct (with the Accept header) the server to return the content using JSON format. But writing production code only for tests can create other kinds of problems.
>
> In any case, even if we parse the HTML, we should try to avoid checks that would fail because of trivial HTML changes like formatting or adding invisible elements. Otherwise, the maintenance of tests would become really bothersome. For this reason, we're parsing the result and comparing only the data displayed with the expected ones. We don't want to have to fix the tests for cosmetic changes to the UI.

Finally, all our tests are passing again, and we can consider this story done.

Extract a Higher-Order Function

To close this chapter on functional domain modeling, let's see a little example of refactoring toward higher-order functions: let's look at how to parse a nullable String to a LocalDate. For the sake of this example, let's assume the String could be either a valid date in ISO 8601 format or be null or empty. In the second case, we must return null:

```
private fun String?.toIsoLocalDate(): LocalDate? =
    if (this.isNullOrBlank())
        null
    else
        LocalDate.parse(this, DateTimeFormatter.ISO_LOCAL_DATE)
```

This works fine, but we can do better.

This function is actually doing two things: checking for null, and transforming the String when not null. We extract the null check logic into a different function, and then compose it with the transformation functions. We will re-use this null check in other cases when we parse nullable fields. In order to do so, we can extract the if and generalize the case for any nonnullable type (bounding U to Any):

```
fun <U : Any> CharSequence?.unlessNullOrEmpty(f: (CharSequence) -> U): U? =
    if (this.isNullOrEmpty()) null else f(this)
```

Now, our LocalDate parser is simpler and clearer:

```
fun String?.toIsoLocalDate(): LocalDate? =
    unlessNullOrEmpty {
        LocalDate.parse(this, DateTimeFormatter.ISO_LOCAL_DATE)
    }
```

One of the little joys of functional programming is being able to identify and extract a generic higher-order function from a seemingly arbitrary piece of code.

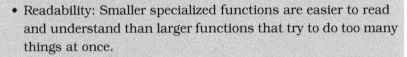

Composing over Smaller Functions

Composing over smaller specialized functions can offer several advantages:

- Readability: Smaller specialized functions are easier to read and understand than larger functions that try to do too many things at once.

- Reusability: By extracting a generic higher-order function, you create a reusable component that can be used in multiple parts of your codebase.

- Testability: The simpler the functions, the easier to test them.

- Flexibility: Composing functions allows you to build up more complex behavior from smaller building blocks. This makes it easier to adapt the code when requirements change.

Recap

In this chapter, we looked in detail at the process of writing a DDT and using it to drive our implementation. We implemented a new story so that we could add items to a list.

We also started using functional dependency injection for our persistence and compared it to the object-oriented approach.

Then we parsed and validated the HTML of the responses to assure that the HTTP layer was correctly working, while the domain-only DDT gave us assurance that we weren't leaking any business logic outside our domain.

Finally, we improved our domain model, learning how to model our data in a functional way.

In the next chapter, we'll look at how to let the user create a new to-do list. We'll also make our acquaintance with events and recursion.

Exercises

The exercises in this chapter will focus on nullable types and partial application.

Here is your friendly reminder that nobody can learn functional programming by just reading code, and the best way to learn is by practicing. You can refer to the exercises folder in the book code repository for the starting point and some hints.

Exercise 4.1: DiscardUnless

For this exercise, let's create a general higher-order function to return null if some predicate is true. Try to implement this function:

```
fun <T> T.discardUnless(predicate: T.() -> Boolean): T? =
```

...in a way that allows these tests to pass:

```
val itemInProgress = ToDoItem("doing something",
                               status= ToDoStatus.InProgress)
val itemBlocked = ToDoItem("must do something",
                               status= ToDoStatus.Blocked)

expectThat(
    itemInProgress.discardUnless { status == ToDoStatus.InProgress }
).isEqualTo(itemInProgress)

expectThat(
    itemBlocked.discardUnless { status == ToDoStatus.InProgress }
).isEqualTo(null)
```

Exercise 4.2: Chain Nullable Functions

We discussed how we can use null to express an unqualified failure. Let's see how we can chain functions that may return nullable result types.

The exercise consists of the implementation of andUnlessNull function, so that if any of the functions in the chain returns a null, the combination should avoid calling the next function if the previous one already returned null.

```
infix fun <A: Any, B: Any, C: Any> FUN<A, B?>.andUnlessNull(
    other: FUN<B, C?>): FUN<A, C?> = TODO()

val processUnlessNull = ::extractListData andUnlessNull
        ::fetchListContent andUnlessNull
        ::renderHtml andUnlessNull
        ::createResponse

fun fetchList(request: Request): Response = processUnlessNull(request)
    ?: Response(404, "Not found")
```

Exercise 4.3: Currying

We have two simple functions that require two parameters and return a result of the same type.

```
fun sum(num1: Int, num2: Int) = num1 + num2
fun strConcat(s1: String, s2: String) = "$s1 $s2"
```

We want to implement a function called curry with this signature:

```
fun <A,B,C> ((A, B) -> C).curry(): (A) -> (B) -> C
```

...so that it will split our function with two parameters in a chain of two functions that require a parameter each:

```
val plus3Fn = ::sum.curry()(3)
expectThat(plus3Fn(4)).isEqualTo(7)

val starPrefixFn = ::strConcat.curry()("*")
expectThat(starPrefixFn("abc")).isEqualTo("* abc")
```

As a second step, we want to compose parameters using an infix function called +++ with this signature:

```
infix fun <A,B> ((A) -> B).`+++`(a: A): B
```

...that can be used in this way:

```
val curriedConcat = ::strConcat.curry()
expectThat(curriedConcat `+++` "head" `+++` "tail")
    .isEqualTo("head tail")

val curriedSum = ::sum.curry()
expectThat(curriedSum `+++` 4 `+++` 5).isEqualTo(9)
```

You can also define a curry function for the case of three, four, and five parameters.

Exercise 4.4: Invokable

The currying function is useful to understand how to consume and produce functions in Kotlin, but a more idiomatic and simple way to do partial application in Kotlin is to use an invokable class.

In this exercise, you need to write a function to get the text for a personalized email using the recipient's first name:

```
class EmailTemplate(templateText: String): (Person) -> String {
  fun invoke(aPerson: Person): String = TODO()
}
```

You need to complete the EmailTemplate class in a way that it uses the templateText argument of the constructor to generate the email text using the details of the Person provided through the invoke function. You can use the template engine from the exercise from Chapter 3.

Write a test to check if the template correctly applies to the email for different persons.

Time is a sort of river of passing events, and strong is its current; no
sooner is a thing brought to sight than it is swept by and another
takes its place, and this too will be swept away.

✍ *Marcus Aurelius*

CHAPTER 5

Using Events to Modify the State

In the previous chapter, we saw how to keep the domain separated from the infrastructure. We also saw how to modify a list, letting DDT drive our design. Now, we'll look more in depth at what instruments functional programming brings to us for manipulating state changes and how to use them.

We'll also examine how to use the *Event Sourcing* pattern, using events to trace the history of our application state. We'll see how this makes it easy to modify our lists without losing the advantages of functional programming.

Creating and Displaying To-Do Lists

In the previous chapter, we managed to modify a to-do list while keeping the domain pure. What we want now is to let users create their lists; for this we also need a page that shows all the user's lists. We drew the mock-up for this page in the first chapter (see Preparing the Mock-Ups, on page 6), and now we can write down the DDTs covering these scenarios:

1. Users start with no lists.
2. Users can see all their lists (and only those).
3. A user can create a new list.

Create a User Lists Page

Let's start with the first two DDTs; we'll look at list creation later. Since these are DDT and not unit tests, we can write both tests together and leave them as work-in-progress:

```
class UserListsPageDDT: ZettaiDDT(allActions()) {

    val carol by NamedActor(::ToDoListOwner)
    val emma by NamedActor(::ToDoListOwner)
```

①

```
    @DDT
    fun `new users have no lists`() = ddtScenario {

        play(
            emma.`cannot see any list`()
        ).wip(LocalDate.of(2023,12,31))
    }

    @DDT
    fun `only owners can see all their lists`() = ddtScenario {

        val expectedLists = generateSomeToDoLists()

        setup {
            carol.`starts with some lists`(expectedLists)
        }.thenPlay(
            carol.`can see the lists: #listNames`(expectedLists.keys),
            emma.`cannot see any list`()
        ).wip(LocalDate.of(2023,12,31))

    }

    private fun generateSomeToDoLists(): Map<String, List<String>> {
        return mapOf(
            "work" to listOf("meeting", "spreadsheet"),
            "home" to listOf("buy food"),
            "friends" to listOf("buy present", "book restaurant")
        )
    }
}
```

❶ We start by defining two actors for our DDT, Emma and Carol.

❷ Without any settings, there are no lists in the system.

❸ Since we added lists attached to Carol, she can see them.

❹ But Emma still can't see any lists.

We added a setup method called starts with some lists to allow for multiple lists for a user, and then we checked that users can see all their lists but only those. We defined it as an extension function on the actor, as we did for the other setup method, starts with a list. To make these tests compile, we need to define the actions for the actor and the tasks for both the domain-only representation and the HTTP one.

The best way to proceed after having written the test is to implement the new methods on the actor. This way, we can clarify which condition we expect to be true for each step. It's easier to do this when we still have the needs of our test fresh in memory.

```
data class ToDoListOwner(override val name: String):
                        DdtActor<ZettaiActions>() {

    fun `cannot see any list`() = step {
        val lists = allUserLists(user)
        expectThat(lists).isEmpty()
    }

    fun `can see the lists: #listNames`(expectedLists: Set<String>) =
        step( expectedLists) {
            val lists = allUserLists(user)
            expectThat(lists)
                .map(ListName::name)
                .containsExactly(expectedLists)
        }
```

❶ allUserLists is a new method on the actions to retrieve all the lists of a user.

❷ To make the step clearer, we use the hash sign to show the expected list names in our tests.

To make the DDT compile, we need to add the methods starts with some lists and allUserLists to the actions interface. We can implement the first using the existing method, start with a list, directly in the interface. For the moment, we can leave a TODO on the implementation of allUserLists in the concrete action classes.

```
interface ZettaiActions : DomainActions<DdtProtocol> {

    fun ToDoListOwner.`starts with some lists`(
                        lists: Map<String, List<String>>) =
        lists.forEach { (listName, items) ->
            `starts with a list`(listName, items)
        }

    fun allUserLists(user: User): List<ListName> = TODO()

    //rest of the methods...
}
```

Switch to the HTTP DDT

As we start working on the HTTP DDT, we need to add a new route to our HttpHandler to return the new page with the list of the user's to-do lists. Continuing with the RESTful approach, we define a route binding the method GET on the user name path to return the page with all the lists of the user:

```
class Zettai(val hub: ZettaiHub) : HttpHandler {

    val httpHandler = routes(
        "/todo/{user}/{listname}" bind GET to ::getToDoList,
```

```
         "/todo/{user}/{listname}" bind POST to ::addNewItem,
❶        "/todo/{user}" bind GET to ::getAllLists
     )

     private fun getAllLists(req: Request): Response {
❷        val user = req.extractUser()

❸        return hub.getLists(user)
❹            ?.let { renderListsPage(user, it) }
             ?.let(::toResponse)
             ?: Response(Status.BAD_REQUEST)
     }

     fun Request.extractUser(): User = path("user").orEmpty().let(::User)

     // rest of the methods...
}
```

❶ Here, we define the new route for fetching all lists.

❷ We created a small extension function to extract the user from the request. For the moment, we don't verify that users do exist.

❸ We need a new method on the hub to get all the lists of a user.

❹ First, we get the lists from the hub, and here, we render the HTML page for the user.

Once we add the new route, we can point our HTTP actions to it. Since we aren't sure about parsing, we'll leave it for later:

```
override fun allUserLists(user: User): List<ListName> {
    val response = callZettai(Method.GET, allUserListsUrl(user))

    expectThat(response.status).isEqualTo(Status.OK)

    TODO("parsing not implemented yet")
}
```

Running the HTTP DDT now, we can verify that the test is actually hitting the application, and it's failing because the hub method is not implemented yet.

Now, we need to introduce a proper interface for the fetcher and a new method on the hub so that we can retrieve all the lists for a single user from our mutable store in memory.

```
interface ZettaiHub {
    fun getList(user: User, listName: ListName): ToDoList?
    fun addItemToList(user: User,
                      listName: ListName, item: ToDoItem): ToDoList?
❶   fun getLists(user: User): List<ListName>?
}
```

```
class ToDoListHub(val fetcher: ToDoListUpdatableFetcher): ZettaiHub {

    override fun getLists(user: User): List<ListName>? =
        fetcher.getAll(user)

    // other methods...
}
```

❶ We declare the list as nullable to distinguish a user without any to-do list (empty list) from a nonexisting user or other errors (null).

❷ The hub will use a new method on the fetcher to get all the lists of a user.

Let the Domain-Only DDT Pass

Once the hub is done, we can complete the domain-only actions:

```
interface ZettaiActions : DdtActions<DdtProtocol> {

    override fun allUserLists(user: User): List<ListName> =
        hub.getLists(user) ?: emptyList()

    // other methods...
}
```

Having implemented the methods in the hub, our DDTs are now passing in the domain protocol; however, we're still missing the rendering of the page in the HTTP protocol.

Generate the User's To-Do Lists Page

To finish the story, we need to generate the HTML page for the lists of a user. Then, as we did with the page with a single list, we use Jsoup to parse the HTML page and return the names of the lists for the DDT validation.

Once done (the full code is in the repository), we can finish the HTTP actions.

```
data class HttpActions(val env: String = "local") : ZettaiActions {

    override fun allUserLists(user: User): List<ListName> {
        val response = callZettai(Method.GET, allUserListsUrl(user))

        expectThat(response.status).isEqualTo(Status.OK)

        val html = HtmlPage(response.bodyString())

        val names = extractListNamesFromPage(html)

        return names.map { name -> ListName.fromTrusted(name) }
    }

    // other methods...
}
```

And now our DDTs are finally passing, as we see here:

Storing the State Changes

The next story is to allow the user to create a new list. We can implement it, continuing to use the ToDoListUpdatableFetcher and at some point later replace it with an implementation that uses a database or some other form of persistence.

While this is a completely valid and sensible approach and has its uses, for Zettai we're going to take a different approach. Rather than storing the state directly, we want to store all the changes in the state, and then recreate the state when we need it, replaying all the changes.

It may seem an unneeded complication, but its benefits will become clear before the end of this chapter.

This is a big change from the normal way of developing applications, and we also need to use functional programming for it. For this reason, we'll analyze this approach now and learn about new functional programming tools. We'll put all this to work on Zettai in the next chapter.

Event Sourcing

Saving the new state every time it changes isn't ideal from the business model point of view. The problem is that when we change the state—for example, adding a new ToDoList to our collection—we don't record when it happened and why. For our application—Zettai—we want to be able to reconstruct the history of our lists so our users can undo the last modification or verify what the list looks like at a certain point in time.

How can we do it? Enter the Event Sourcing pattern![1] The main idea behind event sourcing is that instead of persisting the new state at every change, we persist only the change, specifying the business reason—in other words, the business event. This also gives us an audit flow of who did what on each entity.

This way, we can always reconstruct the history of the entity up to the current state. But, if we want, we can calculate the state of any time in the past; we only need to process all the events up to a certain time. Finally, we can use the stream of events to collect other statistics that can be hard to obtain otherwise. For example, we can select the list with the biggest number of changes. In short, these are the benefits we gain from using event sourcing:

1. The ability to maintain the information about the business event behind the change

2. The ability to collect all the audit data

3. The ability to reconstruct the state at a certain time in the past

4. The ability to easily create multiple different views of the same data

As with everything, there are also some downsides to the event sourcing approach—it's a more complex approach, and it requires the team to learn new techniques.

Moreover, using event sourcing can be a problem with projects where the performance is critical, and it doesn't bring much value for domains where there is little business logic or where we simply don't care much about it. Finally, handling database concurrency and migrations can be a little trickier using event sourcing.

We'll address some of these concerns later in the book, and keep in mind that event sourcing isn't the best solution for every situation. Having said that, when I'm facing an important business domain that's important to model precisely, I consider event sourcing the best solution possible.

But before delving into the details of events, let's consider the bigger picture: how we can handle state changes in functional programming?

Change the State with Immutable Data

Up to this point, we examined the advantages of using immutable types in functional programming. You are forgiven if you think functional style doesn't

---

1. https://microservices.io/patterns/data/event-sourcing.html

have much to offer about changing the state. Actually, the opposite is true. Since we have defined our state using only immutable types, we're now forced to handle explicitly all the changes in our data. This makes us more conscious of what should change and why. Functional programming pushes us to manipulate the state in a more deliberate and sophisticated way.

So now the question is, how can we let immutable data change? The simplest approach is to create a new, immutable copy of the data with the changes we want, and use the new one. This is actually the same thing we do when using primitive types, which are immutable:

```
val name = "frank"
val capitalName = name.capitalize()
println("Hello $capitalName") //Hello Frank
```

In the previous example, name isn't changed; instead, the new capitalized copy has been stored in capitalName.

In the same way, when we add an item in our ToDoList, we do something like this:

```
val toDoList = ToDoList.build("myList", listOf("item1"))
val newToDoList = toDoList.copy(items = items + ToDoItem("item2"))
```

We're not changing the list but creating a copy with the new item.

Now comes the tricky part—at least in the functional world. What if we need to substitute a global reference to the old list with one to the new list?

The preferred strategy is first to try to avoid references to mutable state—in many cases we don't really need them. If this isn't possible, we should at least put the reference at the margins of the system. In this way, most of the code doesn't rely on the mutability and can stay pure. We did exactly this using a MutableMap in the fetcher in Storing Lists Outside the Hub, on page 86. In particular, we must avoid using singleton global objects with mutable state.

What we want is to get rid of the MutableMap and use a different approach: record the changes to the list instead of mutating it directly. This allows us to produce an immutable "snapshot in time" of any list. In other words, we'll replace mutable maps with a growing list of immutable events.

Let's stop a moment to consider the issue we want to solve. The problem isn't that using a mutable map in functional programming breaks some kind of rule. Ultimately, the state has to be kept somewhere, and it has to change, either with a mutable reference in memory or in an external component—a database, for example. What we're trying to do is to put solid boundaries around the mutable and effects part of our code. This will let us easily re-use and compose the majority of our functions.

Let's consider now some strategies to work with mutability.

Temporary Mutability

What can we do if we need some kind of *disposable* temporary state to keep track of a computation? As an example, let's consider the humble loop. Looping on a counter is so common that in the majority of the programming languages we have some kind of construct that allows us to keep updating a temporary state until we have finished, as in this code:

```
var counter = 0
while(true){
    counter++
    if (operation(counter) == null)
        break
}

println("executed $counter operations")
```

But—I can hear you—surely there is nothing wrong in having a mutable counter like this! Well, yes and no. For such a minimal piece of code there is really nothing wrong in using a mutable counter, since there isn't much margin for composition here. On the other hand, we know that code tends to become more complicated as time passes by. Having a mutable local variable in a complex loop is definitely something we want to avoid.

Remove Mutable Local Variables

Let's look at a slightly more complicated example, where we count the bytes on some kind of stream:

```
fun readStream(stream: Stream): Int {

    var totByteRead = 0
    while(true){
        bytesRead = stream.read()
        totByteRead += bytesRead
        if (bytesRead == 0)
            break
    }

    return totByteRead
}
```

This code is still very small, but it's already very error prone. To see why, let's start considering the design problems of this small example.

- Counting the bytes is strictly related to reading them, but here we do it in a different function.

- We need to check if bytesRead is equal to zero to close the stream.

- The local variable, totByteRead, is mutable and it can be changed by mistake.

But the real problem with this code is that it's completely uncomposable. We can't break it down into smaller pieces or re-use it for other similar situations. Everything is tightly coupled together. For example, if we want to put an optional limit to the bytes to read, we need to complicate it considerably, making it even more error prone and inflexible.

How can we improve this? Let's try first to rewrite it using immutable variables:

```
fun readStream(stream: Stream): Int {

    val bytesRead1 = stream.read()
    val bytesRead2 = bytesRead1 + stream.read()
    val bytesRead3 = bytesRead2 + stream.read()
        ...
    val bytesRead10 = bytesRead9 + stream.read()

    return bytesRead10
}
```

This code would solve some of the problems of the previous example, but I hope nobody would seriously think to write code like this. The repetition is terrible, and there is no way to know how many reads we may need.

Looking at the code, we're only interested in the last counter, bytesRead10—and the calls to read the stream—but we aren't interested in the intermediate counters, from bytesRead1 to bytesRead9. What other alternatives do we have? Let's introduce a new tool to treat mutable state in functional programming.

Unleashing the Power of Recursion

Recursion is a very powerful technique that allows us to represent complex algorithms in an elegant and concise way. If we look at the definition of recursion, we see that it's a way of solving a problem by splitting it into smaller versions of itself until they become trivial to solve. A less elegant but more pragmatic definition is solving a problem with a function that calls itself.

For our problem, we would like to have a function that can accept a temporary variable called *accumulator* (in our case, the number of bytes read so far) and an operation (in our case, the call to read from the stream) and return a new accumulator. The accumulator is so called because it "accumulates" the partial results of the operation as it goes.

This kind of higher-ordered function is called a *reducer* because it "reduces" a collection of values down to a single value. We can start defining the signature:

```
fun reduceOperations(accumulator: Int,
                     operation: (Int) -> Int): Int = TODO()
```

...and how we would like to use it:

```
val bytesRead = reduceOperations(0) { it + stream.read() }
println("read $bytesRead bytes")
```

How can we implement it? This seems to be a natural candidate for using recursion. What does using recursion mean? It means that our function will keep calling itself until the stream.read() operation returns 0 bytes, which is the exit condition for this specific example. Let's see it in code:

```
❶ tailrec fun reduceOperations(
      accumulator: Int,
      operation: (Int) -> Int
  ): Int {
❷     val newAccumulator = operation(accumulator)
❸     return if (newAccumulator == accumulator) {
❹         accumulator
      } else {
❺         reduceOperations(newAccumulator, operation)
      }
  }
```

❶ The tailrec keyword will prevent a StackOverflowException. To understand how it works, see Tailrec Keyword, on page 386.

❷ Here, we call the operation and store the returned value.

❸ We check here if it has actually read some new bytes.

❹ If we didn't read new bytes, we return without the recursive call, which means we stop reading the stream.

❺ If we read some new bytes, the function calls itself with the new value as accumulator.

Make It Foldable

Let's now consider a very common case that's quite similar: we want to call an operation on all the elements of a collection and then combine the results in a specific way. As an example, this method downloads all the web pages at the URL specified in a collection and then concatenates them, maybe for some text analysis:

```
fun concatenateHtml(urls: Iterable<URI>): String {
    var html = ""
    for(url in urls) {
        html += fetchHtml(url)
    }
    return html
}
```

Can we rewrite this loop in a recursive way? Here is a way to write it:

```
tailrec fun Iterable<URI>.concatenateHtml(
  initial: String,
  operation: (acc: String, URI) -> String): String {
     val head = firstOrNull()

     return if (head == null)
         initial
     else {
         val html = operation(initial, head)
         drop(1).concatenateHtml(html, operation)
     }
}
```

❶ We read the first element of the URL list.

❷ If the list is empty, we exit with the current accumulator as result.

❸ If we have a valid URL, we fetch the HTML.

❹ Finally, the function calls itself, passing the rest of the list without the first element which we just processed and the new accumulator.

So far so good, but can we make this function more generic and reusable? Yes, we just need to look at our parameters more closely. We're using String and URL, but there is nothing specific about those types in our code; we can replace them with generics.

Let's call our new generic function composeOver:

```
tailrec fun <T, R> Iterable<T>.composeOver(initial: R,
                    operation: (acc: R, element: T) -> R): R {

    val head = firstOrNull()

    return if (head == null)
        initial //if the list is empty
    else {
        drop(1).composeOver(operation(initial, head), operation)
    }
}
```

This is the new signature, and the great thing is that we don't have to change anything in our code (apart from the name of the function); it works correctly with the generic types. Looking at the signature, you can check in the collection standard library, and you'll find an exact match: the fold function.

```
inline fun <T, R> Iterable<T>.fold(
    initial: R,
    operation: (acc: R, T) -> R
): R
```

...

This is not a coincidence; what we just did is commonly called *folding* a collection. The fold function represents one of the more general ways to use recursion.

Fold It Left and Fold It Right

If we examine the code in the Kotlin standard library, we can see that the fold function is implemented without using recursion. This is probably to avoid possible performance issues if collections require a full copy at every step. Regardless of how it's implemented, fold allows us to work on collections with our functions in a safe and composable way.

If we look at our first example in this chapter, fold is the most generic abstraction over the imperative programming loop. All the other abstractions over loops, like map, filter, and so on, can be implemented using only fold.

In our example, we operated by calling the composeOver on increasingly smaller lists (note the drop(1) call) until the list was empty, each time passing the result of operation as accumulator.

The opposite approach is also possible: immediately calling operation, and passing the folding function as a parameter. In this way, we start with the first element, but before calling the operation on it, we do the recursive call, and only after getting the result do we do the operation. So, the first fully processed element will be the last element of the list, and then the second from last, and so on until the first element will be processed. Figuratively, it's proceeding from right to left.

Let's write a new function with this approach called composeOverRight:

```
fun <T, R> Iterable<T>.composeOverRight(
  initial: R,
  operation: (element: T, acc: R) -> R): R {
    val head = firstOrNull()
```

```kotlin
    return if (head == null)
        initial //if the list is empty
    else {
        operation(head, drop(1).composeOverRight(initial, operation))
    }
}
```

Note that the operation here takes first the element and then the accumulator, the opposite of composeOver. Putting the accumulator after the element is the common convention when folding from the right because this way is more convenient for lazy languages like Haskell. In Kotlin, there is no real difference, but it highlights the fact that we're proceeding in the opposite order.

There is a catch here: we can't use tailrec anymore because composeOverRight isn't the last call in our function. To see the difference in the order of the calls, let's try to run both kinds of fold with a simple function that creates a string repeating a character three times, and print it:

```kotlin
fun triple(c: Char): String {
    print(c) //for logs only
    return "$c$c$c "
}

fun main() {
    val chars = listOf('a', 'b', 'c')

    val l = chars.composeOver("") { acc, u -> acc + triple(u) }
    println(" composeOver is $l")

    val r = chars.composeOverRight("") { u, acc -> triple(u) + acc }
    println(" composeOverRight is $r")
}
```

Running it, we'll get this output:

```
abc composeOver is aaa bbb ccc
cba composeOverRight is aaa bbb ccc
```

We can see that composeOverRight is producing the same result as composeOver, but the function triple is called the first time on the last element. Depending on the data structure we're folding over, one way can be better than the other, so let's summarize the difference.

Fold left will combine the first element with the initial accumulator, the second element with the result of the operation, and so on.

Fold right will combine the first element with the result of the fold itself with the rest of the collection.

Note also that usually the order of accumulator and element arguments are inverted in fold and foldRight. A diagram may help to visualize the difference:

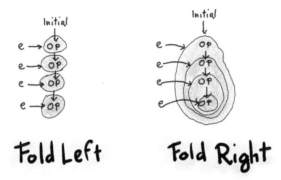

In any case, we don't have to write this code ourselves. In the Kotlin standard library there's a method, foldRight, on all the collections with exactly this signature.

We started looking at recursion and folding to avoid mutable temporary variables in loops, but fold is much more powerful than a simple loop, as we'll see now.

Folding Events

What have we learned after all this folding? Using recursion allowed us to avoid keeping a mutable temporary state and instead keep everything immutable and pure, relying upon the Kotlin stack. What about when it's not possible to keep the state change inside a single computation?

Let's imagine we need to model an entity with different states, like a finite state machine,[2] and that these states also change the behavior of the entity itself. To visualize this, let's consider how we would model a door. It has two states: open and closed. It also has two very different behaviors when it's open versus when it's closed, as anyone who's smacked into a glass door can tell you.

To make the example more interesting, we'll also consider that once closed, it can be locked or unlocked. We then have the following:

- A door can be open or closed (unlocked) or locked.
- It can be opened only when it's closed (unlocked).
- It can be locked only when it's closed (unlocked).
- It can be unlocked only when it's locked.
- When open, it can be swung at different angles, but it stays open.
- When locked, the key can be turned again but it stays locked.

---

2. https://en.wikipedia.org/wiki/Finite-state_machine

How can we model this mutable entity in functional programming?

Implement a Finite State Machine

Let's draw a diagram of all the states and their transitions:

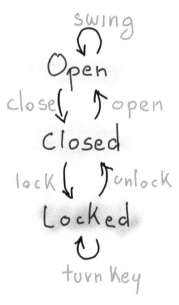

This diagram illustrates how we can represent the entities that change behavior according to their state using a state machine. We map the transitions into domain events, then we constrain each state to accept only some events, and finally, we allow events to change the entity state to another one.

What we want to define at this point is a Type that's the sum of all the States. In other words, we want to define an abstract superclass that can be extended by each of our substates, but only by those.

Kotlin's sealed classes (see Sealed Class, on page 385) are extremely useful for representing this kind of type. They are easy to write and they can't be extended outside their compilation unit, the Kotlin module. Since they are well supported by the when operator, they are also very simple to use. Here is a possible representation of our door:

```
sealed class Door

data class Open(val angle: Double): Door()
object Closed: Door()
data class Locked(val turns: Int): Door()
```

In some cases, we want to have specific information related to the state—for example, the opening angle for an open door and the turn of a key for a locked one. If we don't have any specific information, we can use an object (see Objects and Companion Objects, on page 381) to represent the state instead of a data class. Now, let's consider some characteristics of the Sealed Classes.

Union Types

As we discussed in the previous chapter (see Low Cardinality, on page 93), it is important to keep the cardinality of our types as low as possible. Technically speaking, Sealed Classes are a kind of algebraic data type. More precisely, they are "disjoint union types." As the name suggests, union types are types created by the union of two or more types, where only one is "in use" at any moment.

In some languages, it's possible to simply create types by "unioning" any type. For example, in F# we can create a new type by combining Int and Boolean like this:

```
type IntOrBool =
  | I of int
  | B of bool
```

So in this example, IntOrBool can be an integer or a boolean, but not both— differently from tuples.

Unfortunately, in Kotlin we can't combine existing types directly, but only subtypes of our sealed class. But, we can do something similar using wrappers:

```
sealed class IntOrBool
data class IntWrap(val raw: Int): IntOrBool()
data class BoolWrap(val raw: Boolean): IntOrBool()
```

It's not as elegant and concise as F#, but it's simpler and it will serve the same purpose.

Calculate the Cardinality of Composite Types

We saw in Low Cardinality, on page 93, how to calculate the cardinality of simple types. What's the cardinality of IntOrBool? IntWrap has the same cardinality of Int (2^{32}), and BoolWrap has a cardinality of 2. Since it can be either one or the other, the cardinality of IntOrBool must be the sum of all cardinalities of the subtypes, in this case $2^{32}+2$. For this reason, union types are also called *sum types*.

How can we represent a type that can be an integer or a boolean if we didn't have sealed classes? One possibility is to define a data class with a nullable Int and a nullable Boolean and then set the unused one to null, something like this:

```
data class IntOrBoolTuple(val intWrap: Int?, val boolWrap: Boolean?)
```

Let's try to calculate the cardinality of IntOrBoolTuple. For each value of intWrap, boolWrap can be either true or false. In total, our cardinality would be 2^32*2, that is, roughly the double of the cardinality of our IntOrBool union type. The difference would be much bigger for more complicated types.

For this reason, the data class types can also be called *product types*.

\]/   **Joe asks:**

What Is the Cardinality of Function Types?

This is a very good question!

To calculate the cardinality of a function type such as (Boolean) -> Int we need to take a count of the possible function implementations with the same signature.

We can start enumerating them according to what they return for each possible input. The first function will return 0 if true and 0 if false, the second one 0,1, and so on. The total would be the cardinality of Int (the result type) raised to the power of two (because Boolean has only two possible values), so the cardinality would be (2^32)^2.

For this reason, the function types are also called *exponential types*.

Finally, union types can also be called coproduct types; they really have plenty of names! For a more complete explanation, see Product and Coproduct Types, on page 403.

Define the State Transitions

Going back to our Door example, we can now add methods to the substates to represent all the state transitions we want to allow:

```
sealed class Door {
    data class Open(val angle: Double) : Door() {
        fun close() = Closed
        fun swing(delta: Double) = Open(angle+delta)
    }
    object Closed : Door() {
        fun open(degrees: Double) = Open(degrees)
        fun lock() = Locked(1)
    }
    data class Locked(val turns: Int) : Door() {
        fun unlock() = Closed
        fun turnKey(delta: Int) = Locked(turns + delta)
    }
}
```

This approach allows us to concatenate the state changes in any way we want and still be sure that if it compiles, the state can't be inconsistent. For example:

```
val door = Door.Closed
               .lock()
               .turnKey(3)
               .unlock()
               .open(12.4)
               .swing(34.5)
               .close()
```

If we try to invoke the wrong method on a substate, like closing the door twice or turning the key on an open door, the compiler will stop us.

Discovering the Monoid

If we look at all the base door types, we can represent all our state changes as arrows starting and arriving at the same place:

What we have here is a diagram with only one type and a lot of arrows.

This is similar to the concept of monoid in category theory (see Appendix 3, A Pinch of Theory, on page 391). More precisely, we can say that the door has a monoid instance. We won't cover the theory here, but if you are interested, you can find more information in the appendix section Monoid, on page 396. If we expand the state to all its substates, we can see how events are in relation with the possible states, like in the previous diagram.

Another way to define a monoid is to use the set theory definition. In this case, a monoid is a set of objects that can be combined together plus the neutral element. (A monoid without a neutral element is called a *semigroup*, in case you are interested. And before you ask, a *group* is a monoid where each morphism has its inverse.)

If we look at the elements of the collections of states, we're using a set theory approach. If we look at how functions transform the states, we're using a category theory approach. They are both correct, and you can decide case by case which is more natural for you.

So how we can translate the monoid concept into code with our door example? We'll consider the Door class, ignoring the substates for the moment, and then we should transform the methods on the various substates as functions that transform a Door into another Door:

```
typealias DoorEvent = (Door) -> Door
```

What we can do now is map all the possible transformations to DoorEvent, for example, like this:

```
val unlockDoor: DoorEvent = { aDoor: Door ->
  when (aDoor) {
    is Door.Locked -> aDoor.unlock()
    else -> aDoor //if the state is wrong we ignore the event
  }
}
```

The advantage of this approach is that we can combine multiple functions of type DoorEvent together very easily, since their argument type is the same as the output. We'll see how to take advantage of this in the next chapter.

An interesting consequence of treating our states and events as a monoid is that we deliberately allow for any combination of events to be processed together. If some of the events aren't significant for the current state—like unlocking an open door—we can just ignore them.

Of course we'll aim to not have "rogue" events in our system, but if this happens for any reason, it's better to give priority to the state consistency, and maybe log the issue, rather than raise an error and stop processing the events. We'll see how to put all of this into practice in the next chapter.

Recap

In this chapter, we implemented the story to see all the lists of a user, starting with a DDT and then proceeding with the changes to the hub and the UI.

Then, we learned how to allow for state changes in a functional way. In particular, we examined how recursion can replace loops with mutable variables, and we learned the related monoid concept from the category theory.

In the next chapter, we'll look at how to use commands to generate events and how to connect the HTML UI to the hub.

Exercises

The exercises in this chapter will focus on recursion and folding.

Here is your friendly reminder that nobody can learn functional programming by just reading code, and the best way to learn is by practicing. You can refer to the exercises folder in the book code repository for the starting point and some hints.

Exercise 5.1: Recursion

Let's try to write a function in recursive style to investigate the Collatz conjecture.

We start with a sequence defined in this way: take a positive integer n>1; if it is even, divide it by 2; if it is odd, multiply it by 3 and add 1. Then repeat the process.

The conjecture says that no matter which number you start with, you'll end with 1.

For example, starting with 6, we have this sequence: 6 -> 3 -> 10 -> 5 -> 16 -> 8 -> 4 -> 2 -> 1

The exercise consists of generating the sequence using recursion. Just replace the TODO() here with the correct code to implement the algorithm described earlier.

```
fun Int.collatz() = collatzR(listOf(), this)

tailrec fun collatzR(acc: List<Int>, x: Int): List<Int> = TODO()
```

As proof, we can verify the sequences generated for 8 and 13:

```
expectThat(13.collatz()).isEqualTo(listOf(13, 40, 20, 10, 5, 16, 8, 4, 2, 1))

expectThat(8.collatz()).isEqualTo(listOf(8, 4, 2, 1))
```

Exercise 5.2: Fold

The exercise involves using fold to calculate the current floor of the Elevator based on events that record the directions it has traveled. Given these types:

```
data class Elevator(val floor: Int)

sealed class Direction

object Up : Direction()

object Down : Direction()
```

...our test is taking a list of directions and "folding" them to get the current floor:

```kotlin
val values = listOf(Up, Up, Down, Up, Down, Down, Up, Up, Up, Down)

val tot = values.fold(Elevator(0)){
        TODO("implement this")
}

expectThat(tot).isEqualTo(Elevator(2))
```

You need to replace the TODO with a function that would make this test pass.

Exercise 5.3: Union Types

Union types can be very useful in changing behavior according to the current state of the system. In this exercise, we see how to take advantage of that to strip a JSON string of unnecessary spaces.

Let's define our sealed class hierarchy:

```kotlin
sealed class JsonCompactor{
    abstract val jsonCompacted: String
    abstract fun compact(c: Char): JsonCompactor
}

data class InQuotes(override val jsonCompacted: String): JsonCompactor() {
    override fun compact(c: Char): JsonCompactor = TODO()
}

data class OutQuotes(override val jsonCompacted: String): JsonCompactor() {
    override fun compact( c: Char): JsonCompactor = TODO()
}

data class Escaped(override val jsonCompacted: String): JsonCompactor() {
    override fun compact( c: Char): JsonCompactor = TODO()
}
```

What we want is to strip all the spaces without changing spaces inside the quotes.

```kotlin
val jsonText = """{ "my greetings" :    "hello world! \"How are you?\"" }"""

val expected = """{"my greetings":"hello world! \"How are you?\""}"""

expectThat(compactJson(jsonText)).isEqualTo(expected)
```

Exercise 5.4: Monoid

For the last exercise of this chapter, we need to create a generic data class Monoid<T: Any> that can take a zero and a combination lambda to be able to fold over T.

The exercise consists of implementing a Monoid class, so these tests will pass:

```
with( Monoid(0, Int::plus)){
    expectThat( listOf(1,2,3,4,10).fold() ).isEqualTo(20)
}

with( Monoid("", String::plus)){
    expectThat( listOf( "My", "Fair", "Lady").fold() )
            .isEqualTo("MyFairLady")
    }
}

private val zeroMoney = Money(0.0)
data class Money(val amount: Double){
    fun sum(other: Money) = Money(this.amount + other.amount)
}

with(Monoid(zeroMoney, Money::sum)) {
    expectThat(listOf(Money(2.1), Money(3.9), Money(4.0)).fold())
        .isEqualTo(Money(10.0))
}
```

CHAPTER 6

Executing Commands to Generate Events

In the previous chapter, we saw how we can recreate the current state of an entity from the initial state and a sequence of events. In this chapter, we'll put this approach to work on our application, using commands to capture the user intent and processing them to generate the events.

For that, we're going to implement a new story—to create a new list—using a command. We'll need to transform HTTP requests into commands, generating events from commands, and using events to recreate the state. Then we'll wire it all together in the hub, taking advantage of the functional style of passing functions around and combining them together.

Finally, we'll convert the existing API that adds an item to a list to the new command style.

Creating a New List

We've seen how we can produce a new state combining the current state with a sequence of immutable events that records all the changes, while remaining safely inside functional programming. It's time for us to go back to the Zettai application and apply the lessons we've just learned.

After having completed the HTML page for showing all the lists of the user, we were left with the task of creating a new list. To do this, we need to design an HTML form, also known as a webform, based on the mockup drawings we created in Preparing the Mock-Ups, on page 6.

Add the DDT to Create a New List

As you might guess, we start working on the story by writing a DDT to create a new list. This is the first test we met that sends data to the application—the list details. At this point, we need to make a decision: we can test the creation of a new list by simulating the click of the button in the browser UI, or we can send the HTML form directly from our test.

Simulating the full browser behavior is the safest way of testing our pages. It would require a browser automation tool—also called a headless browser—which is software that operates like a typical browser but lacks the UI part and can be driven by our code. Unfortunately, it's quite slow to run and quite heavy on system resources, so it's better to use this solution only when absolutely necessary, for example, when the UI is heavily dependent on JavaScript functionalities.

Zettai has a very simple UI, at least so far, so we can adopt the easier solution of sending an HTML form request using the HTTP client directly from our test. When in doubt, my motto is: never be afraid to take the easy path, there is always time to complicate things later!

We can add a DDT scenario to our SeeAllTheToDoListsDDT class. It will look like this:

```
val dylan by NamedActor(::ToDoListOwner)

@DDT
fun `users can create new lists`() = ddtScenario {
    play(
        dylan.`cannot see any list`(),
        dylan.`can create a new list called #listname`("gardening"),
        dylan.`can create a new list called #listname`("music"),
        dylan.`can see the lists #listNames`(setOf("gardening", "music"))
    ).wip(LocalDate.of(2023,12,31), "working on it!")
}
```

To make it compile, we need to write the method on the actor:

```
fun `can create a new list called #listname`(listName: String) =
    step(listName) {
        createList(user, ListName.fromUntrustedOrThrow(listName))
    }
```

It's calling a method createList on the actions. We'll leave it empty for the moment, and we'll instead proceed to define our UI and routes. Do you remember the "V" diagram? See Domain-Driven Test Process, on page 75.

Add Buttons to the HTML UI

We need to add a form with a button and text in our UI template to create a new list, following the initial mock-ups (Preparing the Mock-Ups, on page 6).

To keep things simple, we'll start with a simple HTML form, without using JavaScript, to insert the data for the new list. Let's add this HTML snippet on the bottom of our HTML page:

```
fun renderListsPage(user: User, lists: List<ListName>) = HtmlPage(
    """
        <!DOCTYPE html>
        <html>
        <head>
            <link rel="stylesheet" ...bootstrap...>
            <title>Zettai - a ToDoList application</title>
        </head>
        <body>
        <div id="container">
        <div class="row justify-content-md-center">
        <div class="col-md-center">
            <h1>Zettai</h1>
            <h2>User ${user.name}</h2>
            <table class="table table-hover">
                <thead>
                    <tr>
                        <th>Name</th>
                        <th>State</th>
                        <th>Actions</th>
                    </tr>
                </thead>
                <tbody>
                ${lists.render(user)}
                </tbody>
            </table>
            <hr>
            <h5>Create new to-do list</h5>
            <form action="/todo/${user.name}" method="post">
              <label for="listname">List name:</label>
              <input type="text" name="listname">
              <input type="submit" value="Submit">
            </form>
            </div>
        </div>
        </div>
        </body>
        </html>
    """.trimIndent()
)
```

On the browser it looks like the screenshot on page 134.

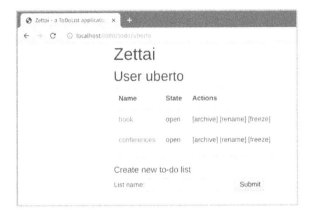

Add Route to the HTTP Handler

To make the HTML form work properly, we need a dedicated route in our HTTP handler. When called, the new route should parse the content and transform it in a new call to the hub:

```
class Zettai(val hub: ZettaiHub) : HttpHandler {

...
    "/todo/{user}" bind Method.POST to ::createNewList
...

    private fun createNewList(request: Request): Response {
        val user = request.extractUser()
        val listName = request.extractListNameFromForm("listname")
        return listName
            ?.let { hub.createToDoList(user, it) }
            ?.let { Response(Status.SEE_OTHER)
                .header("Location", "/todo/${user.name}") }
            ?: Response(Status.BAD_REQUEST)
    }
    private fun Request.extractListNameFromForm(formName: String) =
        form(formName)
            ?.let(ListName.Companion::fromUntrusted)
```

For the moment, we put an empty createToDoList on the hub, but we'll change it soon.

Since our createNewList method is pretty straightforward, just a chain of transformations, we don't have to write unit tests. Regressions will be covered by the HTTP DDTs, and we aren't particularly interested in the error case scenarios here. But, if we had more sophisticated error handling in place, we would have written the unit tests for all the error cases.

With the route in place we can now complete the method on the HTTP actions to create a list, very similar to the method to add an item to a list:

```
override fun createList(user: User, listName: ListName) {
    val response = submitToZettai(
            allUserListsUrl(user), newListForm(listName))

    expectThat(response.status).isEqualTo(Status.SEE_OTHER)
}
```

Running the DDT now, we can see that the HTTP test is failing when calling the hub, but this is OK since it proves that the HTTP routes and the external adapter are working.

Using Commands to Change the State

We could implement the createToDoList method on the hub, as we did for the addItemToList, but it's now time to introduce a new pattern.

We want to treat the operation that can change the state of the system with particular care. To do so, we can use a command-oriented interface for our internal API.[1] Using this style—which incidentally isn't limited to functional programming—gives us more flexibility and control of what will change our state. As Martin Fowler says, this allows us to "easily add common behavior to commands by decorating the command executor. This is very handy for handling transactions, logging, and the like."

Using a command-oriented interface means that instead of having many methods on the hub, we'll define many command data classes, with all the information inside, and we'll pass them to the command executor. Let's see how it works.

We now need to define our commands. For the moment, we have only two of them: adding a new list, and adding a new item to a list (the one we wrote in the previous chapter):

```
❶ sealed class ToDoListCommand

❷ data class CreateToDoList(val user: User, val name: ListName)
        : ToDoListCommand() {

❸     val id: ToDoListId = ToDoListId.mint()
}

  data class AddToDoItem(val user: User,
                        val name: ListName, val item: ToDoItem)
❹       : ToDoListCommand()
```

---

1. https://martinfowler.com/bliki/CommandOrientedInterface.html

❶ All the commands will inherit from the ToDoListCommand sealed class.

❷ This is the command to create a new list, given the user(owner) and the list name.

❸ The command also contains a randomly minted list id. It can be passed from outside, but since it's random we can create it directly in the command.

❹ This is the command to add a new item to an existing list.

Here we're using a sealed class (see Sealed Class, on page 385) because we want to have multiple Commands, but we also want to keep them all together in the same file. This allows us to use exhaustive when conditions while checking the commands. The commands themselves don't have any code. That's because we want to be flexible in handling commands in different ways according to the context and not binding a specific implementation to the command itself.

Our commands are expressing a user's intent—add a new list or add a new item in this case. The system must take care of them and execute the business logic required. If the system can successfully carry out the tasks associated with each command, the commands will succeed; otherwise, they'll fail. So, where do we handle these commands? In a function that we'll call—for lack of imagination—CommandHandler.

So, the command handler will receive commands, but how exactly would that change the state of the system? It's now time to put into practice what we learned about functional state machines in the previous chapter.

Generate Events from Commands

We saw how to define a state as a series of events, but how do we create events? It's simple—they are the result of successful commands. Instead of modifying the state directly, a command will generate one or more events. In some cases, it can even generate zero events if the system is already in the state the command is asking for.

Let's see how to design the CommandHandler function using events. We can return either a failure or a generated list of events.

Modeling the Domain with States and Events

So far, we've discussed the Event Sourcing pattern and how it works, with some examples, and now we need to design our specific domain using them. In the beginning, it can be challenging to model a domain using immutable states and events rather than using mutable objects, but I can assure you

> \\// **Joe asks:**
> ǯ **Why Do We Need Events at All If We Have Commands?**
>
> At the beginning, it can be hard to distinguish between Commands and Events. Still, they are different concepts. The main difference is that commands are messages that arrive from outside, and they are requests to change the state of the system. As a consequence, commands can fail, and they are usually expressed in imperative form: CloseDoor.
>
> Events are the record that the state of the system has changed. Events can't fail (it's already happened) and they are usually expressed in the past form: DoorClosed.

that once you and your team get used to thinking in terms of what has happened and why, mapping a business domain to states and events will become very natural.

In my experience, modeling a domain with event sourcing keeps our source code closer to what actually happens in the real world rather than trying to abstract a model.

We talked about Validating Our Stories with Event Storming, on page 5 which, if you squint enough, can be seen as a meeting format for discovering business events. The events we're discussing here usually have a finer granularity than the ones on the Post-its—unfortunately, an event is a very vague concept—but they are a very useful starting point to defining the commands, the main states of our entities, and what would cause the transitions from one state to another.

A better name for the events of event sourcing would be *state-transitions*, but "state-transition-sourcing" isn't a very catchy term.

Transitional Entities

As we saw, by definition both commands and events work on a single entity, so now is a good time to clarify what an entity is. For example, why is the to-do list an entity but the to-do item is not?

To model something as an entity in our domain, we need to make sure that we can safely update a list without affecting other entities outside the scope of a user transaction. In other words, we need to keep all the state changes of our entities confined in a single transaction.

We can do that with a list, and incidentally also with a user, but we can't do it with a to-do item. For example, updating or removing an item requires a change in the list. The difference is that items are contained inside a list—in the sense of being a collection inside a ToDoList instance—lists aren't contained inside a user, they only have a reference to the UserId. This of course is a design choice, but in our current design, this is what makes the lists and users entities while items are not.

In domain-driven design (DDD) terms, an entity is defined based on its identity, and a set of related entities that can be changed together is called an aggregate. The word "aggregate" comes from the idea of a bunch of objects working together to represent a self-contained state of the system. Correctly defining the (mutable) aggregates is a very delicate task while designing a DDD solution.

In this book, we'll reference the concept of an aggregate—that is, structured data that will change together inside an atomic transaction—as a *transactional entity* or just *entity*. Since all our entities are immutable, they don't have a concept of identity that must be kept across mutation. Each of our entities is really just a snapshot of the state, so we don't have to worry about internal consistency while changing the entities.

Even if having immutable subclasses for each state can be perceived as a complication, in reality, they simplify handling the entity life cycle. As we saw, the functional approach makes it all much more straightforward. Let's see how this works in practice.

Entity States

Once we're sure of our entities, we need to define the state and the events for each of them.

This is an activity that's beneficial to do at the team level, including not only the developers but also all the stakeholders. We can use a technical event-storming session or a big whiteboard session, but we should conclude with a diagram as shown on page 139, similar to this one, to describe all possible states of our to-do lists:

Events Diagram

Once we have drawn a diagram for the state and events of each relevant entity of our domain, I suggest keeping them in a very visible place—either in the office or in some shared repository for remote teams—because everyone in the team will benefit by checking them often, both during the development and while discussing requirements.

Now a note of warning: in a real project we would wait to implement a feature requiring them before implementing the OnHold and Closed state, but for didactic purposes we'll implement now all the states in the domain.

ToDoListEvent

We start the implementation with a type to wrap the ID of any entity and the interface for the base event. The only thing that we're sure of about the generic event is that it's related to a specific entity, so it needs an EntityId field:

```
typealias ToDoListId = EntityId

data class EntityId(val raw: UUID) {
    companion object {
        fun mint() = EntityId(UUID.randomUUID())
    }
}
interface EntityEvent {
    val id: EntityId
}
```

Note that the field id is the id of the entity to which the event refers, not the id of the event itself. This is made explicit by defining the type EntityId.

Also note that to create a new unique id of type UUID we defined a method, mint()— from the verb, not the noun—in the companion object.

We can now define the list of possible events we want to model, following the event/state diagram we just created. Note that each event carries only the information that gets added in its specific state change, plus the entity ID, which is always required.

```
sealed class ToDoListEvent: EntityEvent

data class ListCreated(val id: ToDoListId, val owner: User,
    val name: ListName): ToDoListEvent()

data class ItemAdded(val id: ToDoListId,
    val item: ToDoItem): ToDoListEvent()

data class ItemRemoved(val id: ToDoListId,
    val item: ToDoItem): ToDoListEvent()

data class ItemModified(val id: ToDoListId,
    val prevItem: ToDoItem, val item: ToDoItem): ToDoListEvent()

data class ListPutOnHold(val id: ToDoListId,
    val reason: String): ToDoListEvent()

data class ListReleased(val id: ToDoListId): ToDoListEvent()

data class ListClosed(val id: ToDoListId,
    val closedOn: Instant): ToDoListEvent()
```

ToDoListState

The next step is to define all the possible states of our entity. First, we write the abstract sealed class without any field. A combine method must be implemented in each of the possible states to combine the events. As a side note, having such a method is a strong indication that there is a monoid hidden somewhere in our events.

```
interface EntityState<in E : EntityEvent> {
    fun combine(event: E): EntityState<E>
}

sealed class ToDoListState : EntityState<ToDoListEvent> {
    abstract override fun combine(event: ToDoListEvent): ToDoListState
}
```

Having the combine method and an initial state, we can implement the folding of events, as we saw in the previous chapter:

```
object InitialState: ToDoListState() {
    override fun combine(event: ToDoListEvent) = this // for the moment
}

fun Iterable<ToDoListEvent>.fold(): ToDoListState =
    fold(InitialState as ToDoListState) { acc, e -> acc.combine(e) }
```

The next step is to define all possible states of our entity, with the possible state-transition declared in the combine functions. To define the exact relation between events and states, it's useful and practical to start from unit tests in pure TDD fashion, looking at the diagram as reference.

We start with a test on the create event:

```
internal class ToDoListEventTest {
```
❶
```
    val id = ToDoListId.mint()
    val name = randomListName()
    val user = randomUser()
    val item1 = randomItem()
    val item2 = randomItem()
    val item3 = randomItem()

    @Test
    fun `the first event create a list`() {

        val events = listOf(
```
❷
```
            ListCreated(id, user, name)
        )
```
❸
```
        val list = events.fold()

        expectThat(list).isEqualTo(
                ActiveToDoList(id, user, name, emptyList()))
    }
```

❶ We use random values for our tests. In this case, we don't need multiple runs for each test, since the values aren't particularly relevant for the test success.

❷ As a first test, we only use a single event. We keep this test super simple, so if it fails, it's a signal that something very basic broke.

❸ The extension function, fold, on our events makes it easier to generate the correct list state.

Then, we continue with a test about adding and removing items:

```
@Test
fun `adding and removing items to active list`() {
    val events: List<ToDoListEvent> = listOf(
        ListCreated(id, user, name),
        ItemAdded(id, item1),
        ItemAdded(id, item2),
        ItemAdded(id, item3),
        ItemRemoved(id, item2)
    )

    val list = events.fold()

    expectThat(list)
      .isEqualTo(ActiveToDoList(id, user, name, listOf(item1, item3)))
}
```

Finally, we write the test to put the list on hold. It's not something that's required by the stories we wrote so far, but it's useful to verify we have covered all the states in our diagram:

```
@Test
fun `putting the list on hold`() {
    val reason = "not urgent anymore"
    val events: List<ToDoListEvent> = listOf(
        ListCreated(id, user, name),
        ItemAdded(id, item1),
        ItemAdded(id, item2),
        ItemAdded(id, item3),
        ListPutOnHold(id, reason)
    )

    val list = events.fold()

    expectThat(list).isEqualTo(
        OnHoldToDoList(id, user, name,
            listOf(item1, item2, item3), reason))
}
```

For brevity we'll only show three tests here, but it's a good idea to make sure all the events and the possible states are covered by these tests.

To make the tests pass we need to implement all the ToDoListState subtypes and the functions to switch from one state to another.

First the substates—note that all the constructors are internal (see Internal Visibility, on page 384), so that we're forced to start from an InitialState and then combine events to reach other states:

❶
```
object InitialState: ToDoListState() {
  override fun combine(event: ToDoListEvent): ToDoListState =
    when (event) {
      is ListCreated -> create(event.id, event.name, emptyList())
      else -> this //ignore other events
    }
}

data class ActiveToDoList internal constructor(
  val id: ToDoListId,
  val name: ListName,
```
❷
```
  val items: List<ToDoItem>):  ToDoListState() {
    override fun combine(event: ToDoListEvent): ToDoListState =
      when (event) {
```
❸
```
        is ItemAdded -> copy(items = items + event.item)
        is ItemRemoved -> copy(items = items - event.item)
        is ItemModified -> copy(items = items - event.prevItem + event.item)
        is ListPutOnHold -> onHold(event.reason)
        is ListClosed -> close(event.closedOn)
```
❹
```
        else -> this //ignore other events
      }
}
```

```
data class OnHoldToDoList internal constructor(
  val id: ToDoListId,
  val name: ListName,
  val items: List<ToDoItem>,
  val reason: String):  ToDoListState() {
    override fun combine(event: ToDoListEvent): ToDoListState =
      when (event) {
        is ListReleased -> release()
        else -> this //ignore other events
      }
}

data class ClosedToDoList internal constructor(
  val id: ToDoListId, val closedOn: Instant) : ToDoListState() {
    override fun combine(event: ToDoListEvent): ToDoListState =
      this //ignore other events
}
```

❶ This is the initial state for any list. It's a static object, so it doesn't need to be instantiated every time.

❷ As discussed, the constructors of the data classes are all internal.

❸ For each possible state, we combine the current state with the new event to create the new state.

❹ As we discussed in the Discovering the Monoid, on page 125, we ignore events that don't affect the current state. A potentially safer alternative would be to explicitly enumerate all the irrelevant events instead of applying the else clause.

❺ The final state doesn't react to any event.

This code may seem a little verbose and boring to write. Basically, we're filling a matrix with all possible states and changes. On the other hand, it's easy to read and understand, and it can be used to recreate the state/events diagram at any time. We rely on our unit tests to make sure there are no mistakes.

Finally, we declare the extension functions to switch from one state to another, considering only the transitions our model allows. Since the constructors are defined as internal, we can create a specific state in our code following only the state transitions in the correct order.

Incidentally, I prefer to use extension functions—defined in the same file as the states so they can access the internal constructor—because I can group them together, but it's just a matter of personal preference; using class methods is also perfectly fine.

```
fun InitialState.create(id: ToDoListId, name: ListName,
                        items: List<ToDoItem>) =
    ActiveToDoList(id, name, items)

fun ActiveToDoList.onHold(reason: String) =
    OnHoldToDoList(id, name, items, reason)

fun OnHoldToDoList.release() =
    ActiveToDoList(id, name, items)

fun ActiveToDoList.close(closedOn: Instant) =
    ClosedToDoList(id, closedOn)
```

Writing Functional State Machines

After having prepared events and states, now we start going back to our commands and implementing them, starting from CreateToDoList.

Each command can either generate a list of events or fail. Even if most of the commands will emit a single event, there are cases—as we'll see in the following chapters—where a command needs to generate multiple events. Where should this happen? That would be in our CommandHandler function we started to discuss in Using Commands to Change the State, on page 135.

Let's visualize it with a diagram:

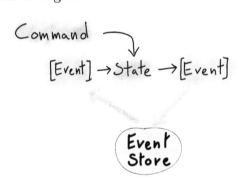

As you see, events determine the state, and commands use the state to generate new events.

This is the skeleton of the invokable class we're going to use:

```
typealias CommandHandler<CMD, EVENT> = (CMD) -> List<EVENT>?

class ToDoListCommandHandler:
        CommandHandler<ToDoListCommand, ToDoListEvent> {

    override fun invoke(command: ToDoListCommand) = TODO()
}
```

Looking at the type, it's clear that the handler will take a command and return a list of events if everything went well, or null in the case of errors.

The handler needs a collaborator to work: someone has to provide the current state for the entity. In the previous diagram, we called it EventStore, but if we examine the handler, it doesn't need the whole event store functionality, it only needs a way to retrieve the list status.

All we need to do is define the signature of a function that fetches an entity by its name. This approach allows us to avoid directly coupling the command handler with the event store, which, truth be told, we haven't defined yet, but we can guess that it will be fairly complicated.

```
typealias ToDoListRetriever =
        (user: User, listName: ListName) -> ToDoListState?
```

Now that we have our types sorted out, we can write a unit test to validate the design and drive the implementation of the CommandHandler:

```
internal class ToDoListCommandsTest {

    val fakeRetriever: ToDoListRetriever = {
        (user: User, listName: ListName) -> InitialState
    }

    @Test
    fun `CreateToDoList generate the correct event`() {

        val cmd = CreateToDoList(randomUser(), randomListName())

        val handler = ToDoListCommandHandler(fakeRetriever)
        val res = handler(cmd)?.single()

        expectThat(res).isEqualTo(
                ListCreated(cmd.id, cmd.user, cmd.name)
        )

    }
}
```

We simulate a retriever that returns the initial state, and we verify the event generated by the CreateToDoList command.

Then we'll inject the retriever in our command handler. Using type aliases instead of interfaces for the dependencies of a class is a bit like duck-typing for functional programming[2]—we don't care what it is, so long as it does what we require.

---

2. https://en.wikipedia.org/wiki/Duck_typing

With the help of the test, we can complete our class to handle commands:

```kotlin
class ToDoListCommandHandler(
    val entityRetriever: ToDoListRetriever
) : (ToDoListCommand) -> List<ToDoListEvent>? {

    override fun invoke(command: ToDoListCommand): List<ToDoListEvent>? =
      when (command) {
         is CreateToDoList -> command.execute()
         else -> null //ignore for the moment
      }

    private fun CreateToDoList.execute(): List<ToDoListEvent>? =
        entityRetriever.retrieveByName(user, name)
            ?.let { listState ->
                when (listState) {
                    InitialState -> {
                        ListCreated(id, user, name).toList()
                    }
                    else -> null //command fail
                }
            }
}
```

❶ The retriever allows us to fetch the current state of a given list, folding all events affecting that list.

❷ Using a when statement with an execute function for each command is a convenient Kotlin idiom.

❸ In this method, we put all the business logic for this command. First, we get the entity state, and then we can decide what to do accordingly.

❹ Differently from when folding the events, if the entity is in an unexpected state, we fail the command. This is because commands can fail safely; they are expected to fail often.

As a side note, using an extension function, CreateToDoList.execute(), makes it easy to navigate from the command class to the handler method using the IDE.

Now we want to test the error cases; handling errors correctly puts as many constraints on the design as the main functionality itself. We start testing the case of what will happen if we try to create a list twice; the second time the command should return an error. Remember that currently we use null to express the error condition.

```kotlin
val handler = ToDoListCommandHandler(entityRetriever)

fun handle(cmd: ToDoListCommand): List<ToDoListEvent>? =
    handler(cmd)?.also(::storeEvents)
```

```
@Test
fun `Add list fails if the user has already a list with same name`() {

    val cmd = CreateToDoList(randomUser(), randomListName())
    val res = handle(cmd)?.single()

    expectThat(res).isA<ListCreated>()

    val duplicatedRes = handle(cmd)
    expectThat(duplicatedRes).isNull()

}
```

❶ This is simulating what the hub will do: generate events from the handlers, and then store them. For this test to pass, the storeEvents function also makes sure that the fakeRetriever returns the new list state.

❷ The first time the command will succeed and we will have created a list.

❸ As we issue the same command again, it will now fail because a list with that name already exists.

This test is failing now. To make it pass, we need to create the event store.

The Event Store

The final piece to make the commands work is having a way to store and retrieve events. We will dedicate a full chapter (Persisting Safely, on page 205) on how to handle the persistence in a functional way, so for the moment, we are going to store events in memory using an atomic reference to an immutable list.

We want to write our ToDoListEventStore class independently from the storage details of the events, so that we won't need to change it once we plug in a proper persistent storage.

Our store needs to implement the EventPersister and the ToDoListRetriever function type, but in Kotlin there are limitations on a class implementing two different functions. The reason is that in a class you can't have multiple invoke methods with the same signature. So for the sake of simplicity, let's transform the retriever into an interface:

```
interface ToDoListRetriever {

    fun retrieveByName(user: User, listName: ListName): ToDoListState?

}
```

And now we can write the store. It doesn't do much, just storing events and folding them to the entity state:

```
typealias EventStreamer<E> = (EntityId) -> List<E>?

typealias EventPersister<E> = (List<E>) -> List<E>

class ToDoListEventStore(
        val eventStreamer: ToDoListEventStreamer
    ): ToDoListRetriever, EventPersister<ToDoListEvent> {

    private fun retrieveById(id: ToDoListId): ToDoListState? =
        eventStreamer(id)
            ?.fold()

    override fun retrieveByName(user: User,
                                listName: ListName): ToDoListState? =
        eventStreamer.retrieveIdFromName(user, listName)
            ?.let(::retrieveById)
            ?: InitialState

    override fun invoke(events: Iterable<ToDoListEvent>) {
        eventStreamer.store(events)
    }
}
```

❶ The event streamer will store and retrieve the events of an entity.

❷ This is the actual place where we fold events in entity state.

❸ Our EventStreamer has a method to retrieve the ID by name, so first we get the ID and then the list of events to fold. In case of no match, we return the initial state as a temporary solution.

❹ The store function is called by the hub to store the events from the command handler.

Finally, we implement the actual event streamer in memory:

```
interface ToDoListEventStreamer : EventStreamer<ToDoListEvent> {
    fun retrieveIdFromName(user: User, listName: ListName): ToDoListId?
    fun store(newEvents: Iterable<ToDoListEvent>): List<ToDoListEvent>
}

class ToDoListEventStreamerInMemory : ToDoListEventStreamer {

    val events = AtomicReference<List<ToDoListEvent>>(emptyList())

// rest of methods using events collection

}
```

With the store and the streamer in place, we can now run our test and prove that everything works.

Joe asks:

Should We Notify Other Systems When an Event Happens?

We need to keep in mind that the events we're using here aren't meant to be shared outside our application.

We'll see in the next chapter how to notify other systems when a significant event happens, but this does not imply sharing the actual event; that's a private concern of our application state.

There is another architectural pattern—called event driven—where we use events to communicate among different applications or services. Event driven and event sourcing are completely independent patterns; even if they work together they'll use different events.

Unfortunately, the word *event* has a very wide meaning in English.

Connecting the Hub

Let's take a step back to look at the big picture—how commands and events work with requests and responses. The diagram below visualizes how a Request gets transformed into a Response using commands and events:

As shown in the diagram, a request gets converted into a command, and then the output becomes the response.

The next step is for the HTTP route to generate our command and pass it to the hub. We need to create a method, handle, on the hub that we can call from the routes. Exactly like the one we wrote in our tests, it will process the command and store the events. Since handle needs the command handler and the event store, we can pass them as constructor dependencies.

```
class ToDoListHub(
    val fetcher: ToDoListFetcher,
    val commandHandler: ToDoListCommandHandler,
    val persistEvents: EventPersister<ToDoListEvent>
) : ZettaiHub {

    override fun handle(command: ToDoListCommand): ToDoListCommand? =
        commandHandler(command)
            ?.let( persistEvents )
            ?.let{ command } //returning the command

    // rest of methods
}
```

Note that the handle method returns the original command in case of success or null in case of any error. We'll see how to improve on the error in the next chapter.

> **Joe asks:**
> # Why Are We Returning the Original Command?
>
> As we'll see later, it's useful to return some information on what has been handled, but if we return the list of events created, we're letting too much information leak outside the domain.
>
> The problem is that if we return the events from the hub they'll become part of the public API of the domain. In general, it's better if events stay hidden inside the domain so that routes or other adapters don't depend on them.

With the hub finished, we can complete the route function to create a new list:

```
class Zettai(val hub: ZettaiHub) : HttpHandler {

...
    fun createNewList(request: Request): Response {
        val user = request.extractUser()
        return request.extractListNameFromForm("listname")
            ?.let { CreateToDoList(user, it) }
            ?.let(hub::handle)
            ?.let { Response(Status.SEE_OTHER)
                        .header("Location", "/todo/${user.name}") }
            ?: Response(Status.BAD_REQUEST)
    }
...
}
```

Read Model

Now, if we try to use the application, we won't see the newly created list in the page with all the lists of the user, even if the command actually works! This is because the page to display the lists is still using the fetcher with the (temporary) mutable map inside.

This is something we want to change, and we'll see (Projecting Our Events, on page 185) how to use the events to create specific views on the system. But to keep things working now, with minimal effort, we'll promote the ToDoListUpdatableFetcher to our *read model* and we will update it when running the commands:

```
class ToDoListCommandHandler(
    val entityRetriever: ToDoListRetriever,
    val readModel: ToDoListUpdatableFetcher // temporary!
) : (ToDoListCommand) -> List<ToDoListEvent>? {

    private fun CreateToDoList.execute(): List<ToDoListEvent>? =
        entityRetriever.retrieveByName(user, name)
            ?.let { listState ->
                when (listState) {
                    InitialState -> {
                        readModel.assignListToUser(
                            user,
                            ToDoList(name, emptyList())
                        )
                        ListCreated(id, user, name).toList()
                    }
                    else -> null //command fail
                }
            }

    // other methods
}
```

With everything in place, not only do the DDTs pass, but we can even verify for ourselves—launching a browser—that the UI allows us to create new lists!

Add an Item to a List

We finished our first command, but it's too early to celebrate. We also need to convert the existing code to add an item to a list to the command and events pattern.

First, we define our new command. As we did with the first one, we verify the happy path and all possible failures in TDD, improving the ToDoListCommandHandler one step at a time. This is what it looks like after the fixes:

```kotlin
class ToDoListCommandHandler(
...
    override fun invoke(command: ToDoListCommand): List<ToDoListEvent>? =
        when (command) {
            is CreateToDoList -> command.execute()
            is AddToDoItem -> command.execute()
        }
...
    private fun AddToDoItem.execute(): List<ToDoListEvent>? =
        entityRetriever.retrieveByName(user, name)
            ?.let { listState ->
                when (listState) {
                    is ActiveToDoList -> {
                        if (listState.items.any { it.name == item.name })
                            null //cannot have 2 items with same name
                        else {
                            readModel.addItemToList(user, listState.name, item)
                            ItemAdded(listState.id, item).toList()
                        }
                    }

                    InitialState,
                    is OnHoldToDoList,
                    is ClosedToDoList -> null //command fail
                }
            }
```

❶ Add the case for the new command. As we proceed, this when expression will grow.

❷ We can only add new items to active lists. If the list is in another state, the command will fail.

❸ Here, we update the read model.

❹ Here, we generate the new event.

❺ In case of other states, we fail. Note that InitialState is a singleton object type so it doesn't need the is.

Finally, we need to add the route. There we create the command from the request, and we pass it to the handle method in the hub:

```kotlin
class Zettai(val hub: ZettaiHub): HttpHandler {

...
    /todo/{user}/{listname}" bind Method.POST to ::addNewItem,
...
    private fun addNewItem(request: Request): Response {
        val user = request.extractUser()
        val listName = request.extractListName()
        return request.extractItem()
```

```
                ?.let { AddToDoItem(user, listName, it) }
                ?.let (hub::handle)
                ?.let { Response(Status.SEE_OTHER).header("Location",
                        "/todo/${user.name}/${listName.name}") }
                ?: Response(Status.BAD_REQUEST)
    }
}
```

Understanding Commands and Events Better

As we conclude this chapter, let's review the design decisions we made, starting with naming.

Our code shows that the `AddToDoItem` command generates an event named `ItemAdded`, and the `CreateToDoList` command generates an event named `ListCreated`. This practice of matching command and event names is a widespread pattern. However, it's not always applicable—it may be that what appears to be a single event is actually a more intricate business scenario. Hence, it's advisable not to blindly adopt this pattern.

In general, commands are linked to the external API and the use-cases, while events reflect the strict logic of the finite state machine. A good rule of thumb is to be generous with events and define many of them—one for each possible change—but be quite stingy when creating new commands.

In the application life cycle, events tend to multiply, and some of them will become obsolete, where commands tend to be more stable. This is the main reason to keep the events internal to the domain, without exposing them to the adapters, much less to other applications. Commands can be considered part of the public API of our system, so it's better if we keep their number low.

If we want to share events between applications, rather than have direct calls, those "public events" will probably have a different level of granularity than the events in Event Sourcing, so it's better to keep the two things separated. Trying to use the same events both to reconstruct the state and share information with external systems is usually a source of many headaches.

Finally, another possible solution to keep track of changes is to store the current state in the traditional way in a database, but at the same time, store all the changes as events in a separate audit persistence. This approach seems a bit like "half-hearted event sourcing" to me, getting all the complication of event sourcing and all the complication of normal state persistence with the added risk of incongruity between the audits and the current status. Still, there are cases where it makes sense, for example, if you need to improve an existing legacy application.

Mutable and Immutable State

Notwithstanding our favorite pattern, sharing a mutable state is a hard problem in any programming style. Functional programming offers a solution that's radically different from the object-oriented one. Functional programming keeps all the state changes at the outskirts of our code, so that the core business logic can ignore them. Object-oriented programming takes the opposite approach: it encapsulates and hides the changes inside the core objects themselves, with the same result.

The object-oriented approach seems more natural because it reminds us of the real world, where things can actually mutate—if I want to paint my wall green, I can do it; I don't need to throw the wall away and get a new green one. The downside of this approach is that we're never totally sure of the possible consequences of our changes.

The functional approach is inspired by mathematics and can be harder to grasp at the beginning, because we aren't naturally mathematicians, or at least most of us aren't. But as with mathematics, once we understand its rules and abstractions, we have an incredibly powerful tool to create complex behavior by composing very simple primitives, keeping our software easy to maintain and expand.

Identity and Entities

The identity is central to the concept of entity. In the words of Eric Evans (*Domain-Driven Design [Eva03]*): "Some objects are not defined primarily by their attributes. They represent a thread of identity that runs through time and often across distinct representations…An object defined primarily by its identity is called an ENTITY."

To clarify, let's assume we're writing software to manage a fleet of freighter ships around the world. In a standard object-oriented approach, we'll probably have a Freighter class and an instance for each of the ships in our system. Then, we need a way to identify if two instances, that may be different, are pointing to the same "real ship" or not. This is quite a complex problem discussed at length in Evans's book.

Identifying the object identity is a problem that's much simpler to solve when all our entities are immutable. They represent just a frozen image in time; they don't pretend to map the mutable behavior of reality. So, we don't have to worry about how to preserve a (semantically) immutable identity between mutable entities.

Since everything is immutable in functional programming, we're forced to solve this problem directly when defining the types, using a unique id for example. So the typical problem with mutable entities—"What should I do if I have two different entities with the same ID?"—must be solved at the type system level once and for all.

Supporting Event Sourcing Applications

Finally, let's have a final word about how you would fix production issues with an application based on event sourcing. What if a user wants to restore a list in a previous state because of some material error?

As a general principle, it's good practice to have events to revert other events so users can solve the errors by themselves. Unfortunately, this isn't always possible for business reasons. In that case, we may use a special "reset" event that allows us to change the state in special circumstances.

What we want to avoid, at any cost, is changing the data directly in the database. We'll discuss this and the migration strategy later in Migration and Versioning Events, on page 259.

Recap

In this chapter, we learned how to implement commands in a functional way.

First, we introduced the Command pattern to better control the changes to our system, and then we used the event sourcing pattern to store all the changes of the state of our system.

Finally, we connected the HTML UI to our commands and events so users can now add and modify ToDo lists.

In the next chapter, we'll look at how to handle errors in a more sophisticated way using functional types.

Exercises

The exercises in this chapter will focus on the functional finite state machine.

Here is your friendly reminder that nobody can learn functional programming by just reading code, and the best way to learn is by practicing. You can refer to the exercises folder in the book code repository for the starting point and some hints.

Exercise 6.1: Modeling an Elevator as a State Machine

For this exercise, try to implement a simple state machine to represent an elevator. You need to define the commands and the states. Commands should represent user interaction, like the button to call the elevator and the ones inside the elevator to stop at some floor. States should be "Doors open at floor x" and "Traveling at floor y." You shouldn't use events yet, just store the current elevator's state.

So, for example, the command would be something like CallElevator, and the command handler function will process a state like ElevatorTraveling to return a new state like ElevatorWaitingAtFloor.

You have to write tests to verify that commands work as expected.

Exercise 6.2: Using Events to Keep the Elevator State

For this exercise, you must continue from the previous exercise example and add events to represent the state changes, things like "button pressed," "elevator moved from floor to floor," and so on.

You need to implement the command handler using the same patterns that we used in Zettai, folding events to determine the current state and generating events from the command handler.

Exercise 6.3: Add an Out-of-Order State

Now you need to add a new state, "out of order," to the elevator state machine. There should be an event, "elevator broken," and a command to "fix the elevator."

Remember to write tests to make sure events state and commands are all working consistently.

Don't panic!

> *Douglas Adams, The Hitchhiker's Guide
to the Galaxy*

CHAPTER 7

Handling Errors Functionally

In this chapter, we'll continue on our journey to the core of functional programming. You'll learn about functors and what wonderfully useful abstractions they are. We'll see how they can help us to better solve our problems.

So far, we've avoided detailed error messages. It's now the moment to see how functors can help us address this and keep detailed error messages without losing our functional totality.

Finally, we'll see how to return nice error pages to the user, keeping the detailed errors for our logs.

Handling Errors Better

What are errors? There could be many definitions, but for our discussion here, we want to concentrate on a somewhat narrow meaning: an error occurs when the software doesn't behave as we expect.

For example, a network call can't connect, an input parameter isn't of the expected type, a component isn't in the right state to perform some work. Our aim is to detect these errors as early as possible and either recover, or failing that, report all the information required to fix the problem back to the client and to the log.

Until now, we have deliberately sidestepped a close examination of errors, but proper error reporting is crucial for maintaining code that's easy to manage and debug. By utilizing Kotlin's explicit nullability, we have ensured the completeness of our functions, but at the expense of detailed information on any errors that may arise.

As a rule of thumb, returning null every time there is an error works well when we don't care much about the why. For example, if we read a text file, we can write a function like:

```
fun readTextFile(fileName: String): List<String>? =
    File(fileName).let {
        if (it.exists()) it.readLines() else null
    }
```

In this case, if the file isn't present, we return null, and the reason is clear enough. There is no more information to add; the file simply isn't there.

If we try to do the same to read a person's details from a remote source, like a REST service or database, we'll have problems:

```
fun getPersonDetails(nickname: String): Person? = ...
  //return null if any error or the person doesn't exist
```

Returning null in this case could mean the nickname isn't present in our database, or we have an error connecting with the database, or maybe we encountered some other issue. In the first case, we should ask the user to check the nickname. In the second case, we should tell the user to retry later or check the configurations. How can we tell which case we're dealing with?

More generally speaking, there are several cases where we need more detailed error messages—for example:

1. We need to distinguish between different failures with different consequences.

2. We need to record details about which step failed in a complex calculation for debugging purposes.

3. We can't use null as an error indication, because null is a valid result of the calculation.

As an example of the last case, let's imagine we need to read the due date of a specific ToDoList. Since the due date field is optional, we need to distinguish the case of the field being empty from any possible error in reading the data. Now, let's consider a more complex scenario in detail.

Handling Errors with Null

Let's assume we're writing a feature to send a greeting email. At some point, we need to read the email text template from an external file using the read-TextFile function mentioned earlier:

```
fun prepareGreetingsEmail(userName: String): Email? {
    val user = getPersonDetails(userName)
    val templateText = readTextFile("myTemplate.txt")
```

```
    if (user != null && templateText != null) {
        val text = replace(templateText, user)
        return Email(user.emailAddress, text)
    } else {
        return null
    }
}
```

Here, we try to read user data and the template text. If any of those fail, (returning null) we make the whole function fail (again returning null).

Although it works, the disadvantage of this style of coding is that we don't know exactly why it failed. Was the user name wrong? Was the template file missing? Was there an error when fetching remote data? We simply don't know.

Returning Errors

As a comparison, let's consider another possibility: we can return the error details together with the result of the calculation. This is a convention common in languages like C and Golang.

Let's use text to describe the error, using the convention that an empty string means success—that is, there are no errors. We can use a Kotlin Pair as the return type and use the destructuring operator to read the result. The previous code rewritten in this style would look like this:

```
fun readTextFile(fileName: String): Pair<String, List<String>?> =
    File(fileName).let {
        if (it.exists())
        {"" to it.readLines() }
        else {
            "file not present" to null
        }
    }


fun prepareGreetingsEmail(userName: String): Pair<String, Email?> {
    val (resUser,user) = getPersonDetails(userName)
    val (resTempl, templateText ) = readTextFile("myTemplate.txt")

    if (user != null && templateText != null) {
        val text = replace(templateText, user)
        return "" to Email(user.emailAddress, text)
    } else {
        return  "Error: $resUser $resTempl" to null
    }
}
```

Here we return an error message together with the nullable result. The implicit pact is that if the result is null, the error message will explain the reason. Otherwise, the error message will be empty.

This code is correct; it preserves totality, and it also gives us detailed information about the error. These are big benefits.

There are two disadvantages, unfortunately:

1. Writing all the code in this way is quite verbose and error prone. We need to return Pair every time, and we still need to check for nullability before using the result.

2. We're forced to represent all possible errors as String (or any other type we choose); this is quite limiting when operating with complex types. If we want to attach a wrong Request to the error, for example, we need to convert it into a string or use a more complex error type that is overkill for other uses. In other words, we're losing flexibility.

Keeping the Exceptions Exceptional

At this point, you may wonder if, after all, we shouldn't reconsider the exceptions? They were there for a reason! Well, before rushing into it, let's review exactly why it's problematic to use exceptions to handle errors in functional programming.[1] To understand the problem in more detail, let's rewrite our snippet using exceptions:

```
fun prepareGreetingsEmail(userName: String): Email {

        val user = getPersonDetails(userName) ?:
            throw RuntimeException("User $userName not found!")

        val templateText = readTextFile("myTemplate.txt") ?:
            throw RuntimeException("Template not found!")

    val text = replace(templateText, user)

    return Email(user.emailAddress, text)
}
```

This code is clear and quite easy to read, but unfortunately, it's misleading. We're declaring a function with return type Email, but in reality it's quite possible that our calculation will terminate with an exception, failing its contract.

To see why this is a big deal, let's say that we want to use this code to send an email to all our contacts from inside a bigger batch job, like this:

---

1. https://docs.oracle.com/javase/specs/jls/se8/html/jls-11.html#jls-11.1.1

```
contactNames
  .map(::prepareGreetingsEmail)
  .forEach(::sendEmail)
```

If at any point we find a missing user, our exception would abort the whole batch job. Still worse, after the exception, the batch job would be left in an unpredictable state, since we aren't sure which emails we sent and which we didn't.

To protect ourselves, we might wrap everything with a try...catch block, like this:

```
contactNames
  .map{
    try {
      val email = prepareGreetingsEmail(it)
      sendEmail(email)
    } catch(e: Exception) {
      log("skipped $it because of $e")
    }
```

You can see how this would make the code more complicated to write and harder to understand. It would also be quite easy to forget it—at least in some places—and we'll discover it only in the worst possible circumstances: while running it in production.

It also would be limiting if we need to pass the throwing exception procedure to another function that doesn't handle the exceptions.

Last but not least, we can't reap the benefit of functional programming if we need to put heavy try...catch clauses around every function; we want our code to be both safe and easy to understand. You can see that even in the small example earlier, the exceptions broke the clean chain of functions, and we have to fall back to imperative code.

Preserving the totality of our functions is important, because it lets us compose safely on top of those functions.

Does this mean there is no role for exceptions in functional programming? No, we'll use exceptions, but only for really exceptional cases. If we're in a situation where there is no way to recover, we'll throw an exception and terminate the program or abort the HTTP call.

For example, if during the web server start-up we discover the port is already taken, we'll throw an exception and stop the application. This is a situation that we don't want to handle because we don't have a possible recovery.

In the earlier examples, on the other hand, we had a perfectly valid business case—a user name not present in our data—that we needed to address correctly.

Joe asks:

Are Checked Exceptions a Possible Solution?

The designers of the Java languages did consider the problem with errors and results, and they came up with an innovative solution.

They split the exceptions into three groups:

- Errors—from which no recovery is possible
- Checked exceptions—which are considered legitimate negative results
- Runtime exceptions—which were intended for cases that shouldn't happen, in other words, only for bugs

What's happened is that in reality it's very difficult to distinguish the last two cases. Moreover, having to handle the checked exceptions separately with catch clauses is quite bothersome, and it caused programmers to hate checked exceptions, so they started using runtime exceptions everywhere.

Now even Java language designers recognize that checked exceptions don't work like they were supposed to, and they are mostly ignored in the recent Java libraries.

The decision also depends on the context. If we were writing a generic web server library, and we had to handle the case of a port already taken in a graceful way, then we can leave to the users of our library the choice to recover the error—choosing another port for example—or stop the application.

In general, if we're unsure, it's always better to not use exceptions.

Functional Error Handling

So if we need good detailed errors, but we can't use exceptions, what should we do? We need a way to preserve details about the errors without making our code clumsy or hard to compose.

Even if this seems strange, mathematics can help us here. To see how, let's first draw a diagram with the arrows for our greetings application, ignoring the errors:

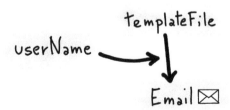

Let's think about how we would like our errors to work. Looking at the previous diagrams, imagine we have some kind of "magic arrows" that allow us to return specific errors but keep the possibility of combining all our functions as before.

If we examine in detail these "error-aware magic arrows," they should work like this:

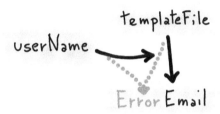

From a functional programming perspective, the solution to our problem is an *algebra* to combine functions aware of errors. Luckily, there is a mathematical tool that allows us to create such an algebra—the magical arrows we defined earlier—called *functors*.

> We defined algebra to mean a collection of functions operating over some data type(s), along with a set of laws specifying relationships between these functions.
>
> —*Functional Programming in Scala* by Paul Chiusano and Rúnar Bjarnason

Learning Functors and Categories

Please bear with me as I explain some theoretical context before we go back to play with the code. Alternatively, feel free to skip ahead and review our approach to error handling in the code (Using Functors to Handle Errors, on page 171) before returning to this section for the theory.

Understanding functors well is a critical step in mastering advanced functional programming. If you fully understand them, you won't have any problems with more complex structures like monads and applicatives, which we'll look at in the next chapters.

To define what a functor is, we need to look first at what a category is. A category is a mathematical concept introduced to define the relation between things in the most abstract way possible.

At first glance, it's just a bunch of arrows and dots where all the dots are connected by arrows. Dots and arrows are abstract representations that can stand for anything. For example, we can create a category with some tourist attractions in New York and the routes that connect them. Let's draw it, from the left: the Statue of Liberty, the Empire State Building, Central Park, Wall Street, and the Brooklyn Bridge.

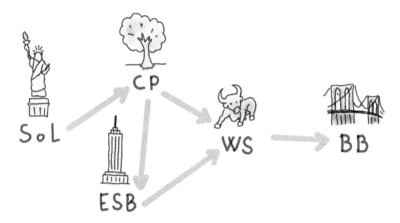

A little note: you have to imagine that each attraction also has an identity arrow that points to itself. They aren't in the diagram for simplicity's sake, but they are important.

What's important in this diagram is the arrows have a direction, and we can compose them together. To form a category, we need to verify some simple rules:

1. We can always combine two arrows (SoL to CP + CP to ESB is identical to Sol to ESB).

2. The order in which we combine arrows isn't important.

3. There is always a special identity arrow from a dot to itself (ESB to itself).

Strictly speaking, the arrows are called *morphisms*, and the dots are called *objects*—they have nothing to do with object-oriented programming.

The concept of *category* is very abstract. It can work with anything that involves relations that can be combined. Its use varies from the study of languages to subatomic physics.

To continue our example, we can draw another category diagram as shown on page 165, for some London tourist attractions that somehow correspond to the New York ones. From the left: Trafalgar Square with the statue of Horatio Nelson, the Shard, Hyde Park, the Bank of England, and the Tower Bridge.

Note that the correspondence is arbitrary, but it should preserve some property that we're interested in, for example, the historic significance or the price of the ticket.

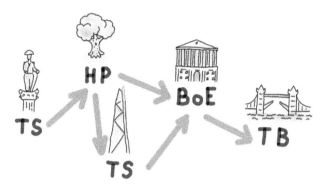

Now we can define a functor. A *functor* is something that maps two categories together. More precisely,

> A functor is a mapping between categories. Given two categories, C and D, a functor F maps objects in C to objects in D—it's a function on objects. If a is an object in C, we'll write its image in D as F a (no parentheses). But a category is not just objects—it's objects and morphisms that connect them. A functor also maps morphisms—it's a function on morphisms. But it doesn't map morphisms willy-nilly—it preserves connections. So if a morphism f in C connects object a to object b, the image of f in D, will connect the image of a to the image of b.
>
> —Bartosz Milewski[2]

This means that if we define a "New York -> London" functor, it has to map all the attractions from New York to the ones in London. Not only that, but it also has to map all of the routes. Let's draw it:

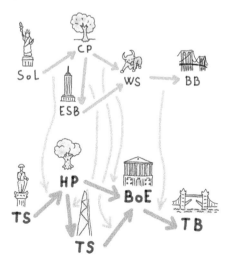

<hr />

2. https://bartoszmilewski.com/2015/01/20/functors/

The idea behind a functor is both simple and powerful: we transform something that we know (New York, in this case) to something that we don't know much about (London, in this example), but thanks to the functor we're able to continue using our knowledge (the arrows).

For a functor to be valid, the two categories don't have to be so similar as in this didactic example. Functors can take different objects in the original category and "squash" them together in the target category, and they can ignore completely parts that aren't relevant. What's important is that all the objects and arrows existing in the source category are mapped to the target in a way that preserves their properties.

You can find a more precise definition of categories and functors in the appendix dedicated to theory (Appendix 3, A Pinch of Theory, on page 391). Even if all this might be a bit too vague and hard to grasp now, hopefully things will become clearer as we examine their application in code. I can assure you that with practice, these concepts will become very familiar to you.

Defining Category in Code

We saw that a category can be used in a number of cases, but what about programming?

A very useful way to define a category in code is to consider the dots representing our types and the arrows representing pure functions (see Category Theory, on page 353).

In this way, we can create a mini category by putting together some functions and some types—for example, to keep things simple, let's consider Int, String, and Double types. We can now verify the three rules of categories using a function for identity and another to combine two other functions, as we did in the exercise in Chapter 2:

```
fun <T> identity(a: T): T = a

infix fun <A, B, C> ((A)->B).andThen(f: (B)->C): (A)->C =
  { a:A -> f(this(a)) }
```

To verify the first rule—we can always combine two arrows—we can do the following:

```
val anyString = randomString()

expectThat( identity( anyString)).isEqualTo(anyString)
```

For the second rule—the order in which we combine arrows isn't important—we can do the following:

```
val l = anyString.length()
val h = half(l) //divide by 2
val halfLength = ::length andThen ::half
expectThat( halfLength(anyString) ).isEqualTo(h)
```

Finally, to verify the third rule—there is always a special identity arrow from a dot to itself—we can combine the three functions in two different ways and still prove that the result is the same:

```
val halfLengthStr1 = (::length andThen ::half) andThen toString
val halfLengthStr2 = ::length andThen (::half andThen toString)
expectThat( halfLengthStr1(anyString) ).isEqualTo(halfLengthStr2(anyString))
```

Does this mean that Kotlin's type system forms a category in itself? Yeah, kind of, but only if we ignore a lot of details, like exceptions, impure functions, mutable singletons, and so on.

Defining Functors in Code

Now that we're beginning to understand what a category is, let's continue creating some functors.

How can we translate the mathematical concept of functors in code? We need to look for a way to transform a set of types into other types, conserving their relations. In other words, if we have a category with types String and Int, plus a function that connects them of type (String) -> Int, our functor must do the following:

1. Create new types based on Int and String or any type we have in our category
2. Allow us to still use our function on the new types

It may be a new way to look at it, but there is a way to create types based on other types in Kotlin—and most other modern languages. It's called *generic programming* and is commonly referred to as "generics."

In Kotlin, we can define a generic type by adding a parametric type to the declaration, like in Java.

For example, if we want to define a generic type Holder that can hold any given value—a bit like a collection that can have only exactly one element—we can write it like this:

```
data class Holder<T>(private val value:T)
```

If, like myself, you've learned about generics in Java, you might be used to thinking of Holder<T> as a type that includes a generic parameter. However, in functional programming, it's more useful to think of it not as a type but as a *type builder*.

Generics Are Type Builders

In other words Holder<Int>, Holder<String>, and so on are all types built by Holder<T>, but Holder<T> isn't a type in itself, it's a type builder.

This might seem like a very abstract distinction, but it will become useful later when we build more complex types in Exploring the Power of Monads, on page 225.

 Joe asks:
Are Functors the Same Things as Generics?

No, but we can say that generics are type builders and that we can use type builders to implement functors in our code.

We can use generics for other reasons—for example, the Comparable interface—and we can create functors that only work on specific types without using generics, although they wouldn't be very useful.

The fundamental idea behind functors is the transformation—you can verify which of your generic types support this notion and which don't.

Transform and Lift

We've addressed the first point using generics, but we still have to address the second requirement: how can we use our function (String) -> Int on the new functor type, Holder<String>?

We can do it in two ways:

1. We apply the function to transform our functor into a Holder<Int>.
2. We use the functor to *lift* our function so that it can operate directly on functors.

Let's look at the first solution. We can define a transform method that would return a new Holder with the value inside:

```
data class Holder<T>(private val value: T) {

    fun <U> transform(f: (T) -> U): Holder<U> = Holder( f(value) )
}
```

The second solution requires defining a higher-order function (see Using Higher-Order Functions, on page 51) to "lift" our function in a way that will allow it to work with any Holder type:

```
data class Holder<T>(private val value: T) {

    companion object {
        fun <T, U> lift(f: (T) -> U): (Holder<T>) -> Holder<U> =
            { c: Holder<T> -> c.transform(f) }
    }
}
```

For example, using transform we take a Holder with a string, and we apply the method String::length that returns an Int:

```
val a: Holder<String> = Holder("this is a string")
val b1: Holder<Int> = a.transform(String::length)
```

Using lift instead, we create a function strLenLifted of type (Holder<String>) -> Holder<Int>, and we can use it directly on our Holder:

```
val strLenLifted = Holder.lift(String::length)
val b2: Holder<Int> = strLenLifted(a)
```

The two results, b1 and b2, are identical.

When Using Lift

When we only need to apply a function to a single functor, transform is usually more convenient than lift. However, when we're working with multiple functors, lifting the function and applying the lifted version directly to the functors can make the code easier to read.

This is similar to the decision of whether to use a function that operates on individual items in a list versus a function that takes the entire list as input.

Finally, a note about names. Our transform method is defined as fmap in Haskell, select in C#, and transform in C++. In most JVM functional libraries in Scala, Kotlin, and Java, it's defined as map, which is unfortunate in my opinion. Anyway, the name isn't really important; what's important is how it works.

The Laws of Functors

There are two laws that functors must adhere to:

1. Functors must preserve identity morphisms.
2. Functors must preserve composition of morphisms.

> \\// **Joe asks:**
>
> ɜʃ **Why Not Call It map?**
>
> In part, it's for didactic purposes; we're so used to using map with the collections that a different name makes it clearer how functors work.
>
> As we'll see, collections can be considered as functors, but that isn't their primary attribute. Collections are designed to hold a group of elements together. Using the same term to describe operations performed on a collection and a functor can create confusion and make it harder to understand their differences.
>
> Moreover, using a name different from map for our transformations has the advantage of making the code easier to understand when we operate on collections of functors or functors of collections, which is quite common.

We can easily translate the first law into code, using the identity function we defined previously—since in functional programming, morphisms are pure functions (Category Theory, on page 353):

```
val a1 = a.transform(::identity)

println(a==a1) //true
```

This verifies that when applying the identity function to the functor, it will return a value identical to the original one.

To verify the second law, we need two functions, splitIntoWords and List<String>::size. We can check that concatenating two transformations gives us the same result as combining the two functions and applying the result in a single transformation:

```
val splitIntoWords: (String) -> List<String> = { s:String -> s.split(' ') }
val c1 = a.transform(splitIntoWords).transform(List<String>::size)

val NumOfWords: (String) -> Int = splitIntoWords andThen List<String>::size

val c2 = a.transform(NumOfWords)

println(c1 == c2) //true
```

We can now be satisfied that our first functor works properly.

As a final note, we're only concerned about *endofunctors* in programming, that is, functors that map a category on themselves. Roughly speaking, the category we're operating on is the Kotlin language itself, so our functors are mapping Kotlin into Kotlin. For a better definition, see Functors Are Mappers, on page 406.

Looking at Lists as Functors

If you've followed along up until now, you may start wondering why we bother discussing functors. Holder doesn't seem to have any use at all.

Let's now look at something more useful, a group of well-known types that work as functors. I'm talking about all the collection types. First, let's consider List, the simplest nontrivial functor.

We can always create a list, or any collection really, from a value. So, a function of type (T) -> List<T> is our functor constructor. Note that it's also possible to create lists of functions—for example:

```
val f: List< (String)->Int > = listOf(String::length)
```

What's the equivalent of our transform? List::map works exactly like a functor's transform, and we can create a liftList function that takes advantage of this:

```
fun <T,R> liftList(f: (T) -> R): (List<T>) -> List<R> =
    { c: List<T> -> c.map(f) }
```

What can we do with such a function? We can transform a function working on elements into a function working on lists, for example:

```
val strFirstLifted = liftList(String::first)
val words: List<String> = listOf(
    "Cuddly","Acrobatic","Tenacious","Softly-purring")

val initials: List<Char> = strFirstLifted(words)
println(initials) // ['C','A','T','S']
```

Lists aren't just a simple "elementary" functor like Holder. We can add to or remove elements from a list, and do a lot of other things.

All these behaviors aren't part of the functor, but this is exactly what makes functors such an interesting concept: we can use them to transform one type into another and still keep the original behaviors.

We started with a well-known type like String, and we transformed it into a List<String> that has new, interesting properties, and we can still use any function that works with String on our list using the map method.

But enough with lists, let's return to our original question: how do functors help us with errors?

Using Functors to Handle Errors

We started our search for a kind of "magic arrow"; functors can work exactly in this way—as you may have already guessed.

To see how this would work, let's look again at the transform method of Holder; it's very simple, but we can add a condition: do the transformation only if the value isn't an error. We can define a class like this:

```
data class ConstantOrErrorF<T>( val value:T?, val isError: Boolean) {

    fun <U> transform(f: (T) -> U): ConstantOrErrorF<U> =
        if (isError || value == null)
            ConstantOrErrorF(null, true)
        else
            ConstantOrErrorF(f(value), false)
}
```

This would work, but we can do better than this.

Handling Errors with Union Types

Instead of using a boolean to represent the possible error, we can define a union type (see Union Types, on page 123) representing the outcome of our calculations, combining two concrete subtypes—success or failure.

Let's start defining our sealed class, Outcome, and the two concrete data classes. Incidentally, it would have been nice to call it Result, but unfortunately there is already a class in the Kotlin standard library called Result, which works in a similar way, but it's somehow limited. Since the IDE will always try to import the standard library Result first, I decided to use a different name for our functor.

```
❶ sealed class  Outcome<T>
❷ data class Success<T>(val value: T): Outcome<T>()
❸ data class Failure(val errorMessage: String) : Outcome<Nothing>()
```

❶ An Outcome can wrap a value of any type (the T parameter), including nullable types.

❷ The actual value is present only in the Success case.

❸ In case of failure, we don't care about the result type, and we use Nothing to avoid having to specify the type in case of failure.

We can now define our tranform only for the successful case:

```
fun <U> transform(f: (T) -> U): Outcome<U> =
    when (this) {
        is Success -> Success(f(value))
        is Failure -> this
    }
```

For our convenience and code readability, we can use two extension functions instead of calling the constructors of Success and Failure:

```
❶ fun String.asFailure(): Outcome<Nothing> = Failure(this)
  fun <T> T.asSuccess(): Outcome<T> = Success(this)
```

❶ In Kotlin, the Nothing type can be used in place of any other type, since you can't instantiate it. Therefore, an Outcome of Nothing can be returned irrespective of the actual type T.

So, this is our functor to manage errors—in other words, our "magic arrow." How can we use it?

Working with Outcomes

We can now rewrite the readTextFile and getPersonDetails methods of the previous greeting email example using an Outcome:

```
fun readTextFile(filename: String): Outcome<String> =
        if (fileExists && canRead)
        readfile(File(filename)).asSuccess()
    else
        "$filename not found".asFailure()


fun getPersonDetails(nickname: String): Outcome<Person> {

        val resp = remoteRead(nickname)

        return if (resp.status == OK)
            Person.parse(resp.bodyString()).asSuccess()
        else if (resp.status = NOT_FOUND )
            "$nickname not found!".asFailure()
    else
        resp.bodyString().asFailure()
}
```

Note that Person.parse and readfile can also fail, and it would be better to make them return an Outcome as well.

So far, so good, but when we rewrite the prepareGreetingsEmail method, we get a compilation error:

```
fun prepareGreetingsEmail(userName: String): Outcome<Email> {

        val userOutcome = getPersonDetails(userName)

    val res = userOutcome.transform { user ->
        readTextFile("myTemplate.txt")
            .transform { templ -> replace(templ, user)}
            .transform { text -> Email(user.emailAddress, text)
    }

    return res // ERROR!
    }
}
```

This code doesn't compile, because the user is now an Outcome, and since we have to do two nested transformations, the final result would be Outcome<Outcome<Email>>, and we don't have (yet) a way to "simplify" two functors nested one inside the other. In the next chapter, we'll learn how to do it, but there is an easier way to solve our problem here.

Break on Failure

We can simplify the problem if we consider that when getPersonDetails is returning an error, we don't need to try to read the text file, we can return immediately. Kotlin inline functions have a useful feature called *non-local return* that allow us to abort the main function from inside a lambda.

We need to add a method to our Outcome class to let us handle the failure case separately by throwing an exception using a non-local return. To do this we need to pass a function without a return type. Kotlin's Nothing type expresses exactly this since it's impossible to create an instance of Nothing (see Nothing, on page 376).

The method should only call the exitBlock in case of error:

```
inline fun <E: OutcomeError, T> Outcome<E, T>.onFailure(
                                exitBlock: (E) -> Nothing): T =
    when (this) {
        is Success<T> -> value
        is Failure<E> -> exitBlock(this)
    }
```

Now that we can directly handle the error case, we can chain two transformations:

```
fun prepareGreetingsEmail(userName: String): Outcome<Email> {

    val user = getPersonDetails(userName)
        .onFailure{ return it } //non local return!

    return readTextFile("myTemplate.txt")
        .transform { templ -> replace(templ, user)}
        .transform { text -> Email(user.emailAddress, text)
    }
}
```

While non-local returns can be beneficial, they have the potential to make the code difficult to read, as they can be easily overlooked. So, it's better to use them judiciously and sparingly.

More Precise Errors

Up to this point, the Outcome type that we've been using has only had a single generic parameter, which represents the type of the successful outcome.

However, this doesn't give us much information about errors that may occur, only a vague, nonspecific error, which is only marginally better than using nullable values to represent errors.

What we really need is a way to precisely model errors as distinct types, just as we do for the successful outcomes. Since Outcome is already a generic type, the question is: how can we specify the error types?

To solve this problem, we can think of generic types as type builders. We need to build a type that not only specifies the success type but also the error type. Therefore, we'll make the Outcome type generic on two types instead of just one.

In this way, our Outcome type will include not only the possibility of success but also the possibility of different types of errors. This allows us to be more specific about the kinds of errors that can occur and handle them accordingly.

```
❶ interface OutcomeError {
       val msg: String
   }
❷ sealed class Outcome<out E : OutcomeError, out T> {

❸     fun <U> transform(f: (T) -> U): Outcome<E, U> =
           when (this) {
               is Success -> f(value).asSuccess()
               is Failure -> this
           }
   }
   data class Success<T> internal constructor(val value: T):
      Outcome<Nothing, T>()
❹ data class Failure<E : OutcomeError> internal constructor(val error: E):
      Outcome<E, Nothing>()

   fun <E : OutcomeError> T.asFailure(): Outcome<E, Nothing> = Failure(this)
   fun <T> T.asSuccess(): Outcome<Nothing, T> = Success(this)
```

❶ We use a generic interface for the error type. Each Outcome can then define a more specific type so far as it implements this interface.

❷ We pass two generic parameters now—the value and the error type. They are in out position, because they are used as the return value by its methods.

❶ The logic of transform method stays the same but allows for more detailed errors.

❹ The failure now requires an error parameter.

> ### Joe asks:
> ## Why Use an Error Base Class?
>
> This is a very good point. It's certainly possible to use a symmetric Either class to map errors. The difference would be that it's up to the user to decide if the left or the right type is the result, even if usually the convention is that the right is "right."
>
> Outcome is an opinionated Either type designed specifically to handle errors. This is done primarily for our convenience, as it helps ensure that we don't accidentally mix up left and right parameters in our codebase. This design ensures that IDE's auto-completion will suggest only compatible types for the value and error generics.
>
> Moreover, in this way we can be more explicit in the naming of the functions that handle failure and success cases, rather than having something like transformLeft and transformRight.

We also need some other functions to operate on the Outcome. First, let's look at how we can implement lift:

```
fun <T,U,E:OutcomeError> lift(f: (T)->U): (Outcome<E,T>)->Outcome<E,U> =
    { o -> o.transform { f(it) } }
```

Another very useful function we can add to our little library is recover. It will allow us to convert the error to the same type as the result and then "merge" them. It looks like this:

```
fun <T,E:OutcomeError> Outcome<E,T>.recover(recoverError: (E)->T): T =
    when (this) {
        is Success -> value
        is Failure -> recoverError(error)
    }
```

We can use it when we have a default value for our calculation:

```
val template = readTextFile("MyTemplate.txt")
    .recover("hello {user_name}!")
```

In this case, if the file "MyTemplate.txt" is missing or corrupt, we'll use a default template.

An even more interesting case is when our calling method must return a value regardless of whether the calculation failed or not. For example, in an HTTP handler we need to create a Response from a generic JSON Request. If everything is correct, we generate a Response with the HTML page; otherwise, we return a bad request Response:

```
fun generatePage(request: Request): Response =
    request.parseJsonRequest()
        .transform { it.toHtmlPage() }
        .transform { Response(Status.OK).body(it) }
        .recover {  Response(Status.BAD_REQUEST).body(it.msg) }
```

Finally, it's convenient to have a method to translate a nullable value in an outcome, mapping the null case to a given failure:

```
fun <T:Any, E:OutcomeError> T?.failIfNull(error: E): Outcome<E, T>
        = this?.asSuccess() ?: error.asFailure()
```

To see an example of its use, let's rewrite the function that extracts the list name from the request:

```
private fun Request.extractListName(): ZettaiOutcome<ListName> =
  path("listname")
    .orEmpty()
    .let(ListName.Companion::fromUntrusted)
    .failIfNull(InvalidRequestError("Invalid list name in path: $this"))
```

In this way, we can combine functions using null as the error with others that use Outcome.

Functional Effects

> Functional programmers often informally call type constructors like Par, Option, List, Parser, Gen, and so on effects. This usage is distinct from the term side effect, which implies some violation of referential transparency. These types are called effects because they augment ordinary values with "extra" capabilities.
>
> —*Functional Programming in Scala* by Paul Chiusano and Rúnar Bjarnason

Our Outcome here is the first "effects" we'll discover in this book. Later, we'll see others when looking at persistence and validation. Using them is the secret sauce of effective functional programming, even if it's not a secret at all.

Clean Up Our Code

Now that we know how to handle the errors, we can improve Zettai error management. Let's look at how to do it using our hub as a concrete example. In the previous chapter, we let the hub methods return nullable results to handle the error cases:

```
interface ZettaiHub {
    fun getList(user: User, listName: ListName): ToDoList?
    fun getLists(user: User): List<ListName>?
    fun handle(command: ToDoListCommand): ToDoListCommand?
}
```

We want to convert them all to Outcome. So, first we'll create some new error classes and a type alias for convenience:

```
sealed class ZettaiError: OutcomeError
data class InvalidRequestError(override val msg: String): ZettaiError()
data class ToDoListCommandError(override val msg: String) : ZettaiError()
...

typealias ZettaiOutcome<T> = Outcome<ZettaiError, T>
```

Now we'll change the signature of all methods, wrapping the result type with Outcome and removing the nullable indication in this way:

```
interface ZettaiHub {
    fun getList(user: User, listName: ListName): ZettaiOutcome<ToDoList>
    fun getLists(user: User): ZettaiOutcome<List<ListName>>
    fun handle(command: ToDoListCommand): ZettaiOutcome<ToDoListCommand>
}
```

The hub implementation must call the command handler as before, but now it passes the events to the event persister using transform:

```
class ToDoListHub(...) : ZettaiHub {

    override fun handle(command: ToDoListCommand) =
        commandHandler(command)
            .transform(persistEvents)
            .transform{ command }
```

In this way, if the command fails for any reason, it won't send events to be persisted. This also means that the command handler now has to return an Outcome with detailed error information instead of a nullable command:

```
typealias ToDoListCommandOutcome = ZettaiOutcome<List<ToDoListEvent>>

class ToDoListCommandHandler(...): (ToDoListCommand)->ToDoListCommandOutcome
...

    override fun invoke(command: ToDoListCommand): ToDoListCommandOutcome =
        when (command) {
            is CreateToDoList -> command.execute()
...
    private fun CreateToDoList.execute(): ToDoListCommandOutcome
```

When the state of the list isn't compatible with our command, instead of a null, we can now return an InconsistentStateError with details about the command and the incorrect state:

```
private fun CreateToDoList.execute(): ToDoListCommandOutcome {

  val listState = entityRetriever.retrieveByName(user, name) ?: InitialState

  return when (listState) {
    InitialState ->
```

```
            ListCreated(ToDoListId.mint(), user, name).asCommandSuccess()

        is ActiveToDoList,
        is OnHoldToDoList,
        is ClosedToDoList -> InconsistentStateError(this, listState).asFailure()
    }
}

data class InconsistentStateError(
                val command: ToDoListCommand,
                val state: ToDoListState): ZettaiError() {
    override val msg ="Command $command cannot be applied to state $state"
}

fun ToDoListEvent.asCommandSuccess(): ZettaiOutcome<List<ToDoListEvent>> =
    listOf(this).asSuccess()
```

We also created a small extension function, asCommandSuccess(), for our convenience.

Finally, we can see how the hub is used by the HTTP handler. Let's consider the method to add a new item to a list. This is how we left it, with the chain of nullable let:

```
private fun addNewItem(request: Request): Response {
    val user = request.extractUser()
    val listName = request.extractListName()
    return request.extractItem()
        ?.let { AddToDoItem(user, listName, it) }
        ?.let(hub::handle)
        ?.let { Response(Status.SEE_OTHER)
          .header("Location", "/todo/${user.name}/${listName.name}") }
        ?: Response(Status.BAD_REQUEST)
}
```

Now we can use functor transformations to produce better errors:

```
① private fun addNewItem(request: Request): Response {
       val user = request.extractUser()
②         .recover { User("anonymous") }
       val listName = request.extractListName()
③         .onFailure { return Response(Status.BAD_REQUEST).body(it.msg) }
       val item = request.extractItem()
           .onFailure { return Response(Status.BAD_REQUEST).body(it.msg)

④     return hub.handle(AddToDoItem(user, listName, item))
           .transform { Response(Status.SEE_OTHER)
                   .header("Location", "/todo/${user.name}/${listName.name}") }
⑤         .recover { Response(Status.UNPROCESSABLE_ENTITY).body(it.msg) }
   }
```

❶ The signature must stay the same, so all Outcome must be converted into a Response.

❷ As a temporary measure, if the user is missing from the request path, we create a default user.

❸ Using the new extractListName function, in case of a failure, we return immediately with a specific error response.

❹ The hub returns an Outcome, and we transform the result from the hub to the successful response.

❺ Using recover, we convert the hub errors into a detailed error response.

There is definitely room for improvement, but at least it now provides more accurate error messages. In the upcoming chapters, we'll make it more elegant and easier to read.

We'll utilize the Outcome type everywhere we require detailed error information. If specific error details aren't necessary, we can leave the result as nullable.

Testing Outcomes

Let's look at how to test functions that return Outcome. First, we define two special assertions—a positive or a negative outcome:

```
fun <E : OutcomeError, T> Outcome<E, T>.expectSuccess(): T =
    onFailure { error -> fail { "$this expected success but was $error" } }

fun <E : OutcomeError, T> Outcome<E, T>.expectFailure(): E =
    onFailure { error -> return error }
        .let { fail { "Expected failure but was $it" } }
```

Using these new assertions, it's very simple to test any function with an Outcome result. For example, we can now verify not only that a user can't create two lists with the same name but also that the exact error is returned:

```
@Test
fun `Add list fails if the user has already a list with same name`() {

    val cmd = CreateToDoList(user, name)
    val res = handle(cmd).expectSuccess().single()

    expectThat(res).isA<ListCreated>()

    val duplicatedRes = handler(cmd).expectFailure()
    expectThat(duplicatedRes).isA<InconsistentStateError>()

}
```

Recap

In this chapter, we started looking at advanced concepts in functional programming. If you have followed along until now, you are no longer a beginner in functional programming!

We analyzed how the functor data structure is a powerful tool that we can use in different ways. This is a really fundamental step to effectively design in a functional way.

A functor is something that allows us to transform types while preserving some properties. This transformation can give us functional effects; for example, separating errors from success is an effect of our Outcome functor.

Then, we looked in detail at how we can use functors to get better error messages, keeping our functions composable without using exceptions.

In the next chapter, we'll progress on our application, making use of functors to project events to query our data in multiple ways.

Exercises

The exercises in this chapter will focus on functors and errors.

Here is your friendly reminder that nobody can learn functional programming by just reading code, and the best way to learn is by practicing. You can refer to the exercises folder in the book code repository for the starting point and some hints.

Exercise 7.1: Combining Functors

We have seen how to create a constant functor, so let's define some further methods on it. The method combine will allow us to combine two Holders passing a function with two parameters.

The exercise consists of implementing the combine method with this signature:

```
fun combine(other: Holder<T>, f: (T, T) -> T): Holder<T> =
  TODO()
```

...so that we can write code like this:

```
val h = Holder("hello")
val w = Holder("world")
h.combine(w){a,b -> "$a $b"} //"hello world"
```

Can you implement it without using the Holder constructor directly?

Exercise 7.2: Verifying Functor Laws

We verified that functor laws worked on Holder.

For this exercise, you need to verify the laws for the Outcome functor instance.

Try to use a random generator to verify each law with 1,000 random values, as we discussed when learning about property testing.

Exercise 7.3: Transform Failure

As we have the transform method to change the type of the success case for our Outcome, let's define a new method to transform the error type from one type to another:

```
fun <F : OutcomeError> transformFailure(f: (E) -> F): Outcome<F, T> = TODO()
```

This is useful if we want to return a specific error type, but we need to use functions that return other kinds of errors.

We can use it to convert the error from one type to another inside a function, sendEmail, in this way:

```
fun sendEmail(fileName: String): Outcome<EmailError, Unit> =
    readFile(fileName)
        .transformFailure { EmailError(it.msg) }
        .onFailure { return@sendEmail it.asFailure() }
        .let(::sendTextByEmail)


class FileError(override val msg: String) : OutcomeError
class EmailError(override val msg: String) : OutcomeError

fun readFile(fileName: String): Outcome<FileError, String> = ...

fun sendTextByEmail(text: String): Outcome<EmailError, Unit> = ...
```

Exercise 7.4: Catching Exceptions

Another useful addition to our Outcome class is a try-catch method that would transform the exceptions in a failure:

```
fun <T> tryAndCatch(block: () -> T): Outcome<ThrowableError, T> = TODO()

data class ThrowableError(val t: Throwable) : OutcomeError {
    override val msg: String = t.message.orEmpty()
}
```

The exercise consists of implementing the method so that this code can work:

```
fun todayGreetings(dateString: String) =
    tryAndCatch { LocalDate.parse(dateString) }
        .transform { "Today is $it" }
        .recover { "Error parsing the date ${it.msg}" }

println(todayGreetings("12/3/2020"))  //Error...

println(todayGreetings("2020-03-12")) //Today is...
```

CHAPTER 8

Using Functors to Project Events

In the previous chapter, you learned about functors. In the next step, as we continue our Zettai application, we'll remove the mutable Fetcher from our application, and instead, generate custom views of our data "projecting" the events. These views are called projections, and they'll work as read-only models for our application.

You'll see how functors allow us to query our projections by simply composing pure functions in a type-safe way and without the risk of leaking resources.

Finally, we'll put it all together to implement the "what's next" feature of our application.

Projecting Our Events

Since we're recording all the changes to our system using events, we should use them not only for the commands (the write model) but also to do queries as well (the so-called read model). In this way, we can also get rid of the last "temporary hack," namely, the ToDoListFetcherFromMap.

The question is, how can we query events? Since each event doesn't contain the whole information of an entity but only what's changed, it would be very hard to run queries directly on top of the event store.

What we're going to do instead is *project* the events in a stateful data structure that we can query like it was a database table. Even better, we can create multiple *projections* with different properties, depending on our needs.

Projections can be stored on a persistence layer, or they can be recreated in memory every time the application starts. In this chapter, we'll consider in-memory projections only, but in the next chapter, we'll learn how to store them in a database without affecting the code that uses them.

The projections will always be a kind of duplication of information already present in the event store; they'll only make it easy for us to search inside it. If for any reason a projection gets corrupted, we can always recreate it by replaying the events from the beginning. This is also very convenient when we want to change our projections. We don't need migration scripts; we only need to replay the events.

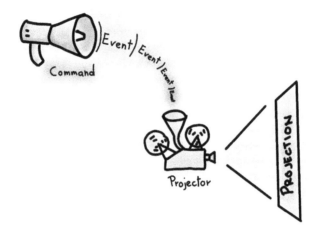

Defining the First Projection

A projection can be compared to a database table: it's a collection of records, also known as rows, that can be queried. The great thing about projections is that they allow us to tailor the rows with precisely the data that we require, denormalized or aggregated, whichever is more convenient for our queries, without worrying about update issues, since they are read-only.

Projections depend on two types:

1. The type of events that generate the projection
2. The type of stored state; in simpler terms, the projection row

Let's create an interface with these two types as generics and with a method update that projects all the new events created since the last update:

```
interface Projection<ROW: Any, EVENT: EntityEvent> {
❶    val eventFetcher: FetchStoredEvents<EVENT>

❷    fun lastProjectedEvent(): EventSeq

❸    fun update() {
        eventFetcher(lastProjectedEvent())
            .forEach{ TODO("project events here") }
    }
}
```

❶ This is the function that will fetch the new events, that is, the ones created after the last update. We'll define it in the next section.

❷ This function will return the last event that has been projected.

❸ This method will fetch the new events and will use them to update the projection.

To keep track of which events have been processed, we need a sequential progressive number associated to each event. In this way, each projection can remember the last processed event and start reading only events after that.

To store this progressive number, representing the sequential identifier of events, we create the EventSeq type. We also define a new generic type, StoredEvent<E>, to keep the event together with its progressive.

```
data class EventSeq(val progressive: Int) {
    operator fun compareTo(other: EventSeq): Int =
        progressive.compareTo(other.progressive)
}

data class StoredEvent<E: EntityEvent>(val eventSeq: EventSeq, val event: E)

typealias FetchStoredEvents<E> = (EventSeq) -> Sequence<StoredEvent<E>>
```

Working with Rows

So, how do we create a projection from the events? With an event projector, of course!

The projector is a function that must update the projection rows, considering each event and the current state of the projection. We need to declare a type that expresses the update of the row.

In other words, a projector takes the stream of events and creates the equivalent of a table with them. Each event will update a row, delete a row, or create a new one.

If you think about it, this is similar to the SQL commands—UPDATE, INSERT, DELETE—and this is because the projector works a bit like an SQL interpreter.

To make it work, the projector will generate a DeltaRow from each event; this class contains all the information to update the projection with the content of the event. In other words, it represents the difference (the delta) between the projection before and after the event.

To model it in code, we can use a sealed class with a subclass for each case:

```
① typealias ProjectEvents<R, E> = (E) -> List<DeltaRow<R>>

② data class RowId(val id: String)

  sealed class DeltaRow<R: Any>

  data class CreateRow<R: Any>(val rowId: RowId,
③                              val row: R): DeltaRow<R>()

④ data class DeleteRow<R: Any>(val rowId: RowId): DeltaRow<R>()

  data class UpdateRow<R: Any>(val rowId: RowId,
⑤                              val updateRow: R.()-> R): DeltaRow<R>()
```

❶ Here, we define the typealias for the projector, generating a list of DeltaRow from an event.

❷ We also need a unique identifier for each row of the projection. It can be the same as the entity key or something more complicated, as long as it's unique for each row of the projection.

❸ Here, we store the information to create a new row.

❹ To delete a row, we only need the row ID.

❺ To update a row, we need to provide a function that takes a row and returns a new one.

Using the just-defined DeltaRow, we can now complete the projection interface with the update method:

```
  typealias FetchStoredEvents<E> = (EventSeq) -> Sequence<StoredEvent<E>>
  typealias ProjectEvents<R, E> = (E) -> List<DeltaRow<R>>

① interface Projection<R: Any, E: EntityEvent> {

②     val eventProjector: ProjectEvents<R, E>

③     val eventFetcher: FetchStoredEvents<E>

      fun lastProjectedEvent(): EventSeq

      fun update() {
          eventFetcher(lastProjectedEvent())
              .forEach{ storedEvent ->
                  applyDelta(storedEvent.eventSeq,
④                     eventProjector(storedEvent.event))
              }
      }

      fun applyDelta(eventSeq: EventSeq, deltas: List<DeltaRow<R>>)

  }
```

❶ Each projection is a type with two type parameters, the event type and the projection row type.

❷ The projector method will only depend on the projection logic and can be a pure function. For this reason, it's more convenient to inject it from outside rather than defining it as an abstract method of the projection.

❸ The event fetcher method will also be injected from outside.

❹ The method to apply the update will depend on the technical implementation of the projection, so we'll leave it as an abstract method here.

Projecting Events on a Map

The nice thing about our projection interface is that it's really generic and can work for any kind of projection. Let's now implement the first concrete projection, which will use a HashMap to store the list of rows in memory. In the next chapter, we'll see an alternative implementation using database persistence.

```
interface InMemoryProjection<R: Any, E: EntityEvent> : Projection<R, E> {
    fun allRows(): Map<RowId, R>
}

data class ConcurrentMapProjection<R: Any, E: EntityEvent>(
    override val eventFetcher: FetchStoredEvents<E>,
    override val eventProjector: ProjectEvents<R, E>
) : InMemoryProjection<R, E> {

    private val rowsReference: AtomicReference<Map<RowId, R>> =
        AtomicReference(emptyMap())

    private val lastEventRef: AtomicReference<EventSeq> =
        AtomicReference(EventSeq(-1))

    override fun allRows(): Map<RowId, R> = rowsReference.get()

    override fun applyDelta(eventSeq: EventSeq, deltas: List<DeltaRow<R>>) {
      deltas.forEach { delta ->
        rowsReference.getAndUpdate { rows ->
          when (delta) {
            is CreateRow -> rows + (delta.rowId to delta.row)
            is DeleteRow -> rows - delta.rowId
            is UpdateRow -> rows[delta.rowId]?.let { oldRow ->
                    rows - delta.rowId +
                    (delta.rowId to delta.updateRow(oldRow))
            }
          }
        }
      }.also { lastEventRef.getAndSet(eventSeq) }
    }

    override fun lastProjectedEvent(): EventSeq = lastEventRef.get()

}
```

Since this is only the first implementation, we don't particularly care about performance, but be aware that operating on big projections in memory can have a significant impact on the overall performance of the system.

The last missing bit for our working in-memory projection is the projector. We now need a function that takes an event and updates the rows of our projection. Now that we've mentioned them, we still have to define what the rows of our first projection will look like.

Our First Projection

Let's take a moment to remind ourselves why we need a projection in our Zettai application. Our goal is to have a collection of rows that can be searched, filtered, and aggregated for analysis. Each row should represent a to-do list, complete with all its details.

The to-do list is also the main entity in our event store, making this the natural projection of our events. To put it another way, if we were using a traditional approach instead of event sourcing, we would have a database table that resembles this projection.

Recreating Event Sourcing Projections

 Event sourcing provides us with several advantages over a traditional database. We now have more information stored in the events; we can examine exactly what's happened and reconstruct the state of the system at any point in time.

Another benefit is that we can recreate the projection from the events whenever we want. This enables us to modify the projection in the future if we need to have a different view of the data. Also, we can create additional projections for specific tasks as needed.

We start by creating the row type, with some utility methods to easily create a modified copy of it:

```
data class ToDoListProjectionRow(val user: User,
                                 val active: Boolean,
                                 val list: ToDoList) {

  fun addItem(item: ToDoItem): ToDoListProjectionRow =
    copy(list = list.copy(items = list.items + item))

  fun removeItem(item: ToDoItem): ToDoListProjectionRow =
    copy(list = list.copy(items = list.items - item))

  fun replaceItem(prevItem: ToDoItem, item: ToDoItem): ToDoListProjectionRow =
    copy(list = list.copy(items = list.items - prevItem + item))
```

```
  fun putOnHold(): ToDoListProjectionRow = copy(active = false)

  fun release(): ToDoListProjectionRow = copy(active = true)
}
```

Note that this projection row has a whole ToDoList—including its items collection—inside one of its fields. So, rather then a relational database table, it's actually more similar to a document database. This may not be always the case; it really depends on how we want to use it. We only have the constraint that we need to update the row from each event.

We now need to define the projector function. This is the core of our projection, a pure function that will generate a list of updates for each event. Since the rows of this projection correspond exactly to entities—they have the same cardinality—we'll generate a single update for each event.

```
fun eventProjector(e: ToDoListEvent): List<DeltaRow<ToDoListProjectionRow>> =
  when (e) {
    is ListCreated -> CreateRow(e.rowId(),
      ToDoListProjectionRow(e.owner, true, ToDoList(e.name, emptyList())))
    is ItemAdded -> UpdateRow(e.rowId()) { addItem(e.item) }
    is ItemRemoved -> UpdateRow(e.rowId()) { removeItem(e.item) }
    is ItemModified -> UpdateRow(e.rowId()) {replaceItem(e.prevItem, e.item)}
    is ListPutOnHold -> UpdateRow(e.rowId()) { putOnHold() }
    is ListReleased -> UpdateRow(e.rowId()) { release() }
    is ListClosed -> DeleteRow(e.rowId())
  }.toSingle()

private fun ToDoListEvent.rowId(): RowId = RowId(id.toString())

fun <T : Any> DeltaRow<T>.toSingle(): List<DeltaRow<T>> = listOf(this)
```

Querying the Projection

We have finally defined all the projection pieces. How should we query it? Let's write some unit tests first, so they can guide us to the best design. What we want to do is create some events, update the projection, run the query, and verify the result:

```
@Test
❶ fun `findAll returns all the lists of a user`() {
    val user = randomUser()
    val listName1 = randomListName()
    val listName2 = randomListName()
❷   val events = listOf(
        ListCreated(ToDoListId.mint(), user, listName1),
        ListCreated(ToDoListId.mint(), user, listName2),
        ListCreated(ToDoListId.mint(), randomUser(), randomListName())
    )
```

```
❸      val projection = events.buildListProjection()

       expectThat(projection.findAll(user))
❹          .isEqualTo(listOf(listName1, listName2))
   }
   private fun List<ToDoListEvent>.buildListProjection(): ToDoListProjection =
       ToDoListProjection { after ->
           mapIndexed { i, e ->
               StoredEvent(EventSeq(after.progressive + i + 1), e) }
                   .asSequence()
       }.also(ToDoListProjection::update)
```

❶ The name of the test should specify the name of the query, that is, the projection method, and what it's expected to do.

❷ We prepare a list of events that will be processed to put the projection in a state that can be queried.

❸ We build the projection projecting the events.

❹ Finally, we verify that the query result is what we expect.

This test isn't working now, because we haven't added the findAll method to our projection yet. Where to start? Since we're using an in-memory projection, we can access allRows, which is a map with all the rows in it. In this way, it's easy to implement the query methods we need, in a way similar to the previous ToDoListFetcherFromMap:

```
class ToDoListProjection(eventFetcher: FetchStoredEvents<ToDoListEvent>):
    InMemoryProjection<ToDoListProjectionRow, ToDoListEvent>
        by ConcurrentMapProjection(eventFetcher, ::eventProjector) {

    fun findAll(user: User): List<ListName>? =
        allRows().values
            .filter { it.user == user }
            .map { it.list.listName }
}
```

Note that we aren't inheriting ToDoListProjection from InMemoryProjection but using delegation (see Implementation by Delegation, on page 382). In this way, ToDoListProjection doesn't have to know anything about how ConcurrentMapProjection works internally.

Similarly, we can implement a method, findList, to retrieve a single to-do list, starting with the test and testing all possible cases. As usual, you can find the full code in the book repository.

To prove that everything works correctly, we can run the tests for the projection we defined earlier and see that they all are green now, as shown in the following image:

We can now add a ToDoListProjection to our hub and remove the need for the old fetcher:

```
override fun getList(user: User, listName: ListName):
                                          ZettaiOutcome<ToDoList> =
    listProjection.findList(user, listName)
        .failIfNull(
            InvalidRequestError("List $listName of user $user not found!"))
override fun getLists(user: User): ZettaiOutcome<List<ListName>> =
    listProjection.findAll(user)
        .failIfNull(InvalidRequestError("User $user not found!"))
```

Unfortunately, it doesn't work yet, because we need to remember to update the projection before querying it.

Moreover, we'll need more than a single projection; adding all of them to the hub isn't ideal. We want to design a new component with the responsibility to keep all the projections together and update them when needed.

In the previous chapter, we created a CommandHandler to handle the commands, and now we need to run our queries. So, we can name our new component, as you may have guessed, a QueryRunner.

Running Queries on Functors

The goal is to have a function that takes a QueryRunner and returns a result of an arbitrary type T. However, to ensure that the QueryRunner is in the proper state when the function is called, we'll execute it as a functional effect in a secure way. To achieve this, we'll create a functor named ProjectionQuery that wraps a function of type (QueryRunner) -> T.

Using a functor offers several advantages. Firstly, it gives us control over when the query is executed. We only want to run the query when it's correct, and at a minimum, we need to ensure that the projections are up-to-date. In the future, there may be additional checks that need to be performed. Functors allow us to separate the technical infrastructure concerns from the business requirements in a clean and organized manner.

In functional design terms, using a functor as a result conveys the message that there is a change of context when running a query, and we restrict the ability to run queries outside of the defined context.

Playing a bit with Kotlin DSL capabilities, the runner will accept a function f that will have the runner itself as receiver, and the runner will wrap the calculation inside a ProjectionQuery functor. In this way, we'll keep control over how and when to run the actual query.

Let's look at QueryRunner first:

```
❶  interface QueryRunner<Self : QueryRunner<Self>> {
       operator fun <R> invoke(f: Self.() -> R): ProjectionQuery<R>
   }

❷  class ToDoListQueryRunner(eventFetcher: FetchStoredEvents<ToDoListEvent>):
                                      QueryRunner<ToDoListQueryRunner> {
❸    internal val listProjection = ListProjection(eventFetcher)

     override fun <R> invoke(f: ToDoListQueryRunner.() -> R) =
❹        ProjectionQuery(setOf(listProjection)) { f(this) }
   }
```

❶ To keep the interface generic, but to allow for invoke to be called on a specific instance of the runner, we use a Self generic parameter.

❷ In our implementation for the to-do list, we pass the event fetcher in the constructor.

❸ Inside the runner, we declare all the projections needed as internal so they can be visible from the DSL.

❹ The invoke will pass the projections to the ProjectionQuery and the function. Note, the receiver of f is ToDoListQueryRunner and not the generic QueryRunner.

Leveraging on Laziness

Another advantage to using a functor for our ProjectionQuery is laziness. Consider a scenario where we need to process thousands of entities with our projection. A naive implementation would require loading all data from the database, keeping it in a list in memory, and copying from that list to a new one for each calculation.

Using a Kotlin sequence (Sequences, on page 387) will allow us to dispense with that, and let each calculation happen only once. There is a catch though: it's very hard to control resources when using a sequence. For example, if we open a file or a connection with the database at the beginning, it could be that the sequence never gets read, and we're left with an open connection. Functors allow us to control both the laziness and how we use external resources. Not only that, functors are very easy to compose together, as we'll see in the next chapter.

Keeping Results Together

Let's write our new functor to run the query on the projection:

```
data class ProjectionQuery<T>(
        val projections: Set<Projection<*, *>>,
❶      val runner: () -> T) {

    fun <U> transform(f: (T) -> U): ProjectionQuery<U> =
❷          ProjectionQuery(projections) { f(runner()) }

❸   fun runIt(): T {
        projections.forEach(Projection<*, *>::update)
        return runner()
    }
}
```

❶ In the constructor, we pass the set of projections and the runner function that will use them.

❷ The transformation returns a new ProjectionQuery that will run f on the result of the existing runner.

❸ This is the method that defines this specific functor; we update the projections first, and then we run the runner function.

Since it's a generic type with a transform method that applies a function and returns a new instance of a different generic type, we can guess that we're dealing with a functor, but how does it work? Before connecting it with our projections, let's try a little example:

```
val naturalNumbers: ProjectionQuery<Sequence<Int>> =
    ProjectionQuery(emptySet()){
        println("Generate a sequence of natural numbers")
        generateSequence(1) { it + 1 }
}
val padded = naturalNumbers
    .transform { it.map(Int::toString) }
    .transform { it.map{ it.padStart(5, '0') } }
```

```
println("still nothing happened here!")

padded
    .runIt()
    .drop(5)
    .take(5)
    .forEach(::println)

println("done")
```

Looking at the output, we can see that the sequence has not been invoked until we called runIt method.

```
still nothing happened here!
Generate a sequence of natural numbers
00006
00007
00008
00009
00010
done
```

Thanks to Kotlin sequences, we can decide how many elements we need without changing the functor. With the drop and take methods, we can avoid processing elements that we don't need. This is useful to implement a pagination functionality, for example.

Removing the Fetcher

We can now put the runner inside our hub, finally remove the fetcher, and connect the methods with the projections.

We don't need to write new tests, since we aren't introducing new behaviors. Everything should work like before, as we can verify by running our tests:

```
class ToDoListHub(
    val queryRunner: ToDoListQueryRunner,
    val commandHandler: ToDoListCommandHandler,
    val persistEvents: EventPersister<ToDoListEvent>
) : ZettaiHub {

//other methods...

    override fun getList(user: User, listName: ListName):
                                        ZettaiOutcome<ToDoList> =
        queryRunner {
            listProjection
            .findList(user, listName)
            .failIfNull( InvalidRequestError(
                "List $listName of user $user not found!"))
        }.runIt()
```

```
override fun getLists(user: User): ZettaiOutcome<List<ListName>> =
    queryRunner {
        listProjection.findAll(user)
            .failIfNull(InvalidRequestError("User $user not found!"))
    }.runIt()
}
```

To visualize how everything works now, a diagram is useful. As shown in the figure, the projector and the projection work as a read model inside the hub:

Thinking in Terms of Functors

At this point, you've seen a few different uses for functors. It's important to understand them very well, because the next chapter will build heavily upon them. Can we abstract some rules about designing with functors and what they can give us? To try to answer these questions, we can consider that functors are useful in these situations:

1. We have some data that's "bound" to something else—for example, a number in a list of numbers, or a result and its failure.

2. We want to operate on the data, ignoring its context.

Functors allow us to keep the two different concerns separated. In other words, they add some kind of effect on a pure function. This is what distinguishes functional effects from nonfunctional side effects.

So far, we've just scratched the surface of functors' possibilities. In the next chapters, we'll see how we can combine them in different ways, like in Exploring the Power of Monads, on page 225, and Sequential Application, on page 287. Modeling our application, taking advantage of functor composition, is really a critical step in switching from an object-oriented mentality to a functional one. Having a solid grasp on functors will help a lot when we see how more advanced data structures work.

Finally, a word of advice: Holder, List, and Outcome can all look like some kind of container, at least if you squint hard enough. This isn't always the case; other functors, like ProjectionQuery, can't be easily thought of as containers. For this reason, it's better to think about relations between different categories rather than functors being some kind of wrapper.[1]

Create the "What's Next" Page

So far in this chapter, we have refactored a lot of code, but we didn't advance with our application. It's now time to implement a new story!

The third story we defined in Preparing the Mock-Ups, on page 6, is about displaying a page with the most urgent items still pending for a user.

Let's proceed for the ones we have already implemented. Let's start writing a DDT to express a possible success scenario of the story:

```
@DDT
fun `What's next show the items in order of urgency`() = ddtScenario {
  setup {
    alice.`starts with some lists`(mapOf(
        gardenList to gardenTasks,
        partyList to partyTasks)
    )
  }.thenPlay(
    alice.`can see that #itemname is the next task to do`(""),
    alice.`can add #itemname to the #listname due to #duedate`(
        "buy present", partyList, LocalDate.now().plusDays(2)),
    alice.`can see that #itemname is the next task to do`("buy present"),
    alice.`can add #itemname to the #listname due to #duedate`(
        "water plants", gardenList, LocalDate.now().plusDays(1)),
    alice.`can see that #itemname is the next task to do`("water plants")
  )
}
```

We can now proceed to implement the methods on the HTTP handler, the hub, and so on using TDD. You can find all the code in the repository, but it's not really worth discussing here, since it's very similar to what we wrote for the other stories.

To make the hub method work though, we need to define a new projection. Let's examine it in detail, because its cardinality is different from the event store entities. In this new projection, we need a row for each item with a due date. So, there could be no rows linked to a list, if it doesn't have any item

---

1. https://byorgey.wordpress.com/2009/01/12/abstraction-intuition-and-the-monad-tutorial-fallacy/

with a due date, or there could be multiple rows, if more than one item on that list has a due date specified.

Let's first see what the projector looks like:

```
data class ItemProjectionRow(val item: ToDoItem, val listId: EntityId)

fun eventProjector(e: ToDoListEvent): List<DeltaRow<ItemProjectionRow>> =
  when (e) {
    is ListCreated -> emptyList()
    is ListPutOnHold -> emptyList()
    is ListReleased -> emptyList()
    is ListClosed -> emptyList()
    is ItemAdded -> CreateRow(
        e.itemRowId(e.item),
        ItemProjectionRow(e.item, e.id)).toSingle()
    is ItemRemoved -> DeleteRow(e.itemRowId(e.item)).toSingle()
    is ItemModified -> listOf(
        DeleteRow(e.itemRowId(e.prevItem))
        CreateRow(e.itemRowId(e.item), ItemProjectionRow(e.item, e.id)),
    )

  }

private fun ToDoListEvent.itemRowId(item: ToDoItem): RowId =
    RowId("${id}_${item.description}")
```

❶ In the row for our item projection, there is the item and the list ID, so we can link it to the correct list.

❷ The projection ignores the events on the list that don't involve items, so it returns an empty list.

❸ Adding an item creates a new row in the item projection.

❹ Removing an item removes the corresponding row.

❺ Modifying an item removes the old row and creates a new one.

We can now write the ToDoItemProjection class, similar to what we did for the previous projection. The new query method, findWhatsNext, accepts two parameters: the maximum number of items to return and the IDs of the lists of the current user. Note that we can't sort a sequence directly—since it's lazy—so we have to transform it into a list:

```
class ToDoItemProjection(eventFetcher: FetchStoredEvents<ToDoListEvent>):
    InMemoryProjection<ItemProjectionRow, ToDoListEvent> by
        ConcurrentMapProjection(
            eventFetcher,
            ::eventProjector
        ) {
```

```kotlin
fun findWhatsNext(maxRows: Int, lists: List<EntityId>):
    List<ItemProjectionRow> =
        allRows().values
            .filter { it.listId in lists }
            .filter { it.item.dueDate != null
                    && it.item.status == ToDoStatus.Todo }
            .sortedByDescending { it.item.dueDate }
            .take(maxRows)
}
```

We can now finish the new method for the hub. First, we find the list of all the current users using the list projection, then we pass them to the items projection to find the most urgent items. Everything is done using functor transformations:

```kotlin
class ToDoListHub(...)
...
  override fun whatsNext(user: User): Outcome<ZettaiError, List<ToDoItem>> =
    queryRunner {
        listProjection.findAllActiveListId(user)
            .failIfEmpty(InvalidRequestError("User $user not found!"))
            .transform { ul -> itemProjection.findWhatsNext(10, ul) }
            .transform { it.map(ItemProjectionRow::item) }
    }.runIt()
```

The functionality is finished, and the new DDT is working, as we can see in the following image:

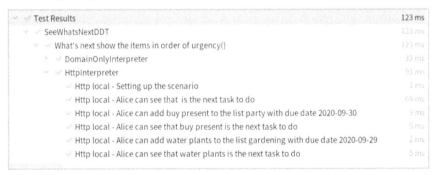

Command and Query Responsibility Segregation (CQRS)

Using commands with events and queries on projections, we implemented an architectural design pattern called Command and Query Responsibility Segregation, CQRS for short.[2] As the name says, the idea behind it is to separate the model we use to read data (query) from the model we use to write data (command).

---

2.   https://martinfowler.com/bliki/CQRS.html

It's important to note that while event sourcing and CQRS are often used together, it's possible to adopt one without the other. However, the two approaches have a natural synergy that makes them well suited for use in tandem.

In particular, the functional approach addresses one of the main challenges associated with CQRS and event sourcing, which is the need to write and manage two separate models and handle events. In my experience, CQRS and event sourcing can be extremely effective in complex application development and, in the long run, require less time and effort compared to traditional approaches.

As a side note, the code examples presented in this book may appear overly intricate at times for the specific task. However, they are intended to also serve as a useful reference for more complex projects.

Recap

In this chapter, you learned how to take advantage of event streams to create event projections that work as read-only models and how they remove the mismatch between data for the user interface and our events. Projections made it possible to implement a killer feature of our application, the "What's Next" page.

We also discussed how functors are useful in querying these projections and using the result of the query without coupling the two things together. Functors allowed us to update the projections at the last possible moment.

In the next chapter, we'll continue exploring the functors' capabilities, looking at how combining them together will open up another trove of possibilities. We'll put them to good use to progress with another critical step for our application: persisting our state using an external database and yet leaving all our functions pure and composable.

Exercises

The exercises in this chapter will focus on lazy sequences and projections.

Here is your friendly reminder that nobody can learn functional programming by just reading code, and the best way to learn is by practicing. You can refer to the exercises folder in the book code repository for the starting point and some hints.

Exercise 8.1: LazyPrimes

Our first exercise is about laziness and Kotlin sequences (Sequences, on page 387). We want to sum the squares of all odd numbers between two positive numbers. This is the code in nonfunctional style using for loops:

```kotlin
fun Long.isOdd(): Boolean =
    this % 2 != 0L

fun sumOfOddSquaresForLoop(numbers: List<Long>): Long {
    var tot = 0L
    for(i in numbers){
        if (i.isOdd()) tot += i*i
    }
    return tot
}
```

Rewriting it using List will make it very slow and it can even run out of memory. Try to reimplement it using Sequence instead.

You can also compare the performance of the three implementations (for loop, list, and sequence). Note that the in-place for loop will likely still be the fastest method.

Exercise 8.2: Stateful Function

We want to create an invokable class named NextFunction, which will function as a stateful function. Essentially, this means it will facilitate the traversal of a list's elements across multiple function calls.

```kotlin
data class NextFunction<T>(val list: List<T>): () -> T? {
    override fun invoke(): T = TODO()
}
```

In this context, "stateful" refers to the class's ability to remember its state (the current position in the list) between function calls.

The exercise consists of implementing the class correctly, so that it can be used in this way:

```kotlin
val names = listOf( "Ann", "Bob", "Charlie", "Dorothy")

val nextName = NextFunction(names)

expectThat( nextName() ).isEqualTo("Ann")
expectThat( nextName() ).isEqualTo("Bob")
expectThat( nextName() ).isEqualTo("Charlie")
expectThat( nextName() ).isEqualTo("Dorothy")
expectThat( nextName() ).isEqualTo(null)
```

Exercise 8.3: Elevator Projection

Continuing from the elevator examples of the event chapter, let's suppose we have multiple elevators operating simultaneously. We want to create a projection to track the current state of each elevator.

A row in the projection could look something like this:

```
data class ElevatorProjectionRow(val elevatorId: Int,
                                 val floor: Int,
                                 val state: ElevatorState)
```

For this exercise, you need to modify the elevator events to include an id, and then process these events to create a projection. This projection should include a row for each elevator, and it should follow the same patterns used in the Zettai application.

To keep things simple, it's not necessary to implement persistence of events, just to implement this interface:

```
interface ElevatorProjection: {
    fun allRows(): List<ElevatorProjectionRow>
    fun getRow(elevatorId: Int): ElevatorProjectionRow?
}
```

Additionally, you should add some unit tests to verify that the projection behaves as expected.

CHAPTER 9

Using Monads to Persist Data Safely

In this chapter, we'll face some of the most powerful concepts of functional programming, which include advanced types of functors and using monads to combine them together.

We'll also learn about PostgreSQL and how to use it effectively in Kotlin with the Exposed library, also learning how to adapt an object-oriented library for functional code to use.

Finally, we'll explore how to make our event storage persistent using an external database without losing our functional perspective. Monads will allow us to keep the code composable and still be sure of not forgetting to commit or rollback a connection or, even worse, leak it out.

Persisting Safely

Looking at the current state of our application, Zettai, we have a final big hurdle to jump before we can start using it realistically. It still doesn't persist the state, so every time the application starts, it will have no users and no list. This is clearly not a viable proposition for launching a new service!

Before jumping to possible solutions, let's further examine what exactly is the issue. One problem we need to solve is to make sure that no state gets lost. So, regardless if the application restarts or crashes, we shouldn't lose any data, and the application must be able to continue from where it was.

This would be quite easily solved locally, for example, storing information using the file system. Unfortunately, this wouldn't be enough because we not only need to store data safely—meaning it must survive a hardware failure— but we also need to share data across multiple instances of our service. We'll discuss distributed architectures in detail later in Deployment Unit, on page

346, but we definitely don't want to paint ourselves into a corner where our application can't scale up when the need arises.

For these reasons, we need to store the information in a separate service that can provide the level of safety we require. Our application will call it remotely to store and retrieve data.

In other words, we need a database! Well, lucky for us, there are a lot of excellent choices available, but we need to decide what kind of database we need. Discussing the pros and cons of different kinds of databases is a topic worth its own book (like *Seven Databases in Seven Weeks [Red18]*), but for our purposes we can just look at two of the most common types of databases: those that are relational and those that are document based.

Kinds of Databases

What's the difference between a relational database and a document-based database? A relational database would need to define a schema for each piece of information with a precise description of what we want to store in the database. Every piece of information needs to be stored in a record, and the collection of similar records is called a table. Relational databases allow us to easily query the data in very sophisticated ways using the relationships between the tables, but they require us to structure our data in advance, following a precise definition that must be identical for all the records in the table.

Document databases, on the other hand, would allow us to store *documents* that can be as complex a nested structure as we want, and it doesn't have to be the same for all documents. However, they have limitations to how we can query the data inside.

Looking at Zettai, we can see that for the write model—storing events—a document database is probably a better fit, because events can be complex, nested structures and we don't need complicated queries on them. On the other hand, for the read model—that is, the projections—a relational database seems a better choice, because the rows can share the same structure and the queries can be very sophisticated. Another factor that will impact our choice is related to the concept of a database transaction.

Database Transaction

 A transaction is a database operation that has four properties—atomicity, consistency, isolation, and durability—also known as ACID.

Database Transaction

- Atomicity means that each transaction, which can be composed of different operations, is either completely executed or none of its statements are executed. What shouldn't be possible is to execute only a subset of statements.

- Consistency means that each transaction should leave the database in a consistent state. Executing valid statements can't corrupt the database; invalid statements should fail the whole transaction.

- Isolation means that even when the transactions are happening concurrently, the result must be the same, as though they were happening sequentially. We'll look into this in more detail in the next chapter.

- Durability means that once a transaction is committed, it will remain stored, even in the case of a system crash or a shutdown.

Not all databases offer the same degree of compliance with these rules; in particular, there could be limitations on what can be atomic in some document databases.

For the examples in this book, we'll use PostgreSQL.[1] PostgreSQL is an open source database that not only has a strong reputation for reliability and performance but also offers some of the best features available.

In particular, although it's a relational database, it allows us to store documents without any schema and do queries on them like a document database. We'll see how to take advantage of this feature when we store events (see Table Schema for Event Store, on page 211).

In any case, whichever database you choose, or may be forced to use for your own project, it's important to know how to use it in a functional way. The rules and techniques you'll learn in this chapter can be applied to any kind of database. Once you understand the principles, you can work with any database.

But, if you're uncertain about which database to use, I highly recommend PostgreSQL. It's one of the most reliable and versatile products out there, and it's both open source and free of charge.

---

1. https://www.postgresql.org/

Joe asks:
What Are NoSQL Databases?

At the beginning of the 2000s, relational databases totally dominated. Then, the necessity of storing and retrieving data without a fixed schema emerged. At the beginning, these "new databases" were collectively called NoSQL because they didn't use the SQL query language typical of relational databases.

Nowadays, the difference is very blurred. Some NoSQL databases are using SQL, and some relational databases allow for schemaless data. Also, NoSQL now means "Not only SQL."

Testing the Integration with PostgreSQL

As we did with Introducing Http4k, on page 25, our approach will be to write some code to see how we can use it, and afterwards we'll look at integrating it with the rest of our application.

As usual, we want to start with the tests. In this case, it's particularly important, as this will introduce a new kind of test for our project—the *integration tests*.

All the tests we wrote so far were either testing a single unit of behavior (a class or a function) or testing the whole system end-to-end (the DDTs). Integration tests, on the other hand, are focusing on the integration between two things—our code and an external system. In this case, we'll test our adapter against the PostgreSQL server. Other typical integration tests are those against other kinds of external services such as email services, Apache Kafka,[2] or other middleware used by your company.

The goal of integration tests is making sure we're using the external service API correctly. Writing them before starting the code ensures that we're considering not only the production environment but also how to access the external system from our local machine right from the start. In this way, we can also evaluate whether the technology we chose can be easily tested and how to do it.

Running PostgreSQL locally is as simple as installing it on our machine or putting it in a Docker container and then starting it before running our tests.[3]

---

2. https://kafka.apache.org/
3. https://www.docker.com/

Using a container is less intrusive, and easier to set up, so it's a widely used practice now. Learning Docker is outside the scope of this book, but all we need for our example is to define a Docker compose file like this:

```
version: '3'
services:
  database:
    image: "postgres:13.1"
    env_file:
      - postgresql.env # configure postgres
    ports:
      - "6432:5432"
    volumes:
      - pg-volume:/var/lib/postgresql/data/
    # a path where to persist data even if container shuts down
  db-test:
    image: "postgres:13.1"
    env_file:
      - postgresql-test.env
    ports:
      - "6433:5432"
    # no need of volumes for test
volumes:
  pg-volume: #
```

This file—you can find it in the scripts directory of the book repository—defines two databases, one for the application itself and one for tests that we can reset every time we run them. They are visible on ports 6432 and 6433; you can change these values if you want to use other ports.

Then we need to define a user, a database, and a password in the env files in this way:

```
# postgresql.env
POSTGRES_USER=zettai_admin
POSTGRES_PASSWORD=zettai!
POSTGRES_DB=zettai_db
```

These are the credentials to run PostgreSQL locally, so it's not a security concern to store them in our source control repository. In the production environment, we'll connect to an external database cluster.

Finally, we need a script to start and stop the local database. The example here is using bash, but it's easy to adapt it for other scripting languages:

start-pg.sh

```
# delete the volumes if they exists
docker volume rm pg-volume || true
# create fresh volumes
docker volume create pg-volume

(docker-compose --file ${BASE_DIR}/bin/docker-compose-local-pg.yml up)
```

The only requirement to run it is to have Docker installed on your machine. If you want to know more about this interesting technology, you can learn more in an online Docker deep-dive course.[4]

To verify that everything is correctly set up, we can use the command line client for PostgreSQL after we start our Docker containers:

```
psql -h localhost -p 6432 --username=zettai_admin --dbname=zettai_db

zettai_db=# \conninfo
>You are connected to database "zettai_db" as user "zettai_admin"
 on host "localhost" (address "::1") at port "6432".

zettai_db=# select * from pg_tables;
```

If everything is correctly configured, we should be able to see the list of system tables.

Connecting to the Database with Kotlin

To access the database with Kotlin, we'll use the Exposed library,[5] which is an open source library that supports many databases, written by the same people who wrote Kotlin itself. To use it, we only need to add the dependencies to our gradle.build file:

```
implementation "org.jetbrains.exposed:exposed-core:${exposedVersion}"
implementation "org.jetbrains.exposed:exposed-jdbc:${exposedVersion}"
implementation "org.jetbrains.exposed:exposed-java-time:${exposedVersion}"
```

On top of Exposed itself, we need to add the PostgreSQL drivers and a library to parse JSON—more about that later.

```
implementation "org.postgresql:postgresql:${postgresqlVersion}"
implementation "com.beust:klaxon:${klaxonVersion}"
```

We're going to use Exposed, not only because it's a nice library that allows us to deal with low-level details of Java interaction with databases, but also

---

4.   https://acloudguru.com/course/docker-deep-dive

5.   https://github.com/JetBrains/Exposed

because it will be a good example of how to use existing nonfunctional libraries inside our functional code.

It would be nice if there were ready-to-use functional libraries for any possible task. The reality is we aren't there yet, and until that happens, we need to smartly re-use object-oriented libraries in our functional code. But, if you are interested let me know, because I'm currently working on one.

Table Schema for Event Store

Using the DSL provided by Exposed, we can now define a table for storing our events and a table for our projection.

Here, we'll take advantage of the document features of PostgreSQL, and we will store all the information specific to events in a 'jsonb' field. This way we can store all events in the same table. Even more, since there is nothing specific about the event type in the table, we can re-use the same data class for different event types, using different tables with the same structure.

Each database column is represented by a field in the Table class; let's see them in detail:

```kotlin
❶ data class PgEventTable(override val tableName: String) : Table(tableName) {
❷     val id = long("id").autoIncrement()
       override val primaryKey = PrimaryKey(id, name = "${tableName}_pkey")

       val recorded_at = timestamp("recorded_at")
❸        .defaultExpression(CurrentTimestamp())
❹     val entity_id = uuid("entity_id")
❺     val event_type = varchar("event_type", 100)
❻     val event_version = integer("event_version")
❼     val event_source = varchar("event_source", 100)
❽     val json_data = jsonb("json_data")
}
```

❶ The table to store the events inherits from open class Table, specifying the name it will have in the database.

❷ This is the field to store the event progressive ID; it's sometimes called the event offset. It's automatically incremented by the database, so we don't have to pass it. It's also defined as the primary key of the database, so there couldn't be two events with the same ID.

❸ In this field, the database stores the time when the event was recorded.

❹ This is the field for the ID of the entity, that is, the unique ID of each to-do list.

❺ We store the type of the event in this field as a string, so we can then correctly extract the data from the JSON field.

❻ All our events will have version 1 at the beginning. If we need to add or remove fields, we'll increment the version so that we can use the right deserializer. See Migrations on page 259.

❼ Here, we store the source of the event, for example, the server IP or some other identifier. It's useful for debugging.

❽ This is the field where we store our event details in JSON format, without using a common schema for all events. PostgreSQL will allow us to query the data all the same.

Note that the event id field can't be a generic UUID like the entity_id. To generate the projections, we need to be able to process all events up to a certain point, so we're going to adopt a progressive id guaranteed by the database. Another possibility would be to implement a similar logic using a timestamp field, but then it would be challenging to ensure its uniqueness.

The Exposed library has already defined all field types that we need apart from the jsonb field. To create a new field type we need to create a new column type, JsonBColumn, that can convert JSON and then call the function registerColumn:

```
fun <T : Any> Table.jsonb(name: String,
                          fromJson: (String) -> T,
                          toJson: (T) -> String): Column<T> =
  registerColumn(name, JsonBColumn(fromJson = fromJson, toJson = toJson))
```

The implementation of JsonBColumn depends on the library details, so it's not relevant here, but you can find the full code—about fifty lines—in the repository of the book.

Convert Events to and from JSON

Now, we're left with the task of converting events between the database and memory. First, we need a generic interface to convert a type to and from a different representation, for example, a JSON string. The data class requires two functions, one to render the type in the representation and another to parse the representation:

```
data class Parser<A, S>(
    val render: (A) -> S,
    val parse: (S) -> Outcome<OutcomeError, A>
) {
```

```kotlin
    fun parseOrThrow(encoded: S) =
        parse(encoded).onFailure { error("Error parsing $encoded ${it.msg}") }
}
```

To represent our events in the database, we need a type with all fields we're going to write to the database:

```kotlin
data class PgEvent(
    val entityId: EntityId,
    val eventType: String,
    val jsonString: String,
    val version: Int,
    val source: String
)
```

Now, we need to convert from our ToDoListEvent to PgEvent and vice versa, but first, we need to write a test for it. The test would be very simple: just generate a good number of random events–let's say 100–and then try to convert them to PgEvent and back. Then, at the end, we verify the new converted event is identical to the original one:

```kotlin
class ToDoListEventParserTest {

    val eventParser = toDoListEventParser()

    @Test
    fun `convert events to and from`() {

        eventsGenerator().take(100).forEach { event ->

            val conversion = eventParser.render(event)
            val newEvent = eventParser.parse(conversion).expectSuccess()

            expectThat(newEvent).isEqualTo(event)

        }
    }
}

fun randomEvent(): ToDoListEvent =
    when (val kClass = ToDoListEvent::class.sealedSubclasses.random()) {
      ListCreated::class -> ListCreated(
                ToDoListId.mint(), randomUser(), randomListName())
      ItemAdded::class -> ItemAdded(ToDoListId.mint(), randomItem())
      ItemRemoved::class -> ItemRemoved(ToDoListId.mint(), randomItem())
      ItemModified::class -> ItemModified(
                ToDoListId.mint(), randomItem(), randomItem())
      ListPutOnHold::class -> ListPutOnHold(
                ToDoListId.mint(), randomText(20))
      ListReleased::class -> ListReleased(ToDoListId.mint())
      ListClosed::class -> ListClosed(ToDoListId.mint(), Instant.now())
      else -> error("Unexpected class: $kClass")
    }
```

```kotlin
fun eventsGenerator(): Sequence<ToDoListEvent> = generateSequence {
    randomEvent()
}
```

The test will fail now since we haven't implemented the parser yet. For the JSON conversions, we'll use the Klaxon library, reading the event class from the event type field of our table:

```kotlin
fun toDoListEventParser(): Parser<ToDoListEvent, PgEvent> =
    Parser(::toPgEvent, ::toToDoListEvent)

fun toPgEvent(event: ToDoListEvent): PgEvent =
    PgEvent(
        entityId = event.id,
        eventType = event::class.simpleName.orEmpty(),
        version = 1,
        source = "event store",
        jsonString = event.toJsonString()
    )

fun toToDoListEvent(pgEvent: PgEvent): ZettaiOutcome<ToDoListEvent> =
    Outcome.tryOrFail {

        when (pgEvent.eventType) {
            ListCreated::class.simpleName ->
                klaxon.parse<ListCreated>(pgEvent.jsonString)
            ItemAdded::class.simpleName ->
                klaxon.parse<ItemAdded>(pgEvent.jsonString)
            ItemRemoved::class.simpleName ->
                klaxon.parse<ItemRemoved>(pgEvent.jsonString)
            ItemModified::class.simpleName ->
                klaxon.parse<ItemModified>(pgEvent.jsonString)
            ListPutOnHold::class.simpleName ->
                klaxon.parse<ListPutOnHold>(pgEvent.jsonString)
            ListClosed::class.simpleName ->
                klaxon.parse<ListClosed>(pgEvent.jsonString)
            ListReleased::class.simpleName ->
                klaxon.parse<ListReleased>(pgEvent.jsonString)
            else -> null
        } ?: error("type not known ${pgEvent.eventType}")

    }.transformFailure { ZettaiParsingError(
        "Error parsing ToDoListEvent: ${pgEvent} with error: $it ") }
```

Klaxon is nice library that utilizes reflection to transform a Kotlin class into JSON. This will serve as a temporary solution. However, we'll tackle the broader issue of how to handle serialization and deserialization in a functional manner later, in Making JSON Functional, on page 318.

Table Schema for Projections

In the same way we did for the events table, we can define a generic projection table, and then save the projection row inside the JSON field.

The kind of table we need for projections is simpler than the table for events. We only need to store the RowId and the timestamp of the last update together with the jsonb field with the row data. Since all the rows are of the same type, we don't need a sealed class hierarchy; we can serialize and deserialize the projection row to a JSON string using our parser:

```kotlin
data class PgProjectionTable<ROW : Any>(
    override val tableName: String,
    val parser: Parser<ROW, String>): Table(tableName) {

    val id = varchar("id", 50)

    override val primaryKey = PrimaryKey(id, name = "${tableName}_pkey")

    val updated_at = timestamp("recorded_at")
        .defaultExpression(CurrentTimestamp())

    val row_data = jsonb("row_data",
        parser::parseOrThrow,
        parser::render.get())
}
```

❶ We pass the table name and the parser for the row directly in the constructor.

❷ In this field, we store the row ID, which must be unique in the projection, and we declare it as primary key.

❸ We store the timestamp of the last update of the row in this field. This is for debugging purposes only.

❹ This is the field for the actual row data, stored in JSON format. We pass the parser functions to the column, so we can directly retrieve the projection row.

Finally, we also need a table to store the sequentially incrementing counter of the last event processed in each projection. For this table, we only need one field, and there will be a row for each projection we need in our read model:

```kotlin
data class PgLastEventTable(override val tableName: String):Table(tableName){
    val last_event_id = long("last_event_id")
    val updated_at = timestamp("recorded_at")
            .defaultExpression(CurrentTimestamp())
}
```

> ### Joe asks:
> ## Why Use a Separate Table for Each Projection?
>
> It's certainly possible to use a single table to store information about the last event of all projections. We have chosen to keep them on separate tables for two reasons:
>
> First, from a technical standpoint, PostgreSQL can more efficiently lock a table than a single row in a table.
>
> Second, from a practical standpoint, when creating a new projection or removing an old one, it's easier to create or drop a table rather than insert or delete a row.

Prepare the Database

We can now create our tables, just passing the names to our table data classes:

```
val toDoListEventsTable = PgEventTable(
        "todo_list_events")

val toDoListProjectionTable =
    PgProjectionTable(
        "todo_list_projection", toDoListProjectionParser)

val toDoListLastEventTable = PgLastEventTable(
        "${toDoListProjectionTable.tableName}_last_processed_event")
```

Then, Exposed will make it very easy for us to create the tables on the database if they don't exist or delete them if we want:

```
fun resetDatabase(datasource: DataSource) {
❶    val db = Database.connect(datasource)

❷    transaction(db) {
❸        addLogger(StdOutSqlLogger)

        dropTables()
        prepareDb()
    }
}

fun prepareDatabase(datasource: DataSource) {
    val db = Database.connect(datasource)

    transaction(db) {
        addLogger(StdOutSqlLogger)

        prepareDb()
    }
}
```

```
private fun Transaction.prepareDb() {
    SchemaUtils.createMissingTablesAndColumns(
        toDoListEventsTable,
        toDoListProjectionTable,
        toDoListLastEventTable
    )
}

private fun dropTables() {
    SchemaUtils.drop(
        toDoListEventsTable,
        toDoListProjectionTable,
        toDoListLastEventTable)
}
```

❶ First, we need to create a database connection passing the DataSource.

❷ Then, we can call the operations inside a transaction block.

❸ This line is to see the actual SQL commands in the logging console.

❹ To create missing tables and missing columns in existing tables, we just need to pass our table objects.

❺ This lets us drop, or delete, the tables.

In this code, we can see the main problem of using Exposed from a functional point of view. We must call the SchemaUtils function inside a transaction block, otherwise, we'll get an exception at runtime: java.lang.IllegalStateException: No transaction in context. Unfortunately, there is no control at compile time to enforce this, but we can fix it.

Effects and Side Effects

Internally, Exposed is using a thread local variable to store the transaction manager so it can find the transaction "under the hood." As we'll discuss soon, this kind of magic does not work well with functional programming, because it makes it difficult to compose and re-use functions. We aim for our software to fail to compile if we forget to pass the transaction; having a runtime error can lead to a lot of headaches.

While we don't care if our libraries are written in functional style or not, as long as they work, we do care that they work without using *spooky actions at a distance*.

To understand this concept better, let's consider that a pure function (see Keep Your Functions Pure, on page 355) has an effect, which is the return value. If the function isn't pure and it has other effects, like modifying the transaction manager of the current thread for example, those effects are called side effects, or sometimes "actions at distance." This is because they cause changes in other parts of the system without any apparent connection, like in quantum mechanics.

We'll discuss in the next section a better and fully functional way to manage the transaction life cycle without resorting to using side effects. But, now we need to look at how we can explicitly pass the current transaction to the functions of the Exposed library.

And now the good news: since Exposed is completely open source, we can write small, focused functions that operate on an explicit transaction! It's quite easy, because Exposed is very modular and open to being extended.

As a general rule, source availability and modularity are also very important factors to consider when adopting a third-party library for our projects.

Read and Write from a Table

The best way to model the small, focused functions we need is to write some tests using the existing function of Exposed, and then refactor them, passing the transaction explicitly and then adapting them until we're happy with the result. Since Kotlin allows us to write extensions to the Exposed Table class, we can make our new functions look like regular methods.

You can find all the tests on the repository. Let's look at the test to read and write events:

```
❶ val dataSource = pgDataSourceForTest()

  @Test
  fun `can read and write events from db`() {

    val db = Database.connect(dataSource)
❷    transaction(db) {

      val listId = ToDoListId.mint()
      val event = ListCreated(listId, user, list.listName)
❸      val pgEvent = toPgEvent(event)

❹      val eventId = toDoListEventsTable.insertIntoWithReturn(this, stored(event))
          { newRow ->
              newRow[entity_id] = pgEvent.entityId.raw
              newRow[event_source] = pgEvent.source
              newRow[event_type] = pgEvent.eventType
              newRow[json_data] = pgEvent.jsonString
              newRow[event_version] = pgEvent.version
          }.eventSeq
```

```
⑤      expectThat(eventId.progressive).isGreaterThan(0)
       val row = toDoListEventsTable.selectWhere(this,
⑥         toDoListEventsTable.id eq eventId.progressive)
          .single()
⑦      expectThat(row.get(toDoListEventsTable.entity_id)).isEqualTo(listId.raw)
   }
}
```

❶ First, we need the data source for the test database.

❷ To open a session in the database and start a transaction, we need to use this block.

❸ Here, we create an event and then translate it to PgEvent.

❹ To store data in the database and read the auto-generated ID, we use the new insertIntoWithReturn function.

❺ Then, we verify that the ID is correctly returned.

❻ To read data from the table, we use selectWhere, using the Exposed syntax to write simple queries using Kotlin DSL.

❼ Finally, we verify that the ListId we started with has been correctly saved.

Exposed Extensions

Looking at the Exposed library code, it's not difficult to write our implementation, and we can mostly re-use existing methods and classes. The actual code isn't that important, and you may finish with a different design. The important part here is how to work with a library that isn't particularly functional friendly.

So, what we want is to create new functions that would present a functional API to work with the library. With functional, I mean as referentially transparent as possible, as explained in the appendix, under Think in Morphisms, on page 360.

In this specific case, we have to make sure to always pass the transaction explicitly instead of relying on the standard hidden singleton for managing transactions that Exposed seems to prefer:

```
fun Table.selectWhere(
    tx: Transaction,
    condition: Op<Boolean>?,
    orderByCond: Column<*>? = null
): List<ResultRow> =
```

```
    tx.exec(
        Query(this, condition).apply {
            orderByCond?.let { orderBy(it) }
        }
    )?.iterate { toResultRow(this@selectWhere.realFields) }
        ?: emptyList()

fun queryBySql(tx: Transaction, fields: List<Expression<*>>,
               sql: String): List<ResultRow> =
    tx.exec(SqlQuery(sql))
        ?.iterate { toResultRow(fields) }
        ?: emptyList()

fun ResultSet.toResultRow(fields: List<Expression<*>>): ResultRow  {
    val fieldsIndex = fields.distinct().mapIndexed { i, field ->
        val value = (field as? Column<*>)
            ?.columnType
            ?.readObject(this, i + 1)
            ?: getObject(i + 1)
        field to value
    }.toMap()
    return ResultRow.createAndFillValues(fieldsIndex)
}

fun <T, Self: Table> Self.insertIntoWithReturn(
    tx: Transaction,
    postExecution: InsertStatement<Number>.() -> T,
    block: Self.(InsertStatement<Number>) -> Unit
): T =
    InsertStatement<Number>(this).apply {
        block(this)
        execute(tx)
    }.let { postExecution(it) }

fun <Self: Table> Self.insertInto(
    tx: Transaction,
    block: Self.(InsertStatement<Number>) -> Unit
) {
    insertIntoWithReturn(tx, {}, block)
}

fun Table.updateWhere(
    tx: Transaction,
    where: Op<Boolean>? = null,
    block: Table.(UpdateStatement) -> Unit
) {
    UpdateStatement(targetsSet = this, limit = null, where = where).apply {
        block(this)
        execute(tx)
    }
}
```

A final word of caution: it may be possible that a future version of Exposed would break our solution, so this is something you must take into consideration. On the other hand, if the alternatives are to abandon our functional principles or to write a database library from scratch, this can be a good compromise.

Now that we know how to read and write from a database, we need a better way of working with it, rather than passing transactions all the time, which is boring and can result in errors.

Our objective is to implement a system that allows functions to work inside transactions in a safe manner, without requiring any additional logic. In essence, we aim to abstract away the transaction itself and create a mechanism for operating in any "context" that facilitates the reading and writing of data.

Accessing Remote Data in a Functional Way

Now we need to understand how to safely access remote data in a functional way. This is a harder problem than just sending stateless requests remotely, like using HTTP, because for our data, we need to keep using the same session and transaction for related calls, since they are executed atomically—either all of them or none.

Since a simple call won't work, and we want to abstract on the actual database transaction, a solution is to put database operations in some kind of context where they can be used safely and passed around. Looking at the problem in this way, functors seem like a good fit.

From the definition, functors (see Learning Functors and Categories, on page 163) are transformations from one category into another, so we can look at our problem in this way: we want to transform calls to access data into calls inside a transaction on remote data storage. In other words, what we need is a way to read and write stuff "over the wire."

Let's play a bit with some pseudocode. As a typical case, we would like to read a value, calculate a new value from it, and then store it, something like the following:

```
a = readA(id)      //impure computation
b = calculateB(a) //pure function
writeB(b)          //impure computation
```

This is easy to read; actually it's deceptively easy, because it's clear that readA and writeB computations aren't pure functions, but it's not clear at all where they get the data from. So, following the functional style, we want to make the fact that we're using some kind of storage explicit. Let's try introducing a generic Context parameter that allows reading and writing:

```
val context = remoteStorageContext("config") //impure computation
val a = readA(context::read, id)              //pure function
val b = calculateB(a)                         //pure function
writeB(context::write, b)                     //pure function
```

This code is much better from a functional point of view, since readA and writeB can be pure functions now. Still, it's not very easy to read, and another problem is that remote access can fail for a lot of reasons, but there is no indication here of what can fail and why.

If you remember from when we discussed Using Higher-Order Functions, on page 51, a HOF is pure if it stays referentially transparent when its arguments are pure functions. In other words, we want to maintain readA pure even if we'll use it eventually with an impure input—the context::read.

The Context Reader

For the moment, we'll concentrate on the first problem—how to avoid passing the context explicitly every time—and we'll leave the error handling for later. Let's see how we can create a generic functor that reads the context, a ContextReader; it should work more or less like this:

```
fun readA(id: String): ContextReader<CTX, A> =...

fun calculateB(a: A): B = ...

fun writeB(b: B): ContextReader<CTX, Unit> =...

reader = readA(id)
    .transform{ a -> calculateB(a) }
    .transform{ b -> writeB(b) }

reader.runWith{ TODO("Here we need the context") }
```

The idea is to wrap any computation that needs the context with a ContextReader, and then run them all together at the end with the context.

Actually, there is a problem with the second transform—the one around writeB—but let's pretend we didn't spot it yet. We'll find it out soon enough.

With this approach, we aren't committing ourselves to any specific context. It would work with a connection to a database, or a CSV file we want to modify, or a structure in memory. Another way to look at it is that we're using a functor to inject the context into the chain of transformations.

```
❶ data class ContextReader<CTX, out T>(val runWith: (CTX) -> T) {
❷     fun <U> transform(f: (T) -> U): ContextReader<CTX, U> =
           ContextReader { t -> f(runWith(t)) }
   }
```

❶ CTX is the type of the generic context, and T is the type of the result we want. We need a function that can read a value of type T from a context of type CTX.

❷ To run the transform method, we create a new function that applies the new function to runwith, and then we put the just-created function inside a new reader.

The main difference from most of the functors we've looked at is that we're wrapping around a function, not a value. The functor we used for Running Queries on Functors, on page 193, was similar, but now we're taking a more general approach.

It may be a bit more difficult to understand it at the beginning, but it also opens a lot of interesting possibilities, as we'll soon see.

To finish this example, we need a way to provide the context, so let's create a ContextProvider:

```
❶ interface ContextProvider<CTX> {
❷     fun <T> tryRun(reader: ContextReader<CTX, T>): Outcome<ContextError, T>
   }
```

❶ Also, the provider is generic over the context. The CTX parameter has to match between reader and provider in order to work.

❷ This function needs to be implemented differently by different providers.

The ContextProvider will provide a context to the ContextReader, and it will return an Outcome with the result. This way, the provider can also handle the failure case without letting exceptions leak out.

The main responsibility of the provider is to correctly handle the context even in case of failures—for example, closing the file descriptor in case of a file or releasing the database connection for a database.

This looks very promising, so let's try to implement our functor and use it to store the projections.

Storing the Projections in the Database

Let's try to translate the previous example to something more concrete. Let's see how to update a row in our projection using the just-defined ContextReader. We need the equivalent to readA and writeB functions for our ToDoListProjectionRow, and we also need some kind of context, for example, a Transaction type. For the moment, we just care about the type signature, not the implementation:

```
fun readRow(id: String):
    ContextReader<Transaction, ToDoListProjectionRow> = TODO()

fun writeRow(row: ToDoListProjectionRow):
    ContextReader<Transaction, Unit> = TODO()

val remoteStorageProvider: ContextProvider<Transaction> = TODO()
```

Note that readRow, instead of returning a ToDoListProjectionRow, is returning a ContextReader with the row inside. Same for writeRow, returning Unit inside the context reader. We still don't care about the implementation; for the moment we focus on how these functions can be composed together. But if you prefer, you can read Accessing the Database with Monads, on page 237.

The previous example in pseudocode would translate to the following in this regular Kotlin code example:

```
❶ val listUpdater = readRow("myRowId")
❷     .transform { r-> r.copy(active = false) }
❸     .transform { r -> writeRow(r) }

❹ remoteStorageProvider.tryRun(listUpdater).expectSuccess()
```

❶ We start reading the row with a given ID, using the function just defined.

❷ We then deactivate the row, creating a copy with the active flag set to false.

❸ Here, we save the new deactivated row, returning a new ContextReader.

❹ Finally, we run the reader in a transaction to actually change the database. We also check that the operation succeeded.

This code compiles, but it doesn't work as we expected. We wanted for listUpdater to be of type : ContextReader<Transaction, Unit>, but it actually is a ContextReader<Transaction, ContextReader<Transaction, Unit>>. We have a ContextReader too many!

We had the same issue when composing over Outcome (see Break on Failure, on page 174); it's now time to see how to solve this problem, and it will require a new type of data structure. Let's look at the (in)famous monad.

Exploring the Power of Monads

You may have heard the terms *monads* as a reference to something very hard to understand. In a famous keynote, Douglas Crockford referred to them as cursed:[6]

> The monad in addition to it being useful, it is also cursed and the curse of the monad is that once you get the epiphany, once you understand—"oh that's what it is"—you lose the ability to explain it to anybody.

Once you understand functors, monads are just a natural follow up, as monads are essentially a specific type of functor that can be "combined" together. Without a solid understanding of functors, comprehending monads can be challenging. I suspect that much of the "curse" derives from trying to understand monads without having fully digested functors. So, let's go back to them.

What's a Functor?

From a programmer perspective, a functor can be understood as a type constructor—that is, a generic type—that can be transformed using a function.

When you see a generic type in the form of Foo<T> with a method with a signature similar to this:

Foo<T>.bar(f: (T) -> U): Foo<U>

Then it's highly likely that you are looking at a functor—or at least a type that has the potential to be one.

To qualify as a functor, it must also satisfy certain conditions, which we discussed in the previous chapter, but this is the gist of it.

When we looked at functors, we left this case unsolved—what if we finish with a functor inside another functor? For example, if we have a function that reads a file and another that sends an email, and both of them return an Outcome, we can't simply combine them:

```
fun readFile(fileName: String): Outcome<FileError, String> = TODO()

fun sendEmail(text: String): Outcome<EmailError, Unit> = TODO()

fun processEmailFile(fileName: String): Outcome<OutcomeError, Unit> =
    readFile(fileName)
        .transform { text -> sendEmail(text) } //compiler error!
```

---

6.   https://www.youtube.com/watch?v=dkZFtimgAcM

A simple workaround we've used is to force a non-local return in case of errors, like this:

```
fun processEmailFile(fileName: String): Outcome<OutcomeError, Unit> =
    readFile(fileName)
        .transform { text -> sendEmail(text)
            .onFailure{ return@processEmailFile it.asFailure() }}
```

But, it would be useful to be able to "bind" the two functions together into a single functor, like this:

```
fun Outcome<ERR, T>.bind(f: (T)-> U): Outcome<ERR, U> = TODO()

fun processEmailFile(fileName: String): Outcome<OutcomeError, Unit> =
    readFile(fileName)
        .bind { text -> sendEmail(text) }
```

And this is exactly what monads allow us to do. Or more precisely, if a functor can be combined with another functor (of the same type), we can say that it forms a monad.

What's a Monad?

Keeping our programmer perspective, a monad can be considered a functor that comes equipped with an additional method allowing two functors to be bound together using a function.

In other words, if you come across a generic type that takes the form of Foo<T> and has a method with the following signature:

Foo<T>.barbar(f: (T) -> Foo<U>): Foo<U>

Then you are most likely dealing with a monad.

However, note that there are certain rules that it must follow, which we'll explore in more detail shortly.

It doesn't seem so difficult in the end! For a more comprehensive explanation, you can look at how Category Theory defines The Mysterious Monad, on page 410.

Still, there are some subtleties we need to keep in mind when using monads. To see why, let's look a bit deeper at how functors work.

Endofunctors

We implemented functors using generics. This means that the generic type of a functor can be another functor. So, we can always create a functor on top of an existing functor. For example, from a List<Int> we can create a List<List<Int>> or a Outcome<MyError, List<Int>>, going on without limits.

\//
ʒ̈ƒ   **Joe asks:**
Shouldn't the bind Function Be Called flatmap?

In some languages, like Scala, the monadic composition is called flatmap, but since we already have map and flatmap methods in all the Kotlin collections, using different names for the functorial and monadic composition would make them stand apart and easier to understand.

In other languages it's called collect, but the operation is the same. When in doubt, you look at the signature; it will be the same in any language, regardless of the name.

So, the functors we're describing here are all mapping any type of the Kotlin type system (which forms a category if we squint hard enough) to other types in the same category. We defined functors as a mapping between two categories, which is correct, only in our case the two categories are the same. Functors that map a category into itself are called endofunctors.

We'll continue to call them just functors for simplicity, but this fact is important, because we can combine two of them together only when the two categories are the same. And since monads need to combine two functors, we can only create monads from endofunctors.

What's a Monad?

So, we need some kind of endofunctor, and we need to combine two instances of them together. Note that they must be of the same type; we can flatten a List<List<Int>> or a Outcome<E, Outcome<E, Int>> but—in the general case—we can't flatten a List<Outcome<E, Int>> to a single outcome. At most we can switch the two functors around to a <Outcome<E, List<Int>>>. (See Sequence, on page 285.)

Now, if we consider the category of all functions of type (T) -> EF<T> where T can be any type and EF is an endofunctor, can you combine these functions? In other words, does this category have a monoid instance? If so—it really depends on which endofunctor we choose—then EF is also a monad. If you remember, a category of arrows is a monoid only if we can combine all of them together (see Discovering the Monoid, on page 125).

> A monad is a monoid in the category of endofunctors, what's the problem?
>
> —jokingly attributed to Philip Wadler[7]

You may have observed that the term "monad" bears resemblance to "monoid" since both can combine things together. However—as we just saw—while

---

7. http://james-iry.blogspot.com/2009/05/brief-incomplete-and-mostly-wrong.html

monoids work on functions, monads work on functors. In other words, monads are those functors that can be bound together.

It may be helpful to see it visually. Let's look at a diagram to see how transform and bind work for the Outcome monad:

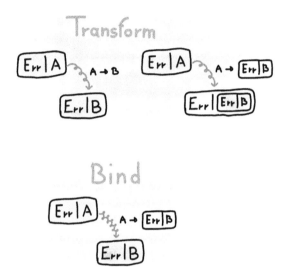

Monads are often described as "programmable semicolons," implying that they enable a chain of transformations that involve effects. In this context, "programmable" means that each monad can determine its own behavior based on the specific context in which it's used. For instance, if an Outcome fails in a chain, the subsequent bind operations won't be executed.

What Isn't a Monad

So far, all the functors we saw are also monads, but this isn't always the case. To better understand what a monad is, let's see a counterexample of a functor that isn't a monad. Let's consider a functor that keeps a value associated with a tag, related to its origin:

```
enum class ValueOrigin {internal, external, generated}

data class TaggedValue<T>(val value: T, val tag: ValueOrigin){
    fun <U> transform(f:(T) -> U): TaggedValue<U> = TaggedValue(f(value), tag)
}
```

With such a functor, we can attach a tag to any value and transform it to other values. But, what would be the result of the following?

```
TaggedValue(5, internal)
    .bind{ x -> TaggedValue(x*2, external) }
```

It can't be TaggedValue(10, internal) or TaggedValue(10, external), and TaggedValue(10, generated) would be even more confusing.

There is no sensible way we can make this work. Even if—fortunately for us—these are quite rare cases, we need a way to determine if our monad is a legit one. To be so, it has to follow three simple laws.

Monad Laws

The first law is the *left identity*, which says that if we apply a plain monad to a value and we bind a function that creates a new monad, the result would be the same as applying that function to our initial value.

Let's see two examples, with List and with our Outcome. The equivalent of bind for collections is the flatmap method:

```
val a = Random.nextInt()

fun `List left identity`(){
    val f: (Int) -> List<Int> = {x -> listOf(x * 2) }
    val ma = listOf(a).flatMap(f)

    expectThat(ma).isEqualTo(f(a))
}

fun `Outcome left identity`(){
    val f: (Int) -> Outcome<OutcomeError, Int> = { (it * 2).asSuccess() }
    val ma = a.asSuccess().bind(f)

    expectThat(ma).isEqualTo(f(a))
}
```

The second law is the *right identity*, which says that if we have a monadic value and we bind it to a function that returns the plain monad, the result would be the same as our initial monadic value.

Let's see how it works with the same two examples:

```
val a = randomText(10)

fun `List right identity`() {
    val ma = listOf(a).flatMap { listOf(it) }

    expectThat(ma).isEqualTo(listOf(a))
}

fun `Outcome right identity`() {
    val ma = a.asSuccess().bind { it.asSuccess() }

    expectThat(ma).isEqualTo(a.asSuccess())
}
```

The third law is *associativity*, which says that if we have a chain of functions to bind, it shouldn't matter how we nest them.

And now the examples:

```
val a = Random.nextInt()

fun `List associativity`(){
    val f: (Int) -> List<Int> = { listOf(it * 2) }
    val g: (Int) -> List<Int> = { listOf(it + 5) }

    val ma1 = listOf(a).flatMap(f).flatMap(g)
    val ma2 = listOf(a).flatMap{ x -> f(x).flatMap(g) }

    expectThat(ma1).isEqualTo(ma2)
}

fun `Outcome associativity`(){
    val f: (Int) -> Outcome<OutcomeError, Int> = { (it * 2).asSuccess() }
    val g: (Int) -> Outcome<OutcomeError, Int> = { (it + 5).asSuccess() }

    val ma1 = a.asSuccess().bind(f).bind(g)
    val ma2 = a.asSuccess().bind{ x -> f(x).bind(g) }

    expectThat(ma1).isEqualTo(ma2)
}
```

For example, an ImpureMonad that writes something on the console every bind would break these laws.

The same is true for our previous TaggedValue functor, even if we agreed on some arbitrary convention.

 Joe asks:
Can We Make a Monad out of TaggedValue?

We can't make a monad out of TaggedValue...unless the tag is of a type with a monoid instance.

A possible way could be changing the tag from an enum to a list of enum; so we can compose them together in the bind function.

Outcome Monad

Enough theory, let's write some code! We can start from our Outcome functor, and let's make it a monad. As we saw, we need to combine two outcomes together. Let's consider two cases: combining an outcome with a function that would return a new outcome—which is our bind—and flattening an outcome nested inside another one—this operation is called join.

Here are the tests:

```
val genericFail = DivisionError("generic error").asFailure()
val divFail = DivisionError("You cannot divide by zero").asFailure()
```

❶
```
private fun divide100by(x: Int): Outcome<DivisionError, Int> =
    if (x == 0)
        divFail
    else
        (100 / x).asSuccess()
```

```
@Test
fun `binding two outcome together`() {
    val valid = 5.asSuccess()
```
❷
```
    expectThat(valid.bind(::divide100by)).isEqualTo(20.asSuccess())

    val invalid = DivisionError("generic error").asFailure()
```
❸
```
    expectThat(genericFail.bind(::divide100by)).isEqualTo(invalid)

    val zero = 0.asSuccess()
```
❹
```
    expectThat(zero.bind(::divide100by)).isEqualTo(divFail)
}
```

```
@Test
fun `joining two outcome together`() {
    val valid = 10.asSuccess().asSuccess()
```
❺
```
    expectThat(valid.join()).isEqualTo(10.asSuccess())

    val invalid = genericFail.asSuccess()
```
❻
```
    expectThat(invalid.join()).isEqualTo(genericFail)
}
```

❶ Here, we have a function that can return a success or a failure.

❷ If we bind two successes together, we have a single success.

❸ A failure will remain a failure even if bound to a success.

❹ A success will become a failure if bound to one.

❺ When we join two successes, we get a single success.

❻ But, when we have a failure inside the success, the result will be a failure.

The implementation of bind is pretty elegant:

```
inline fun <T, U, E : OutcomeError>
        Outcome<E, T>.bind(f: (T) -> Outcome<E, U>): Outcome<E, U> =
    when (this) {
        is Success -> f(value)
        is Failure -> this
    }
```

If the current outcome is a success, we run the f function with the value; otherwise, we return the current failure.

The implementation of join is even simpler:

```
fun <T, E : OutcomeError> Outcome<E, Outcome<E, T>>.join(): Outcome<E, T> =
    bind { it }
```

It may be hard to understand how this can possibly work, but in a nested outcome, the value is another outcome, so you can bind it directly. You may want to try and debug it yourself to fully appreciate it.

 Joe asks:
Should We Avoid Using onFailure Now?

Having the binding methods offers an elegant way to combine together nested functors, but there are still situations where the code is more readable using onFailure, as we'll see.

What's important is keeping the code compact and easy to read, rather than striving for theoretical perfection.

Reader Monad

We can now answer the question at the beginning of the chapter: how can we combine two ContextReaders?

Let's first see how it should work with a diagram:

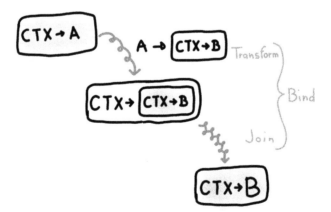

To make bind work, we need to create a new reader that will run the original runWith as input for the function f, then the result of f will be the new runWith:

```kotlin
data class ContextReader<CTX, out T>(val runWith: (CTX) -> T) {

    fun <U> transform(f: (T) -> U): ContextReader<CTX, U> =
        ContextReader { ctx -> f(runWith(ctx)) }

    fun <U> bind(f: (T) -> ContextReader<CTX, U>): ContextReader<CTX, U> =
        ContextReader { ctx -> f(runWith(ctx)).runWith(ctx) }
}
```

Regarding the name, ContextReader is also called the Reader monad or the Environment monad.

Type Classes and Interfaces

Let's look at a final consideration before going back to Zettai. Looking at all our functors, it's tempting to try to extract interfaces for the functor and the monad themselves, something like this:

```kotlin
interface Functor<T> {
    fun <U> transform(f: (T) -> U): Functor<U>
}

interface Monad<T>: Functor<T> {
    fun <U> bind(f: (T) -> Monad<U>): Monad<U>
}
```

Unfortunately, this won't go very far, because the return type can't be the generic interface, but must be the implementing concrete class. For example, if we make our simple functor, Holder, implement this interface, we'll get this:

```kotlin
data class Holder<T>(val value: T): Monad<T> {
    override fun <U> transform(f: (T) -> U): Functor<U> =
        TODO("Not yet implemented")

    override fun <U> bind(f: (T) -> Monad<U>): Monad<U> =
        TODO("Not yet implemented")
}
```

But this isn't what we want; transform should return a Holder<U>, not a generic functor, and the same for bind. What we actually want is a way to define a group of types with some methods, without abstracting them to a common interface.

These kinds of abstractions are called type classes, and we don't have a way to define them in Kotlin.

So, we're stuck with manually adding the methods to each of our functors and monads, relying on self-discipline rather than compiler checks. This is unfortunate, but since they are just a few functions, it's not a big burden.

A Final Word About Monads

I think that, at least in part, the mystical connotations that are often associated with monads might result from a lack of understanding about how functors operate.

I hope it's now clear that monads aren't magical entities that allow impure stuff to become pure, but instead they are a useful tool to make functional code as convenient as impure code but maintaining its purity and composability. In other words, they save us some typing and duplication, they don't inherently make our code more functional. In the words of one of their main advocates:

> Say I write an evaluator in a pure functional language.
>
> - To add error handling to it, I need to modify each recursive call to check for and handle errors appropriately. Had I used an impure language with exceptions, no such restructuring would be needed.
>
> - To add a count of operations performed to it, I need to modify each recursive call to pass around such counts appropriately. Had I used an impure language with a global variable that could be incremented, no such restructuring would be needed.
>
> - To add an execution trace to it, I need to modify each recursive call to pass around such traces appropriately. Had I used an impure language that performed output as a side effect, no such restructuring would be needed.
>
> Or I could use a monad.
>
> —Philip Wadler, "Monads for Functional Programming"

Recap

We covered a lot in this chapter!

We looked at databases and in particular how to leverage the capabilities of PostgreSQL to store and retrieve events and projections. We also learned how to adopt a nonfunctional library—JetBrains's Exposed—for our project and adapt it to be more functional friendly.

Then we looked at the properties of monads and how we can use them to solve problems. Monads enable the combination of operations, providing us with versatility in how we integrate pure functions. Additionally, we learned why they are sometimes called "programmable semicolons."

In the next chapter, we'll make our Zettai application persist and retrieve events, putting into practice what we've learned so far.

Exercises

The exercises in this chapter will focus on how to use monads.

Here is your friendly reminder that nobody can learn functional programming by just reading code, and the best way to learn is by practicing. You can refer to the exercises folder in the book code repository for the starting point and some hints.

Exercise 9.1: Monad Laws for ContextReader

We wrote some tests to verify monad laws for Outcome and List. For this exercise, you need to write the same three tests for our ContextReader monad, one for each law.

Exercise 9.2: Implementing bind from join

In our monads, we implemented join in function of bind. It's also possible to do the opposite. For this exercise, try to reimplement ContextReader.join without using bind and then implement bind using join.

```
fun <U> ContextReader<CTX, T>
    .bind(f: (T) -> ContextReader<CTX, U>): ContextReader<CTX, U> = TODO()

fun <CTX, T> ContextReader<CTX, ContextReader<CTX, T>>
    .join(): ContextReader<CTX, T> = TODO()
```

Fixation is the way to death. Fluidity is the way to life.

    Miyamoto Musashi, The Book of Five Rings

CHAPTER 10

Reading Context to Handle Commands

In the previous chapter, we examined how the Reader monad can assist us in executing computations that rely on data from an external context.

We'll apply this concept by using it to incorporate persistence into the event store and projections. Since these operations are decoupled from the context, we can keep projections in memory or store them in the database depending on our requirements. The best part is that we won't have to modify the projector code.

At the end, we'll look at some good practices on how to approach designing and managing changes of an event-sourcing system.

Accessing the Database with Monads

It's now time to put the monads to work on the database library we started before. Using the ContextReader we wrote in the previous chapter, we can now combine the read and write operations in the same transaction:

```
val listUpdater = readRow("myRowId")
  .transform { r-> r.copy(active = false) }
① .bind { r -> writeRow(r) }
② runInTransaction(listUpdater).expectSuccess()
```

❶ With the bind method, we're able to make the writeRow call compile and work correctly without using a non-local return.

❷ Until we run the ContextReader in a transaction, ContextReader is only maintaining a record of the operations we intend to carry out on the database, without performing them. All the actual database calls happen in this line.

Now that we have the functions to access the database, and we have a way to read and write from it safely and in a functional-friendly way, we need to put all this together.

First, we have to finish implementing the readRow and writeRow functions, using a ContextReader working with the transaction:

```
① typealias TxReader<T> = ContextReader<Transaction, T>

② fun readRow(id: String): TxReader<ToDoListProjectionRow> = TxReader { tx ->
③     toDoListProjectionTable.selectWhere(tx, toDoListProjectionTable.id eq id)
          .map { it[toDoListProjectionTable.row_data] }
④     .single()
}

⑤ fun writeRow(row: ToDoListProjectionRow): TxReader<Unit> = TxReader { tx ->
⑥     toDoListProjectionTable.insertInto(tx) { newRow ->
          newRow[id] = row.id.toRowId()
          newRow[row_data] = row
      }
}
```

❶ We start by defining a type alias for our convenience.

❷ We wrap the result of readRow inside a transaction reader.

❸ Then, we select all rows from the projection table where the row ID is equal to requested ID.

❹ Finally, we check that the query must return a single row.

❺ We wrap writeRow inside a reader in the same way.

❻ We insert a new row on the projection table using the transaction from the reader.

To complete our task, we need to implement the ContextProvider for the transaction. The goal here is to control the way transactions are used by the database, so that we roll them back in case of errors, and we always close the database connection. We also want to decide the isolation level to use to run the reader case by case:

```
data class TransactionProvider(
            private val dataSource: DataSource,
            val isolationLevel: TransactionIsolationLevel,
            val maxAttempts: Int = 10): ContextProvider<Transaction> {

    override fun <T> tryRun(
        reader: ContextReader<Transaction, T>): Outcome<ContextError, T> =
①     inTopLevelTransaction(
②         db = Database.connect(dataSource),
```

```
                transactionIsolation = isolationLevel.jdbcLevel,
                repetitionAttempts = maxAttempts) {
❸           addLogger(StdOutSqlLogger)

            try {
❹               reader.runWith(this).asSuccess()
            } catch (t: Throwable) {
❺               rollback()
                TransactionError("Transaction rolled back: ${t.message}", t)
                    .asFailure()
            }
        }
    }
```

❶ inTopLevelTransaction from Exposed does exactly what we need here.

❷ We pass the database connection, the isolation level, and the max attempts parameters from the constructor.

❸ Exposed will log out all the SQL commands to the console.

❹ We run our reader inside a try...catch block. Note that runWith is a field storing a function, not a method of the ContextReader.

❺ In case of exceptions, we'll rollback the transaction.

We can now successfully run the full test on the projection row with actual code that can run on the database:

```
class TxContextReaderTest {

    @Test
    fun `write and read from a table`() {
        val user = randomUser()
        val expectedList = randomToDoList()
        val listId = ToDoListId.mint()
        val row = ToDoListProjectionRow(listId, user, true, expectedList)

        val listReader: TxReader<ToDoList> =
            writeRow(row)
                .bind { readRow(listId.toRowId()) }
                .transform { row -> row.list }

        val list = transactionContextForTest().tryRun(listReader)
            .expectSuccess()

        expectThat(list).isEqualTo(expectedList)
    }

}
```

We need to start the PostgreSQL Docker container or another database instance before running the tests, otherwise, they'll fail.

If everything has been set up correctly, we can now successfully run our test and see the generated SQL commands in the console, as in this figure:

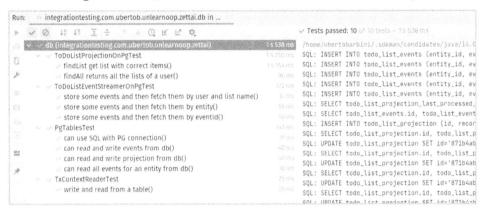

EventStreamer with ContextReader

With all the necessary components in position, we're now able to run our event store in a database instead of relying on in-memory maps. What's more, our persistence framework has been designed in a manner that allows for its operation in memory, with a database, or with alternative persistence solutions, provided they can be incorporated within a ContextReader.

In other words, we defined an algebra of data and functions to manage the persistence of our system using functional effects.

Let's briefly recap where we are. Every domain operation that needs some kind of persistence should return a ContextReader. We can then combine them, and once we assemble enough pieces to complete a task—something that should atomically work or fail—we can run it in a ContextProvider to obtain the final result or a detailed error.

All the domain logic should ignore the actual context that will be used, because it will be something injected from an outside adapter (see Separating the Domain from the Infrastructure, on page 53).

Let's look again at our EventStreamer interface. Its role is to read and write events to the repository. It shouldn't know about entity and the rest of the model:

```
interface EventStreamer<E : EntityEvent, NK: Any> {
    fun fetchByEntity(entityId: EntityId): List<E>?
    fun fetchAfter(eventSeq: EventSeq): Sequence<StoredEvent<E>>
    fun retrieveIdFromNaturalKey(key: NK): EntityId?
    fun store(newEvents: Iterable<E>): List<StoredEvent<E>>
}
```

Typically, each entity has a *natural key* that should be unique, like the combination user and list name in Zettai. A good practical consideration is to add a method to retrieve events using the natural key from our database. We could use projections for this, but it's faster and safer to directly query the events.

Joe asks:
Why Is Using a Projection Not Safe?

The problem is that the projections are created by observing the events created by the command handler. So, there is always a risk that they aren't completely up-to-date.

This is called eventual consistence, and it's usually not a problem for the read model, but it can be problematic for the event store. Depending on the domain, the risk can be quite small or not of much consequence. But in general, it's better to avoid having the write model depend on projections.

It's now time we put into practice what we learned about monads! We need to change the interface to return ContextReader, also making the EventStreamer generic over the context:

```
interface EventStreamer<CTX, E : EntityEvent, NK : Any> {
  fun fetchByEntity(entityId: EntityId): ContextReader<CTX, List<E>>
  fun fetchAfter(eventSeq: EventSeq): ContextReader<CTX, List<StoredEvent<E>>>
  fun retrieveIdFromNaturalKey(key: NK): ContextReader<CTX, EntityId?>
  fun store(newEvents: Iterable<E>): ContextReader<CTX, List<StoredEvent<E>>>
}
```

Rewrite the In-Memory Event Streamer

Rather than writing a new database event streamer for the database from scratch, it's preferable to split the work into two parts: first, we convert the current streamer to use the ContextReader operating with a list of events in memory, and second, we can migrate it to an external database.

By proceeding in this way, we can validate each step separately and minimize the potential for errors.

For this we need to move the event lists from the in-memory event streamer to the ContextProvider for in-memory events:

```
typealias ToDoListInMemoryRef = AtomicReference<List<ToDoListStoredEvent>>

❶ typealias InMemoryEventsReader<T> = ContextReader<ToDoListInMemoryRef, T>

class InMemoryEventsProvider() : ContextProvider<ToDoListInMemoryRef> {
```

```
❷    val events = AtomicReference<List<ToDoListStoredEvent>>(listOf())

     override fun <T> tryRun(reader: InMemoryEventsReader<T>) =
         try {
❸            reader.runWith(events).asSuccess()
         } catch (e: Exception) {
             ToDoListEventsError("Operation failed: ${e.message}", e)
❹                .asFailure()
         }
 }
```

❶ First, we define the alias for the in-memory events reader.

❷ The list for events is now in the in-memory provider; it will be shared to all the readers.

❸ Here, we run the reader inside a try...catch block as inside the transaction provider. In this way, we're sure that no exception can leak outside.

❹ In case of exception, we return a failure with the exception details.

We also need to adapt the EventStreamerInMemory using the list from the context instead of the private field. Let's just look at the store method since the rest are quite similar:

```
class EventStreamerInMemory : ToDoListEventStreamer<ToDoListInMemoryRef> {

    override fun store(newEvents: Iterable<ToDoListEvent>) =
        InMemoryEventsReader { events ->
            newEvents.toSavedEvents(events.get().size.toLong())
                .also { ne -> events.updateAndGet { it + ne } }
        }
//... similar changes to rest of the methods

}
```

Stream Events from Database

We now need a new implementation of the EventStreamer interface working with database and transactions. Let's call it EventStreamerTx. We start by writing a test for the fetchByEntity method. The test will consist of storing some events and then fetching them using the EntityId:

```
fun transactionProviderForTest() = TransactionProvider(
❶          pgDataSourceForTest(), ReadCommitted)

❷ fun createToDoListEventStreamerOnPg(): EventStreamerTx = TODO()

class ToDoListEventStreamerOnPgTest {

    val user = randomUser()

    val streamer = createToDoListEventStreamerOnPg()
```

```kotlin
private val txProvider = transactionProviderForTest()

@Test
fun `store some events and then fetch them by entity`() {
    val newList1 = randomListName()
    val newList2 = randomListName()
    val newList3 = randomListName()
    val listId1 = ToDoListId.mint()
    val listId2 = ToDoListId.mint()
    val listId3 = ToDoListId.mint()
    val item1 = randomItem()
    val item2 = randomItem().copy(dueDate = LocalDate.now())

    val eventsToStore = listOf(
        ListCreated(listId1, user, newList1),
        ListCreated(listId2, user, newList2),
        ItemAdded(listId2, item1),
        ItemAdded(listId2, item2),
        ListCreated(listId3, user, newList3)
    )

    val storeAndFetch = streamer.store(
        eventsToStore
    ).bind {
        streamer.fetchByEntity(listId2)
    }

    val events = txProvider.tryRun(storeAndFetch).expectSuccess()

    expectThat(events).isEqualTo(
        listOf(
            ListCreated(listId2, user, newList2),
            ItemAdded(listId2, item1),
            ItemAdded(listId2, item2)
        )
    )
}
```

❶ This method provides a context for working on our test database.

❷ Here, we'll create the new streamer.

❸ We store a list of events to create three lists.

❹ We bind the store call to the fetchByEntity call, so they'll run on the same transaction.

❺ We run the reader on the test database, and we expect that it runs successfully.

❻ At the end, we'll verify that we fetched all the events of the correct entity, and only those.

To make the test compile, we need to implement the EventStreamerTx, and we need to add some custom methods to the PgEventTable. Being able to add methods to custom tables is a nice feature of Exposed. For example, we can directly convert the table records to domain events:

```kotlin
fun PgEventTable.queryEvents(
        condition: Op<Boolean>): TxReader<List<StoredEvent<PgEvent>>> =
    TxReader { tx ->
        selectWhere(tx, condition, id).map(::rowToPgEvent)
    }
```

Now we can write the EventStreamerTx class. We pass some parameters to the constructor, so that it can work with any general event table, not only our todo_list_events:

```kotlin
class EventStreamerTx<E : EntityEvent, NK : Any>(
    private val table: PgEventTable,
    private val eventParser: Parser<E, PgEvent>,
    private val naturalKeySql: (NK) -> String
) : EventStreamer<Transaction, E, NK> {

    private fun pgEventsToEvents(pgEvents: List<StoredEvent<PgEvent>>) =
        pgEvents.map {
            StoredEvent(it.eventSeq, it.storedAt,
                eventParser.parseOrThrow(it.event))
        }

    override fun fetchByEntity(entityId: EntityId): TxReader<List<E>> =
        table.queryEvents(table.entity_id eq entityId.raw)
            .transform { pgEvents ->
                pgEventsToEvents(pgEvents).map(StoredEvent<E>::event) }

    override fun fetchAfter(
            eventSeq: EventSeq): TxReader<List<StoredEvent<E>>> =
        table.queryEvents(table.id greater eventSeq.progressive)
            .transform(this::pgEventsToEvents)

    override fun retrieveIdFromNaturalKey(key: NK): TxReader<EntityId?> =
        table.getEntityIdBySql(naturalKeySql(key))

    override fun store(events: Iterable<E>): TxReader<List<StoredEvent<E>>> =
        table
            .insertEvents(events.map { eventParser.render(it) })
            .transform(this::pgEventsToEvents)

}
```

①
②
③
④
⑤

❶ In the constructor we pass the table to use, the parser for the events, and the specific SQL to use for the natural key search.

❷ Here, we query all events with a given EntityId.

❸ This is the call used by projections; we fetch all events with a progressive greater than the eventSeq parameter.

❹ For the natural key search, we pass the SQL to fetch the EntityId.

❺ The insertEvents method also gets the auto-generated ID and timestamp from the database.

This is how we can use it to fetch the entity ID of a list from events using a PostgreSQL JSON query:

```
typealias ToDoListEventStreamerTx =
            EventStreamer<Transaction, ToDoListEvent, UserListName>

fun createToDoListEventStreamerOnPg(): ToDoListEventStreamerTx =
    EventStreamerTx(toDoListEventsTable, toDoListEventParser()) { natKey ->
    """
    SELECT  entity_id
    FROM    todo_list_events
    WHERE   event_type = 'ListCreated'
            AND json_data ->> 'owner' = '${natKey.user.name}'
            AND json_data ->> 'name' = '${natKey.listName.name}'
    """.trimIndent()
}
```

In the same way, we can now write the tests for the other methods of the event streamer; as usual, you can see the full code in the book repository.

Handling Commands with Context Reader

It's now time to put the event streamer to work inside the command handler. In our event store implementation, we split the responsibilities in this way:

- EventStreamer knows the events—clearly—it knows the database (or the in-memory list), and it knows how to search for data in it, but it doesn't know the domain entity.

- EventStore knows how to convert events into entities and how to use the event streamer. It doesn't know about the actual persistence and can work with both streamers, and it doesn't know about commands.

- CommandHandler manages the logical transactions; it knows how to use event store, but it doesn't know anything about the streamer.

Let's visualize it:

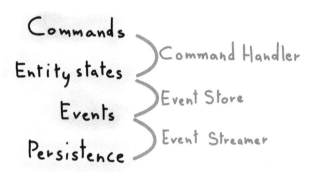

To work with a context, CommandHandler needs a context provider and an event store passed as constructor dependencies. Since they have to work together, CommandHandler must be generic over the context type.

The Command::execute methods will return a ContextReader, so they need to be bound together with the storing of events at the end of the operation:

```
class ToDoListCommandHandler<CTX>(
    private val contextProvider: ContextProvider<CTX>,
    private val eventStore: ToDoListEventStore<CTX>
) : (ToDoListCommand) -> ToDoListCommandOutcome {

    override fun invoke(command: ToDoListCommand): ToDoListCommandOutcome =
        contextProvider.tryRun(
            when (command) {
                is CreateToDoList -> command.execute()
                is AddToDoItem -> command.execute()
            }.bindOutcome(eventStore)
        ).join()
            .transform { storedEvents -> storedEvents.map { it.event } }
            .transformFailure { it as? ZettaiError
                                ?: ToDoListCommandError(it.msg) }

    private fun CreateToDoList.execute() =
        eventStore.retrieveByNaturalKey(UserListName(user, name))
            .transform { listState ->
                when (listState) {
                    null -> ListCreated(ToDoListId.mint(),
                            user, name).asCommandSuccess()
                    else-> InconsistentStateError(this, listState).asFailure()
                }
            }
}
```

```
private fun AddToDoItem.execute() =
    eventStore.retrieveByNaturalKey(UserListName(user, name))
      .transform { listState ->
          when (listState) {
            is ActiveToDoList ->
                if (listState.items.any {
                  it.description == item.description })
                    ToDoListCommandError("two items with same name!")
                      .asFailure()
                else {
                    ItemAdded(listState.id, item).asCommandSuccess()
                }
            else -> InconsistentStateError(this, listState).asFailure()
          }
      }
}
```

❶ In the constructor, we pass a context provider and the event store for the same CTX.

❷ We bind the combination of two operations, fetching the entity and saving the events but only if the command is successful. We'll analyze this function better soon.

❸ Now, we have two outcomes nested, one from executing the command and another from running the context reader, so we join them together.

❹ We use transformFailure from Exercise 7.3 to report the database error as a command error.

❺ It's quite straightforward to translate the existing commands to make them work with the context reader.

A Monad Transformer

The bindOutcome function is quite interesting, because it works as a monad transformer:

```
fun <CTX, E : OutcomeError, T, U> ContextReader<CTX, Outcome<E, T>>
        .bindOutcome(f: (T) -> ContextReader<CTX, U>):
                            ContextReader<CTX, Outcome<E, U>> =
    ContextReader { ctx ->
        val outcome = runWith(ctx)
        when (outcome) {
            is Success -> f(outcome.value).runWith(ctx).asSuccess()
            is Failure -> outcome
        }
    }
```

I said that different monads can't be combined together; in other words, we can't bind an Outcome to a ContextReader, but hey, we're doing exactly that here! How is this possible?

Well, it's true that it's *generally* not possible to combine monads of different types, but we can write specific ad hoc functions like this. They are called monad transformers, and you need to write one for each pair of monads you want to combine.

Execute Commands Concurrently

Before moving on to how to use the database with the read model, let's consider what happens if two commands arrive at the same time and the command handler starts processing them in parallel.

What are our constraints in doing concurrent operations? Looking at the events, we need to make sure we start the transaction before we fetch the entity at the beginning of the command handler, and we commit it at the end once we emit the events, or we roll it back if the command fails.

Command Concurrency

 While it's possible (and desirable) to process multiple commands on different entities simultaneously, it's important to avoid processing two commands for the same entity key in parallel. Note that this is a business constraint, not a technical one.

Even if we have multiple instances of our service running on different machines, we still need to ensure that we don't allow the processing of two commands for the same entity at the same time. Failing to do so could result in corrupting the flow of events and leaving the entity in an inconsistent state.

The easiest way to make sure we respect this constraint is to set the database isolation level to *Serializable*. This way, PostgreSQL would make sure that "any concurrent execution of a set of Serializable transactions is guaranteed to produce the same effect as running them one at a time in some order."[1]

This means that we don't have to worry about concurrency, because PostgreSQL will take care of it for us. The only downside is that it can become a bottleneck if we have very high traffic on our service.

In such cases, we may need to implement a more advanced locking system to enable simultaneous execution of commands on different entities. One

---

1. https://www.postgresql.org/docs/current/transaction-iso.html

common strategy is to utilize optimistic locking on the events of the same entity. We can verify that no new events have occurred for the entity when committing the transaction. If new events are detected, we reload them and reprocess the command.

Wiring It All Together

We have all the pieces ready, and we can wire them together in our main function. It's easy, because we just need to pass a different implementation of our EventStore in the hub, and everything will work:

```
fun main() {

    val dataSource = prepareProductionDatabase()

    val streamer = createToDoListEventStreamerOnPg()
    val eventStore = ToDoListEventStore(streamer)
    val txProvider = TransactionProvider(dataSource,
                            TransactionIsolationLevel.Serializable)

    val commandHandler = ToDoListCommandHandler(txProvider, eventStore)

    //...
}
```

Since we removed the initial data setup, we can verify that everything is working correctly running the application. We can create and delete lists, and even if we stop it and restart it, Zettai now remembers all the data.

We can also look in the database tables and see our lists stored there as a stream of events, as shown in the following figure:

In our DDT, we can use the test database for the HttpActions and the in-memory event store for the DomainOnlyActions. As you can see, it's pretty simple to set up the in-memory event store:

```
val streamer = EventStreamerInMemory()
val eventStore = ToDoListEventStore(streamer)
val inMemoryEvents = InMemoryEventsProvider()

val cmdHandler = ToDoListCommandHandler(inMemoryEvents, eventStore)
```

With this, we finished handling the commands. The next step is to store the projections in a database.

Querying Projections from Database

Before looking at how we can store our projections in a database, we should ask ourselves, should we keep our projections in memory or not?

In case of events, we don't really have a choice, we need to store them in a database before going live with our application. However, for projections, we also have the option of keeping them in memory in the final application.

In this case, when the application starts, we create the projection by replaying all the events from the beginning, reading them from the database, and then we must keep the projections always up to date by reading new events from the database before every query.

The advantage of keeping projections in memory is the speed of access and flexibility. Reading data from memory is several orders of magnitude faster than getting it from a remote database. For some applications, getting data from memory can be a crucial requirement. Moreover, it's easier to do complex searches on structures in memory than using SQL.

On the other hand, in-memory projections usually require a substantial amount of memory, which can be expensive depending on the RAM plans offered by our cloud provider.

They also have other limitations, the biggest one being the start-up time. If we have a lot of events, reading them all can take several minutes. Depending on the application, this could be acceptable or not. It's also possible that for some projections, we don't need to read all events—for example, we may create a special projection with only the to-do lists created in the last month.

On the other hand, database projections have their own advantages: they can be used as a base for reports and joined with other tables like in a normal relational database. This may create some misalignment issues if all projections aren't up-to-date, but this can be acceptable for batch reporting, for example.

Since they are created from the events, we can change them without impacting our domain model—the events—and we can share them directly between applications without having to write and expose an HTTP API.

So at the end of the day, what's better, in-memory projections or database ones? It depends on the system requirements. It's a delicate balance as is often the case with architectural decisions.

We'll now proceed with converting one of our two projections to use a database, leaving the other one in memory, so you can see how to work with both kinds.

Persist a Projection

We don't need to change the ToDoListProjection interface, since it only has the update and query methods. We also don't need to change the projector, because its logic is independent of the persistence details. We only need to write a new projection implementation with the correct SQL to run the queries.

Since we have the test for the in-memory version of the projection, instead of writing a new test, we'll make it abstract over the actual projection implementation. So, the same test will run twice, first on the in-memory projection and then on the database one:

```
❶  abstract class ToDoListProjectionAbstractTest {

        abstract fun buildListProjection(
❷                       events: List<ToDoListEvent>): ToDoListProjection

        val user = randomUser()

        @Test
        fun `findAll returns all the lists of a user`() {

            val listName1 = randomListName()
            val listName2 = randomListName()

❸          val projection = buildListProjection(
                listOf(
                    ListCreated(ToDoListId.mint(), user, listName1),
                    ListCreated(ToDoListId.mint(), user, listName2),
                    ListCreated(ToDoListId.mint(), randomUser(), randomListName())
                )
            )

❹          expectThat(projection.findAll(user).expectSuccess())
                .isEqualTo(listOf(listName1, listName2))
        }
    //other tests ...
    }
```

⑤
```kotlin
internal class ToDoListProjectionOnPgTest : ToDoListProjectionAbstractTest() {
    val dataSource = pgDataSourceForTest()
    val txProvider = TransactionProvider(dataSource,
                        TransactionIsolationLevel.ReadCommitted)
    val streamer = createToDoListEventStreamerOnPg()
    val projection = ToDoListProjectionOnPg(txProvider)
```
⑥
```kotlin
                    { txProvider.tryRun(streamer.fetchAfter(it)) }

    override fun buildListProjection(events: List<ToDoListEvent>) =
        projection.apply {
```
⑦
⑧
```kotlin
            txProvider.tryRun(streamer.store(events)).expectSuccess()
            update()
        }
}
```

❶ This is the abstract class where all tests are. It's extended by ToDoListProjectionOnPgTest and the equivalent for in-memory projection. Only one test is listed here for brevity.

❷ This is the abstract method that needs to be overridden in the concrete classes. It receives a list of events and will get a projection back.

❸ In each test, we get the projection calling the buildListProjection method.

❹ Here, we call the actual projection method under test, and we verify the expected result.

❺ This is the concrete class for the database projection. It contains no tests, just the abstract method implementation.

❻ The method to fetch events from the streamer must run inside txProvider now.

❼ To prepare the projection for the test, first we store the events into the database.

❽ Then, we update the projection. Now it's ready to use.

Update the Projection from Database

With new tests in place, we need to update the Projection interface to work with ContextReader and ContextProvider:

```kotlin
typealias FetchStoredEvents<E> =
            (EventSeq) -> Outcome<OutcomeError, List<StoredEvent<E>>>
typealias ProjectEvents<R, E> = (E) -> List<DeltaRow<R>>
```
❶
```kotlin
interface Projection<CTX, R : Any, E : EntityEvent> {
```
❷
```kotlin
    val contextProvider: ContextProvider<CTX>
    val eventProjector: ProjectEvents<R, E>
    val eventFetcher: FetchStoredEvents<E>
```

```
❸     fun readRow(rowId: RowId): ContextReader<CTX, R?>
      fun saveRow(rowId: RowId, row: R): ContextReader<CTX, Unit>
      fun deleteRow(rowId: RowId): ContextReader<CTX, Unit>
      fun updateRow(rowId: RowId, updateFn: (R) -> R): ContextReader<CTX, Unit>
      fun lastProjectedEvent(): ContextReader<CTX, EventSeq>
      fun updateLastProjectedEvent(eventSeq: EventSeq): ContextReader<CTX, Unit>

❹     fun update() {
        contextProvider.tryRun { ctx ->
❺           eventFetcher(lastProjectedEvent()
              .runWith(ctx))
              .transform {
                  it.onEach { storedEvent ->
❻                     applyDelta(eventProjector(storedEvent.event))
                        .runWith(ctx)
                  }.lastOrNull()?.apply {
❼                     updateLastProjectedEvent(eventSeq)
                        .runWith(ctx)
                  }
              }
        }.recover {
❽           println("Error during update! $it")
        }
      }

      fun applyDelta(deltas: List<DeltaRow<R>>): ContextReader<CTX, Unit> =
❾ ❿     deltas.fold(ContextReader {}) { reader, delta ->
            reader composeWith delta.transformation()
        }
⓫     fun DeltaRow<R>.transformation() =
        when (this) {
            is CreateRow -> saveRow(rowId, row)
            is DeleteRow -> deleteRow(rowId)
            is UpdateRow -> updateRow(rowId) { oldRow -> updateRow(oldRow) }
        }
    }
```

❶ Now, the projection interface is also generic on the context.

❷ We need a contextProvider, because each projection will manage its own database transactions. This will replace the in-memory list of rows.

❸ All the functions to modify rows and the counter for the last updated event must return a ContextReader, so we can combine them in a single transaction.

❹ The update operation is implemented in the interface, calling the abstract methods.

❺ First, we open a transaction and fetch all the events from the last update.

❻ Then, we update the projection for each of them using applyDelta method.

❼ Finally, we update the counter of the last projected event and close the transaction.

❽ In case of an error, we log it, but we don't throw an exception, because it's better to run the query with a slightly stale projection than to fail the whole call.

❾ To apply the delta, we use fold on the ContextReader, so we have a single reader at the end.

❿ To compose the two readers together, we created a new infix function.

⓫ We extracted the row transformation into a extension function to make it easier to read.

The new composeWith function on ContextReader is simply a shorthand for a bind operation where we're solely concerned with both operations succeeding, and we can ignore the value passed from the first reader:

```
infix fun <CTX, T> ContextReader<CTX, T>.composeWith(
                    other: ContextReader<CTX, T>) = bind { other }
```

Joe asks:

When Should We Call the Projection Update?

This is a very good question!

For in-memory projections we need to update the projection before each query, because there could be new events in the database written by another instance of the service—unless we're sure there is only one instance running.

For database projections, there is also the option to update the projections immediately after we save events on the database. What's the best solution? As usual, it depends. If the application query performance is very important, it's probably a good idea to update them when saving the events. In that case, make sure to use a different transaction, as a failure updating the projection shouldn't roll back the new event.

An alternative approach is to update the projections at regular intervals, such as every few minutes or hours, using a timer. This can help alleviate the system's workload, but the drawback is that the projection may not always reflect the most current data. However, this may not be a problem for some use-cases.

UnaryPlus Operator DSL

Looking at the update method, we have three runWith(ctx) calls. Ideally, we would like to combine all our ContextReader together using bind or join, because, this way, our code will stay declarative; we specify how to combine them without writing the control flow.

But, sometimes the imperative approach is the most straightforward way to express certain logic. For example, I attempted to use a fold in the update call, but it did not work as well as I had hoped; the declarative code was too convoluted.

Calling runWith multiple times and using temporary variables is an example of what we can call the functional imperative approach—so far as we preserve the purity of our functions, it's OK.

Nevertheless, we can leverage the Kotlin DSL capabilities to make the code a bit nicer to read. Using a method, doRun, the ContextProvider will pass a ContextWrapper that can capture the current context using unary Operators, on page 388.

```kotlin
interface ContextProvider<CTX> {
    fun <T> tryRun(reader: ContextReader<CTX, T>): Outcome<ContextError, T>

    fun <T> doRun(block: ContextWrapper<CTX>.() -> T) =
        tryRun(ContextReader { ctx -> block(ContextWrapper(ctx)) } )
}

data class ContextWrapper<CTX>(val context: CTX) {
  operator fun <T> ContextReader<CTX, T>.unaryPlus(): T = runWith(context)
}
```

This allows us to rewrite the update method using little + signs instead of run-With(ctx):

```kotlin
fun update() {
    contextProvider.doRun {
      eventFetcher(+lastProjectedEvent())
        .transform {
            it.onEach { storedEvent ->
                +applyDelta(eventProjector(storedEvent.event))
            }.lastOrNull()?.apply {
                +updateLastProjectedEvent(eventSeq)
            }
        }
    }.recover {
        println("Error during update! $it")
    }
}
```

Is it better this way? Not necessarily. It's a matter of personal taste, but it's an interesting technique. The advantage of using the unaryPlus operator, rather than another operator, is that it has no other possible use.

Write Queries in SQL

Finally, to complete our projection, we need to implement the queries in SQL. Let's see how the findAll query would work from the database. The other query methods are all similar:

```
class ToDoListProjectionOnPg(
    txProvider: ContextProvider<Transaction>,
    readEvents: FetchStoredEvents<ToDoListEvent>
) : ToDoListProjection,
    Projection<Transaction, ToDoListProjectionRow, ToDoListEvent> by
        PgProjection(
            txProvider,
            readEvents,
            ToDoListProjection.Companion::eventProjector,
            projectionTable = toDoListProjectionTable,
            lastEventTable = toDoListLastEventTable
        ) {

    override fun findAll(user: User): Outcome<OutcomeError, List<ListName>> =
        contextProvider.tryRun(
            toDoListProjectionTable.selectRowsByJson(findAllByUserSQL(user))
        ).transform { it.map { row -> row.list.listName } }

    private fun findAllByUserSQL(user: User): String =
        """SELECT *
        FROM    ${toDoListProjectionTable.tableName}
        WHERE   row_data ->> 'user' = '${user.name}'
        """.trimIndent()

//other methods...
}
```

❶ We get the context provider in the constructor.

❷ We need to get readEvents separately, because events can use a different context than the projection—for example, using database events with an in-memory projection.

❸ We delegate most of the methods to the generic PgProjection.

❹ We use the JSONB query capabilities of PostgreSQL to find the correct rows.

❺ Exposed doesn't help us with JSONB queries, so we need to write the full SQL as a string.

Wiring the Query Handler

Now that we have converted the event streamer to using a database, the fetcher function needed by our projection is pretty cumbersome:

```
val fetcher = { lastEvent ->
    txProvider.tryRun(streamer.fetchAfter(lastEvent)) }
```

What we can do to improve it is add a method to the interface ContextProvider to run a reader created from a specific input, in this case, the lastEvent. We can call the method runWith:

```
fun <A, T> runWith(readerBuilder: (A) -> ContextReader<CTX, T>):
    (A) -> Outcome<ContextError, T> =
        { input -> tryRun( readerBuilder( input )) }
```

And now we can fit the query handler quite nicely in the main method:

```
fun main() {

    val dataSource = prepareProductionDatabase()

    val streamer = createToDoListEventStreamerOnPg()
    val eventStore = ToDoListEventStore(streamer)
    val txProvider = TransactionProvider(dataSource, Serializable)

    val commandHandler = ToDoListCommandHandler(txProvider, eventStore)

    val fetcher = txProvider.runWith(streamer::fetchAfter)

    val queryHandler = ToDoListQueryRunner(
        ToDoListProjectionOnPg(txProvider, fetcher),
        ToDoItemProjection(fetcher)
    )

    val hub = ToDoListHub(queryHandler, commandHandler)

    Zettai(hub).asServer(Jetty(8080)).start()

}
```

Zettai has full persistence now, and even if it's not completely finished, it's finally a perfectly usable application. Hurray!

Let's visualize what the overall application design looks like with a diagram. The diagram shows that the EventStreamer and the Projection persist their state using the ContextReader:

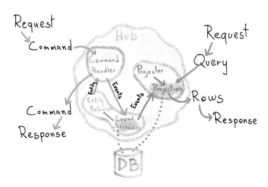

Modeling the Domain with Event Sourcing

Even if this book is about functional programming, it's worth reviewing some best practices to create a solid system based on CQRS and Event Sourcing. We now have all the elements to understand how to build a system-based event sourcing, but how should we design it?

Define the State Machine

The first consideration is that each event and each command should work on a single entity (aka, the aggregate). For this reason, the entity of an event sourcing model must coincide with the *transactional scope*, so that we can always change it inside a single transaction.

Identifying these transactional entities is the first and most important task when designing our model. The Event Storming technique is very useful to identify these entities and the commands that we need to pass to them.

The second step is to list all the commands that we need to complete our requirements. With the commands we can identify all the possible states of our entity. Each state must represent a behavior, that is, a different way in which our entity will respond to inputs.

A good rule of thumb is that different behaviors should be mapped on different states. In other words, there shouldn't be ifs in our code where the same state would do different things depending on internal attributes. Symmetrically, identical behaviors should be mapped to the same state.

Sometimes it's tempting to use different states for the same behavior depending on what happened before, but if there are no changes in behavior, it's better to have a single state regardless of the past history of the entity. States must be determined by what can happen after, that is, their behavior, not by what happened before.

The third step is to draw and keep updating the state diagram for each entity. This lets the whole team quickly refer to it while writing the code or discussing requirements. In the diagrams, states are connected by arrows, which correspond to the events. Each event must have a single destination but can have multiple origins. The arrows can fan in but they shouldn't fan out.

Finally, naming commands, states, and events can be challenging. Commands must be named using the imperative form. Try to avoid *meek commands* like TryToPublish or EnsureCorrectPayment. Just call them Publish or ProcessPayment.

States are *situations* with a definite behavior. If there is no good noun for the specific situation, they can be expressed with verb+ing. Like "waiting for xxx" or "listening at xxx."

Migration and Versioning Events

Once events are saved in the database, changing their format, for example, adding fields or removing them, can be problematic. A good practice is to save the version of each event on the database table—as we did. This way, when deserializing events, we can migrate them to the latest version on the fly. To learn more, I suggest the book *Versioning in an Event Sourced System* by Greg Young.[2]

If an event can't be migrated to the new version, it's better to consider the new one a completely new event type, and stop using the old event. Keep it only for compatibility purposes.

As for projections, in-memory ones can be modified at any time without issue. However, projections that are persisted in a database aren't as easily changed. But, since they can be recreated by replaying events from the start, rather than migrating projection tables, it's easier to create a new table for the updated projection, and allow the update to recreate the projection from scratch with the new schema.

Recap

In this chapter, we looked at how to let our system interact with the database without losing the benefits of functional programming, using the Reader monad.

Then, we put this into practice, making our Zettai application able to persist and retrieve events from database without losing the benefits of our functional approach.

Finally, we analyzed pros and cons of in-memory and persistent projections and learned how to easily switch from one type to the other.

In the next chapter, we'll continue our application, looking at how to better validate the user input and exploring the power of applicative functors.

Exercises

The exercises in this chapter will focus on different types of monads.

---

2. https://leanpub.com/esversioning

Chapter 10. Reading Context to Handle Commands • 260

Here is your friendly reminder that nobody can learn functional programming by just reading code, and the best way to learn is by practicing. You can refer to the exercises folder in the book code repository for the starting point and some hints.

Exercise 10.1: Logger Monad

We saw how a TaggedValue functor can't be a monad unless the tag type has a monoid instance. Now, we consider something similar, replacing the tag enum to a list of strings that we want to use as an operation log.

For this exercise, you have to implement the Logger monad and add a test to prove it honors the monad's laws:

```
data class Logger<T>(val value: T, val log: List<String>) {
    fun <U> transform(f: (T) -> U): Logger<U> = TODO()
    fun <U> bind(f: (T) -> Logger<U>): Logger<U> = TODO()
}
```

Exercise 10.2: Console Monad

Let's consider an interface, ConsoleContext, with methods to read and write from arbitrary streams:

```
interface ConsoleContext {
    fun printLine(msg: String): String
    fun readLine(): String
}
```

For this exercise, you should write a SystemConsole that implements the Console-Context so that this program can work:

```
fun contextPrintln(msg: String) =
        ContextReader<ConsoleContext, String>{ ctx -> ctx.printLine(msg) }

fun contextReadln() =
        ContextReader<ConsoleContext, String>{ ctx -> ctx.readLine() }

fun main() {

    contextPrintln("Hello, what's your name?")
        .bind { _ -> contextReadln() }
        .bind { name -> contextPrintln("Hello, $name") }
        .runWith(SystemConsole())
}
```

You should verify that it works on the command line, but also write unit tests for it using System.setOut() and System.setIn() methods to redirect the streams.

Exercise 10.3: Console Monad RPN Calculator

If you remember, we did an RPN calculator as an exercise in the second chapter. For this exercise, you need to reimplement it here using the same calculator code but using the ConsoleContext to manage the IO.

Bonus points if you manage to ask the users if they want to do new calculations using recursion for the inner loop.

I don't think it's weak to admit you made a mistake. That takes
strength, if you ask me.

> *Terry Pratchett*

CHAPTER 11

Validating Data with Applicatives

In this chapter, we'll meet a new type of functor called applicatives. They are particularly useful when we need to use functions with multiple parameters or combine functors together, like our outcomes.

We'll discover them when working on a new story—renaming a list. Then, we'll meet them again when we discuss validation for user input for our forms. We'll look at the concept of applicative functors, and we'll delve into some of their uses. Applicatives allow us to compose function results in a new way that can be convenient for solving a new kind of problem.

At this point in the book, we're now working with quite sophisticated functional programming concepts. Our code will look less and less familiar, but after a while, you'll appreciate its terseness and clarity.

In the course of the book, you've progressed from a total functional programming beginner to an intermediate one, and we're now going to get into pretty advanced stuff. We started out being very prescriptive, but now we'll see how the design process actually happens, so in these last two chapters, we'll spend more time discussing possible alternative solutions.

In the final part of this chapter, we'll see how to improve our HTML pages to allow for a better user experience. To do that, we need to write a simple template engine. It's a good chance to put into practice what we've learned so far about functional design and see how to take advantage of its benefits.

Renaming a List

Our application is now fully working and the whole event-sourcing infrastructure is completed. We can now progress to picking up a new user story from the ones we defined at the beginning of Defining Our User Stories, on page 3.

The process should be quite familiar; we let the DDT guide us through the implementation. The story we're going to pick up now is about renaming a list. So, let's start writing the new DDT, and let's also introduce a new actor—Ben—who has a list of vegetables to buy and wants to rename the list:

```
@DDT
fun `the list owner can rename a list`() = ddtScenario {
    setup {
        ben.`starts with a list`("shopping", emptyList())
    }.thenPlay(
        ben.`can add #item to the #listname`("carrots", "shopping"),
        ben.`can rename the list #oldname as #newname`(
            origListName = "shopping",
            newListName = "grocery"
        ),
        ben.`can add #item to the #listname`("potatoes", "grocery"),
        ben.`can see #listname with #itemnames`(
            "grocery", listOf("carrots","grocery")
        )
    ).wip(LocalDate.of(2023,12,31))
}
```

❶ We start with an empty list called "shopping."

❷ We add an item and rename the list as "grocery."

❸ We add an other item and verify we can see both the items in the list.

❹ We put the test as work-in-progress until it passes.

To make it compile, we need to create the rename step on the actor and a method renameList in the ZettaiActions, like this:

```
interface ZettaiActions : DomainActions<DdtProtocol> {
//... other methods
    fun renameList(user: User, oldName: ListName, newName: ListName)
}
```

Rename List Command

The implementation of the domain-only action is straightforward—we only need to define a new command to rename a list, specifying both the old list name and the new list name:

```
data class RenameToDoList(
        val user: User,
        val oldName: ListName,
        val newName: ListName): ToDoListCommand()
```

As soon as we create the command, the compiler will tell us we need to handle its case inside ToDoListCommandHandler. We'll leave a TODO() there for the moment, and implement the new method on the DomainOnlyActions, passing the new command to the hub:

```
class DomainOnlyActions: ZettaiActions {
//other methods...
    override fun renameList(
            user: User,
            oldName: ListName,
            newName: ListName) {
        hub.handle(RenameToDoList(user, oldName, newName))
    }
}
```

For the HTTP actions, we need to create a new webform where we put the new list name and pass the data:

```
data class HttpActions //other methods...

    private fun renameListForm(newName: ListName): Form =
        listOf("newListName" to newList.name)

    override fun renameList(
            user: User,
            oldName: ListName,
            newName: ListName) {
        val response = submitToZettai(
                renameListUrl(user, oldName), renameListForm(newName))

        //if success we redirect to the same page
        expectThat(response.status).isEqualTo(Status.SEE_OTHER)
    }
```

We're proceeding from the DDT to the web app and then to the domain. We can complete the HTML page before starting the DDT or after finishing it, whichever you prefer. In this case, we'll leave the user interface as the last thing.

Now, we need to add a new route for the web server to connect the request to the command, using a new path segment, rename, under the single list location:

```
"/todo/{user}/{listname}/rename" bind POST to ::renameList,
```

The renameList adapter function will take care of converting the HTTP request to the command. Let's start writing it like the others:

```
private fun renameList(request: Request): Response {
    val user = request.extractUser()
            .onFailure { return Response(BAD_REQUEST).body(it.msg) }
    val listName = request.extractListName()
            .onFailure { return Response(BAD_REQUEST).body(it.msg) }
```

```
    val newListName = request.form("newlistname")
        ?.let(ListName.Companion::fromUntrusted)
        ?: return Response(BAD_REQUEST).body("missing new listname in form")

    return hub.handle(RenameToDoList(user, listName, newListName))
        .transform { Response(SEE_OTHER)
                       .header("Location", todoListPath(user, newListName))}
        .recover { Response(UNPROCESSABLE_ENTITY).body(it.msg) }
}
```

We'll be using an HTML form to do the renaming, so the method will be a POST, and we can get the old list name from the path and the new list name from the form. This makes it easy to implement the user interface in HTML.

We can now remove the TODO() we left in the command handler, and we can implement the handing for RenameToDoList:

```
private fun RenameToDoList.execute(): CommandOutcomeReader<CTX> =
  eventStore.retrieveByNaturalKey( UserListName(user, oldName) )
    .transform { listState ->
      when (listState) {
        is ActiveToDoList -> {
          ListRenamed(listState.id, user, newName).asCommandSuccess()
        }
        null -> ToDoListCommandError("list $oldName not found").asFailure()
        else -> InconsistentStateError(this, listState).asFailure()
      }
    }
```

We put a note to ourselves that we need to test this. Yeah, I know, it's not very TDD! It happens sometimes that in writing the code to make a high-level test pass (our DDT), I write some nontrivial logic that deserves some tests. Ideally, I should pause and write the test before proceeding, but sometimes I prefer not to stop, but finish the current task first.

Next, we need to define the new event to make it compile.

Renamed List Event

Let's write down the new event and decide which fields it needs:

```
data class ListRenamed(
    override val id: ToDoListId,
    val owner: User,
    val newName: ListName): ToDoListEvent()
```

We put both the old name and the new name in the command, but this isn't necessary in the event, since we only need the new name once we have the list id. In the command, we used the old name to retrieve the correct list, but the event already has it.

More interestingly, we added the owner to the event, even if we don't strictly need it to reconstruct the state. The fact is that the list name and owner must be unique, and keeping them in the same event would make it easier to check it quickly in our database.

Generally, in an ideal world, we don't want to base our events on database requirements, but this isn't an ideal world, and we need to find a good balance between them. All in all, this isn't a bad compromise, because there is a domain-specific reason to keep the owner and list name together, as the second alone isn't enough to identify a specific list.

Now, the projections can't compile, because they don't know how to project the new event. We can put a temporary TODO() there and promise to come back soon.

Everything compiles now, and the tests will remind us to add a new case to the function toToDoListEvent for the new event. After that, we need a test to assure us that the folding of the event is working as intended:

```
@Test
fun `renaming the list`() {
    val newName = randomListName()
    val events: List<ToDoListEvent> = listOf(
        ListCreated(id, user, name),
        ItemAdded(id, item1),
        ListRenamed(id, user, newName)
    )

    val list = events.fold()

    expectThat(list)
        .isEqualTo(ActiveToDoList(id, user, newName, listOf(item1)))
}
```

The test is now failing because we didn't add the ListRenamed event case to the ActiveToDoList. To fix it, we only need to handle a new case in the when, and add the new function to modify the state of the list when we have a rename:

```
fun ActiveToDoList.rename(newName: ListName) = copy(name = newName)
```

Project Rename Event

Now that the event folds correctly, we need to go back to the projections; we promised it just a few pages ago. We have two projections; let's consider them one by one.

First, the ToDoItemProjection has only two fields in its row—the list ID and the item details—so it isn't interested in the list rename event. In other words, processing the ListRenamed event should return an empty list of DeltaRow, because we don't have to change anything in this projection when a list is renamed.

On the other hand, the ToDoListProjection needs to take the rename into consideration, so add a test to verify that it's able to handle the new event correctly.

Here is the test:

```
@Test
fun `findList get a renamed list`() {
    val listName = randomListName()
    val id = ToDoListId.mint()
    val item1 = randomItem()
    val newListName = randomListName()

    val projection: ToDoListProjection = buildListProjection(
        listOf(
            ListCreated(id, user, listName),
            ItemAdded(id, item1),
            ListRenamed(id, user, newListName)
        )
    )

    expectThat(projection.findList(user, listName).expectSuccess())
        .isNull()

    expectThat(projection.findList(user, newListName).expectSuccess())
        .isNotNull()
        .isEqualTo(ToDoList(newListName, listOf(item1)))
}
```

To make it pass, we need to change how to handle the new event in the projector as well:

```
data class ToDoListProjectionRow(
        val id: ToDoListId,
        val user: User,
        val active: Boolean,
        val list: ToDoList) {
//  ... here are the other methods ...
    fun rename(newName: ListName): ToDoListProjectionRow =
            copy(list = list.copy(listName = newName))
}

interface ToDoListProjection {

    companion object {
        fun eventProjector(e: ToDoListEvent) =
            when (e) {
```

```
//  ... here are the other events ...
            is ListRenamed -> UpdateRow(e.rowId()) { rename(e.newName) }
        }.toSingle()
    }
}
```

Now, all the projection tests are passing, both within the memory projection and the persisted one.

Invalid Rename Errors

We're not finished yet. So far, we've only considered the happy path; we now need to verify any possible errors. How can a rename fail?

One possible way is if we picked up a name for the list that's already used. We can quickly add a test for it on the command handler:

```
@Test
fun `Rename list fails if a list with same name already exists`() {

    handler(CreateToDoList(user, name)).expectSuccess()

    val newName = randomListName()
    handler(CreateToDoList(user, newName)).expectSuccess()
    val res = handler(RenameToDoList(user, name, newName)).expectFailure()
    expectThat(res).isA<ToDoListCommandError>()
}
```

Since we didn't consider this case until now, we shouldn't really be surprised that the test fails. We forgot to consider if the new name was already taken when implementing the command! What we need to do is to search the database for both a list with the old name and one with the new name. If the former is present and the latter isn't, we can proceed.

Otherwise, we'll return an error:

```
fun RenameToDoList.execute(): CommandOutcomeReader<CTX> =
❶  retrieveOldAndNewListName()
❷    .transform { (listState, newNameList) ->
        when (listState) {
            is ActiveToDoList -> {
❸              if (newNameList != null)
                    ToDoListCommandError("list $newName already exists")
                        .asFailure()
                else
                    ListRenamed(listState.id, user, newName)
❹                      .asCommandSuccess()
            }
            null -> ToDoListCommandError("list $oldName not found")
                        .asFailure()
            else -> InconsistentStateError(this, listState).asFailure()
```

```
        }
    }
fun RenameToDoList.retrieveOldAndNewListName():
        ContextReader<CTX, Pair<ToDoListState?, ToDoListState?>> =

    eventStore.retrieveByNaturalKey(UserListName(user, oldName))
        .bind { currList ->
            eventStore.retrieveByNaturalKey(UserListName(user, newName))
                .transform { currList to it }
    }
```

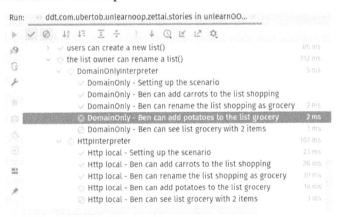

❶ We created a new function called retrieveOldAndNewListName.

❷ It returns a pair of nullable list states. The first is the current state, and the second is the state of the list with the new candidate name, if the name exists.

❸ If the new name is already used by another list, we return a failure.

❹ In case of success, we return the new event.

❺ Here, we need to create a pair from two readers. We'll look more at this function in the next section.

Let the DDT Pass

We're now fairly confident that our DDT will pass, so we can run it and...oops! It actually fails at the last step:

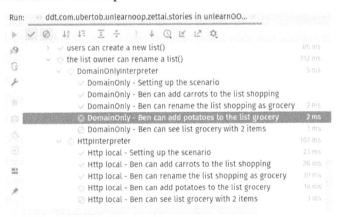

We can see the error message:

org.opentest4j.AssertionFailedError: Failure(error=ToDoListCommandError(msg=list   List-
Name(name=grocery) not found)) expected success but was   ToDoListCommandError(msg=list
ListName(name=grocery) not found)

It seems that once we renamed the list, the commands were not able to find it with the new name. Since it's failing for both the HTTP and the domain-only protocols, it seems to be an error in our domain logic. In this case, it's better to investigate using the domain-only version since it's easier to debug and faster to run.

Looking at the existing code, now that we know what to look for, it's clear that the problem is that we didn't change the logic after adding the rename event:

```
override fun retrieveIdFromNaturalKey(key: UserListName) =
    InMemoryEventsReader { events ->
        events.get()
            .map(ToDoListStoredEvent::event)
            .firstOrNull { it == ListCreated(it.id, key.user, key.listName) }
            ?.id
    }
```

When we wrote it, we only considered the list name in the initial ListCreated event.

So, first we write a unit test that highlights the problem and fails:

```
@Test
fun `RetrieveIdFromNaturalKey considers the most recent ListName`() {
    handler(CreateToDoList(user, name)).expectSuccess()
    val newName = randomListName()
    handler(RenameToDoList(user, name, newName)).expectSuccess()
    val newNewName = randomListName()
    handler(RenameToDoList(user, name, newNewName)).expectSuccess()

    handler(AddToDoItem(user, name, randomItem())).expectFailure()
    handler(AddToDoItem(user, newName, randomItem())).expectFailure()
    handler(AddToDoItem(user, newNewName, randomItem())).expectSuccess()
}
```

Then, we need to rewrite retrieveIdFromNaturalKey, taking into consideration both ListCreated and ListRenamed events and making sure we filter them based on the last rename for each list:

```
override fun retrieveIdFromNaturalKey(key: UserListName) =
    InMemoryEventsReader { events ->
        events.get()
            .mapNotNull {
                when (val e = it.event) {
                    is ListCreated -> if (e.owner == key.user)
                            e.id to e.name else null
                    is ListRenamed -> if (e.owner == key.user)
                        e.id to e.newName else null
```

```
                    else -> null
              }
        }
        .groupBy({ it.first }, { it.second })
        .filter { it.value.lastOrNull() == key.listName }
        .keys.singleOrNull()
}
```

Now the new test and the domain-only DDT are passing, but the HTTP DDT is still failing. At this point, we have a strong hint that the remaining problem must be in the SQL query. Before fixing the code as usual, let's write the equivalent of the former test for the SQL integration:

```
@Test
fun `RetrieveIdFromNaturalKey considers the most recent name of a list`() {
    val name = randomListName()
    val newName = randomListName()
    val newNewName = randomListName()
    val listId = ToDoListId.mint()

    val eventsToStore = listOf(
        ListCreated(listId, user, name),
        ListRenamed(listId, user, newName),
        ListRenamed(listId, user, newNewName)
    )

    transactionProvider.doRun {
        +streamer.store(eventsToStore)

        expectThat(
          +streamer.retrieveIdFromNaturalKey(UserListName(user, name))
        ).isNull()

        expectThat(
          +streamer.retrieveIdFromNaturalKey(UserListName(user, newName))
        ).isNull()

        expectThat(
          +streamer.retrieveIdFromNaturalKey(UserListName(user, newNewName))
        ).isEqualTo(listId)
    }.expectSuccess()
}
```

The new test is failing. We probably should have written the command test the same way we wrote the projection abstract tests (Persist a Projection, on page 251), to make it run it twice—first with a stubbed in-memory only version and then on the actual database. Well, this is a good idea for a future refactoring!

To make this test pass, we'll use a more sophisticated SQL that considers also the ListRenamed event and picks up the most recent rename name for each list. The logic is the same as the memory-only version but written in SQL instead of Kotlin:

```
fun createToDoListEventStreamerOnPg(): ToDoListEventStreamerTx =
    EventStreamerTx(toDoListEventsTable, toDoListEventParser()) { """
SELECT entity_id
FROM   todo_list_events INNER JOIN (
        SELECT MAX(id) as maxid
        FROM   todo_list_events
        WHERE  json_data ->> 'owner' = '${it.user.name}'
               AND event_type in ('ListCreated', 'ListRenamed')
        GROUP BY entity_id) lastRename ON id = lastRename.maxid
WHERE
    json_data ->> 'owner' = '${it.user.name}'
    AND (json_data ->> 'name' = '${it.listName.name}'
        OR json_data ->> 'newName' = '${it.listName.name}')
""".trimIndent()
}
```

Now, finally, all our tests pass, including the DDTs. Hurray!

The nice part of this process is that the compiler and the DDTs guide us on what we need to do next. In this way, we can add the new functionality quickly and safely. When all the DDTs are finally passing, we're quite confident that our application is working as intended.

Transforming Functions with Two Parameters

The main topic of this chapter is exploring ways to compose functions together. For our first example, let's consider the function we've just written—retrieveOldAndNewListName. This is the piece of code where we combined two readers and returned a tuple with their results:

```
// retrieveOldAndNewListName
  eventStore.retrieveByNaturalKey(UserListName(user, oldName))
    .bind { currList ->
      eventStore.retrieveByNaturalKey(UserListName(user, newName))
          .transform { newList -> currList to newList }
    }
```

Is there something more generic that can be extracted here? Let me show you a good technique—let's extract local variables for each functor and the combining function:

```
// retrieveOldAndNewListName
    val cr1: ContextReader<CTX, ToDoListState?> =
        eventStore.retrieveByNaturalKey(UserListName(user, oldName))
    val cr2: ContextReader<CTX, ToDoListState?> =
        eventStore.retrieveByNaturalKey(UserListName(user, newName))
```

```
    val f: (ToDoListState?, ToDoListState?) ->
                       Pair<ToDoListState?, ToDoListState?> = ::Pair

    return cr1.bind { v1 ->
        cr2.transform{ v2 -> f(v1, v2)}
    }
}
```

Looking at the last line, it seems we have found something quite generic. We created a new ContextReader using a function with two input parameters. We can continue, extracting that last line into a new function that we can call transform2, because it transforms two functors to a new one using a function that combines their generic types:

```
fun <CTX, A, B, R> transform2(
    first: ContextReader<CTX, A>,
    second: ContextReader<CTX, B>,
    f: (A, B) -> R
): ContextReader<CTX, R> =
    first.bind { a ->
        second.transform { b ->
            f(a, b)
        }
    }
```

If we inline, the bind is probably even clearer:

```
fun <ERR : OutcomeError, A, B, R> transform2(
    first: Outcome<ERR, A>,
    second: Outcome<ERR, B>,
    f: (A, B) -> R
): Outcome<ERR, R> =
    when (first){
        is Failure -> first
        is Success -> second.transform {b -> f(first.value, b) }
    }
```

As a comparison, if we write down transform as a pure function instead of a member function, we can see how similar their signatures are:

```
//transform
(Outcome<ERR, A>, f: (A)-> R) -> Outcome<ERR, R>

//transform2
(Outcome<ERR, A>, Outcome<ERR, B>, f: (A,B)-> R) -> Outcome<ERR, R>
```

Keep this in mind, because we'll return to tranform2 multiple times in this chapter.

For the moment, let's finish the refactoring of retrieveOldAndNewListName:

```
private fun RenameToDoList.retrieveOldAndNewListName() =
    transform2(
```

```
            eventStore.retrieveByNaturalKey(UserListName(user, oldName)),
            eventStore.retrieveByNaturalKey(UserListName(user, newName)),
            ::Pair
    )
```

The result is clearer now, so for the moment we can be satisfied.

User Inputs Validation

For another example of combining functors, let's consider validation. All applications need some kind of user input validation. The goal of validation is to intercept the data inserted by the user of our application, and make sure that it's correct before processing it.

Let's start from validating the name of a new list; this will be useful for both new list creation and renaming. We have some requirements to verify:

1. The list name is at least three characters long.
2. It's no longer than thirty characters.
3. It shouldn't contain spaces, slashes, and other characters not valid in URLs.

We can surely write a function that verifies all these requirements, but it would definitely be easier to read and use if we have a few smaller functions, one for each rule, that we can use to verify each validation independently.

Not only will our code be neater, we'll be able to show users all the errors together, so they can fix them in one go rather than having to fix the name length only to discover that it also contains invalid characters.

Collect Errors

This is the current check to validate the name of the list:

```
fun fromUntrusted(name: String): ListName? =
    if (name.matches(pathElementPattern) && name.length in 1..40)
        fromTrusted(name) else null
```

We already had written a test to validate this, but rather than a generic null, we want to return an Outcome with the specific reason for the failure. Let's start writing a test for it:

```
@Test
fun `Names longer than 40 chars are not valid`() {
    stringsGenerator(validCharset, 41, 200)
        .take(100)
        .forEach {
```

```
        val failure = ListName.fromUntrusted(it).expectFailure()
        expectThat(failure.msg).contains("is too long")
    }
}
```

Where to start? First, we need to split the validation into smaller functions.

As you may remember, we defined a nice little function in one of the exercises in Exercise 4.1: DiscardUnless, on page 103, to return null if a Boolean condition was false, and we called it discardUnless:

```
fun <T> T.discardUnless(predicate: T.() -> Boolean): T? =
    takeIf { predicate(it) }
```

Using it together with failIfNull, we can rewrite our functions in a more concise and maybe clearer way:

```
fun nameTooShort(name: String): Outcome<ValidationError, String> =
    name.discardUnless { length >= 3 }
        .failIfNull(ValidationError("Name is too short!"))

fun nameTooLong(name: String): Outcome<ValidationError, String> =
    name.discardUnless { length <= 40 }
        .failIfNull(ValidationError("Name ${name} is too long"))

fun nameWithInvalidChars(name: String): Outcome<ValidationError, String> =
    name.discardUnless { matches(pathElementPattern) }
        .failIfNull(
            ValidationError(
                "Name ${name} contains illegal characters:" +
                " only letters, digits, and hyphen are allowed"
            )
        )
```

Which is better? Using if or the discardUnless syntax? It's a matter of personal taste and familiarity. Personally, I find the fluent style easier to read in this specific case. The important thing is that you can choose, and it's always worth trying both options to see which one fits better in your code.

Validating with Validations

Getting back to validating the name for a to-do list, how can we combine these functions? What we want is to apply each of them to the same input, and then combine all the errors together, or return success if there isn't any error.

Combining errors is something that we haven't done yet. Every time we've looked at Outcome, we've concentrated on the success case, which is more natural. Still, there are cases like this one where we don't particularly care for the successful result, and instead we want to focus on error composition.

> ⑁ **Joe asks:**
> # Why Not Use a Single faillf Function?
>
> Using a single function that combines the discardUnless and the faillfNull is a possibility for sure, but sometimes using two functions with a single parameter each make the code easier to read. In this case, I think that specific function with two parameters doesn't work very well.
>
> You may disagree of course. It's important to experiment and explore the possibilities. And let me know if you find a better solution.

How can we write such a function in a generic way? A useful technique in functional programming is writing the function with the signature we want and then trying to implement it and seeing how far we can go. In this case, we want to combine two outcomes—if we can combine two, we can can easily reduce a list to a single outcome.

Since we'll focus on failures, let's call it combineFailures:

```
fun <E: OutcomeError, T> combineFailures(
        first: Outcome<E, T>,
        second: Outcome<E, T>): Outcome<E, T> =
    when (first) {
        is Success<*> -> second
        is Failure<E> -> when (second) {
            is Success<*> -> first
            is Failure<E> -> ??? a failure with first.error + other.error
        }
    }
```

We start easily enough, writing down two nested whens to take care of all cases. But, then we get stuck figuring out what to do if we have two errors; we don't have a generic way to combine them. To progress further, we need to add a function that combines two errors as a new input parameter. This way, the caller will decide how the errors will be combined.

But wait a minute! We already have a function with almost the same signature—two outcomes and a function:

```
fun <A, B, R, ERR : OutcomeError> transform2(
    first: Outcome<ERR, A>,
    second: Outcome<ERR, B>,
    f: (A, B) -> R
)
```

The main difference is that now we need to combine the two errors instead of the two success values. However, observe how the generic types have changed. In the success, transform2, the error must stay consistent while the two success types can vary. By contrast, in this case, the success type remains constant while the errors are distinct.

So, let's write a more general transform2Failures function that applies a transformation function to the failures of any two outcomes with the same parameters:

```
fun <ER : OutcomeError, E1 : ER, E2 : ER, T> transform2Failures(
    first: Outcome<E1, T>,
    second: Outcome<E2, T>,
    f: (E1, E2) -> ER
): Outcome<ER, T> =
    when (first) {
        is Success<*> -> second
        is Failure<E1> -> when (second) {
            is Success<*> -> first
            is Failure<E2> -> f(first.error, second.error).asFailure()
        }
    }
```

Note that the types of the errors E1 and E2 need to inherit from ER. Can you see why?

The next step is to define a reduceFailures to collect all the failures and a special ValidationError where we can store them:

```
fun <E : OutcomeError, T> List<Outcome<E, T>>
                .reduceFailures(f: (E, E) -> E): Outcome<E, T> =
❶   reduce { acc, r -> transform2Failures(acc, r, f) }

data class ValidationError(val errors: List<String>) : ZettaiError() {
❷   constructor(error: String) : this(listOf(error))

❸   override val msg: String = errors.joinToString()

    fun combine(other: ValidationError): ValidationError =
❹       ValidationError(errors + other.errors)
}
```

❶ Reduce is a fold, where the result type is the same type as the elements of the initial collections.

❷ The main constructor takes a list of errors. For our convenience, we also create an alternative constructor that takes a single error.

❸ We create the final error message, chaining all the errors together.

❹ We combine two validation errors, merging their error lists.

To go further, we can extract a validateWith generic function so that we can re-use it in other places:

```
fun <T, E: OutcomeError> T.validateWith(
        validations:List<(T) -> Outcome<E, T>>,
        combineErrors: (E, E) -> E): Outcome<E, T> =
    validations
        .map { it(this) }
        .reduceFailures(combineErrors)
```

We can now use reduceFailures with our validation functions to validate the list name and replace the original fromUntrusted function, returning a nullable result, with the new one:

```
typealias ListNameValidation = (String)->Outcome<ValidationError, String>

typealias ListNameOutcome = Outcome<ValidationError, ListName>

data class ListName internal constructor(val name: String) {
    companion object {
// other methods...

        fun fromUntrusted(name: String): ListNameOutcome =
            name.validateListName(
                ::nameTooShort,
                ::nameTooLong,
                ::nameWithInvalidChars)
    }
}

fun String.validateListName(vararg validations: ListNameValidation) =
    validateWith(validations.toList(), ValidationError::combine)
        .transform { ListName.fromTrusted(it) }
```

The new method is working like the old one, but in case of a name being invalid for more than one reason, it will now return the full explanation, and we have a test in place to verify that we're producing the correct error.

Return Errors to the User

We'll see later in Better Validation Errors, on page 297, how to display the errors directly on the form for a better user experience. For the moment, we show the failed validation on the error page. But first, we need to change the extractListNameFromForm function of the routes to return an Outcome instead of a nullable.

```
private fun Request.extractListNameFromForm(formName: String) =
    form(formName)
        .failIfNull(InvalidRequestError("missing list name in form!"))
        .bind { ListName.fromUntrusted(it) }

private fun createNewList(request: Request): Response {
```

```
val user = request.extractUser()
    .onFailure { return Response(BAD_REQUEST).body(it.msg) }

val listName = request.extractListNameFromForm("listname")
    .onFailure { return Response(BAD_REQUEST).body(it.msg) }

hub.handle(CreateToDoList(user, listName))
    .transform { allListsPath(user) }
    .transform { Response(SEE_OTHER).header("Location", it) }
    .recover { Response(UNPROCESSABLE_ENTITY).body(it.msg) }
}
```

So, what have we gained with the ListName validation? We can show to users a much more detailed reason why their input was not correct. This can be very important from a user experience point of view.

 However, returning null in case of errors can be good enough. Combining validations together is a powerful technique, but it's also quite complicated. In our applications, we always need to find a balance between simplicity and powerful features.

We can proceed in a similar way with renameList—we extract the old list name from the request path and the new list name from the web form. The rest is very similar:

```
private fun renameList(request: Request): Response {
    val user = request.extractUser()
        .onFailure { return Response(BAD_REQUEST).body(it.msg) }
    val listName = request.extractListName()
        .onFailure { return Response(BAD_REQUEST).body(it.msg) }
    val newListName = request.extractListNameFromForm("newListName")
        .onFailure { return Response(BAD_REQUEST).body(it.msg) }

    return hub.handle(RenameToDoList(user, listName, newListName))
        .transform { Response(SEE_OTHER)
                .header("Location", todoListPath(user, newListName)) }
        .recover { Response(UNPROCESSABLE_ENTITY).body(it.msg) }
}
```

Are we happy with this? Well this code isn't bad, but all those onFailures with the non-local returns are repetitive and make the code somewhat hard to read. It's now time to combine our outcomes in a better way.

Get Rid of Non-Local Returns

To improve our code, we should strive to express our intentions more precisely and eliminate redundancies. The goal isn't merely to reduce the number of lines of code but rather to enhance the signal-to-noise ratio of our code. When our code contains identical or nearly identical parts, our brains tend to skip over them, which can lead to errors.

These are two of the Four Rules of Simple Design,[1] which also include a focus on passing tests and minimizing the number of elements in the code. These rules apply regardless of whether we're working with object-oriented or functional code.

So, what can we do to remove the repetitions? A possibility is to put all the outcomes together in a generic product type (see Product and Coproduct Types, on page 403); in this case, we can use the Triple from the Kotlin standard library.

```
val triple: Triple<ZettaiOutcome<User>,
        ZettaiOutcome<ListName>,
        ZettaiOutcome<ListName>> =
Triple(
    request.extractUser(),
    request.extractListName(),
    request.extractListNameFromForm("newListName")
)
```

OK, this was easy, but now we have a Triple of three outcomes, which isn't a big improvement.

What we want to do is, if any of these is an error, return it as a failure; and if there are none, to return the three values as a Triple. To achieve this, we can consolidate all the outcomes into a single new outcome:

```
val outcome: Outcome<ZettaiError, Triple<User, ListName, ListName>> =
    triple.first.bind { a ->
        triple.second.bind { b ->
            triple.third.transform { c ->
                Triple(a, b, c)
            }
        }
    }
```

This seems promising. What we did was to convert a Triple<ZettaiOutcome<User>,ZettaiOutcome<ListName>,ZettaiOutcome<ListName>> into a Outcome<ZettaiError, Triple<User, ListName, ListName>>. Essentially, we swapped the position of Outcome and Triple.

We can further improve this code, making it generic:

```
fun <A, B, C, ERR: OutcomeError> swapOutcomeAndTriple(
        first: Outcome<ERR, A>,
```

```
          second: Outcome<ERR, B>,
          third: Outcome<ERR, C>): Outcome<ERR, Triple<A, B, C>> =
②    first.bind { a ->
          second.bind { b ->
③            third.transform { c ->
                Triple(a, b, c)
            }
        }
    }
```

❶ Instead of passing a Triple as input, we ask for three parameters to simplify the calling code.

❷ Then, we use bind on the first and second parameters in the result of the next operation.

❸ Finally, we transform the third parameter with the Triple creation.

It's now time to practice our functional eye. Looking closer at the type signature, now that we have removed the initial Triple, what's the reason for keeping the final one? Presumably, another function will consume the Triple, so it's possible to replace it with a function that takes three parameters. So, this will be the signature:

```
( Outcome<ERR, A>,
  Outcome<ERR, B>,
  Outcome<ERR, C>,
  f: (A,B,C)-> R) -> Outcome<ERR, R>
```

But wait a moment, this function looks exactly like transform2, which we saw before in Transforming Functions with Two Parameters, on page 273, but with three parameters instead of two. We can easily implement this in the same way:

```
fun <A, B, C, R, ERR : OutcomeError> transform3(
    first: Outcome<ERR, A>,
    second: Outcome<ERR, B>,
    third: Outcome<ERR, C>,
    f: (A, B, C) -> R
): Outcome<ERR, R> =
    first.bind { a ->
        second.bind { b ->
            third.transform { c ->
                f(a, b, c)
            }
        }
    }
```

Even more interestingly, we can implement it using transform2 and the partial application:

```
fun <ERR : OutcomeError, A, B, C, R> transform3(
    first: Outcome<ERR, A>,
    second: Outcome<ERR, B>,
    third: Outcome<ERR, C>,
    f: (A, B, C) -> R
): Outcome<ERR, R> =
    transform2(first,
        transform2(second, third) { b, c -> f.partial(c).partial(b) })
            { a: A, fa: (A) -> R -> fa(a) }
```

Now, putting it all together we have:

```
private fun renameList(request: Request): Response =
    transform3(
        request.extractUser(),
        request.extractListName(),
        request.extractListNameFromForm("newListName"),
        ::RenameToDoList
    ).bind { cmd ->
        hub.handle(cmd)
            .transform { Response(SEE_OTHER)
                .header("Location", todoListPath(cmd.user, cmd.newName)) }
    }.recover { Response(UNPROCESSABLE_ENTITY).body(it.msg) }
```

Now, the whole method is a single expression. This is a further improvement, but we're still depending on transform3. If we had four parameters, we'd need a new function. Let's see how we can make it even more generic.

Combining Applicative Functors

So, what we have found so far? You may have noticed that until now we've tried to always use functions with a single parameter, because they are simpler to compose. But, now we have a type of functor that can do transformations using functions with multiple parameters. Functors that can do this are called *applicative functors*.

We can continue to explore the nature of this kind of functor by looking back at what we did for Validating with Validations, on page 276. We started with a list of functions returning outcomes and returned a single outcome with a list of errors inside. Can you already spot the similarity with transform2? Don't worry if you can't. We'll look at it in detail now.

Traverse

What we did with validateWith is map all the validation functions over the same input—that is, our list name—and then combine all the failures so we had a single outcome, either the success or a combination of failures.

In other words, we started with a collection of functor builders and traversed it to produce a single functor with a collection inside. The fact that we collected failures instead of results is a detail; it just depends on which side of the Outcome we focus on.

This operation is called *traverse* and types that support it are called traversables. The signature of the traversable where Functor is a generic functor is this:

```
fun <A,B> Iterable<A>.traverse(f: (A) -> Functor<B>): Functor<List<B>>
```

You can see how similar it is to a map over a collection, where the target type is a Functor<B>:

```
fun <A,B> Iterable<A>.map(f: (A) -> Functor<B>): List<Functor<B>>
```

The only difference is how the two types are swapped at the end! This is very similar to what we did with the validations.

Let's now try to define traverse for the simple Holder functor we used in Defining Functors in Code, on page 167. Let's first implement transform2:

```
data class Holder<T>(private val value: T) {
    fun <U> transform(f: (T) -> U): Holder<U> = Holder(f(value))

    companion object {
        fun <A, B, R> transform2(
            first: Holder<A>,
            second: Holder<B>,
            f: (A, B) -> R
        ): Holder<R> =
            Holder(f(first.value, second.value))
    }
}
```

Using tranform2, we can fold the element of the collection into a Holder with a list inside:

```
fun <A, B> Iterable<A>.traverse(f: (A) -> Holder<B>): Holder<List<B>> =
    fold(Holder(emptyList())) { acc, e ->
        transform2(acc, f(e)) { list, el -> list + el }
    }
```

❶ We start with a collection of some type and then we apply a functor to it, in this case Holder.

❷ We proceed with folding the elements, starting with an empty list inside the functor as accumulator.

❸ We use transform2 to combine the accumulator with the new functor instance created by f.

We can generalize the Iterable<A> here to any foldable structure, including trees, sequences, and so on. The traversable itself has to be a functor, and more precisely an applicative, because we need the transform2 method to combine the values.

Sequence

As we saw, the difference between map and traverse are the two results, List<Functor<A>> and Functor<List<A>>. Now, we should ask ourselves, what if we already have the first result and we want the second one?

In other words, we want to define a generic function that swaps the position of a collection and a functor:

```
(List<Functor<A>>) -> Functor<List<A>>
```

This operation is called *sequence* in Haskell, but since sequence is already a function in the Kotlin standard library, creating a Kotlin sequence() using the same name would have been confusing. So instead, we can call this function swapWithList(), to highlight that it swaps the positions of the list inside the functor with the functor itself.

It's simple to implement if we already have the traverse function. Let's see how it looks with the simple Holder functor:

```kotlin
fun <A> Iterable<Holder<A>>.swapWithList(): Holder<List<A>> =
    traverse { it }
```

Surprised? It could be a bit hard to understand how it works at first. The best option may be to try to run it yourself to understand how it works.

The same is true with Outcome. We could implement swapWithList as a single function, but if we split the logic into two smaller functions, we gain in flexibility:

```kotlin
fun <T, ERR: OutcomeError, U> Iterable<T>.foldOutcome(
    initial: U,
    operation: (acc: U, T) -> Outcome<ERR, U>
): Outcome<ERR, U> =
    fold(initial.asSuccess() as Outcome<ERR, U>)
        { acc, el -> acc.bind { operation(it, el) } }

fun <E: OutcomeError, T, U> Iterable<T>.traverseOutcome(
    f: (T) -> Outcome<E, U>
): Outcome<E, List<U>> =
```

```
    foldOutcome(emptyList()) { list, e ->
        f(e).transform { list + it }
    }
fun <E: OutcomeError, T> Iterable<Outcome<E, T>>.swapWithList(
): Outcome<E, List<T>> =
    traverseOutcome {it}
```

Let's compare the two with a diagram of map and traverse:

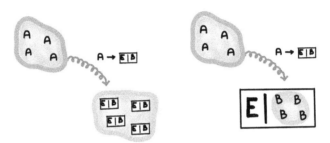

Our swapWithList function directly transforms the result on the left into the one on the right.

Finally, here's a general consideration: all functors are also foldable, which means that if the inner one is traversable—as they usually are—we can write a function to swap the position of any two functors, for example, from ContextReader<CTX, Outcome<ERR,T>> to Outcome<ERR, ContextReader<CTX,T>>; the swapability isn't limited to collections.

Performance Warning

A note about performance of our traverseOutcome implementation. Building a list calling repeatedly list + element can have a significant impact on performance if you have a collection of thousands of elements or more, because it will allocate and copy the list thousands of times. In that case, it's better to stoop down from our immutability stand and implement it using a mutable list:

```
fun <E: OutcomeError, T, U> Iterable<T>.traverseOutcome(
    f: (T) -> Outcome<E, U>
): Outcome<E, List<U>> =
    foldOutcome(mutableListOf()) { list, e -> f(e).transform { list.add(it) } }
```

Less elegant but much faster!

Sequential Application

So far we've looked at transform2 and traverse, but there is another more funda-mental function that demonstrates more than anything else the nature of applicatives: the *sequential application*. This is its signature using a generic Applicative:

```
typealias sequentialApplication<A,B> =
    (Applicative<(A)->B>) -> (Applicative<A>) -> Applicative<B>
```

This type alias is very elegant, and in looking at it you can see that applicatives are functors that preserve arrows.

Still, it doesn't seem to be that useful, does it? But, appearances can be deceiving.

What it does is take a functor encapsulating a function from A to B and returns a new function that accepts a functor of A and returns a functor of B. In a sense, it extracts the function from within the original functor and enables it to directly interact with functor instances.

This provides us with the capability to generate interesting functional effects, as we'll discover soon.

The name *applicatives* itself comes from this application. They were first described in the paper, "Applicative Programming with Effects,"[2] and in mathematical terms they are *lax monoidal functors*. It would be too complicated to try to explain its full meaning here, but if you're interested you can read an explanation in Bartosz Milewski's blog.[3]

Intuitively, from the name, you can guess that they are related to monoids. More precisely, monoidal functors are functors that preserve all the structure of a monoidal category. As we saw in Discovering the Monoid, on page 125, they are all about composing arrows, and intuitively, you can imagine a monoidal category as a category where functors can operate on multiple morphisms, so it can map functions with any number of arguments as we saw with transform2.

Going back to our sequential application, we need to implement it now for some functor. We need to choose a name, and since apply is already a function in the Kotlin standard library, let's call it andApply to suggest the idea that we can use it in a sequential way. Let's start with the functor List:

```
fun <A,B> List<(A)->B>.andApply(a: List<A>): List<B> = flatMap { a.map(it) }
```

---

2.   http://www.staff.city.ac.uk/~ross/papers/Applicative.pdf
3.   https://bartoszmilewski.com/2017/02/06/applicative-functors/

To see how it works, let's try with a simple function to convert an Int to a String, and let's apply it to a list of strings:

```
val l = listOf(Int::toString)
        .andApply( listOf(1,1,2,3,5,8) )

println(l.joinToString()) //1, 1, 2, 3, 5, 8
```

Well, maybe it's not incredibly useful, but it works. To make things more interesting, let's try with a function that takes two parameters. We want to apply them separately, and to do that we need to curry it first.

Do you remember currying? We did an exercise with it in Exercise 4.3: Currying, on page 104. Currying is a technique that converts a function that takes multiple arguments into a chain of multiple functions, where each one takes a single argument. This is how we define it in Kotlin:

```
fun <A,B,R> ((A,B)->R).curry(): (A)->(B)->R =
        { a -> { b -> invoke(a, b) } }

fun <A,B,C,R> ((A,B,C)->R).curry(): (A)->(B)->(C)->R =
        { a -> { b -> { c -> invoke(a, b, c) } } }

//and so on...
```

We can continue up to five or six arguments, but if a function needs even more arguments, it's probably better not to use it with applicatives, since we can't easily distinguish the arguments.

If we curry the function to append two strings, we can apply it to two separate lists of strings:

```
val l = listOf( String::plus.curry() )
        .andApply( listOf("hmm", "ouch", "wow") )
        .andApply( listOf("?", "!") )

println(l.joinToString()) //hmm?, hmm!, ouch?, ouch!, wow?, wow!
```

Things are becoming interesting now! What's happening here? Applying a list of three elements and then a list of two will give us a list of six elements. We're getting all possible combinations. This is similar to what we did for validations at the beginning of this chapter.

Looking at the code, it seems pointless to put our curried function into a list just to use the applicative. A better way is to start with one of the lists of expressions, and then apply the function, as a normal functor. Like this:

```
val l = listOf("hmm", "ouch", "wow")
        .map(String::plus.curry())
        .andApply( listOf("?", "!"))

println(l.joinToString()) //hmm?, hmm!, ouch?, ouch!, wow?, wow!
```

This is more efficient, but the code was clearer before, with the function first and then the two lists. What we can do is create a new function that does the functor transformation on the right-hand argument, and while we're at it, we can also curry it. Let's call it transformAndCurry since it's a transformation on the right parameter. Let's define it for two, three, and four parameters:

```
fun <A, B, R> ((A, B) -> R)
    .transformAndCurry(other: List<A>): List<(B) -> R> =
        other.map { curry()(it) }

fun <A, B, C, R> ((A, B, C) -> R)
    .transformAndCurry(other: List<A>): List<(B) -> (C) -> R> =
        other.map { curry()(it) }

fun <A, B, C, D, R> ((A, B, C, D) -> R)
    .transformAndCurry(other: List<A>): List<(B) -> (C) -> (D) -> R> =
        other.map { curry()(it) }
```

Unfortunately, we have to redeclare it for each number of parameters, but at least the code is the same for all. We can now rewrite our small example in a more readable way:

```
val l = String::plus
        .transformAndCurry( listOf("hmm", "ouch", "wow"))
        .andApply( listOf("?", "!"))

println(l.joinToString()) //hmm?, hmm!, ouch?, ouch!, wow?, wow!
```

Infix Notation

To give even more relevance to the lists and the functions, we can also define an alias with a very short symbol as an infix function. This is a common idiom in other functional languages, like Haskell, Scala, and F#. It's a matter of familiarity and personal taste, but I think it's worth experimenting with it.

For our applicatives, I've chosen the exclamation mark (!) and the star symbol (*) between backticks as infix functions. Feel free to adopt other symbols if these don't suit your taste:

```
infix fun <A, B, C, R>
        ((A, B, C) -> R).`!`(other: List<A>): List<(B) -> (C) -> R> =
    transformAndCurry(other)

infix fun <A, B> List<(A) -> B>.`*`(a: List<A>): List<B> =
    andApply(a)
```

So, we can now rewrite our example in an even more concise form, one that's arguably easier to read:

```
val l = String::plus `!` listOf("hmm", "ouch", "wow") `*` listOf("?", "!"))

println(l.joinToString()) //hmm?, hmm!, ouch?, ouch!, wow?, wow!
```

We can implement the infix applicative methods to other functors as well, starting with Outcome. With a diagram, it's easier to see how the curried function and the sequential application work together:

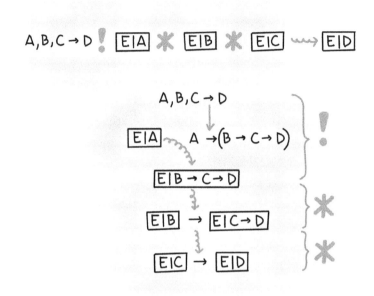

Applicative Laws

To recap, if we want to define an applicative functor we need a type constructor to create the applicative from any type and then the implementation of andApply, or alternatively, of transform2. Note that you can always define the functor transform function in terms of transform2 or andApply, but not vice versa. This is because all applicatives are functors, but the opposite isn't true.

To ensure we're implementing our applicative functions correctly, we need to verify we're respecting the applicative laws, as we did for functors and monads. There are four of them. Let's look at the first two: identity law and the homomorphism law.

The identity law says that if we apply an applicative with the identity function to another applicative, the result would be equal to the other applicative alone. Maybe it's easier to see it in code, using both the compact and verbose version as reference:

```
val x = randomString(text, 1, 10)
val id: (String) -> String = { it }
```

```
@Test
fun `Identity law`() {
    expectThat(listOf(id) `*` listOf(x)).isEqualTo(listOf(x))
}

@Test
fun `Identity law verbose`() {
    expectThat(
        listOf(id).flatMap { f -> listOf(x).map(f) }
    ).isEqualTo(listOf(x))
}
```

The homomorphism law says that if you apply the applicative of a function to the applicative of a value, the result must be equal to the applicative of the function applied to the value. We can translate into code in this way:

```
val f: (String) -> Int = { it.length }

@Test
fun `Homomorphism law`() {
    expectThat(listOf(f) `*` listOf(x)).isEqualTo(listOf(f(x)))
}
```

Note that String and Int and the String::length function here are just an example. For the law to be valid, it should work with any combination of types and pure functions.

The last two laws are the interchange law and the composition law. They are enforcing the same concept, namely, that the sequential application must be completely transparent. The code is a bit too complicated to be discussed here, but you can find the code to verify all four laws inside the file ApplicativeLawsTest.kt in the book repository.

Monads and Applicatives

As a final reflection, let's think about the similarities and differences between monads and applicatives.

With monads, we can set up a chain of operations where each one can influence the next. Applicatives, on the other hand, allow us to execute the operations independently and then combine their results.

In a sense, applicatives are less powerful than monads, but this comes with advantages: we couldn't have done validation with monads, because the first failure would have prevented the others.

It's also common to talk about monadic effects when the Functional Effects, on page 177, of our types work with a monad instance, so they are applied one after the other, and the first failure will fail them all. The term applicative effects is used when they work with an applicative instance, and they are applied independently from each other.

As a last consideration, we have observed that both applicatives and monads are functors, but how do they relate? The answer is that not all applicatives are monads. This is the reason why we can implement functions such as andApply and transform2 without utilizing bind. Conversely, we can always implement these functions using bind, which is why all monads are also applicatives.

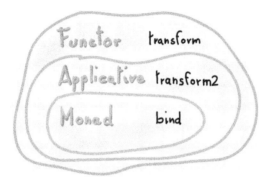

It's now time to go back to Zettai! We can put all that we learned to good use.

A Pattern to Handle Commands

We left our renameList function using a transform3 function. Let's see how it would look if we used the infix applicative form:

```
fun renameList(request: Request): Response =
    ( ::RenameToDoList `!` request.extractUser()
                       `*` request.extractListName()
                       `*` request.extractNewListName())
    .bind { cmd ->
        hub.handle(cmd)
            .transform { Response(SEE_OTHER)
            .header("Location", todoListPath(cmd.user, cmd.newName)) }
    }.recover { Response(UNPROCESSABLE_ENTITY).body(it.msg) }
```

Once you get used to it, the infix application reveals the intent clearly. We can use the same pattern for all the other requests that need to be mapped to a command.

Looking at the other requests, we can extract a convenient function to handle a command, passing it to the hub and binding the result:

```
fun <C: ToDoListCommand>
    executeCommand(command: ZettaiOutcome<C>): ZettaiOutcome<C> =
        command.bind(hub::handle)
```

Finally, to further improve the code, we can extract a function to centralize all possible error responses. The advantage of using a sealed class for ZettaiError is that we can be sure to capture all possible errors here:

```
fun errorToResponse(referrer: String?): ZettaiError.() -> Response = {
    when (this) {
        is ValidationError -> Response(BAD_REQUEST).body(msg)
        is InvalidRequestError -> Response(NOT_FOUND).body(msg)
        is ZettaiParsingError -> Response(BAD_REQUEST).body(msg)
        is QueryError, is ToDoListCommandError,
        is InconsistentStateError, is ZettaiRenderError ->
            Response(UNPROCESSABLE_ENTITY).body(msg)
    }
}
```

This is the final version of renameList:

```
fun renameList(request: Request): Response =
    executeCommand(
            ::RenameToDoList
            `!` request.extractUser()
            `*` request.extractListName()
            `*` request.extractListNameFromForm("newListName"))
        .transform { Response(SEE_OTHER)
            .header("Location", todoListPath(it.user, it.newName)) }
        .recover(errorToResponse(request.referer))
```

We can use the same pattern for all the other commands—for example, createNewList:

```
fun createNewList(request: Request): Response =
    executeCommand(
            ::CreateToDoList
            `!` request.extractUser()
            `*` request.extractListNameFromForm("listname")
    ).transform { allListsPath(it.user) }
        .transform { Response(SEE_OTHER).header("Location", it) }
        .recover(errorToResponse(request.referer))
```

Improving the User Interface

We're finally happy with the code, at least for the moment, but we still need to connect the list renaming with the user interface.

At this point, we can make our user interface more pleasant to look at. As in a real project, to improve the aesthetics, we can't continue to rely on HTML pages hardcoded in our application. Instead, we must switch to serving some static content, including CSS files, fonts, scripts, and so on.

We may also need to use HTML templates to generate our dynamic content.

Let's start by adding a new /static route to serve static content from the resource folder of our application:

```
val httpHandler = routes(
    "/" bind GET to ::homePage,
    "/todo/{user}" bind GET to ::getAllLists,
    "/todo/{user}" bind POST to ::createNewList,
    "/todo/{user}/{listname}" bind GET to ::getTodoList,
    "/todo/{user}/{listname}" bind POST to ::addNewItem,
    "/todo/{user}/{listname}/rename" bind POST to ::renameList,
    "/whatsnext/{user}" bind GET to ::whatsNext,
    "/static" bind static(Classpath("/static"))
)
```

The advantage of putting the static content into the resources is that it will be always be deployed together with our application, making deployment simpler. The disadvantage is that the content will be deployed together with our application, so we can't change it independently. But for a simple application, this is probably the best solution.

A Functional Template Engine

> "Treat every problem as if it can be solved with ridiculous simplicity. The time you save on the 98% of problems for which this is true will give you ridiculous resources to apply to the other 2%."
>
> —Dr. Paul MacCready[4]

We did two exercises in the previous chapters to build a functional template engine. It's very simple, but simplicity is a value in itself, so far as it solves our problem. We can now put it to good use to generate the HTML pages.

For a more complete solution of a similar problem, check out my GitHub repository, templatefun.[5]

Let's refresh our memory on what will be the interface of our template engine. The main function is renderTemplate, which takes the template string and a map of tags that will substitute the special markers in the template with the correct values.

We need three kinds of tag: StringTag for simple string replacement, ListTag to handle collections, and BooleanTag to show or hide a block of text:

❶ **typealias** Template = CharSequence

❷ **typealias** TagMap = Map<String, TemplateTag>

---

4. https://wiki.c2.com/?RidiculousSimplicityGivesRidiculousResources
5. https://github.com/uberto/templatefun

Joe asks:
Why Reinvent the Wheel?

It's true that there are many open source template libraries available, but we'll write our own for two reasons. One is for its didactic value in learning how to write and use a simple library according to functional principles. The other is that if the choice is between solving a problem with fifty lines of code or importing and learning a big, complex library, I tend to prefer the first choice.

It isn't a question of trying to reinvent the wheel but rather to assemble a customized solution that suits our particular requirements, instead of selecting a needlessly complex one off the shelf.

```kotlin
❸ sealed class TemplateTag
   data class StringTag(val text: String?) : TemplateTag()
   data class ListTag(val tagMaps: List<TagMap>) : TemplateTag()
   data class BooleanTag(val bool: Boolean) : TemplateTag()

❹ infix fun String.tag(value: String?): Pair<String, TemplateTag> =
       this to StringTag(value)

   infix fun String.tag(value: List<TagMap>): Pair<String, TemplateTag> =
       this to ListTag(value)

   infix fun String.tag(value: Boolean): Pair<String, TemplateTag> =
       this to BooleanTag(value)

❺ fun Template.renderTemplate(data: TagMap): TemplateOutcome =
       applyAllTags(data).checkForUnappliedTags()
```

❶ CharSequence is an interface that represents a sequence of characters. We're using it here so Template can be either a String or a StringBuilder.

❷ This is how we specify which string in the template corresponds to which tag.

❸ This is the sealed class with the three tag types we use.

❹ Three infix functions make it easier to create a map with tags.

❺ This is the main method to render a template. It returns an Outcome with either the final text or the error.

Let's see how to use it. Since the template text is inside the resources of our application, we don't need to worry too much about the file system access:

```kotlin
fun renderTemplatefromResources( fileName: String,
                                 data: TagMap): ZettaiOutcome<Template> =
    TemplateTag::class.java.getResource(fileName)
```

```
        .failIfNull( TemplateError("Template not found $fileName"))
        .transform(URL::readText)
        .bind { it.renderTemplate(data) }
        .transformFailure { ZettaiRenderError(it) }
```

We need three templates for our pages, and since this isn't a book about HTML or JavaScript, we're now going to discuss the new, fancier user interface. The goal is to show how to integrate with the work of graphics rather than win a prize for web design. The amount of JavaScript is minimal and you can see the actual code in the repository.

To use the page templates, we can rewrite our render functions, taking advantage of the infix notation for tags, like this:

```
❶ fun renderListPage(
        user: User,
        toDoList: ToDoList,
        errors: String? = null
   ): ZettaiOutcome<HtmlPage> =
❷      mapOf(
            "user" tag user.name,
            "listname" tag toDoList.listName.name,
❸          "items" tag toDoList.items.toTagMaps(),
            "errors" tag errors,
            "if_error" tag (errors != null)
❹      ).renderHtml("/html/single_list_page.html")

❺ fun TagMap.renderHtml(fileName: String): ZettaiOutcome<HtmlPage> =
        renderTemplatefromResources(fileName, this)
            .transform(Template::toString)
            .transform(::HtmlPage)

❻ private fun List<ToDoItem>.toTagMaps(): List<TagMap> =
        map {
            mapOf(
                "description" tag it.description,
                "dueDate" tag it.dueDate?.toIsoString().orEmpty(),
                "status" tag it.status.toString()
            )
        }
```

❶ To render a single list page, we pass the user, the list, and an optional error message.

❷ Then, we create a map with the tags using the infix functions.

❸ For the items, we need to generate a map of tags for each item.

❹ We also specify the name of the template file in the resources.

❺ Finally, we render the template and we transform it into an HTML page.

❻ This function maps a list of items to a list of hashmaps with tag and value that will be used to render the items.

I have to thank my friend Asad Manji for the actual HTML and CSS design. This is how the page with the complete list of a user looks now:

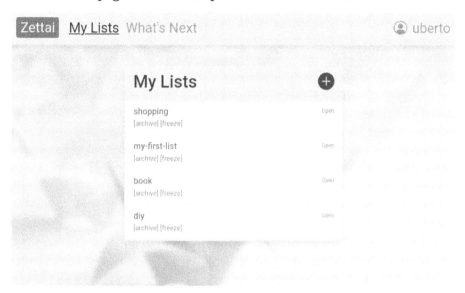

We now need to do the same for renderListsPage and renderWhatsNextPage. In the code repository, you can also find the tests I used to ensure everything keeps working and the changes to the HTML parsing inside the DDT.

Better Validation Errors

As the final touch, we should display our validation errors in a better way so that users can input data correctly without leaving the form. To do this, we'll use flash attributes.

Flash attributes are useful when we want to display a one-time notification to the user. They are set inside a request cookie so that the browser can send them back to the server after a redirect, and they'll be deleted afterward.

To take advantage of that, we only need to set up the FlashAttributesFilter in front of the routes:

```
val httpHandler = FlashAttributesFilter.then(
    routes( /* routes definition here */ ))
```

...and include the error message in the flash attribute of the response:

```
fun errorToResponse(referrer: String?): ZettaiError.() -> Response = {
    when (this) {
```

```
        is ValidationError -> Response(SEE_OTHER)
                .header("Location", referrer)
                .withFlash("Validation error: $msg")
//rest of the errors...
```

To verify it, we can input an invalid name when renaming a to-do list:

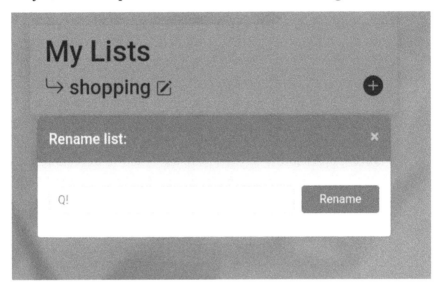

We can see the errors now:

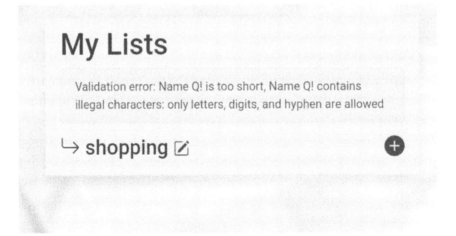

Have we completely finished with validations? To be honest, there is still something missing. Once we add JavaScript to our user interface, we should test that logic by interacting directly with the user interface, rather than only scraping HTML.

A possibility is to implement a new DDT protocol that uses a headless browser to interact with the application. This would cover us for HTML or JavaScript errors, but it will also lengthen the build process. It's probably an overkill for a simple application like Zettai, but it's a possible strategy for more complicated applications.

Another possibility is to keep all the DDT at HTTP level and use JavaScript tests to test the UI over a stubbed version of the back-end API.

Recap

We started this chapter with a complete implementation of a new user story, including making some mistakes and learning how to fix them. I hope it's becoming more evident how the functional approach simplifies finding bugs and shortens the time needed to fix them.

Then, we considered how to do the validation of user input. That drove us to the concept of traverse and how to swap the place of a collection inside a functor.

Generalizing on traverse, we arrived at the concept of applicative functors—a very useful data type pattern for handling functions with more than a single parameter in a functional way. We also experimented using infix functions to make the code easier to read, and we adopted them in the Zettai routes.

Finally, we put a better user interface on Zettai, using a template engine we created in the previous exercises.

In the next chapter, we'll consider how to monitor operations and how to parse and serialize JSON in a functional way.

Exercises

The exercises in this chapter will focus on how to combine multiple outcomes using applicative functors.

Here is your friendly reminder that nobody can learn functional programming by just reading code, and the best way to learn is by practicing. You can refer to the exercises folder in the book code repository for the starting point and some hints.

Exercise 11.1: Reduce Outcomes

We defined reduce for combining failures, but it can be done for successes as well. For this exercise, try to implement this function in a way that it will return the reduction of all outcomes in a success if they were all successful or in an error if at least one was a failure:

```
fun <E : OutcomeError, S, T: S> List<Outcome<E, T>>
        .reduceSuccess(f: (S, T) -> T): Outcome<E, S> = TODO()
```

Exercise 11.2: Applicative Context Reader

We only defined applicative for Outcome and List. For this exercise, try to implement ! and * for ContextReader, and then test them.

You can also reimplement the retrieveOldAndNewListName() function in Zettai using ! and * instead of bind and transform.

Exercise 11.3: Edit List Items

To make our application fully functional, we also need to be able to edit the list items. For this exercise, you need to implement a new story to allow the user to edit a single list item.

You should start writing the DDT first, and then try to make it pass, as we saw in past chapters.

The command EditToDoItem is present but commented out, so you can de-comment it and make the adjustment to compile. Note that you don't need to create new events for this story, just emit them in the right order.

To finish the story, you need to add tests for projections, and add the HTML UI for the user.

Exercise 11.4: Delete List Items

This exercise also consists in implementing a new story, in this case, deleting a simple item from a list.

You must start with the DDT and progress as specified in the previous exercise.

CHAPTER 12

Monitoring and Functional JSON

In this chapter, we'll finish our application and learn new functional concepts.

First, we'll see why monitoring is important and how to produce good logs in our application in a purely functional style.

Then, we'll put this into practice logging all the operation of our hub. The functional approach allows us to do it cleanly, without affecting our domain and with little centralized code, which will be easy to change and maintain.

Next, we'll see how we can parse and serialize our types using JSON format without using reflection and exceptions, in a completely safe, functional way. We'll also look at how to map relations using profunctors in functional programming.

Finally, we'll also add logs for our database layer, completing the Zettai application.

Monitoring Our Application

As professional developers, we should keep in mind that simply ensuring our applications work isn't enough. We need to monitor what's going on, and to be able to do that, our applications need to tell us what they are doing.

Broadly speaking, this process of releasing information is referred to as logging. The simplest solution for logging is to append the significant events on a local file, line by line. This file would be the log file of the application. In the old days, when our applications were running on only one or two servers, it was common to directly access that file and dig for information.

The debugging activity consisted mainly of walking through the application code and the log file together to see the point where things went pear shaped.

And if it was not clear, we'd add some more logging statements in the code and run the application again trying to reproduce the issue.

Those log files tended to become very big, and trying to understand what happened was a time-consuming activity, especially when there were multiple threads logging in parallel.

Cloud-Monitoring Platforms

The general activity of reading logs to extract relevant information in real time is called *monitoring*. With the advent of the cloud and microservices architecture, monitoring has become more difficult, because it's no longer sufficient to read a log file; we need to aggregate logs from multiple machines across the net.

Luckily for us, aggregating logs is a common issue for distributed architectures, and a new kind of service was born to specifically solve this problem. Now, there are several ready-to-use solutions available. They are all based on the idea to send any new log row to a central server that will store the information in some kind of fully searchable database.

Some solutions are open source, like ELK-stack,[1] and some are commercial, like Splunk.[2] They usually have a user interface to allow users to search through the aggregate log data but also to generate alerts, reports, and visualizations from the information logged.

This is important because we can use the logs not only for helping us with debugging but also to constantly get updates on critical business indicators.

For example, we can measure how many new users subscribed each day and how often they use our application. These reports can be automatically sent to the stakeholders, to evaluate sales strategy, UI changes, and so on.

Finally, we can also use logs to record timings so we can constantly check if the system performs well. A look at any dashboard can tell us when the system started having problems—maybe because it had too much load or because a bug was present in the last commit. (Yes, it does also happen in a functional code base.)

For the purposes of this book, we'll assume someone else did the monitor platform for the log aggregator, and we'll just make sure that our application

---

1. https://www.elastic.co/what-is/elk-stack
2. https://www.splunk.com

writes its log on a local file that will somehow be aggregated in a centralized monitoring dashboard.

Functional Logging

So, why are we talking about monitoring in a book on functional programming? The reason is that logging is a very important requirement for every application and the functional approach requires specific solutions.

We need to analyze two things: where to put the logging in a functional application and how to design and implement a functional logger.

But before we start designing our functional solution, let's examine what's problematic in the industry standard approach of logging, especially from a functional point of view.

Traditional Logging

In all honesty, my personal opinion is that the standard way in which logging is implemented in most JVM-based applications is one of the worst "best practices" of our industry.

As a representative example of what I mean, we can look at the library SLF4j, which is considered the gold standard of logging libraries. It's described on its web page as follows: "The Simple Logging Facade for Java (SLF4J) serves as a simple facade or abstraction for various logging frameworks (e.g., java.util.logging, logback, log4j) allowing the end user to plug in the desired logging framework at deployment time."[3]

This is a brief example of its use:

```
import org.slf4j.Logger;
import org.slf4j.LoggerFactory;

public class HelloWorld {
  public static void main(String[] args) {
    Logger logger = LoggerFactory.getLogger(HelloWorld.class);
    logger.info("Hello World");
  }
}
```

As you can see, it's based on a static method, getLogger, that returns the logger singleton for the class passed—HelloWorld in our case. The logger has multiple functions depending on the severity of the log (debug, info, error, and so on).

---

3. https://www.slf4j.org/manual.html

Since the logger is associated with the class where it's called from, it's possible to configure the log level externally with a selection on the packages hierarchy.

The advantage of this approach is that it's very easy to add new loggers and log messaging and then set up the log level—the severity threshold that determines which messages are recorded—of each one using an external configuration, usually an XML file.

Unfortunately, this approach to logging has several disadvantages:

1. There is no easy way to test that our methods are generating the right logs or not, unless we parse the log files or use a special configuration for tests.

2. Configurations can be very obscure, and it's easy to make mistakes.

3. Since all logs are string messages, it's not straightforward to log complex data structures.

4. The log severity levels are decided by the programmers when writing the code, but they often don't fit the monitoring requirements when the application is running.

5. The package hierarchy can be quite opaque and coarse grained. It's hard to understand what we want to enable and disable.

6. Security concerns: many logger libraries have little known features that can be exploited for malicious intents.

Moreover, there is another concern for functional programmers: loggers are completely referentially opaque, and we have no idea if a method will log something without checking all its code and the code of the functions it calls.

Apart from the purity point of view, making log calls in the application critical path can have serious performance impact; likewise, missing the logging of an important operation can make it hard to debug production issues. As functional programmers, we don't like these kinds of surprises.

Let's provide our wish list of what our logger functions should look like:

1. There should be no global singletons referenced everywhere; loggers should be created at the top level and explicitly passed where needed.

2. Each log message should be typed so we can make sure that all the data we need is included and not just concatenating strings.

3. Instead of log levels, we want to define why we're logging something. (Did we successfully complete something important? Are there actions to be taken for this error?)

4. For errors, we want to attach to the log entry all the relevant data to make it easier to reconstruct the cause of the problem.

Pepperdine's Law of Logging

If we think from a fresh point of view about the logging operation, we can see that there are only two possible things we want to log: what we did if everything went well—the success case—and exactly what went wrong—the error case. In the first case, we log data because we want to collect metrics (performance, KPIs, and so on), and in the second case, we log them because we want to be notified of errors, and we want all the information that can be useful to fix them.

> Log as much as you can when things go wrong, log as little as you dare when things go well.
>
> —Kirk Pepperdine

Kirk Pepperdine is one of the top experts on performance tuning of the JVM. His job often requires him to quickly fix bugs and performance bottlenecks on big projects without having the time to get familiar with their code. As you can imagine, having good logs makes his job much easier. He gave me the quoted advice when discussing debugging and logs, and I've found this advice very useful on numerous occasions.

To apply this principle, we must consider its underlying assumption, which is that we can invariably determine whether things went well or not so well.

Fortunately, in our application, the way we use outcomes makes our job here very easy. The reason is that we need not be concerned about the types of exceptions that could be thrown, nor their significance, since we have already captured them in outcomes at the source.

Moreover, since our errors constitute a sealed hierarchy, adding supplementary information, when required, to enrich the context of each error is quite straightforward.

Test-Driven Logging

Since we said that logging is an important requirement of our application, we want it covered by tests. Let's start writing a couple of tests to verify that we're logging the result of a command for both the success case and the error case.

As we did many times before, we'll listen to these tests to determine the best way to design the functionality. Let's start with the simplest possible test:

```
internal class LoggerTest {
    val failingHub = TODO()
    val logger = TODO()
    val logs: List<String> = emptyList()

    @Test
    fun `commands log when there is a failure`() {
        Zettai(failingHub, logger)
            .httpHandler(Request(Method.POST, "/todo/AUser"))

        expect {
            that(logs.size).isEqualTo(1)
            that(logs[0]).startsWith("error!")
        }
    }
}
```

❶ We prepare a hub that returns an error for any method.

❷ The purpose of this test is to guide the design of logger.

❸ We expect to find here the list of logged events.

❹ Call an existing route to simulate an error from the hub.

❺ Verify we logged the error.

To make this compile, we need to pass a logger to the Zettai class. This is already an important design decision: we keep the logger outside the hub.

The reason is that logging isn't a business domain concern; users don't care if a website has good monitoring or not, as long as it's working. It's a non-functional requirement for operation and all the other uses we discussed, so it shouldn't enter into our domain—which is represented by the hub.

Logging Pure Functions

Typically, pure functions hardly need any logging—basic calculations like "two and two gives four" aren't worth logging. We usually are interested in things that happen at the edge of our system— we received a command from a user, we sent a notification to an external system, we stored or retrieved something from the database. All these kind of operations are worth logging, but they are done by the adapters, not by the domain.

Since the hub methods will always return the outcome with all the error information, it's safe to log it from outside. Another advantage, as we'll see later, is that if we write the log inside the external adapters (HTTP in this case), we have more information on the external technical details that aren't visible inside the hub.

Considering all we've discussed so far, the simplest possible definition for our logger is a function that takes an Outcome and returns Unit—in other words, it doesn't return anything.

In a diagram, it will look like this:

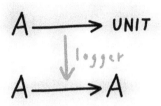

 Joe asks:
Why Return Unit? Is It a Side Effect?

The caller of a log function isn't interested in its result—in other words, even if the logs failed for whatever reason, we don't want to fail our main operation, so a Unit result is correct here.

It's impossible to avoid an impure operation when logging, but we'll try to minimize the opaque bits as much as possible in our logger.

So, to compile the tests, we need to define a type alias for our logger function and pass it to the constructor of our Zettai:

```
typealias ZettaiLogger = (Outcome<*,*>) -> Unit

class Zettai(val hub: ZettaiHub, val logger: ZettaiLogger) : HttpHandler {
```

Now, to compile our tests, we need to provide an instance of the hub with failing methods:

```
val failingHub = object : ZettaiHub {
    override fun <C : ToDoListCommand> handle(command: C) =
        InvalidRequestError("failing test").asFailure()

    override fun getList(userListName: UserListName) =
        InvalidRequestError("failing test").asFailure()
```

```
override fun getLists(user: User) =
    InvalidRequestError("failing test").asFailure()

override fun whatsNext(user: User) =
    InvalidRequestError("failing test").asFailure()

}
```

And, we can add a minimal implementation that outputs a message according to the outcome:

```
val logs = mutableListOf<String>()

val logger: ZettaiLogger = {
    val msg = when(o){
        is Failure -> "error! $it"
        is Success -> "success! $it"
    }
    logs.add(msg)
}
```

At this point, our test is compiling but failing, so the next step is to make good use of the logger inside the Zettai class.

A simple logIt() method calls the logger with the outcome of our commands and queries:

```
class Zettai(val hub: ZettaiHub, val logger: ZettaiLogger): HttpHandler {

// other methods...

    fun <C: ToDoListCommand> executeCommand(command: ZettaiOutcome<C>) =
        command.bind(hub::handle)
            .logIt()

    fun <QP, QR> executeQuery(
        queryParams: ZettaiOutcome<QP>,
        query: (QP) -> ZettaiOutcome<QR>
    ): ZettaiOutcome<Pair<QP, QR>> =
        queryParams.bind { qp -> query(qp).transform { qp to it } }
            .logIt()

    private fun <T> ZettaiOutcome<T>.logIt(): ZettaiOutcome<T> =
        also { logger(it) }
}
```

Note that a single function can work with any type of result since we're only interested in printing them, at least for the moment.

We can now add tests for success case and for the queries, just as we did for the failing command.

Since we want to test the log for the hub calls in case of success and failures, we need to know what the hub will return. Rather than setting up complex mocks or building a FakeHub with some test logic inside, I prefer to set up a failingHub that returns a failure for any call and a happyHub that always returns success.

This makes it easier to write and understand the test. This is our happyHub:

```
val happyHub = object : ZettaiHub {
    override fun <C : ToDoListCommand> handle(command: C) =
        command.asSuccess()

    override fun getList(userListName: UserListName) =
        randomToDoList().asSuccess()

    override fun getLists(user: User) =
        listOf(randomListName()).asSuccess()

    override fun whatsNext(user: User) =
        randomToDoList().items.asSuccess()
}
```

We can now write all the remaining tests and verify they are all passing OK.

```
internal class LoggerTest {

// declarations...

    @Test
    fun `commands log when there is a failure`() {
        Zettai(failingHub, logger)
            .httpHandler(Request(Method.POST, "/todo/AUser"))

        expect {
            that(logs.size).isEqualTo(1)
            that(logs[0]).startsWith("error!")
        }
    }

    @Test
    fun `commands always log successful calls`() {
        val times = Random.nextInt(5, 20)
        val zettai = Zettai(happyHub, logger)
        repeat(times) {
            zettai.httpHandler(
                Request(Method.POST, "/todo/AUser")
                    .form("listname", "newList")
            )
        }
        expect {
            that(logs.size).isEqualTo(times)
            that(logs[0]).startsWith("success!")
        }
    }
```

```
@Test
fun `queries log when there is a failure`() {
    Zettai(failingHub, logger)
        .httpHandler(Request(Method.GET, "/todo/AUser"))

    expect {
        that(logs.size).isEqualTo(1)
        that(logs[0]).startsWith("error!")
    }
}

@Test
fun `queries always log successful calls`() {
    val times = Random.nextInt(5, 20)
    val zettai = Zettai(happyHub, logger)
    repeat(times) {
        zettai
            .httpHandler(Request(Method.GET, "/todo/AUser"))
    }
    expect {
        that(logs.size).isEqualTo(times)
        logs.forEach {
            that(it).startsWith("success!")
        }
    }
}
}
```

Note that the actual command or query called is irrelevant. It would also be possible to write tests to make sure the logs work for all the possible routes, but our goal now is to determine the design of our logger, rather than exhaustively test the functionality, so this would be enough for the moment.

> **Joe asks:**
> ## Won't We Risk Losing All the Logs in the Event of a Crash?
>
> It's a fair question, since we log only after the hub—the domain—returns an outcome. If the system goes down during the elaboration, we won't have any log.
>
> In reality, there isn't much cause for concern for two reasons:
>
> First, if we have a catastrophic crash, like OutOfMemoryError, it's better to investigate it from JVM logs and using a thread dump rather than rely on our own logs.
>
> Second, all external communications—such as HTTP requests, database connections, file-system access—happen outside the hub, and we should log those as soon as they happen.

> Finally, keep in mind that this is just a rule of thumb. If you happen to do something potentially risky inside the domain, for example, allocating a big chunk of memory, it's certainly worth it to log it immediately.

Logging on a Stream

Now that we're happy with how the logger is called, we can continue implementing a logger that can write to any kind of output stream, like a file or StdOut.

To do this, we need a class to keep the state of the stream, which will implement our function type. Note that we'll need to override the invoke method with the same signature of ZettaiLogger type alias.

```
data class StreamLogger(val stream: OutputStream): ZettaiLogger {

    val writer = PrintWriter(stream, true)

    override fun invoke(outcome: Outcome<*,*>) {
        when (outcome) {
            is Success -> "success! ${outcome.value}"
            is Failure -> "error! ${outcome.error.msg}"
        }.let(writer::println)
    }
}
```

To test it, we only need to change the declaration of our test and run our tests again:

```
val outputStream = ByteArrayOutputStream()
val logger = StreamLogger(outputStream)
val logs by lazy { outputStream.toString().trim().split('\n') }
```

It works, but it's not a great design. The class StreamLogger is doing too much, even if it's only ten lines of code. But, it would be easier to extend it if we separate the logic of composing the log message from the details of how to write on the output stream.

To do this, we'll change StreamLogger to receive the functions for formatting the log message in the constructor:

```
data class StreamLogger(
    val stream: OutputStream,
    val successFn: (Any?) -> String,
    val failureFn: (OutcomeError) -> String
) : ZettaiLogger {
```

```
override fun invoke(outcome: Outcome<*, *>) {
    outcome.transform(successFn)
        .recover(failureFn)
        .let(stream::appendLine)
}
}
```

Then, we can create a SimplerLogger using delegation:

```
data class SimpleLogger(
    val stream: Appendable
) : ZettaiLogger by StreamLogger(
    stream = stream,
    successFn = { "success! ${it}" },
    failureFn = { "error! ${it.msg}" }
)
```

More Detailed Errors

Remember the principle: we want to log as much information as possible when there is a failure so that we can investigate it better. In our functional code, all failures are captured in OutcomeError, so we can create a new type to capture the error with some more information about it.

In the case of Zettai router, it would be very useful to have the complete HTTP request from the user when reporting an error. This way, we can easily check if there is something wrong in the request or in our code:

```
data class LoggerError(
        val error: ZettaiError,
        val request: Request): OutcomeError {

    override val msg: String = "$error - processing request: ${request}"
}
```

Then, let's change the logIt method to add the additional info in case of error:

```
fun <T> ZettaiOutcome<T>.logIt(request: Request): ZettaiOutcome<T> =
    also { //the result of logger is ignored
        logger(
            transformFailure {
                LoggerError(it, request) //we log request in failures
            }
        )
    }
```

Since the request isn't available in the executeCommand method, we have to move the call to logIt to every route. As we'll see later, this will also bring some other advantages.

So far, we've only discussed logging in the HTTP adapter of our application. It's a good idea to have a logger in all adapters of our ports and adapter architecture, because this way, we can log all the information from the technical layer before losing it. We'll discuss this more later when we add logging to the database adapter.

Putting It All Together

We can now wire our logger into the real application from the main function:

```
fun main() {
//... setup
    val zettai = Zettai(hub, stdOutLogger())
    zettai.asServer(Jetty(8080)).start()
    println("Server started at http://localhost:8080/todo/username")
}
```

We define a function to create a simpler logger on the standard output:

```
fun stdOutLogger() = SimpleLogger(System.out)
```

Joe asks:

Why Are We Not Using a Monad of Some Kind Here?

It may be surprising that we just write on Sysout. The reason we do that is because of the use we're planning for our logger. A monad would be an unnecessary complication since we're calling the impure logging function just once.

On the other hand, if we need to preserve the status between logger calls (closing the file, getting connections, and so on), using a monad would make a lot of sense, as we did with the database connection.

Generally speaking, monads are a super powerful but quite heavy solution that's better to use only when absolutely needed. When possible, we should strive to write our code as simply as we can.

Looking Back

Let's pause a second and consider what we achieved so far: leveraging on the functional principles of our design, we added the log as a function for each domain operation.

Our logs are pretty simple; they consist of a few lines of very easy-to-understand code. Moreover, having all logs happening at the end of a chain of transformations makes it easy for us to keep them uniform and easy to change.

Finally, we added additional information in case of errors—the full HTTP request—to help us understand what caused the error.

Not bad at all!

Joe asks:
What about the Log Levels?

Although it may sound surprising, based on my experience, log levels are often unnecessary. In fact, they tend to be either too detailed for effective production monitoring or useless for debugging purposes.

I also recommend avoiding enabling debug or trace level logs in a production environment. Instead, it's more effective to rely on additional information to identify and troubleshoot errors when they occur.

For debug purposes when running locally, it's easier to write directly on the standard error and then remove the calls once the problem is fixed. Hopefully, good unit tests make this quite a rare occurrence anyway.

In the next section, we'll look at how to add other information that is much more detailed than a log level to our logs.

What's next? So far we just logged our information as a stream of plain strings, but we can improve our monitoring if we add more structure to our logging.

Structured Logging

The idea is that if we structure the information better, it would make it easier to search for specific details. For example, the previously mentioned ELK and Splunk log monitoring products allow us to search in our log data using indexes and aggregate relevant indicators in graphs and dashboards. But to take advantage of this, we need to write out logs in a JSON format.

Even more importantly, a JSON format would make it easier to store and retrieve complex structured data using a consistent schema.

LogEntry

We start by defining a LogEntry type that will contain the details of what we want to log. We can log the current time, the machine hostname, and the log message; of course, each application will need a different set of details logged.

Since we're here, we can also log some domain-related context data wrapped on a LogContext type that we'll define soon:

```
sealed interface LogEntry {
    val time: Instant
    val hostname: String
    val msg: String
    val logContext: LogContext
}
```

We defined LogEntry as a Sealed Interface, on page 385, rather than using a sealed class, because this makes it simpler to share some fields in all sealed classes.

We then define two data classes for the success and failure case:

```
data class LogSuccess(
    override val time: Instant,
    override val hostname: String,
    override val msg: String,
    override val logContext: LogContext
) : LogEntry

data class LogFailure(
    override val time: Instant,
    override val hostname: String,
    override val msg: String,
    override val logContext: LogContext
) : LogEntry
```

Using the LogEntry type, we'll be sure this info will be saved in all log entries.

LogContext

We mentioned that we want to log a domain context as well. Logging the domain context is particularly useful for collecting business intelligence information. For example, how often do our users use the application? How long is the average session? How many lists does each user create?

To make it easy to collect this data, we define the LogContext type with an OperationKind and fields for user and the list name. We'll keep these nullable, because in some cases we won't be able to determine them:

```
data class LogContext(
    val desc: String,
    val kind: OperationKind,
    val user: User?,
    val listName: ListName?)

enum class OperationKind { Command, Query }
```

To make use of the LogContext, we need to change our ZettaiLogger type alias and the StreamLogger class, since we can't infer it from the outcome of the operations:

```
typealias ZettaiLogger = (Outcome<*,*>, LogContext) -> Unit
```

JsonLogger

Now, we can write a new JSON logger that can use the LogEntry extending StreamLogger. We'll leave the issue of the actual JSON serialization for later:

```
data class JsonLogger(
    private val stream: OutputStream,
    private val clock: Clock,
    private val hostName: String
) : StreamLogger(stream) {
    override fun onSuccess(value: Any?, logContext: LogContext) =
        LogSuccess(
            clock.instant(),
            hostName,
            value.toString(),
            logContext
        ).toJson()

    override fun onFailure(error: OutcomeError, logContext: LogContext) =
        LogFailure(
            clock.instant(),
            hostName,
            error.toString(),
            logContext
        ).toJson()

    private fun LogEntry.toJson(): String = this.toString
}
```

❶ We pass the stream to the StreamLogger.

❷ We use a clock to record the timing of events.

❸ Since the hostname won't change between requests, we pass it in the constructor.

❹ We return the specific log entry type for the success case.

❺ We do the same for the failure case.

❻ We don't know how to write JSON yet, so we use the toString temporarily.

It's also easy to define a function to create a logger that saves the data to a file:

```
fun fileLogger(fileName: String) =
    JsonLogger(
```

```
        FileOutputStream(fileName),
        Clock.systemUTC(),
        getLocalHost().hostName
)
```

Passing the Context

We need to pass the context and some description of the operation to each of the hub methods. This allows us to put more specific information, but it's a more verbose solution than calling logIt only in the executeCommand and executeQuery methods.

There is no perfect solution; as usual it depends on our needs. Assuming we want more detailed logs, we need to change the logIt functions, adding more parameters:

```
private fun <T> ZettaiOutcome<T>.logIt(
    kind: OperationKind,
    description: String,
    request: Request,
    describeSuccess: (T) -> String
): ZettaiOutcome<T> =
    also {
        logger(
            transform(describeSuccess)
                .transformFailure {
                    LoggerError(it, request)
                },
            LogContext(
                description,
                kind,
                request.extractUser().orNull(),
                request.extractListName().orNull()
            )
        )
    }
```

❶ This is the enum with the kind of operation we're logging.

❷ Here, we put a longer description of the operation.

❸ The full HTTP request is logged only in case of errors.

❹ This function renders the return value as text.

❺ In the logger call, after the outcome, we add the LogContext.

Here is how we call it, taking a couple of methods as an example:

```
private fun getAllLists(request: Request): Response =
    executeQuery(
```

```
        request.extractUser(),
        hub::getLists
    ).logIt("getAllLists", request) { "Found ${it.second.size} lists" }

private fun addNewItem(request: Request): Response =
    executeCommand(
        ::AddToDoItem
                `!` request.extractUser()
                `*` request.extractListName()
                `*` request.extractItem()
    ).logIt("addNewItem", request) { "Item added ${it.item}" }
```

Now we're done with the logger, but we still have to convert the LogEntry in JSON format.

Making JSON Functional

We already used a library to render and parse Kotlin objects in JSON in the database chapter. It worked, but it was not an ideal solution, so we'll do something better now.

Let's consider what the problems are with that solution:

1. It's based on reflection; changing the name of one of our classes would break the database layer.

2. It's based on exceptions; we trap them but it's not ideal.

3. It does not handle Kotlin sealed classes, so we had to write and register our own serializers or use annotations.

So let's see how we could design an ideal functional JSON library. At the end of the day what we want is to be able to serialize objects of a given type into a JSON string and be able to parse them back. We can translate this into code starting with two functions:

```
fun toJson(value: T): String
fun fromJson(json: String): Outcome<JsonError, T>
```

We use an Outcome for the parsing, because it may be impossible to map a given JSON to our type; instead, we assume it's always possible to serialize our types in JSON.

The next step is to define two interfaces for the operations and also make them generic on the output type (that can be different from a String):

```
interface ToJson<T, S> {
    fun toJson(value: T): S
}
```

```
interface FromJson<T, S> {
    fun fromJson(json: S): JsonOutcome<T>
}
```

So, if we want to implement a JSON converter, it needs to implement both these interfaces for a given type. So, we can define another interface:

```
interface JsonConverter<T> : ToJson<T, String>, FromJson<T, String>
```

So, a class implementing JsonConverter<LogEntry> is a type that can convert a LogEntry to and from JSON.

Now, as you can imagine, it would be quite burdensome to manually write the code to parse and produce JSON for each type. What we can do is to take advantage of some of the Kotlin DSL capabilities to autogenerate the converters from a type that knows their schema.

How can we write such a library?

KondorJson Library

As it happens, I did already write it, with the help of other people in my team, to solve a specific problem in our project: we had to map domain objects to different JSON schema.

It worked very well for us, so we made it open source. This is the second library in this book written by me (the other is Pesticide), so I was a bit wary of introducing it, but considering that there is no other fully functional JSON library for Kotlin, overall, I think it could be useful to present it as an example of what a functional JSON converter would look like.

The library is called KondorJson, and you can find the full documentation about how to use it on the GitHub page[4]. Its main advantages are:

1. It's fully functional and doesn't throw any exceptions; instead, it has very clear error results.

2. It makes it easy to map complicated JSON schemas directly to the domain classes, without DTO and annotations.

3. It's not based on reflection, so changing the domain class name and packages has no impact on the JSON format.

4. It makes it possible to have different JSON schemas for the same domain type.

---

4.   https://github.com/uberto/kondor-json

Its main drawback is that we need to create a type (usually a singleton Object) for each class to be rendered in JSON. There is a tool to generate them using reflection, but you probably still need to manually adjust them.

On the bright side, this job is only needed once, and it's actually faster than creating dedicated classes just for the JSON serialization (Data Transfer Objects) or adding annotations and custom serializers.

JSON Converters

Now, let's look at the converters. First, let's consider our tiny domain types, which are just a wrapper around a String: we don't want to render them as JSON objects but instead use them directly as if they were strings. Since Kondor already knows how to render and parse a String, we only have to provide two functions to a JStringRepresentable class to convert our domain type to a string:

```
object JUser : JStringRepresentable<User>() {
    override val cons: (String) -> User = ::User
    override val render: (User) -> String = User::name
}

object JListName : JStringRepresentable<ListName>() {
    override val cons = ::ListName
    override val render = ListName::name
}
```

Note that you can pass any function, so it's not a problem if the class has a custom constructor or private fields.

As the next step, let's look at how we create a converter for a normal data class:

```
❶ object JLogContext: JAny<LogContext>() {

❷     private val kind by str(LogContext::kind)

❸     private val description by str(LogContext::desc)

❹     private val user by str(JUser, LogContext::user)

       private val list_name by str(JListName, LogContext::listName)

❺     override fun JsonNodeObject.deserializeOrThrow() =
           LogContext(
               description = +desc,
               kind = +kind,
               user = +user,
               listName = +list_name
           )
}
```

❶ For mapping an object, we inherit from JAny and specify the type we want to convert to JSON.

❷ For each of the JSON fields, we specify the name of the field in the JSON format and its type using Kotlin DSL. In this case, we're mapping the desc attribute of our type using a string field. The conversion with enum is automatic.

❸ For the description, we're using a different name for the JSON field.

❹ When an attribute is an object, we need to provide its converter. Since the converter is a JStringRepresentable, it will be mapped to a JSON string.

❺ We also need to provide the constructor method to Kondor converter, using a unary plus operator.

Sealed classes (and class hierarchy in general) are usually hard to convert in JSON. Kondor has a special converter that uses a discriminator field to know which concrete class to use in the conversion.

This is how we can write the converter for LogEntry:

```
object JLogEntry : JSealed<LogEntry>() {

    override val discriminatorFieldName: String = "outcome"

    override val subConverters = mapOf(
        "success" to JLogSuccess,
        "failure" to JLogFailure
    )

    override fun extractTypeName(obj: LogEntry): String =
        when (obj) {
            is LogSuccess -> "success"
            is LogFailure -> "failure"
        }
}

object JLogSuccess : JAny<LogSuccess>() {

    private val hostname by str(LogSuccess::hostname)

    private val time by str(LogSuccess::time)

    private val log_context by obj(JLogContext, LogSuccess::logContext)

    private val log_message by str(LogSuccess::msg)

    override fun JsonNodeObject.deserializeOrThrow(): LogSuccess =
        LogSuccess(
            hostname = +hostname,
            logContext = +log_context,
            msg = +log_message,
            time = +time
        )
}
```

```
object JLogFailure : JAny<LogFailure>() {

    private val hostname by str(LogFailure::hostname)

    private val time by str(LogFailure::time)

    private val log_context by obj(JLogContext, LogFailure::logContext)

    private val error by str(LogFailure::msg)

    override fun JsonNodeObject.deserializeOrThrow(): LogFailure =
        LogFailure(
            error = +error,
            hostname = +hostname,
            logContext = +log_context,
            time = +time
        )
}
```

❶ To convert a sealed class or interface, we need to inherit from JSealed converter.

❷ Overriding discriminatorFieldName, we can specify the name of the field in JSON containing the label associated with the concrete class.

❸ Here, we associate the converters with the labels.

❹ And here, we associate the labels with the types. The labels must be the same!

Now that we've written the converters, we can output the log as well-formatted JSON. Each converter implements the FromJson and ToJson interfaces, so we only need to call the correct method in our JsonLogger:

```
private fun LogEntry.toJson(): String = JLogEntry.toJson(this)
```

Now, when we use the application, we can see a series of JSON entries like this in the log file:

```
{
    "hostname": "pop-os",
    "time": "2022-04-07T09:47:25.345322334Z",
    "log_context": {
        "kind": "Query",
        "description": "getToDoList",
        "user": "uberto",
        "list_name": "shopping",
    },
    "log_message": "Got list shopping",
    "outcome": "success"
}
```

As a final improvement, we can simplify our JSON a bit. Since we're using Kondor, let's take advantage of the flatten field feature to remove the log_context section of the JSON.

If we change the type of the field in this way:

```
private val log_context by flatten(JLogContext, LogFailure::logContext)
```

...we'll get this JSON format:

```
{
    "hostname": "pop-os",
    "time": "2022-04-07T09:47:25.3453223342",
    "kind": "Query",
    "description": "getToDoList",
    "user": "uberto",
    "list_name": "shopping",
    "log_message": "Got list shopping",
    "outcome": "success"
}
```

For a complete overview of how to use the Kondor library, please refer to its home page and the unit tests included with the source.[5]

Meeting Profunctors

So far in the book I've always presented functional programming concepts as solutions to specific problems. But now we're near the end, and for once, we can take a more theoretical approach—let's try to identify our abstraction after we've already solved the problem!

The risk with the theoretical approach is that it introduces unnecessary abstractions, but sometimes that can be illuminating and very useful in the long term. So, let's have some fun together and try to carve out a functor from our converters.

We define a converter as the union of two functions, and we learned that a functor is defined by the transform operation.

Let's try to define a type, FromJsonF, that would work as functor for the parsing operation. Have a go; it's not too difficult:

```
data class FromJsonF<T>(
        val parse: (String) -> JsonOutcome<T>): FromJson<T> {

    override fun fromJson(json: String): JsonOutcome<T> = parse(json)
```

```
    fun <U> transform(f: (T) -> U): FromJson<U> =
        FromJsonF { fromJson(it).transform(f) }
}
```

For a concrete example of how to use FromJsonF, let's say we have a function that parses a JSON file and returns a Customer instance, and then we have a function that takes a Customer and returns an Address type. We can combine them to obtain a parser that returns an Address from the Customer JSON. Maybe it's not super useful, but it's kind of interesting. So far, so good.

Contravariant Functor

Can we do the same with the ToJson function? Let's try the same method:

```
data class ToJsonF<T>(val serialize: (T) -> String) : ToJson<T> {
    override fun toJson(value: T): String = serialize(value)
    fun <U> transform(f: (T) -> U): ToJson<U> = ToJsonF { ??? }
}
```

Hmmm, we got stuck. There is no way that we can combine a function from T to U with another one from T to String. Thinking about it actually makes sense: in the case of the parser, we can parse and then transform the result if successful in the new type, but in the case of the serializer, we can't do the transformation after having converted it into a string. But neither could we apply the transformation before, because we don't know how to serialize an arbitrary U type.

So, is this the end of the story? Not really...if we look again at the types, we don't have any use for a function from T to U, but we could use a function from U to T. We can apply such a function to an arbitrary U, convert it into T, and then serialize it.

Does this thing have a name? As a matter of fact, all the functors we considered so far are technically called *covariant functors*. There is another type of functor in which the transformation works in the opposite way, exactly as we wanted for the ToJsonF; they are called *contravariant functors*.

A diagram shows how they work in an opposite way:

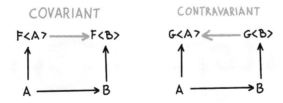

We can render the idea in code this way:

```
data class ToJsonF<T>(val toJson: (T) -> String) : ToJson<T> {

    fun toJson(value: T): String = toJson(value)

    fun <U> contraTransform(f: (U) -> T): ToJson<U> = ToJsonF { toJson(f(it)) }
}
```

Now, the names aren't very important, but the concept of the contravariant functor can be really useful.

Intuitively, a covariant functor is something that contains or produces another type. Our `Outcome` contains a result; our `ContextReader` produces the read values.

A contravariant functor, instead, is something that consumes an arbitrary type to produce a given type. In the case of the serializer, it consumes a type to produce a `String`. Another example is predicates—functions that return a `Boolean` from an arbitrary type—like those used in filters. You may stumble upon other types of contravariant functors when writing functional programs.

To continue with the study of our JSON converter, we finished with two related functors, one covariant and another contravariant. Is there anything we can do with this thing?

Profunctors

It does happen that couples of covariant and contravariant functors are quite common in the study of categories. They have a fancy name (of course they have!)—they are called *profunctors*.

A profunctor is composed of a covariant functor and a contravariant functor that work together as a relation between two categories. They are very important in category theory.[6]

The characteristic of profunctors is a double map function called `dimap`. It's defined with this interface in Kondor:

```
interface Profunctor<A, B> {

    fun <S, T> dimap(contraMap: (S)->A, coMap: (B)->T): Profunctor<S, T>

    fun <S> lmap(f: (S)->A): Profunctor<S, B> =
        dimap(contraMap = f, coMap = { it })
    fun <T> rmap(g: (B)->T): Profunctor<A, T> =
        dimap(contraMap = { it }, coMap = g)
}
```

---

6. https://bartoszmilewski.com/2016/07/25/profunctors-as-relations/

By definition, a profunctor comes with two types, here A and B, and it's contravariant on A and covariant on B. To define a concrete instance of it, we must define the dimap function that accepts two mapping functions and returns a new profunctor with the new types—in our case S and T.

Now, considering our JSON converters, how can we treat them as profunctors? Each converter has the two functions, FromJson and ToJson, but they are both working on the same type; otherwise, we would have a converter that parses one type but can only render a different type. In other words, in our JSON converters A and B are the same type—the domain class—and also S and T are the same type—the String representation of JSON.

To be more accurate, FromJson returns an Outcome<T>, not just the generic T. However, due to Kotlin's lack of support for higher-kinded types, we can't make Outcome<T> into a <RESULT<T>> generic type. So, for the sake of practicality, we'll ignore the outcome type. As such, the Kondor converters are defined as profunctors with a single generic parameter T:

```
interface JsonConverter<T, JN: JsonNode> :
    Profunctor<T, T>,
    ToJson<T>, FromJson<T> {...}
```

Note that the actual converter interface is also generic over the kind of JSON node it needs for the JSON representation, but we can ignore it for this discussion.

All the converters implement the method dimap, so one possible application is this: suppose we need to invoke an external web service named BXT from our application, to obtain some user data. However, BXT employs an excessively verbose JSON schema that contains forty-two fields for each user.

Since we don't use all those fields, we can define a couple of functions to convert from our User type to BxtUser type and vice versa.

Then, after having defined JBxtUser, use dimap to create a converter that uses the BXT JSON format but parses and renders our User:

```
val JUserForBxt = JBxtUser.dimap(
    User::toBxtUser,
    BxtUser::toUser
)
```

Arguably, we could have done the same with a custom mapping without using dimap. However, by using dimap, we have the flexibility to re-use the same technique in case we need to use other fields from BxtUser in the future.

Looking at this example, we have defined a way to go from User to BxtUser and back; in other words, we created a relation between these two types. Intuitively, we can see how profunctors are an abstraction over relations.

But now it's time to come back to earth with our logging.

Logging Database Calls

So far we've only considered logging for calls from the HTTP routes to the hub and its responses. But, logging isn't limited to the HTTP layer or incoming requests. We also need to log other types of external adapters, for example, client to external REST services or messaging systems.

As an example of an outgoing adapter, let's look at our database adapter. We already used a logger on stdout that was part of the Exposed library, and now we want to replace it with our JsonLogger. We're lucky, because Exposed has a very nice interface for logging called SqlLogger.

Let's first add a new operation type, SqlStatement, to our enum:

```
enum class OperationKind { Command, Query, SqlStatement }
```

We just need to implement SqlLogger and translate the call to ZettaiLogger:

```
data class SqlJsonLogger(val logger: ZettaiLogger) : SqlLogger {
    override fun log(context: StatementContext, tx: Transaction) {
        logger(
            context.expandArgs(tx).asSuccess(),
            LogContext(
                "txId: ${tx.id} duration: ${tx.duration}",
                OperationKind.SqlStatement,
                null,
                null
            )
        )
    }
}
```

We can pass our logger when we create the transaction in the TransactionProvider class:

```
data class TransactionProvider(
    private val dataSource: DataSource,
    private val logger: SqlLogger,
    val isolationLevel: TransactionIsolationLevel,
    val maxAttempts: Int = 10
) : ContextProvider<Transaction> {

    override fun <T> tryRun(reader: TxReader<T>) =
        inTopLevelTransaction(
```

```
            db = Database.connect(dataSource),
            transactionIsolation = isolationLevel.jdbcLevel,
            repetitionAttempts = maxAttempts
        ) {
            addLogger(logger)
//...rest of the method
```

And finally, we can wire it to the main method:

```
val logger = fileLogger("zettai-${System.currentTimeMillis()}.log")

val txProvider = TransactionProvider(
    dataSource = dataSource,
    logger = SqlJsonLogger(logger),
    isolationLevel = TransactionIsolationLevel.Serializable
)
```

Now, every time we access the database, we'll have an entry in our log file
with the exact SQL called the transaction id, and the duration of the operation
in milliseconds:

```
{
    "hostname":"pop-os",
    "time":"2022-04-07T09:47:25.336500578Z",
    "kind":"SqlStatement",
    "desc":"txId: 62ebb7ab-88ea-4374-a100-b92d53475f61 duration: 1",
    "msg":"SELECT * FROM todo_list_projection WHERE ...",
    "outcome":"success"
}
```

So, our final log will show both SQL statements and domain actions in a well-
formed JSON:

Recap

We have learned how to add logs to our application for better observability and monitoring. The approach for logging presented here is unconventional, but it makes it possible to get most of the information on what the application is doing without touching the domain code itself.

We also considered how a functional JSON library should work, and we looked at how to adopt it for our JsonLogger.

Finally, we got a taste of profunctors and contravariant functors, learning some theory that can be useful in future projects.

This is the final chapter of our application. We went a long way together and Zettai is now fully working. Now you are able to add new features by yourself following the functional paradigm.

In the next chapter, we'll look at how functional programming influences architectural decisions at a broader scale, and we'll explore how to develop a distributed system split in a modular way.

Exercises

The exercises in this chapter will focus on the logging and completing new stories.

Here is your friendly reminder that nobody can learn functional programming by just reading code, and the best way to learn is by practicing. You can refer to the exercises folder in the book code repository for the starting point and some hints.

Exercise 12.1: Improve Monitoring

As a first exercise, try to add more information to the logger. From the user HTTP request, extract the header with the user's browser information and add it to all of the hub logs.

Exercise 12.2: Remove Klaxon

For this exercise, you have to remove the Klaxon library used to serialize and deserialize events into the database and replace it with Kondor converters for the required classes so that you can remove all the uses of reflection from Zettai.

The final step should be removing the dependency on Klaxon in the Gradle file:

```
implementation "com.beust:klaxon:${klaxonVersion}"
```

Exercise 12.3: Allow Users to Change Item Order

As a new feature, let the user change the order of the items in any list. This would require writing a new DDT, then implementing the back-end logic and finishing with the changes to the user interface.

Exercise 12.4: Introduce a New List State

There are two commands that we didn't implement yet, FreezeToDoList and RestoreToDoList. As the names indicate, they'll introduce a new frozen state in our to-do lists, and the commands will put a list in this state or they'll return the list in normal state. Once a list is in a frozen state, it can't be modified and its items shouldn't appear in the reports. (Or maybe they'll appear with a different color?) You can define the exact requirements.

This exercise will be a recap of all the things you've learned so far. You need to define a story, write a DDT, and then implement a new state in the domain and adapt the user interface to support it.

CHAPTER 13

Designing a Functional Architecture

In this chapter, we look at how the functional approach can help when designing a complete solution too big to be contained as a single service or set of APIs.

First, we'll discuss what software architecture is and what its goals are. Then, we'll focus on how modularity can help us to deliver software that's easy to maintain, functional modularity in particular. Then we'll continue with suggestions on how to make our application modular and how to set up the project. Finally, we'll look at the choices we have for deployment: microservices, monolith, or serverless.

In this chapter, there will be no code example, but we'll use our application Zettai as an example of how to iteratively implement a complex architecture.

Chasing Simplicity

What is software architecture? A surprising place to find an answer is a book by Vitruvius, an architect from ancient Rome. In the first century BC, he wrote the oldest book we have about the art of architecture. He defines architecture as the fulfillment of three goals: firmitas, utilitas, and venustas, which are Latin for strength, utility, and beauty.

These three goals are the essential pillars of software architecture, especially if we can see beauty in code that's easy to understand and enjoyable to utilize. In other words, we can consider a software architecture as effective only if it not only manages the workload but also is easily comprehensible to the entire team. Otherwise, it will likely break at the first change of requirements.

When we design our system, we can't predict what the future changes will be, but we can be sure that there will be a lot of them. So the real challenge isn't to design a system that works perfectly with the current requirements, but to design it in a way that can be easily changed when necessary.

How can we design a system in a way that will remain easy to change even when growing? Let's keep in mind that, everything else being equal, a simple solution is always easier to change than a complicated one. In a more catchy form: simple beats smart every time! We can hold in our minds a small application written in a complicated way. But, once it becomes too big for any single mind to work on, simplicity becomes really important.

So, the trick is to model something complicated while writing simple code, which may not be easy. Functional programming can help us here, because breaking down a problem into small, pure functions is already a step in the right direction. If we continue in this way, it's easier to solve complex problems if we Prefer a Declarative Style, on page 364, instead of imperative style. Generally speaking, writing imperative code accessing a mutable state makes the code easy to write, but much harder to read and change later, since each step relies on the previous steps and the current state at that point. As we saw many times in this book, it's much easier to combine pure functions.

Joe asks:
Err...Is Functional Code Really Easier to Read?

OK, fair enough! To the untrained eye, functional code like the examples in the chapters of this book may appear as obscure as Egyptian hieroglyphics.

However, this is to be expected since functional programming is like learning a new language, and fluency is necessary to fully appreciate its simplicity. Once you become accustomed to it, you'll be able to recognize its patterns in various computer languages without difficulty, and it will be much clearer and easier to read than the equivalent imperative code. Trust me on this.

Also, remember that there is no such thing as "premature simplification"—at least if the application is already working. Every time we have a chance to simplify our architecture, we should take it immediately; the results will pay out in the not-so-long term.

But how can we simplify the whole architecture of an application? We have a powerful tool available—modularization.

Modules and Subdomains

The term "module" in this book refers to a group of functions and data structures that work closely together to fulfill a common goal and can be compiled and released independently. Ideally, a module should be easier to understand than the sum of its parts and should expose a limited number of published APIs to be called by the other modules. In technical terms, it can be a Gradle subproject or a Java module,[1] but it doesn't have to be—a policy shared by all members of the team can be just as effective.

To see how modules can help us, let's analyze our problem a bit deeper. We can visualize how complicated our architecture is with a diagram that illustrates all of its components. The greater the number of components and the more intricate their interconnections, the more challenging it will be to modify and comprehend the software.

You can see in this diagram the typical spaghetti code; everything is connected with everything else.

If we group some of these moving parts into discrete blocks, or modules, then we can easily understand how the application works without having to look at all the details. If we need to, we can focus just on each module and forget the rest of the application. But, this works only if we respect two rules:

1. There must be few and very clear connections between modules. Just putting all the spaghetti in separate boxes won't work.

2. Modules must communicate with the rest of the system using only explicit APIs that work as contracts, and don't, for example, share a common database.

The following diagram shows how introducing three modules that mask the internal connections—still present but not shown anymore—simplifies the architecture; we need to understand only six connections rather than thirteen.

Our goal is to find the natural boundaries that minimize the need to communicate between modules. In other words, we want to discover the smallest blocks of our application that can work independently. If we consider our business domain, we can call these blocks the subdomains of our application.

It may sound easy, but in reality it's a very hard problem to solve. At first, it's tempting to group similar things together—for example, everything related to the User entity. Unfortunately, this approach usually won't produce good modules. The problem with this approach is that we would probably have to expose all the possible ways to manipulate the User entities, finishing either with a module that's way too big or that has too many connections between modules.

A better idea is to look at our intention or the use-case we're trying to solve. If we keep together all the code needed to solve one or a few related use-cases (for example, authentication), we have a better chance of discovering natural boundaries between modules.

Other use-cases related to the user—for example, the subscription payments—will form other modules and will share little data with the authentication module.

Another good technique is to look at the extent of any business transactions. Atomic transactions shouldn't spread across modules, so they can help us to identify them. A module can contain more than a business transaction scope, but the scope can't be shared between modules. Note that there may be high-level transactions that span over multiple modules, but those transactions must be treated as a chain of single transactions that can be reversed with an opposite transaction—for example, using the Saga pattern.[2]

If we model our code in modules that map those groups of related atomic transactions, we can drastically reduce the calls among different modules and make them independent from each other.

---

2. https://www.infoq.com/articles/saga-orchestration-outbox/

With well-defined modules that mirror how the business domain is structured, we can further reduce the number of connections between them and completely hide their internal parts. In many cases, these modules align with the *bounded contexts* of our domain.

> A bounded context is a defined part of software where particular terms, definitions and rules apply in a consistent way.
>
> —Eric Evans

This allows us to successfully split a system into modules or components that we can easily assemble and change independently. This won't only provide us with a simpler view of the system, it will also introduce a new level of flexibility.

Building with Modules

Having our application broken down into separate modules has a critical impact in our productivity as well. This may sound surprising, but to use a familiar metaphor, it's like building something with Lego blocks. We can combine our modules to build different things and quickly add or remove features in our application.

 Joe asks:
What Is the Right Size for a Module?

There is no such a thing as the right size for a module. However, there are a couple of considerations: modules should be significantly smaller than the whole application to be useful, and they should be big enough to represent a meaningful unit of work.

Another interesting characteristic of a modular design is its fractal nature—bigger modules can be composed of smaller modules that can be broken into even smaller modules and so on.

As much as we carefully plan, though, at some point we'll end up with modules that are too small or too big. In the former case, there is no problem; we can easily merge two of them together if it makes sense. Breaking up a module that's too large, on the other hand, is more complicated and time consuming, so we want to make sure that it's necessary before we start working on it.

When Breaking a Module

There is no hard rule, but there are some hints that suggest a module has grown out of proportion.

One is having problems with naming things because we're using the same name with different meanings inside our module (incidentally, using the same name is okay if it's done inside different modules).

As a simple example, if in our module we have an "AuthenticatedUser" and a "NonAuthenticatedUser", but in other parts of the module we don't care if the user is authenticated or not, maybe it's time to extract the authentication logic to form a smaller module by itself.

Another good sign that we need to break up our module is when our module is used by many other modules for different reasons. We find some modules require the authentication API of our module, and other modules require a different subset of the API. We can try to define them the best we can initially, and then keep them up to date. Later, we'll see a good approach for defining them at the beginning in Using a Zettai Example, on page 339.

Functional Modularization

Let's talk now about one of the most challenging problems of a modular design, namely, managing the global state of our application. We want fully independent modules, so they can't share a state, but we also want to avoid too many interactions between modules.

Lucky for us, a functional programming approach can help us here. Going back to the basics, the defining characteristic of a module is to keep a significant chunk of logic, expressed by code, behind a small interface. Ideally, from a functional point of view, we would like each module to behave just like a single function or a small set of closely related functions. Inside, the module can be completely pure—for example, if it's only doing calculations from the inputs—or it can use external storage for memoization (cache) or even implement a full-state machine.

What's important is that, from an external perspective, we don't need to concern ourselves with the internal intricacies of each module, and we can treat the public APIs as completely independent from each other. This means that we shouldn't have functions that must be called only in a given sequence or that have hidden dependencies between them.

In this context, the whole Zettai application we finished writing in the previous chapter can be seen as just two functions: one to execute a command and one to query the state.

This is what I mean with the fractal functional design. We can zoom out and consider all commands as single functions, or we can zoom in and look at the specific functions for each command, and so on. At any scale, we don't need to consider the details of smaller scale to comprehend the picture of the system that we're looking at.

As an example, let's consider the user authentication. Instead of having a public call like `authenticateUser(UserId)` that changes the current state of the user as a side effect without returning anything, we can model it with a function of type `NonAuthenticatedUser -> Outcome<AuthenticatedUser>`, and then we can just use the `AuthenticatedUser` for all functions that require an authenticated user, without the need to keep a mutable state somewhere. Note that we almost don't need to know the name of the call in this second case to understand what it does, since it's already clear from its type signature.

This example may sound oversimplified, but it shows the importance of not having hidden dependencies among calls (for example, `authenticateUser` must be called before `getUserLists`) and instead using the type system to clarify how to call the API. The first advantage is that we'll need to write (and read) much less documentation, which is a big productivity boost, but there are others.

Shared Data Structures

Data structures are a critical component of a modular system. To reduce coupling between modules, we should keep most of them hidden inside the module. However, it's inevitable that types used by public functions need to be exposed. So, we must be very careful with the data structure that each module uses in its API. We won't be able to change them later without impacting other modules—specifically those that are using them. Therefore, we should consider these types as "published," and we must model them with double care.

There will probably be some types and functions specific to the application's business domain that are genuinely used by all modules, so it makes sense to create a module to group all the common logic. But we should aim to keep it as small as possible and question every single addition. In particular, we should avoid generic terms that can mean different things in different modules. For example, a `User` in the authentication module will probably be quite different from a `User` in the payment module. It's better to have two separate types, with some functions to transform one into another, if needed, rather than try to model a universal User that can be used everywhere.

Synchronous and Asynchronous Protocols

Finally, let's keep in mind that even if we used the HTTP protocol exclusively in the form of a function of type (Request) -> Response in this book, it's only one of the possible choices. The same principles can be applied to any other communication mechanism, like Kafka,[3] gRPC,[4] ZeroMq,[5] and so on.

From an architectural point of view, it doesn't matter what protocol we're using, as long as we can represent it with a transformation from an input to an output. Even more surprisingly, it doesn't even matter if we're using a synchronous or an asynchronous communication method. The fact that the response is immediate or will come later is a technical detail that doesn't matter much in the high-level picture.

Of course, in the implementation phase, the choice of protocol and a synchronous or asynchronous communication method can make a huge difference in the performance and stability of our application. An asynchronous function may look like something whose result is to wait for a response and then do something else, but a more useful point of view is to focus on the ultimate result: fundamentally, asynchronous functions are just functions with a delayed effect. Or, we can also consider synchronous functions as just asynchronous functions with a zero delay.

The goal of the call is to produce some kind of result for the user, so instead of considering "waiting for a response" as our goal, we should concentrate on what we need to produce as a final result (a report? an email?), and look at the whole flow as a single computation instead of "independent actors" that talk to each other. Making it asynchronous changes the flow of the calls needed to complete the task and, most importantly for us, it allows the system to scale and to nicely handle peaks of demand. But at the end of the day, it won't change the nature of the functions.

It's always possible, even if not painless, to change the communication protocols without changing the business logic and the general architecture. Making some process asynchronous shouldn't impact (much) the domain model code, only the technical adapters. As always, a good approach is to try the simplest thing that can satisfy the current needs of the project first, and keep the door

---

3. https://kafka.apache.org/
4. https://grpc.io/
5. https://zeromq.org/

open to more complex options for the future. Once we define our architecture following these principles, the granularity of the deployment doesn't really matter. We can aggregate some handlers and deploy them as a single (not-so-micro) service.

Going further, functional modules also match serverless architecture patterns very well. Serverless computing is based on the idea of letting the cloud provider worry about instantiating the computing resources depending on the load, freeing the developers to focus on their servers. It's still a young technology, but it's a very promising model, not least because of the economical advantages over traditional solutions.

Having the code already organized in independent functions makes it very easy to adopt the serverless model.

Designing a Whole System

Enough with pure theory. Let's see a concrete example of how to architect our application with functional modules. So far, we've developed only the core service for Zettai, but if we plan to launch it as a product we need to create other services for support. Let's have a go with how to design and develop such an architecture.

Using a Zettai Example

At this stage, Zettai is a rather minimal application that isn't yet ready for public release. However, we can use it to learn more about our users and the features they would like in a complete product. One approach is to run a campaign where we offer interested users free access to the current version of Zettai, letting them test and explore its functionalities. By collecting feedback on their usage and impressions, we can improve our product, abandon the idea entirely, or move forward with developing a full-fledged version.

So, for argument's sake if nothing else, let's imagine our campaign was an encouraging success and we now need to figure out how to make Zettai into a full product. As I mentioned, Validating Our Stories with Event Storming, on page 5, is a good tool to use to identify the missing pieces and where the modules' boundaries lie.

The developers participating in the Event Storming workshop will write all the technical stuff that's still needed, the head of finance will focus on the events bringing in revenue, like user registration and subscriptions models, and the marketing team will be interested in related events, like user sharing on Twitter and importing lists from external applications. The security expert will write events about authentication and password recovery, and so on. In other words, anybody who is involved can contribute.

In the end, we'll probably have something chaotic, but once we regroup the events around common entities, our different modules start to emerge. Of course, this is only a high-level view, and when we delve into the details, we may discover that we have to change some things. Still, overall, it gives us a great first draft for our architecture.

Let's look at the following diagram. If we consider all the possibilities, we'll need an authentication module, a UI for user support, a user preferences page, the user onboarding process, plus integration with several external applications (such as Twitter, Slack, and so on).

We'll also need a mobile version that will talk to the RESTful API, so we may want to extract the HTML rendering from the core application and have a server-side rendering module, and maybe in the future, expansion features like a wiki and a calendar. So, even for such a small thing like a to-do list application, we'll finish with a not-so-trivial modular system.

Before concluding the planning workshop, there is another important step: we should describe each use-case, drawing all the function calls between modules needed for it. Once we have finished the use-cases, we can look at the rough map of our API. If we note too many connections between two specific modules, it could be that they should be unified. If a module has too many connections with other modules, maybe we should split it.

This API map is a very useful diagram that we should keep up-to-date each time we add a new module or a new use-case. Developers and stakeholders can also use it when discussing problems and improvements. As a real-world example see the diagram on page 341. It is a map of the calls for a project where we adopted the approach discussed in this book, after a few iterations.

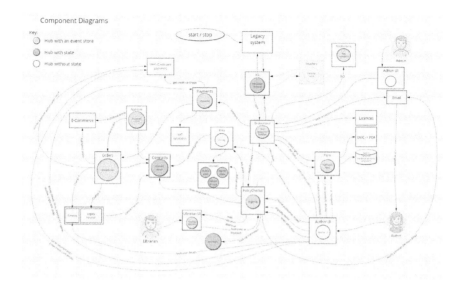

Evolution

Realistically, we won't have the resources to start to implement everything at the same time, and even if we had them, it's still better to develop our application one step at a time and validate it with real users at each step before deciding what to do next.

So it's entirely possible, even probable, that we won't incorporate all the features that popped up in the big-picture diagram in the final product. But on the other hand, it's still important to plan them. As a great strategist allegedly said:

> Plans are worthless, but planning is essential.
>
> —Dwight Eisenhower

When our diagram becomes obsolete, it's time to call for a new workshop to update it. What's important is to prioritize what the team has to build right now—in other words, to keep the backlog short—and make sure we can go live as soon as possible with a product that, even if not complete in terms of functionality, is still viable, that is, can solve a real problem for the customers, even if it's still a bit painful to use. Continuing with frequent small releases afterward, even after releasing the first version, maximizes the chances of success.

For example, we can draw a plan like this:

- Step 1: Adding authorization and onboarding
- Step 2: Adding a user interface for support

- Step 3: Adding a separate back end and a mobile application
- Step 4: Integration with multiple external services
- And so on

But, keep in mind that the feedback after each release can affect the plan, and each release will also change existing functionality, not just add new ones. The usefulness of such a plan is in keeping the team focused on the next feature to deliver, while allowing for changes as we better understand our customers.

Multimodule Application

When we built the Zettai application, in order to keep the domain separated from the adapters, we put them in different packages. This is adequate for a small application, but once we start using modules, we should put each subdomain and each adapter in a different module. In this way, we can keep them separated from each other, and we can also enforce that domain modules shouldn't depend on adapter modules in the building dependencies of Gradle.

A module is akin to a compiled and released entity, such as a jar in the JVM ecosystem, that can operate autonomously. However, it isn't a self-contained application.

In general, a single deployable service—which functions independently—usually comprises one or multiple domain modules, all necessary adapter modules (HTTP, database, and so on), and a module that contains service-specific configuration details, such as the HTTP routing table.

If each service contains a single subdomain, contained in the hub, it can communicate with other subdomains only through the adapters, as shown in this diagram:

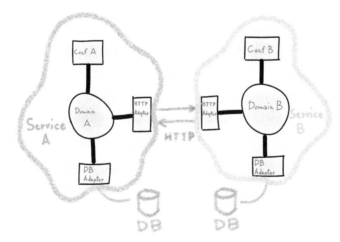

If we have more than a subdomain module inside a service, we can connect the hubs directly, without using adapters, as described by this diagram:

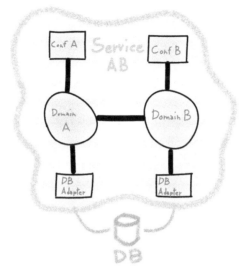

This is particularly useful during development, because we can aggregate all our modules in a single service and start it from the IDE to have the full application running locally, without using Docker or virtual machines. It also allows us to put breakpoints anywhere and speed up the debugging, or use the hot-deploy to see code changes reflected in real time, as I describe in this blog post.[6]

Translating to Code

Now that we have a plan, we can start implementing it.

How can we translate this into code? There are a few choices we need to make: how to organize our code, how to set up a continuous integration and a build pipeline, and how to deploy it in production. Even if these aren't topics strictly related to functional programming, it's useful to learn how to work with multiple modules.

Let's start from the code repository.

Monorepo

Since we're building an application with multiple modules, we can organize our code repository in two ways: either we keep all the modules in a single repository or we use a different repository for each module. In the first case,

---

6.   https://www.javaadvent.com/2020/12/composable-microservices-http4k.html

we can be sure that all the modules are working correctly together in every commit, at least if we run the tests. On the other hand, it would make things more complicated to build them independently. Using separate repositories instead makes it very easy to maintain independent builds for each module, but we have to figure out a way to specify the correct versions of all dependent modules.

All in all, I prefer the first approach: independent builds aren't hard to configure with modern continuous integration software. Instead, keeping all the module's versions aligned is a much harder problem. Moreover, this approach has other advantages: it's faster to update all the code locally every day, it's easier to explain the application to a new joiner, and last but not least, it's very easy to run tests on multiple modules, starting with our DDTs.

Keeping all the modules of the same project together in the same repository is usually called the monorepo approach.[7] Not only can we keep the different subdomains of our application separate, but we can also separate the domain logic from the various adapters needed for our architecture. Subdomains should not depend on each other, if possible, but there will be a need to have a common domain module with the shared public interfaces and data structure used to communicate between domains. It's important to keep the common parts as small as possible so we don't have to change them often, because every change in the common interfaces will imply a full rebuild of all our modules.

Adapters also can see the public part of the domain, but subdomains shouldn't depend on the adapter. In this way, if we want to change a JSON representation in an HTTP call, for example, we only need to rebuild the HTTP adapter module. Similarly, if we need to change some domain logic, we should only be recompiling the specific subdomain. In this way, even with a big repository with many modules, we can keep the compiling time reasonably low. Using a functional approach with immutable types and stateless functions can also help minimize coupling between modules and the execution time of unit tests.

The whole repository structure should make the role of each module easy to understand. The diagram on page 345 shows a way to organize multiple modules inside a single source repository.

Many modern JVM tools are optimized to work with monorepos. In particular, Gradle allows us to declare module dependencies at source level, without

---

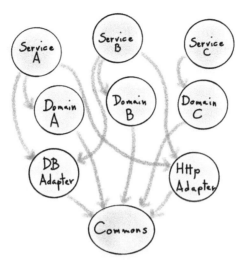

using a version, and can take advantage of the build cache to reduce compilation times.

Continuous Building and Integration

Every time someone commits new code to the common repository, a good practice is to build all the modules that changed and the module that depends on them, and then run all the tests. If the builds or the tests fail, we can notify the author so that they can promptly fix it.

This is the task of the continuous integration system. It's beyond the scope of this book to discuss such a vast argument, but if you are interested, a great book on the topic is Dave Farley's *Continuous Delivery [HF10]*.

What's important to highlight here is that we must set up the pipeline so that it builds each module independently before running the acceptance tests (or DDTs) on a dedicated environment at the end. This will let us know that our application works correctly after each commit. If we have written DDTs for all the important use-cases, we can be sure that the application mostly works. There could be corner cases and things we didn't think about, but for most users it should continue to work, even if we deploy in production after every commit. Which, incidentally, should be our goal.

In this context, we can also appreciate the particularity of DDTs over normal acceptance tests: they run fast locally in the domain-only mode and also not too slowly in the local HTTP mode. All the other solutions I know for the same problem are slower to run and more complicated to set up.

In our continuous integration server, we need to run our DDTs using the same infrastructure setup as in production. Only in this way can we be sure they'll catch all possible issues. In the end, the pipeline will be something like this:

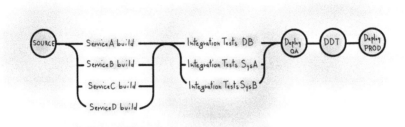

Now, let's briefly discuss how we're going to deploy our modules.

Deployment Unit

So far, I've managed to avoid the divisive question, "Microservices: yes or no?"

Ultimately, the decision boils down to how many distinct services we choose to deploy for our modules. While I don't believe that dividing our application into multiple independent microservices is always the optimal solution, it may be the best for your unique circumstances.

A prudent approach would be to try to minimize the number of services in the beginning, even releasing the whole application as a single monolith, as long as it's composed of smaller modules. Once the load for our application increases, we can start breaking down the monolith into separate microservices. The advantage of having multiple services is that we can finely tune the requirement for each, optimizing the use of resources and the general reliability of the platform. Handling microservices may be simple when we have a few instances (still more complicated than a single monolith), but it requires a lot of work and money to keep hundreds or thousands of services running.

> I'll keep saying this…if people can't build monoliths properly, microservices won't help.
>
> —Simon Brown

But then again, using the network as a boundary of our subdomains forces teams to think properly in terms of modularity. But, at the end of the day, using modularity and a stateless approach makes the choice easily reversible, and it's only a matter of which deployment strategy fits our requirements better.

A more extreme approach would be to deploy our modules as a number of independent stateless functions, the so-called "serverless" architecture. In theory, it would be very friendly to our functional design, but in practice, there are limitations due to the different proprietary approaches. One thing that seems certain is that for relatively low-load applications, the serverless approach is significantly cheaper to run on the cloud. This alone can be a good reason to adopt it.

In conclusion, one of the main benefits that a modular design can give us is the freedom to choose the deployment strategy at the last moment and to change ideas later.

Final Considerations

I think that the most important thing for a software architect to do is to embrace change. When I started writing applications, my aspiration was to write the "perfect" application using all the best practices together and distilling all the requirements into a definitive design that could be configured for any purpose, while remaining entirely future-proof.

Now I think that this is not only impossible, but fundamentally wrong. We should aim to write as little code as possible and be more willing to throw parts away rather than add new lines. We should aim to help users and stakeholders in achieving their goals, rather than writing software merely for its own sake.

In my experience, when writing software, flexibility is a far more important quality than striving for perfection or brilliance. I prefer to have rugged modules that may not fit perfectly but that I can rearrange at will, rather than a very polished, and very smart framework that can only do what its architects planned for.

Even more generally, I have found that, at least for the kind of applications I work on, the functional approach, with transformations of types and compositions, gives me more freedom and productivity than the object-oriented design approach, where everything tends to be related to everything else.

Now that we've reached the end of our journey, I hope you've found something useful in this book, maybe more than something. Before parting, my message to you is, "Keep coding, trust no authority, learn, and experiment yourself."

Exercises

The book is finished, but there is a final exercise.

Exercise 13.1: Final Exercise

Take the functional approach and apply the lessons learned in this book to create an application similar to Zettai from scratch, using your preferred programming language, keeping all the DDTs from this book, and starting from there.

What Is Functional Programming?

We're asking a big question here: "What is functional programming?" To understand it better, we need to look at where it came from and when it first started. Even though it seems like everybody's talking about it only recently, you might be surprised to know that it's not new. It has a long story behind it.

In this appendix, we're going to show you how functional programming works in real life. We'll take a little application that was written in an object-oriented style and change it to the functional paradigm. This will help us see what's different between the two ways of writing code.

But first, let's dive into the history of functional programming.

The Origins

Although the concept of "functional programming" can be traced back to the 1950s, it was John Backus that brought significant recognition to the term through his Turing Award lecture in 1977, "Can Programming Be Liberated from the von Neumann Style? A Functional Style and Its Algebra of Programs."[1]

It's interesting because John Backus is the inventor of the FORTRAN language, one of the first high-level languages, yet he has become one of the fiercest critics of his own creation. He says that "von Neumann Style" languages—what we would call nonfunctional languages now—have four basic defects. In his own words:

1. Their close coupling of semantics to state transitions

2. Their division of programming into a world of expressions and a world of statements

---

1.   https://dl.acm.org/doi/pdf/10.1145/359576.359579

3. Their inability to effectively use powerful combining forms for building new programs from existing ones

4. Their lack of useful mathematical properties for reasoning about programs

He was calling for a new style of programming, based on mathematical ideas, so that it would be possible to create programs composing simple elements using an *algebra* similar to mathematics.

John Backus's vision is very close to what modern functional programming can offer us. It's still impressive how it took almost fifty years before his ideas became mainstream. His paper is insightful and well worth reading, if you have the opportunity to do so, perhaps after finishing this book.

The first point in that list is particularly interesting. What Backus is saying here is that if we assign a specific meaning—a semantic value—to each state change, then we lose some of the flexibility to combine and re-use the components in new programs, because the state change is coupled to that specific behavior.

To see what he means, let's look at Bob Martin's Bowling kata as an example of typical object-oriented code:[2]

```
public class Game {
  private int rolls[] = new int[21];
  private int currentRoll = 0;

  public void roll(int pins) {
    rolls[currentRoll++] = pins;
  }

  public int score() //some logic to calculate score from rolls
}
```

In order to continue calculating the score, objects of this class modify their hidden fields each time we log the number of pins that have been knocked down in a roll. Although the code works well, and its intent is relatively clear, the underlying logic is closely linked to the changes in the domain state. This strong connection makes it challenging to modify them independently. For example, if we want to do a five-pin bowling game score, we can't easily re-use the same code. By rewriting it using the functional approach, we'll gain the ability to manipulate the rules of the game independently of its state.

---

2. http://www.butunclebob.com/ArticleS.UncleBob.TheBowlingGameKata

> ### Joe asks:
> ## What about Design Patterns?
>
> The book, *Design Patterns: Elements of Reusable Object-Oriented Software [GHJV95]*, popularized a set of general, reusable solutions to solve common problems in object-oriented design.
>
> Reusing object-oriented code is definitely possible, but it requires anticipating the need for re-use and designing the code accordingly or performing a refactor later to incorporate a specific pattern.
>
> Throughout the book, we'll compare this method with code re-use in functional programming, and the results may surprise you—functional code is typically more composable and reusable.

Finally, the last point—being able to reason about the mathematical properties of our software—is a key element of adopting functional programming. This may seems bizarre to you now, but I hope it won't be by the end of this book. To get an inkling of what he meant, let's have a quick look at lambda calculus and category theory.

Lambda Calculus

Lambda calculus was invented by mathematician Alonzo Church in the 1930s. It's a formal way to express computations in a way that can be analyzed in mathematical terms.

It's important for us because it puts the fundamental concept of functional programming on a firm, theoretical ground. To give you an idea of how lambda calculus works, you can imagine that any computation is a series of anonymous functions that can be composed and calculated at the end, substituting the variables with actual values.

For example, let's start with an expression that adds one to the product of two numbers:

```
x*y + 1
```

What lambda calculus is requiring us to do is to declare the variables we need to bind, in this case, x and y. To express the binding of a variable to a function, Church chose the greek letter lambda. So our expression can be written as shown in the figure on page 352.

$$\text{Head-declaration} \qquad \text{Body-expression}$$

$$\lambda x . \lambda y . \ xy+1$$

$$\lambda y. \ 5y+1 \qquad \text{replaced x with 5}$$

$$5 \cdot 6+1 \qquad \text{replaced y with 6}$$

$$31$$

The same expression in Kotlin would look like this:

```kotlin
val lambda: (Int) -> (Int) -> Int = { x -> { y -> x*y + 1}}

//usage
val r = lambda(5)(6)
println(r) // 31
```

If you aren't familiar with Kotlin lambdas, see Lambda Variables, on page 377. You can see how composing anonymous functions can completely remove the need for local variables.

Lambda calculus is based on the idea that even the most intricate computations can be resolved by replacing a subexpression with its value in the primary calculation, a process known as beta reduction. This notion is then extended into mathematical theorems and proofs, which we don't necessarily have to fully understand in order to benefit from them.

In the words of Backus: "In introducing the assignment statement, which can change the value of a variable in the middle of its scope, they have broken the basic ground rules of mathematical notation. Instead of being *referentially transparent*, programming languages are *referentially opaque*."

Referential Transparency

Backus mentioned the concept of "referential transparency," a term coined by the philosopher of language, Willard Van Orman Quine, in reference to the significance of words and their utilization. This term has been promptly embraced by computer scientists to indicate if a function can be substituted with its output without altering the behavior of the entire application.

If you think about it, we can apply the lambda calculus reduction only if our code is referentially transparent, otherwise we would get unpredictable results. For example, looking at the previous bowling code, we can't substitute the call to roll(5) with a value, because it was not returning any value.

Even if we change the method roll() to return the score, we still can't use the substitution principle, because if we call it multiple times with the same input, we'll get different results on each call—depending on the current score.

This is another useful criteria to distinguish transparent from opaque code: we can call the former multiple times, always getting the same result for the same input, and without affecting the rest of the system.

Joe asks:
What Does "Affecting" Mean Here?

Well, in an ideal computer there shouldn't be any difference calling referentially transparent code multiple times, but in reality, calling it multiple times will probably affect the CPU utilization and the memory consumption and this can potentially impact other parts of the system. Having said that, the JVM is optimized to reduce this risk as much as possible.

The important principle is that calling the function multiple times shouldn't change the state of the application in any way.

Category Theory

Let's go back to mathematics: if lambda calculus gave us a definition of what functional programming is, then category theory helps us change the way we think about types and functions.

Category theory has been defined, in typical mathematical humor, as "general abstract nonsense" in the sense that it studies how structures are preserved across transformations without looking at the actual content of the structures. In functional programming, we aim to do the same: be able to define our software as a composition of transformations.

These transformations are called *morphisms*, and they are usually represented as arrows. To form a category, we need arrows connecting dots. But not just any arrows will do—they must be composable. Composition of two arrows means creating a new arrow that's equivalent to applying the first arrow to the second.

Categories had a profound impact on functional programming. We discussed them when talking about Learning Functors and Categories, on page 163, and in even more detail in Appendix 3, A Pinch of Theory, on page 391.

Translating this into computer programming, the dots are types—not object instances (keep this in mind!)—and the arrows are functions that transform a type into another one; more precisely, they transform an element of a type into an element of another type. As with morphisms, composing two functions f and g means to create a new function h = g(f). Visually we can represent it like this:

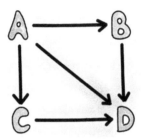

In this diagram, we have four arrows representing operations on four types A, B, C, and D. If we compose the functions A -> B and B -> D, the resulting function will be equivalent to a function A -> D. Similarly, if we compose the functions A -> C and C -> D, we'll also obtain the same function A -> D. When this happens, we say that the diagram "commutes." It's important to note that there may be multiple functions with the A -> D signature, but only one will make the diagram commute.

What does it mean for us to think in morphisms? Imagine building complex applications using transformations like they are toy construction blocks, putting one on top of the other, except that it's both harder and more powerful because our blocks aren't just static things but they are transformers themselves—that is, functions—and they can also transform other transformers!

You can now understand how thinking in terms of morphisms has the potential to greatly increase both flexibility and power. By utilizing functions as building blocks and allowing them to also transform other functions, we can create more dynamic and adaptable solutions.

So, how can we put all this into practice? It may seem impossible at first, but it's not. On the other hand, if it were that easy, I wouldn't have needed to write a book about it.

Achieving Referential Transparency

So, if the essence of functional programming is referential transparency, is there any easy rule to follow to preserve it? Yes, there are three *functional principles* we need to follow: *purity*, *immutability*, and *totality*.

The exact definitions of "referential transparency" and "purity" aren't universally agreed upon even in academic literature. However, for the purposes of this book, achieving referential transparency is the primary goal of functional programming. In other words, we can measure how functional a piece of code is by its level of referential transparency.

What I mean is that referential transparency is what makes functional programming work. If someone discovers a way to achieve it without using pure functions, I would abandon them. Similarly, I consider immutability and totality as important principles to maintain referential transparency but not as goals in themselves.

Let's examine them one by one in more detail.

Keep Your Functions Pure

How does *purity* apply to functions? A pure function is an operation that works like a mathematical function, which makes it easier to understand and re-use it.

It has two characteristics. First, it has to return a result. Some languages distinguish between function, which returns a value, and procedure, which executes a computation without returning a value. In Java, procedures are methods that return void; in Kotlin, they return Unit (see Unit, on page 376).

Note that there could be cases where Unit is a perfectly valid value to be deliberately returned, but here we're talking about having no semantic value.

In the bowling example, the roll method was changing the internal state without returning anything. If we want to write a BowlingGameFP class in a functional way, we need to return something from the roll method. Since roll changes the state of the game, the simplest thing is to return the new game state:

```
data class BowlingGameFP(val rolls: List<Int>) {

    fun roll(pins: Int): BowlingGameFP = BowlingGameFP(rolls + pins)
// rest of the class
}
```

For Kotlin's data class syntax, see Data Classes, on page 381.

Remember the definition: a function is referentially transparent if its value can be substituted for the function without altering the behavior of the program. If substitution isn't possible, the function is referentially opaque.

It's easy to prove with a test that the new roll is referentially transparent:

```
val g1 = BowlingGameFP(emptyList()).roll(5).roll(4)

val g2 = BowlingGameFP(listOf(5)).roll(4)

val g3 = BowlingGameFP(listOf(5,4))

assertEquals(g1, g2)
assertEquals(g1, g3)
```

More precisely, a pure function can't have other effects than the calculation of its return value. So, our pure functions can't modify any state external to the function, like global variables or mutable singletons. If the return value is the effect of the function, any other change that it makes on the system is considered a *side effect*, and we should limit them as much as possible.

Side Effects

You'll often hear the term *side effect* when discussing functional programming. It may be surprising because it doesn't refer to the common meaning of "unwanted result," like in medicine.

In computer science, its meaning includes every effect on the system that's different from the function's explicit result. So, for example, writing to standard output is a side effect of the println function, because its result value is Unit, which has nothing to do with the standard output.

Other common side effects are writing to the screen, transmitting data on the net, reading or writing a file, and so on.

The other characteristic of pure functions is that the result must only depend on their inputs. This means we also have to make sure we aren't using anything other than the function inputs to calculate the result. In other words, any reading or writing of global variables, singleton stateful objects, or external resources like files or network sockets inside a pure function would qualify as a side effect. This would violate the principle of referential transparency, since you could potentially get different results with the same inputs.

In this book, pure functions will be called functions and impure functions will be called computations. Eric Normand calls them calculations and actions, respectively. The names aren't important, but it's important to keep in mind the fundamental difference.

> ### \\/ Joe asks:
> ### Can I Write an Application Without Side Effects?
>
> Of course you can, just write an application that performs no actions whatsoever! But, this isn't particularly useful or interesting.
>
> Jokes aside, we can't avoid performing impure computations in a useful program, but it's possible to avoid side effects.
>
> In this book, we'll explore various techniques that can be employed to achieve this goal. In essence, this requires explicitly indicating when an effect is taking place using the type system, making them apparent, and transforming them from side effects into functional effects.

A final consideration about syntax: when a function consists of just a single expression, Kotlin lets us completely avoid curly brackets, like we did for roll, and instead use an = sign. When writing pure functions, it's a good idea to use this expression syntax to make it more evident that this is a function returning something. For more details, see Functions, on page 375.

Don't Trust Mutable Types

The second principle is *immutability*. Even if we don't refer to global state, the use of mutable data structure is an impediment to referential transparency.

Mathematical entities, like numbers, are immutable, but computers use memory cells, which have to be mutable. Low-level programming needs to stay very close to how hardware works, so it needs to use mutable structures. There is nothing wrong with that, but for our high-level code, if we want to keep it referentially transparent, we need a way to treat all data as immutable.

Let's see with a little example why it's important for the data to be immutable. In our Bowling kata, we made the data class immutable. What if instead we write a mutable version of it?

```
data class BowlingGameMutable(private val rolls: MutableList<Int>) {

    fun roll(pins: Int): BowlingGameMutable {
        rolls.add(pins)
        return this
    }
}
// rest of the class
}
```

In this version, the roll function will return the current instance, and it will change the mutable list of rolls inside. Our previous test would still pass, since g1, g2, and g3 are all the same instance. But we can write another test:

```
val g1 = BowlingGameMutable(emptyList()).roll(5)

val expected = BowlingGameMutable(emptyList()).roll(5).roll(4)

assertEquals(expected, g1.roll(4))

assertEquals(expected, g1.roll(4))
```

Here, we're asserting that it doesn't matter how many times we call g1.roll(4), we'll always get the same result. This test would pass with BowlingGameFP, but it fails with BowlingGameMutable.

Working with pure functions and immutable data also makes it easier to debug the code and avoid errors in the first place. This is because we don't have to keep all the possible states in our mind when looking at functional code.

Creating a new instance of a data structure with only a few fields altered is such a common task that data classes provide a convenient method called copy for this exact purpose. We can refactor our roll function in this way:

```
fun roll(pins: Int): BowlingGameFP = copy(rolls = rolls + pins)
```

How can we make sure our data is immutable? Unfortunately, there is no easy way to ensure we're using immutable data. Even if our classes are immutable, we need to check that each field they have is of an immutable type. It's even possible to declare data classes with mutable fields, declaring them using var instead of val, but it's better to avoid using mutable fields in data classes as much as possible.

The architects of Kotlin shared the opinion that using mutable temporary variables isn't a great idea, and since they know very well how much programmers hate to see underscored elements in the code, IntelliJ underscores all var variables, to discourage developers from using them. It can be disabled from the editor configuration, but while writing functional code, using a mutable variable is almost always a sign of a design flaw.

As a bonus, using immutable data simplifies sharing data between tasks running concurrently—since the data can't change, there is no need for memory locks and CPU cache invalidations.

As a final consideration, Kotlin collections aren't really immutable but they only use read-only interfaces;[3] this means that you can usually modify an

---

3.   https://proandroiddev.com/the-mystery-of-mutable-kotlin-collections-e82cbf5d781

> \/ /   **Joe asks:**
> ~~   **Does Allocating New Instances Every Time Have an Impact on Performance?**
>
> Yes, for critical pieces of code, mutable structures may be faster. But in general, the JVM is pretty fast at allocating objects, and the overall impact is often negligible.
>
> Allocating time isn't everything, though. Having immutable objects simplifies the job of the just-in-time compiler and the garbage collector. Depending on how long they live and how often they change, immutability can improve overall performances.

"immutable" collection, casting it to a mutable one. There is a project for creating really immutable optimized Kotlin collections that can make the copy operation more efficient; you can check out Kotlin's immutable collections library on GitHub.[4]

Consider All the Possible Inputs

The final condition we need to meet in order to make our functions safe to compose is what is called *totality*. The full definition of totality is: a total function is a function that, for any input, terminates with a result in finite time.

To return results for any input, we have to follow two rules. The first rule is quite reasonable: total functions can't have infinite loops. The second rule is more tricky: total functions must process all the possible inputs; in other words, they can't throw exceptions.

If a function uses exceptions to reject invalid input parameters, it's called *partial*, because it works only on a subset of possible input values.

Let's say we want to add a check to reject invalid inputs in our Bowling kata. One way is to throw an exception:

```
fun roll(pins: Int): BowlingGameFP =
    if (validPins(pins))
        copy(rolls = rolls + pins)
    else
        error("Invalid number of pins!")
```

A very simple way to avoid exceptions is to ignore the invalid input and return the current version of our BowlingGameFP like this:

---

4. https://github.com/Kotlin/kotlinx.collections.immutable

```
fun roll(pins: Int): BowlingGameFP =
    if (validPins(pins))
        copy(rolls = rolls + pins)
    else
        this //ignore it
```

This may or may not be acceptable, depending on our software, and we'll see more sophisticated solutions later in the book in Handling Errors Better, on page 157, but it's important to avoid using exceptions to handle the flow of our programs.

Exceptions are very useful for handling unexpected errors in our code, but we should limit their use to really *exceptional* circumstances, like out-of-memory errors, essential services (for example, databases) not being available, and so on. These are also cases that involve external systems and probably they won't involve pure functions.

From now on, when talking about functions in this book, it's in the sense of "pure, total function working on immutable type." Otherwise, they'll be called computations or actions.

Think in Morphisms

Following the three functional principles, we can be sure to write functional code, but they can only tell us what code we should avoid, not how to design our application. We need to start thinking in functional terms, but how?

This is extremely different from object-oriented design. Alan Kay—who invented the term object-oriented—described his idea in a famous email:[5] "I thought of objects being like biological cells and/or individual computers on a network, only able to communicate with messages (so messaging came at the very beginning—it took a while to see how to do messaging in a programming language efficiently enough to be useful)."

To give an intuitive idea of the differences, in a pure object-oriented design, everything is based on the exchange of messages between entities with a hidden internal state, a bit like cells in living organisms:

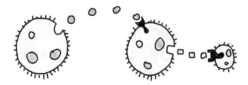

---

5. http://userpage.fu-berlin.de/~ram/pub/pub_jf47ht81Ht/doc_kay_oop_en

Instead, in a pure functional design, everything is based on transformations and compositions, somewhat closer to a mathematical style:

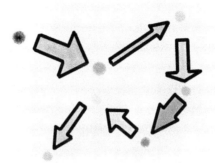

We'll now look at four very important heuristics that can help us effectively design our software with a morphism-friendly mindset:

1. Treat functions as data.
2. Define your types precisely.
3. Prefer a declarative style.
4. Try to be lazy.

Treat Functions as Data

We're used to considering functions as distinct from data: functions are something that use data type as input and as results. In the functional world, functions are first-class citizens—they can be treated like any other variable—so we can take functions as input parameters and return new functions.

Functions that work by treating other functions as data are called *higher-order functions*. They are one of the most powerful tools for functional programmers, and they are used a lot in this book.

Using HOF can be challenging at first, but with experience and practice, you'll gain a better understanding of them and they'll become natural to you.

For example, in the bowling class, we can inject the function to calculate the score from outside, as a dependency:

```
data class BowlingGameFP(
        val rolls: List<Int>,
        private val scoreFn: (List<Int>) -> Int) {

    val score = scoreFn(rolls)

    fun roll(pins: Int): BowlingGameFP = //..

    companion object {
```

```
        fun newBowlingGame() = BowlingGameFP(emptyList(), ::calcBowlingScore)
    }
}
fun calcBowlingScore(rolls: List<Int>): Int { //...
```

In Kotlin, we can declare stand-alone Functions, on page 375, which are like static functions in Java minus the class, and their type is the combination of inputs and outputs—in this case (List<Int>) -> Int.

Here, the advantage is the possibility to easily change the logic of the score. For example, if we need to score a game of five-pin bowling, we can keep the same class and just add a different scoring function:

```
fun new5PinBowlingGame() = BowlingGameFP(emptyList(), ::calc5PinBowlingScore)
```

Another advantage is that we can test the scoring function alone or by comparing the results of different algorithms. On the other hand, it makes our code a bit more complicated to use, so the final decision always depends on the specific circumstances. What's important is the principle that functions can be treated as data.

We can also write a function that takes functions as input and returns a new function as a result. For example, let's say we need to consider two kinds of scoring rules. A way to proceed is to create a new function to score with a new Boolean parameter:

```
fun chooseAndScore(
    is5pinBowling: Boolean,
    rolls: List<Int>
): Int =
    if (is5pinBowling)
        calc5PinScore(rolls)
    else
        calc10PinScore(rolls)
```

Another way is taking the two different scoring functions as input and returning one of them depending on another parameter. The caller can use the function for the score directly or store it to use multiple times:

```
fun chooseScoringFn(
    is5pinBowling: Boolean,
    fn10PinScore: (List<Int>) -> Int,
    fn5PinScore: (List<Int>) -> Int
): (List<Int>) -> Int =
    if (is5pinBowling)
        fn5PinScore
    else
        fn10PinScore
```

Returning a function from a function is a bit like answering a question with a new question. It may seem strange at first, but this way of thinking helps to elegantly solve many problems, and it's very commonly used in functional programming, as we discussed in Using Higher-Order Functions, on page 51.

Finally, let's consider our rules for functions: is the chooseScoringFn function pure? The definition says: a higher-order function f is pure if the expression f(g) (where g is another function) is referentially transparent for all referentially transparent g. In other words, to consider chooseScoringFn pure, we only need to verify it using other pure functions as input.

Similarly, if we treat functions as data, we can ask ourselves what an immutable function is. For all practical purposes, an immutable function is a function that returns the same output for a given input. So all pure functions are also immutable functions.

Define Your Types Precisely

If we start designing our software as a chain of transformations between types, we need to represent different things with different types, in a very precise way.

Defining precise types will make our functions more specific and easier to find from their signature. As a matter of fact, when we write code in a functional way, we rely much more on the functions' signatures rather than on their names. But if we use generic types for our domain, we have to rely only on the function name to understand what they are for, and since there are practical limits on how long a function name is, there will be possibility of confusion.

For example, let's consider the signature of our score function: (List<Int>) -> Int; it's very generic. It's the same for List<Int>::sum and List<Int>::size, and it'd be easy to pass a wrong function by mistake.

Instead, if we define a specific type for the pins knocked down in a roll—let's call it Pins—our score function signature would become: (List<Pins>) -> Int, which is more precise and tells us something about it.

Using domain classes instead of primitive types like String or Int isn't specific to functional programming. Wrapping all built-in type in domain specific classes is called the TinyType pattern.[6] And there is also a correspondent antipattern called "primitive obsession" to condemn using primitive data types to represent domain ideas.[7]

---

6. https://darrenhobbs.com/2007/04/11/tiny-types/
7. https://wiki.c2.com/?PrimitiveObsession

Another advantage of defining specific types for our domain is that it can help us achieve totality. For example, there are only eleven possible values for the Pins type, representing throwing down a number of pins from zero to ten. Instead of wrapping an integer, we can use an enum:

```
enum class Pins(val number: Int) {
    zero(0),
    one(1),
    two(2),
    three(3),
    four(4),
    five(5),
    six(6),
    seven(7),
    eight(8),
    nine(9),
    ten(10)
}
```

This way, we drastically reduce the possibility of introducing an error, and we can remove input validation, which in turn will make it easier to enforce totality. This may seem just a case of moving the problem around, from inside our function to the Pins creation. The advantage is that the compiler itself will check that we aren't using invalid values.

Prefer a Declarative Style

Broadly speaking, there are two ways we can tell someone to do a task for us: either we can specify exactly all the steps needed to accomplish it, or we can describe what the ultimate goal is.

For example, if we need to instruct someone to bring us a container of milk, we can say: "Go out, turn left, go ahead 50 meters, enter the store, find the container of milk, get one, bring it to the cash register, pay for it," and so on.

Or we can say: "Here is the money. I want a container of milk."

It's easy to imagine what can go wrong in the first case. If we forgot to mention a required step of the instructions, the agent can't complete the task because they don't have enough information to correct the mistake. If the milk shop is just a few meters further off, the instructions will fail. In the second case, the agent can figure out how to find the store and complete the task without problems.

On the other hand, there is always a risk of missing information in the second case, and we could end up waiting for hours because the agent didn't know about the store around the corner and went somewhere else.

In programming, we call the detailed-steps style *imperative* and the goal-oriented one *declarative*.

The imperative style consists of a sequence of statements and can be quite hard to read. As an example, let's look at the algorithm for calculating the score of our bowling application:

```
fun calcBowlingScore(rolls: List<Pins>): Int {

    fun getRoll(roll: Int): Int = rolls.getOrElse(roll){ Pins.zero }.number

    fun isStrike(frameIndex: Int): Boolean =
        getRoll(frameIndex) == 10
    fun sumOfBallsInFrame(frameIndex: Int): Int =
        getRoll(frameIndex) + getRoll(frameIndex + 1)
    fun spareBonus(frameIndex: Int): Int =
        getRoll(frameIndex + 2)
    fun strikeBonus(frameIndex: Int): Int =
        getRoll(frameIndex + 1) + getRoll(frameIndex + 2)
    fun isSpare(frameIndex: Int): Boolean =
        getRoll(frameIndex) + getRoll(frameIndex + 1) == 10

    var score = 0
    var frameIndex = 0
    for (frame in 0..9) {
        if (isStrike(frameIndex)) {
            score += 10 + strikeBonus(frameIndex)
            frameIndex++
        } else if (isSpare(frameIndex)) {
            score += 10 + spareBonus(frameIndex)
            frameIndex += 2
        } else {
            score += sumOfBallsInFrame(frameIndex)
            frameIndex += 2
        }
    }
    return score
}
```

The names of the methods are quite clear and they mirror the rules, but the frameIndex variable is tricky to understand, because sometimes we advance a frame, sometimes two frames. Also, the number of the frames is hard-coded in the for-loop and it's not very clear how it relates to the rolls.

The main issue with this code, however, is that it ties the logic with a mutable state. Therefore, when you have to modify it, you must keep all these aspects in mind, which can be quite challenging.

Even after rewriting it in Kotlin, I wouldn't be able to change this code with confidence. Having tests in place makes changing it safe enough, but wouldn't it be better to work with easy-to-predict code?

Now, let's try to rewrite it in a more declarative style. How can we express the bowling rules? Here is my take:

1. Let's start with frame 1.

2. If the roll is a strike (all pins down) then score 10 points plus the next two rolls.

3. If the next two rolls are a spare (all pins down in two rolls) then score 10 points plus the roll after.

4. Otherwise, just add the next two rolls to the score.

5. Go to the next frame; if we have less than 3 rolls or it's frame 10, just add the last rolls.

We can translate this in code with a recursive function. You can see that each of the rules corresponds to a line of code:

```kotlin
fun calcBowlingScoreRec(rolls: List<Pins>): Int {
  val lastFrame = 10
  val noOfPins = 10
  fun List<Int>.isStrike(): Boolean = first() == noOfPins
  fun List<Int>.isSpare(): Boolean = take(2).sum() == noOfPins

  fun calcFrameScore(frame: Int, rolls: List<Int>): Int =
    when {
      frame == lastFrame || rolls.size < 3 -> // 5
        rolls.sum()
      rolls.isStrike() -> // 2
        rolls.take(3).sum() + calcFrameScore(frame + 1, rolls.drop(1))
      rolls.isSpare() -> // 3
        rolls.take(3).sum() + calcFrameScore(frame + 1, rolls.drop(2))
      else -> //4
        rolls.take(2).sum() + calcFrameScore(frame + 1, rolls.drop(2))
    }

  return calcFrameScore(1, rolls.map(Pins::number)) // 1
}
```

You may have a better solution in mind, and it doesn't have to be recursive, but arguably, having removed all the mutable variables made it simpler to understand the rules of the game, which is our intention.

You may have heard that functional programming is declarative and object-oriented is imperative. This isn't strictly correct, because we can write declarative object-oriented code (for example, domain-specific languages) and functional imperative code (see UnaryPlus Operator DSL, on page 254).

But then again, functional programming allows for a wider and more powerful use of declarative style than procedural programming, and we should adopt it where possible over the imperative style. Ultimately, our aim as programmers is to follow Tony Hoare's suggestion:

> There are two ways of constructing a software design: One way is to make it so simple that there are obviously no deficiencies, and the other way is to make it so complicated that there are no obvious deficiencies. The first method is far more difficult.
>
> —Tony Hoare

Try to Be Lazy

It's true that programmers are often lazy people, at least I am for sure. But here we're talking about a different kind of laziness: *lazy evaluation.*

The idea is to defer the evaluation of some expressions until the last possible moment, when we need their result. Sometimes we don't need the result after all, so we can save unnecessary computations and external calls. This works very well with functional programming, because lazy operations are usually passed around as functions that we call only when we need their result.

For example, we can use laziness to calculate the score in the bowling game only if it's required and store the value so any subsequent call doesn't have to recalculate it. This is very easy with Kotlin as we'll cover in Delegated Properties, on page 383.

```
data class BowlingGameFP(
        val rolls: List<Pins>,
        val scoreFn: (List<Pins>) -> Int) {

    val score by lazy{ scoreFn(rolls) } //lazy score

    // rest of the class
}
```

But this is just a taste of what laziness can give us. There is an interesting example of Leveraging on Laziness, on page 194.

On the other hand, laziness can make the code harder to debug, since the actual call can happen in a completely different place from where we create it. It's always better to ponder the pros and cons before using it, just like any other technique in programming.

Recap

In this appendix, we looked at the origins of functional programming and its mathematical foundations. Then we discussed the benefits of adopting it in our code.

From mathematical foundations, we have derived three functional principles for writing code:

- *Purity*: The same inputs always produce the same results.

- *Immutability*: All data structures are immutable.

- *Totality*: Functions return a result for any input, without throwing exceptions.

We have also derived four heuristic rules:

- *Prefer a declarative style.* Express what you want to achieve with your code rather than the how.

- *Define your types precisely.* Make the signature of your function meaningful.

- *Treat functions as data.* Define behavior combining simpler functions together.

- *Try to be lazy.* Defer calculations until the last possible moment.

Following the rules isn't enough, so we also considered the changes functional programming brings to the way we design our applications: thinking in morphisms and writing referentially transparent code.

Looking at the full code of this exercise, what have we learned?

```kotlin
data class BowlingGameFP( val rolls: List<Pins>,
                          val scoreFn: (List<Pins>) -> Int) {

  val score by lazy{ scoreFn(rolls) }

  fun roll(pins: Pins): BowlingGameFP = copy(rolls = rolls + pins)

  companion object {
    fun newBowlingGame() = BowlingGameFP(emptyList(), ::calcBowlingScoreRec)

    fun calcBowlingScoreRec(rolls: List<Pins>): Int {
      val lastFrame = 10
      val noOfPins = 10

      fun List<Int>.isStrike(): Boolean = first() == noOfPins

      fun List<Int>.isSpare(): Boolean = take(2).sum() == noOfPins

      fun calcFrameScore(frame: Int, rolls: List<Int>): Int =
```

```
    when {
      frame == lastFrame || rolls.size < 3 ->
        rolls.sum()
      rolls.isStrike() ->
        rolls.take(3).sum() + calcFrameScore(frame + 1, rolls.drop(1))
      rolls.isSpare() ->
        rolls.take(3).sum() + calcFrameScore(frame + 1, rolls.drop(2))
      else ->
        rolls.take(2).sum() + calcFrameScore(frame + 1, rolls.drop(2))
    }

    return calcFrameScore(1, rolls.map(Pins::number))
  }
 }
}
```

We roughly halved the lines of code, and we arguably made the rules to calculate the score more clear. On top of this, we also made it easier to change
the score algorithm if we need to score games with different rules.

The most crucial aspect is that the new code is arguably much easier to test
and maintain. This is because it does not have the complexity of an internal
mutable state, which can often cause issues and headaches for developers.

About Functional Kotlin

Kotlin is a modern language, aimed at making development fun and our job easier.[1] It's concise, safe, interoperable with Java, and can target different platforms. This book is mainly focused on the JVM implementation of Kotlin, but keep in mind that there is also a compiler to native executables and a transpiler to JavaScript to run Kotlin in the browser.

The first time I saw some Kotlin code was in 2013, while I was basking in the Crete sun for a Java conference there. My first impression was that it was too good to be true. At the time, other languages seemed better positioned to become a more modern version of Java: Scala, Ceylon, Groovy, and so on. From the start, I really liked the pragmatic approach of Kotlin: let's copy what works in other languages, and let's keep it as close as possible to Java. I think this is still its main selling point today.

The goal of this appendix is to offer a quick way to familiarize yourself with Kotlin by providing the Java equivalent of idiomatic syntax in Kotlin. We'll focus on functional programming constructs, specifically those utilized inside this book that may catch Java programmers off guard.

It isn't meant as a complete course, but if you already know Java, you can use this appendix as a reference to understand the Kotlin code featured in this book.

Setting Up Kotlin

For your first taste of Kotlin, you can try the online REPL site.[2] It contains many examples and exercises to help you learn the language.

---

1. https://kotlinlang.org/
2. https://play.kotlinlang.org

The easiest way to use Kotlin is with the IntelliJ IDE. You can download the free Community version at the JetBrains site.[3] To set up your Kotlin working environment, you can follow the instruction on their Get Started page.[4] If you prefer Eclipse as your IDE, there is a plugin for Kotlin.[5] It's possible to also use Kotlin with other Java IDEs or editors (Emacs, VScode, and so on) and also compile it from the command line, but that's outside the scope of this book.

This book uses the latest Kotlin version, which in February 2023 is Kotlin 1.8.0.

Gradle

We're using Gradle as our build tool.[6] It's very easy to use and requires little configuration. It's possible to use Gradle from the command line or launch the commands directly from the IDE.

You don't need to install anything to build the examples of this book; just launching the build with gradlew build in the project root will download and build the project. If you need the full Gradle distribution, I suggest using a management tool like SDKMAN!.[7]

To use Gradle, we need to write a build file using its own DSL. The original DSL language was Groovy, but it's now possible to use Kotlin as Gradle script language as well. The code in this book uses the Groovy language. Learning Gradle DSL is outside the scope of this book, but you can find many tutorials online.[8]

Hello World

Let's start with the traditional hello world example, one of the smallest possible Kotlin programs:

```kotlin
fun main() {
  println("Hello Functional World!")
}
```

You can type these three lines in a Kotlin file—let's call it "Hello.kt"—and you can run them from the IDE by clicking on the little green arrow in the gutter area, as shown on line 3 in the screenshot on page 373.

---

3.   https://www.jetbrains.com/idea/download/
4.   https://kotlinlang.org/docs/getting-started.html
5.   https://kotlinlang.org/docs/eclipse.html
6.   https://gradle.org/kotlin/
7.   https://sdkman.io/
8.   https://gradle.org/guides/#getting-started

> ### Joe asks:
> # Why Use Groovy in Gradle Files?
>
> It may seem like a strange choice to use Groovy in the Gradle files in a book about Kotlin.
>
> Since the Gradle DSL was born with Groovy, I find it more natural to continue to define them in Groovy. Moreover, I'm not entirely convinced that a static typed language is the best choice to write build scripts, but maybe this will change with future versions of Gradle. However, in my personal experience, sticking to Groovy in build files is more productive. Your experience may differ, so please experiment with it yourself.

```
Project ▾                    ☰ ÷ ⚙ —   Hello.kt
  gradle
  kotlin
    out                              fun main() {
    src                                  println("Hello Functional World!")
      main                           }
        kotlin
          Hello.kt
    build.gradle
Run:   HelloKt
       /home/ubertobarbini/.sdkman/candidates/java/14.0.1.hs-adpt/bin/java ...
       Hello Functional World!

       Process finished with exit code 0
       |
```

As a result, it will print the phrase "Hello Functional World!" on the standard output, as you can see in the terminal window.

What we did is equivalent to the following Java public method:

```java
public static void main(String[] args) {
    System.out.println("Hello Functional World!");
}
```

But, in Kotlin you don't need to define a class to attach your static method. We can create stand-alone functions (in the general sense of procedures or methods).

To see how the Kotlin JVM compiler works, we can look at the generated bytecode by using the javap command-line tool or the IntelliJ menu command Tools | Kotlin | Show Kotlin Bytecode.

A helpful trick is to use the button in the bytecode window to decompile it to Java. In practice, we can see the equivalent Java of our Kotlin code. If we do this with our main function, we can see something like this (the details might be different):

```
public final class HelloKt {
   public static final void main() {
      String var0 = "Hello Functional World!";
      System.out.println(var0);
   }

   public static void main(String[] var0) {
      main();
   }
}
```

You can see here that, behind the curtains, Kotlin creates a static class with the name of your file (HelloKt) and then provides the functions as static methods.

Automatic Converter

Another useful tool in the IntelliJ IDE is the automatic converter from Java to Kotlin. It doesn't always produce great code, but it's very useful as a starting point for converting a codebase to Kotlin. To use it, select a Java file and then click on the menu command Code | Convert Java File to Kotlin File.

The converter tool can also be used to learn Kotlin: just copy some Java code to the clipboard that you are unsure how to translate into Kotlin, and when you paste it into a Kotlin project, IntelliJ will ask to convert it for you.

Kotlin 101

Let's see what Kotlin looks like, comparing the basic syntax constructs with their Java equivalents.

Temporary Variables

In Java, to declare a temporary variable, you have to write the type before the name of the variable. Starting with Java 10, it's also possible to use the keyword var, and let the compiler figure out the exact type. For example:

```
int a = 4;
var b = 5;
b = a + b;
```

In Kotlin, the type is always optional if it can be inferred, and is declared after the variable name, but there are two variable keywords: val for immutable (that is, not reassignable) variables and var for variables that can be reassigned, like this:

```
val a: Int = 4;
var b = 5;
b = a + b;
```

As a rule of thumb, it's better to avoid using the var keyword as much as possible since variable reassignments are a common cause of bugs, on top of being against functional programming principles.

Functions

Functions in Kotlin don't need to be declared inside a class; they are really first-class citizens of the Kotlin language:

```
fun plusOne(a: Int): Int { return a + 1 }
```

If the function is a single expression, we can use the terser expression syntax, putting an equal sign after the declaration:

```
fun plusOne(a: Int) = a + 1
```

You can reference functions directly by putting a double colon in front of the name, like ::plusOne. This way, it's very clean to assign a function to a variable and pass it around:

```
val intFun = ::plusOne

fun plusTwo(a: Int) = intFun(intFun(a))
```

The (almost) equivalent code in Java would be this:

```
class Functions {

    static Integer plusOne(Integer a) {
        return a + 1;
    }

    static Function<Integer,Integer> intFun = Functions::plusOne;

    static Integer plusTwo(Integer a) {
        return (intFun.apply(intFun.apply(a)));
    }

}
```

Function Types

As we saw in the previous example, you can use a generic interface to represent the type of functions in Java, depending on the parameters. For example, the type of a function that takes a String and returns an Integer is this:

```
Function<String,Integer> stringLen = ...
```

If we add a second parameter, we need to use a different interface:

```
Function2<String, Integer, String> leftString = ...
```

and so on until Function22.

In Kotlin, there is a more elegant way to declare the type of a function, using an arrow, like this:

```
val stringLen: (String) -> Int = ...
```

Or in case of two parameters, like this:

```
val leftString = (String, Integer) -> Int
```

The Kotlin compiler will translate these types to the expected JVM types when generating the bytecode.

Unit

So what is the return type of a statement without an explicit return in Kotlin? For example:

```
fun hello(){ println("Hi!") }
```

There is a special singleton type defined in Kotlin for cases like the above; it is called Unit. We can rewrite any statement without return type as an expression returning Unit:

```
fun hello(): Unit = println("Hi!")
```

The Unit type in Kotlin is roughly equivalent to the void type in Java, but differently from void, it's a real type inheriting from Any.

Nothing

If Unit is the type of a statement in Kotlin, what is the type of a function without a return? You may be surprised, but there is a type exactly for this case: it's called Nothing. It's a special type that represents the absence of a value.

In other words, it indicates that a function doesn't return a value, either because it throws exceptions for all possible inputs or because it has an infinite loop.

The TODO() function of the Kotlin library has a return type of Nothing. The TODO() function is intended to be used as a placeholder for code that hasn't been implemented yet or as a way to temporarily disable code that you don't want to run.

Since Nothing is a subtype of all other types, you can use it in places where any other type is expected. This is convenient, because we can use TODO() anywhere, regardless of the function declared return type.

Lambda Variables

A lambda is just a small function that can be inlined directly without giving it a name. We can define an anonymous function and assign it to a variable, exactly as we did with functions. For example, in Kotlin you can write:

```kotlin
val plusOneL = fun(x: Int): Int { return x + 1 }
```

Note that in this case, plusOneL is the name of the variable, but the function itself is anonymous.

This is a bit verbose; fortunately, we can skip the fun keyword and the explicit return if we use the simplified lambda syntax:

```kotlin
val plusOneL: (Int) -> Int = {x: Int -> x + 1}
```

We can simplify it further if we use it as the implicit parameter:

```kotlin
val plusOneL: (Int) -> Int = {it + 1}
```

Depending on the context, using it can be confusing, so it's better not to abuse it.

A big benefit of this syntax is that lambdas can be passed directly as parameters to other functions. For example, to find the first element of a list of strings that start with "A", we can do this:

```kotlin
val names = listOf("Bob", "Mary", "Ann", "Fred")
val aName = names.firstOrNull { it.startsWith("A") }
```

firstOrNull method also shows a nice Kotlin convention: if the last argument of a function is a lambda, we can put it outside the function's parentheses. And even if you forget about it, IntelliJ will suggest the fix.

Lambdas were introduced for the first time in Java with version 8. In Kotlin, they were present from the start, and as you can imagine, they are more integrated with the rest of the language.

The last example in Java would be:

```
String aName = names.stream()
        .filter(name -> name.startsWith("A"))
        .findAny()
        .orElse(null);
```

Extension Functions

Extension functions are one of those little things that makes using Kotlin so nice. They are just stand-alone functions which take the first parameter in the receiver position. For example, instead of writing:

```
fun plusOne(a: Int) = a + 1

//---

println( plusOne(5) ) //6
```

...we can write it as an extension function:

```
fun Int.next() = this + 1

//---

println( 5.next() ) //6
```

This is arguably much easier to read! Also, note the use of this to refer to the receiver argument.

The overall effect is like we're adding methods to existing classes without touching them, even if they are final (like Int in the example).

There is a catch, of course, since they are just a bit of syntax sugar over static methods—we can't access nonpublic fields or methods of the receiver class.

Extension functions are compiled exactly as the stand-alone functions, as Java static methods of a hidden class with an implicit parameter. They can be referenced by Class::method like normal methods of that class.

The type of an extension function is declared differently from normal functions; to indicate that the argument is a receiver, we put it outside the parenthesis. For example:

```
val nextFn: Int.() -> Int = Int::next
```

An interesting use of extension functions is to define them inside another class or interface as methods. By doing this, we're adding methods to an existing type *but only inside our class*.

To learn more about it, you can read my blog post about advanced uses of lambdas and extension functions.[9]

In version 1.7 of Kotlin, they introduced a more powerful construct called *multiple receivers* to allow more than a single parameter in the receiver position. Since they are still experimental in Kotlin 1.8, we won't use them in this book, but they may play an important role in the future.

Return New Functions

Another use of lambda literals is when we want to return a new function as result of a function. For example, to create a function that adds x to any number, we can write:

```kotlin
fun plusX(x: Int): (Int) -> Int = { x + it }
```

Or more verbosely:

```kotlin
fun plusX(x: Int): (Int) -> Int {
    return fun(y: Int): Int = x + y
}
```

Please note that plusX isn't returning a number but a new function. It can be used like this:

```kotlin
val plus12 = plusX(12)
val answer = plus3(30) //42
```

For the equivalent Java, we need to implement the Function functional interface with a lambda:

```java
Function<Integer, Integer> plusX(int x){
    return num -> num + x;
}
```

Scope Functions

Scope functions are four useful functions in the Kotlin standard library that allow us to compose functions and lambdas in a flexible way. It's worth it to remember them, because we use them often in the book.

---

9. https://medium.com/@ramtop/kotlin-pearls-lambdas-with-a-context-58f26ab2eb1d

They are all extension functions, and they get a single lambda as argument. Then we can distinguish them depending on what they do with the result of the lambda:

- let, run: call the lambda and return the result
- also, apply: call lambda and ignore the result

And, how they pass the external object inside the lambda:

- let, also: use argument inside the lambda (it)
- run, apply: use receiver inside the lambda (this)

Using them, we can often avoid temporary variables, making the code more concise. For example, to check a user's age, we can do the following:

```kotlin
fun checkMajority(userName: String): Boolean {
    val user = getUser(userName)
    val age = currentYear - user.dateOfBirth.year
    return age < 21
}
```

The apply scope function can avoid some repetition:

```kotlin
fun checkMajority(userName: String): Boolean =
    getUser(userName).apply{
        currentYear - dateOfBirth.year < 21
    }
```

Introducing an implicit scope (apply and run) can make the code obscure as it becomes unclear which objects the methods are being called on, so it's better to limit their use to simple cases. I also wrote a blog post with more examples of scope functions.[10]

Classes

Declaring a class in Kotlin is very similar to Java, but the main constructor parameters are passed directly after the name.

```kotlin
class User( val name: String,
           val surname: String) {

    fun initials() = "${name.first()}${surname.first()}"

}
val fred = User("Fred", "Flintstone")
println(fred.name)
println(fred.initials())
```

---

10. https://medium.com/@ramtop/kotlin-scope-functions-c8c41f09615f

Class, methods, and fields are all final by default in Kotlin. If we want to modify them, we need to add the open keyword to them:

```
open class User(
    open val name: String,
    open val surname: String) {

    open fun initials() = "${name.first()}${surname.first()}"

}

class JapaneseUser(
  override val name: String,
  override val surname: String): User(name, surname) {

    override fun initials() = "${surname.first()}${name.first()}"
}
```

Generally speaking, inheritance can create too much coupling between classes. For this reason, it's better to avoid open classes and instead limit inheritance using abstract classes or sealed classes.

Objects and Companion Objects

In Kotlin, there is no static keyword, and we can't declare static methods in our objects. So how can we create static methods? We can attach them to the class companion object, which is an implicit singleton invoked by the class name:

```
class User(
...

    companion object {
        fun fromString(fullName: String) =
            fullName.split(" ")
                .let { User(it.get(0), it.get(1)) }
    }
}

val fred = User.fromString("Fred Flintstone")
```

We can also create objects that aren't a companion of any class, in which case, they behave as a type with their own singleton instance.

Data Classes

Kotlin data classes are similar to records in Java (introduced in Java 15), and more generally, they are useful to represent value objects. Just by declaring a data class, Kotlin will generate the three methods required for comparison and equality: equals, toString, and hashCode.

Fields of a data class are immutable by default but, unlike Java's record, by using the var keyword they can be made mutable. But, as you may remember, that isn't a good idea in functional programming.

```
data class User(
    val name: String,
    val surname: String
)
```

In addition to the three methods mentioned, data classes implement another very useful method to create a copy of the instance with only one or more fields modified:

```
val fred = User("Fred", "Flintstone")
val wilma = fred.copy(name = "Wilma")
```

With a data class with only two fields, like here, they aren't making a big difference, but with more complicated classes, copy method is very convenient.

Implementation by Delegation

Another great feature of Kotlin that lets you avoid writing unnecessary code is delegation. Let's say we have an interface and a class that implements it fully:

```
interface UserStore {
    fun saveUser(user: User)
    //other methods...
}
class UserStoreDb(val conn: String): UserStore {
    override fun saveUser(user: User) {...}
    //other methods...
}
```

Now we want to add some more behavior to our UserStoreDb class. Instead of inheriting from it—which would force us to make it open—we'll use delegation, passing an instance of UserStoreDb to our new class and delegating the methods to it.

The problem in using delegation in other languages (for example, Java) is that we need to write a lot of boring code to delegate the methods. In Kotlin, the compiler will do the job for us.

Here is how we add our logging to a UserStore without extending it, using the by keyword:

```
class UserStoreLog(
    private val store: UserStore,
    private val logger: Logger
```

```
) : UserStore by store {

    override fun saveUser(user: User) {
        logger.info("saving $user")
        store.saveUser(user) //calling
        logger.info("saved  $user")
    }

}
val dbStore = UserStoreDb("mydb")
val loggedStore = UserStoreLog(dbStore, mylogger)
```

We only need to override the methods that we want to change; the rest will be automatically delegated.

This way, if we have multiple implementations of our store, we can add logging capabilities on all of them with a single class.

Delegated Properties

In Kotlin, it's also possible to delegate some behavior of object properties to avoid code duplication. This is a very powerful tool with many uses—for example, we can write a delegate to read the properties from a configuration file using reflection, or from a JSON, and so on.

Another very useful delegate is lazy. We can avoid doing some calculations until someone requires the property value. For example:

```
val lazyAnswer: Int by lazy {
    superLongComputation()
    42
}
```

Our field lazyAnswer will only be initialized when someone tries to read its value. After that, any other call will return the same value without recalculating it, but if nobody reads it, it won't be unnecessarily initialized.

Type Alias

Type aliases are just an alias for a type. In this way, we can avoid long types and make the code clearer and more compact. For example:

```
typealias Bookings = Map<User, List<LocalDate>>
```

Keep in mind that they are just an alias, not a different type, so for example, we can declare an alias for a String and use it in a parameter:

```
typealias UserId = String
```

```
fun findUser(id: UserId): User = ...
```

But we can still call findUser, passing any variable of type String or any other alias of String; it doesn't have to be a UserId.

There is no equivalent of type aliases in Java (so far), and they are completely resolved at compile time with the equivalent type declaration.

Internal Visibility

Functions, properties, classes, objects, and interfaces in Kotlin can have different visibility levels, like in Java. Private, public, and protected visibility modifiers work like in Java, but package is missing.

In its place there is internal, which is a new kind of visibility modifier that makes something visible only within the same module. A Kotlin module is a set of files compiled together, like a project or an IntelliJ module or a Gradle sourceset.

What's happening internally is that the internal elements are compiled with a mangled name, so they can't be accessed outside from other modules, at least not without some hacking.

Talking about visibility, another difference to keep in mind is that in Kotlin, the default visibility is public and not package like in Java.

When

In Kotlin, when works like switch in Java or a chain of if. It works as an expression, returning the value of the selected choice.

```kotlin
fun isTheAnswer(x: Int): String =
    when (x) {
        42 -> "the answer"
        else -> "not the answer"
    }
```

The equivalent Java code is something like this:

```java
String isTheAnswer(int x) {
  String res;
  switch(x) {
  case 42:
    res = "the answer";
    break;
  default:
    res = "not the answer";
  }
  return res;
}
```

Java 12 introduced a new switch syntax that doesn't require the break but is still quite verbose when compared to Kotlin.

There are other features in the Kotlin when: it supports smart-casting, destructuring, and a somewhat-limited pattern matching. It's particularly useful together with sealed classes.

Sealed Class

The concept of a sealed class is a class that can be inherited only inside the same package and the same module. In other words, all the hierarchy must be compiled at the same time.

The sealed class itself is abstract, and it can't be instantiated directly. Its children can be objects, final classes, or other abstract classes, but they can't be open classes:

```
sealed class MyError()

class GenericError(val msg: String): MyError()

class HttpError(val status: Int, val response: String): MyError()

object UnexpectedError : MyError()
```

Since all its children are known at compile time, we can use when to check for all the possible implementations and use smart cast to access their properties:

```
fun checkError(e: MyError): String =
    when(e){
        is GenericError -> e.msg
        is HttpError -> "${e.status}"
        UnexpectedError -> "Unexpected Error!"
    }
```

Sealed classes have been added to Java in version 15, but they were present in Kotlin from the start.

Sealed Interface

In addition to sealed classes, Kotlin 1.5 introduced sealed interfaces and removed the restriction of having all the sealed class hierarchy in a single file.

Sealed interfaces are particularly useful when all the sealed instances have some fields in common. The typical case is when all the types of the union have some common contract to honor, like in the following example:

```
sealed interface MyErrorWithMsg {
    val msg: String
}
```

```
class GenericError(override val msg: String): MyErrorWithMsg

class HttpError(val status: Int, val resp: String): MyErrorWithMsg {
    override val msg = "$status - $resp"
}

object UnexpectedError : MyErrorWithMsg {
    override val msg = "Unexpected Error!"
}
```

In this way, we force any concrete implementation of MyErrorWithMsg to have a msg field of type String.

The same result can be reached using abstract fields in the sealed base class, but interfaces make it more elegant and easier to read.

Tailrec Keyword

In Java, there is a limit to the number of recursion calls, since each call will use an entry on the stack and at some point (in order of thousands of recursions) the stack will exhaust its space.

If the recursive call is the last function call of the function, though, the compiler can drop the current stack frame and replace with the new call, since there will be no need to come back, being the call at the end.

To see how it works, let's try with a very silly function that calculates the sum of all numbers up to x in a recursive way:

```
fun recursiveSum(acc: Long, x: Long): Long =
    if (x = 1) acc else recursiveSum(acc + x,x-1)
```

If we try to call it with an x big enough—about 10000 with standard JVM parameters—it will generate a java.lang.StackOverflowError.

Adding the tailrec modifier removes the stack frame before calling itself, so it can be used with any value of x:

```
tailrec fun recursiveSum(acc: Long, x: Long): Long =
    if (x = 1) acc else recursiveSum(acc + x,x-1)
```

I also wrote a blog post with a deeper analysis of Kotlin recursion.[11]

In Kotlin 1.6, they introduced DeepRecursiveFunction for allowing deep recursion functions, not tail recursive, using the heap to maintain its own calling stack.[12]

---

11. https://medium.com/@ramtop/kotlin-pearls-8-recursion-tailrecursion-and-ycombinator-in-kotlin-3ec6975e9b6
12. https://kotlinlang.org/api/latest/jvm/stdlib/kotlin/-deep-recursive-function/

Sequences

Sequences are special iterators in Kotlin that work like a collection. This lets us create infinite lists and then generate only the elements that we need.

```
val powersOfTwo = generateSequence(2) { it * 2 }

powersOfTwo
    .take(10)
    .forEach(::println)
```

Since our powersOfTwo sequence is infinite, we need to make sure to take only the elements that we need. Without the take(10) line, this program would never end.

The other characteristic of sequences is that map and the other collection higher-order functions work in a lazy way on them, which can be faster because it avoids copying intermediate collections. A good explanation can be found in this blog post.[13]

Exploring the Kotlin Type System

In my opinion, the single main advantage of Kotlin over Java is the powerful type system. We'll cover some of its features here, but for a general overview there is a nice blog post by Nat Pryce.[14]

Nullable Types

The first thing a Java programmer usually notices when looking at Kotlin code for the first time is that there are a number of question marks interspersed in the code. They are used to specify that something can be nullable.

A nullable type is a type created by the union of a nonnullable type with the null. It has a question mark ? appended after the type name:

```
val maybeAString: String? = null
val definitelyAString: String = null //doesn't compile!
```

There are two rules with nullable types:

1. You can't assign null to a nonnullable type.
2. You can't call a method on a nullable type, without null-checking it first.

Following these rules, we can completely get rid of NullPointerExceptions in Kotlin.

Putting a question mark before the dot is a shortcut to call a method on a nullable object only if it's safe to do.

---

13. https://medium.com/androiddevelopers/collections-and-sequences-in-kotlin-55db18283aca
14. http://www.natpryce.com/articles/000818.html

```
maybeAString.length //doesn't compile

maybeAString?.length //return Int?
```

Finally, let's meet the Elvis operator, a question mark followed by a colon (which looks a bit like the King if you bend your head), which returns the value on the right if the object on the left is null:

```
maybeAString?.length ?: 0 // return Int
```

The equivalent Java code would be this:

```
if (maybeAString == null) {
    return 0;
} else {
    return maybeAString.length();
}
```

Infix Functions

Another nice feature of Kotlin is how it makes it effortless to define a Domain Specific Language. For example, as we saw, we can put the lambda parameters outside the parenthesis. Infix functions allow us to go further in the same direction.

What is an infix function? It's a function that stays in the middle of the two operands rather than to the left. To define them, you add the infix keyword on the left of an extension function with only one parameter.

For example, we can use it to build our types in a DSL style. Let's say we have a Pizza data class with two fields.

```
data class Pizza(val name: String, val price: Double)
```

We can create an infix function that calls the constructor:

```
infix fun String.costs(price: Double): Pizza = Pizza(this, price)
```

So, we can now define our menu in a way closer to a natural language:

```
val menu = listOf(
    "Marinara" costs 5.8,
    "Margherita" costs 6.2,
    "Capricciosa" costs 8.5
)
```

Operators

Some languages, like C++ and Scala, allow you to override the behavior of operators on types, and some don't allow that, like Java. Overriding the operators is a very powerful technique, but it can result in hard-to-read code.

Kotlin takes an intermediate way and allows you to override a well-defined set of operators, but not create new ones.

As an example, we create a data class, Order, to keep track of pizzas and we'll override the + operator. Each operator has a method associated, in this case, the plus method:

```kotlin
data class Order(val pizzas: List<Pizza> = emptyList()) {

    operator fun plus(pizza: Pizza): Order {
        return Order(pizzas + pizza)
    }

}
```

Using the new operator, we can define an order adding up some pizzas:

```kotlin
val mari = "Marinara" costs 5.8
val capri = "Capricciosa" costs 8.5
val order = emptyOrder + mari + capri
```

We've only scratched the surface of Kotlin's DSL possibilities here. To learn more about it, I recommend the book, *Programming DSLs in Kotlin [Sub21]*.

A Pinch of Theory

In this appendix, we'll examine the mathematical principles that underlie functional programming. Additionally, we'll revisit some of the concepts we have previously covered and provide a more rigorous definition of them.

This appendix isn't a comprehensive explanation of the topic; rather, it serves as a gentle introduction that does not require any mathematics knowledge. It aims to bridge the gap between introductory and more advanced material and serve as a stepping stone for further study of category theory in traditional textbooks.

Here, I have attempted to write down what I wish someone had told me when I first began studying the mathematical fundamentals of functional programming.

Category Theory

Category theory is a branch of mathematics that studies how things are related to each other. Its fundamental idea is that we can capture the essential features of a system using a bunch of dots and arrows.

Since its requirements are so minimal and abstract, category theory can be applied in a lot of fields that are apparently unrelated, for example:

- Biology: Category theory has been used to model biological systems, such as networks of gene interactions and protein folding pathways.

- Linguistics: Linguists have used category theory to study the structure of language, including the relationships between words and grammatical structures.

- Philosophy: Category theory has been used in philosophy to study concepts such as causation and ontology.

- Economics: Category theory has been used to study economic systems, including supply and demand relationships and game theory.

- Music: Category theory has been used to study the structure of musical composition and improvisation.

The power of category theory is its ability to abstract away the specific details of a given system or process and focus instead on the relationships between its parts. By creating a category that captures these relationships, we can utilize the rich toolkit of category theory to analyze the system as a whole.

For example, suppose we have a complex biological network consisting of many genes and proteins that interact with one another in intricate ways. By constructing a category that captures the interactions between them, we can apply the theorems and proofs of category theory to gain insights into the behavior of the network as a whole, regardless of the specifics of each individual gene or protein.

In the same way, in linguistics, we can represent the relationships between words and grammatical structures using a category, so we can use it to analyze the structure of language and its use in communication.

While our main focus in this appendix will be the application of category theory to functional programming, it's important to keep in mind how everything we discuss here can have many other applications.

Talking about our field, functional programming does not require an understanding of category theory, but familiarity with category theory can help you to understand why certain things work better than others.

What studying category theory gave to me is a fresh approach to problem-solving—a kind of new perspective that, although it may not be 100 percent accurate from a mathematical point of view, has proven very useful in my day-to-day work.

It's not about understanding a particular concept from category theory and immediately applying it to my code; rather, the concepts of categories have allowed me to better recognize patterns within my codebase.

I firmly believe that the real big change in adopting functional programming happens when it becomes second nature to solve problems by abstracting simple functions, rather than relying on a sequence of imperative instructions.

In this regard, studying category theory has certainly improved my ability to think in terms of abstract structures and relationships, rather than focusing on specific cases. This has led me to adopt a more systematic approach to problem solving, aiming to create solutions that are more sustainable and manageable over time.

To draw a comparison, engineers undoubtedly benefit from mathematics, but they aren't concerned with the impossibility of precisely calculating pi; a reasonable approximation is all they need.

In this appendix, we'll focus on some aspects of category theory that may be interesting to programmers and gloss over some of the technicalities. Hopefully you'll be intrigued enough to learn more. For further reading there is a list of materials I found useful in Appendix 4, Additional Resources, on page 417.

Let's start with some definitions.

Sets and Functions

Let's first introduce the concept of a *set* in mathematics. We don't need a formal definition because we aren't focusing on sets, and, strictly speaking, categories aren't based on sets. Still, we'll refer to sets often, so it's better to refresh ourselves with some concepts first.

For the purposes of this appendix, we can consider a set as a collection of unique elements. It can contain a finite number of elements—for example, a set of your classmates—or it can contain an infinite number of elements—for example, the set of natural numbers, which are positive integers starting from one.

In mathematics, a function is a relation between two sets: a set of all possible input values, which is called the *domain* of the function, and a set of all possible output values, which is called the *codomain* of the function.

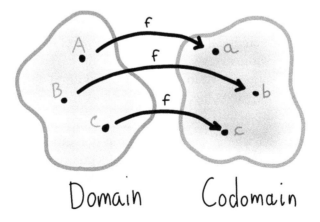

For example, let's consider the squared function and the square root function in the context of the set of natural numbers. The squared function takes a natural number and produces its square as the output. For instance, when we input 3, the squared function outputs 9, which is the square of 3.

The domain of the squared function is the set of all natural numbers, because we can input any natural number into the function and obtain a valid output. However, the codomain of the squared function is restricted to the set of perfect square numbers, which are the numbers that can be expressed as the square of some other integer. For example, 1, 4, 9, 16, 25, and so on.

On the other hand, the square root function takes a perfect square number as its input and produces the number whose square is equal to the input as its output. For instance, when we input 25, the square root function outputs 5, because 5 multiplied by 5 equals 25. So the domain of the square root function is the set of perfect square numbers, and its codomain is the set of natural numbers.

As a programming example, we can define a function, isTaller(), that will return true or false depending on whether a classmate is taller than you. This function maps all our classmates to the Boolean set—that is, a set composed of the two elements true and false.

We can say that a function is total if it's defined for all possible input values in its domain and therefore has no "gaps" or undefined values. We'll see later why this is important.

What Is a Category?

Previously in the book, we defined a category as a bunch of dots and arrows (see Learning Functors and Categories, on page 163). However, we now require a slightly more precise definition.

A category is a mathematical construct consisting of some dots, which are called objects, and some arrows connecting them, called morphisms. These morphisms must satisfy certain properties, including the existence of an identity morphism for each object, and the ability to compose morphisms in a way that's associative.

Now you may wonder what's so exciting about dots and arrows? Well, there is a lot to be excited about actually. Using objects and morphisms, we can reproduce the fundamental shape of different structures so that we can study their relationships in a unified way.

A central theme in category theory is the study of structures and structure-preserving maps. A map f:X -> Y is a kind of observation of object X via a specified relationship it has with another object, Y.

—An Invitation to Applied Category Theory

We can consider a category as something similar to a set, but instead of being interested in its elements, we're mostly interested in how those elements relate to each other. For simplicity, we'll focus on *locally small categories*, which are categories where the collection of arrows between any two objects forms a set.

The corresponding elements of a set are the objects of a category—that is, the dots in our diagrams. The objects are connected by arrows, which are the morphisms.

Similar to functions, in a morphism from A to B, we call A the domain object and B the codomain object. We can compose two morphisms f and g if the codomain of f is equal to the domain of g. The composition operator is represented with a dot, and it reads from right to left. In other words g . f is equivalent to g(f())—first we apply f and then g to the result.

Morphism composition needs to satisfy the associative law. To understand what the associative law is, think of the analogy "the mother of your grandmother is the grandmother of your mother." In other words, in the earlier diagram, it doesn't matter the order in which we compose the arrows. We can express this by writing: h . (g . f) = (h . g) . f.

The final characteristic of a category is that every object must be associated with an identity morphism. The identity morphism is a special type of morphism that maps an object to itself—in other words, has the object both as domain and codomain—and is denoted by the symbol "id". We can draw it as a little circular arrow around every object, but in most diagrams they are skipped for clarity.

One important point is that an object can have multiple morphisms to itself, known as *endomorphisms*. However, there is only one endomorphism that serves as the identity—the one that maps the object back to itself exactly.

Let's now familiarize ourselves with the concept of categories by examining some examples.

Empty Category

The simplest possible category is the *Empty* category. This is a category with no objects and no morphisms, and it's related to the empty set. It's not particularly interesting in itself, but is a valid category, which means that it can be used as a starting point for constructing more complex categories.

Monoid

You already learned about the category with only one object (see Discovering the Monoid, on page 125): the *Monoid*. In this category, since there is a single object, all morphisms are endomorphisms that can be composed together.

However, it's important to note that not all of these endomorphisms are identity morphisms. Since there is only one object in this category, there is only one identity morphism as well.

To provide an example of a monoid, you can consider the Rubik's cube, where the endomorphisms represent moves that can be made on the cube. The identity morphism in this case would be the "no move" action, while all other moves are endomorphisms that change the state of the cube.

Set Category

The category of all sets is called *Set*. Every possible set is an object in Set. This may seem confusing, but each object in Set—the category—is a set, not an element of a set.

Note that you can't define a set of all sets; that would result in the well-known Russell's paradox. However, the category of all sets can be defined without any problem.

Since functions connect two sets, or a set with itself, every total function is a morphism in Set. The identity function of each set is the identity morphism of that set.

Totality is a requirement, because if a function isn't defined for all elements in the input set, it may not produce a valid output set. Therefore, partial functions can't be considered morphisms, because they don't always preserve the structure and relationships between objects. Set is a very important category and we'll use it again.

Computer Language Category

For the functional programmer, the most interesting categories are the ones that reflect computer languages. It's possible to create a category with all the types in a programming language: the objects are the different types, and the morphisms are pure total functions between two types, one as input and one as output.

For example, let's imagine a toy programming language with only three types: Int, String, and Boolean. These are the objects in our category; the morphisms are the functions that take one of these types as input and produce another type as output—for example: intToString: (Int) -> String, isOdd: (Int) -> Boolean, reverse: (String) -> String, and so on.

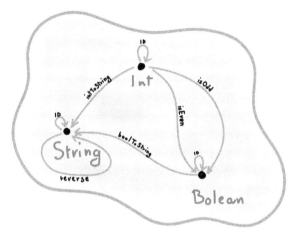

In this example, reverse() is an endomorphism, but it's not the identity. The identity function will always return the argument received.

In relation to Kotlin, we can consider a category where objects are all the possible Kotlin immutable types, and the morphisms connecting them are pure total functions with one argument.

For this to work, we need to consider a kind of idealized version of Kotlin, purified from mutable objects, global state, side effects, and exceptions. We can call this category *PK* (Pure Kotlin). Even if it's only a subset of the Kotlin language's capabilities, it's useful to know that if we stick with those limitations, as we did in this book, we can successfully apply intuitions from category theory.

What benefit can we gain with this? Generally speaking, mapping a computer language to a category with all its types allows us to study it in the context of category theory. This could be useful for better understanding its structure and the relationship between types and functions, and it will likely give us insights on new methods and approaches for combining these types and functions—in other words, what's been discussed during the course of this book.

> **Joe asks:**
> # What about Class Methods?
>
> In the context of category theory, what we care about are the properties of morphisms, rather than the specific syntax used in a programming language such as Kotlin. For our purposes, methods are simply a convenient means of defining a function with an additional implicit argument, which is the object referenced by this.
>
> The only constraint on methods is that they must return an output value without modifying the object itself.
>
> Similarly, for functions with multiple parameters and receivers, we can consider the tuple formed by their arguments and receivers as an implicit product type that serves as the only input parameter for the function.

Subcategory

In general, a subcategory is a category that contains a subset of the objects and morphisms from the main category. It must be a well-defined category in its own right: self-contained and following the rules about associativity and identity.

Speaking of computer languages, we can create a subcategory from some types and functions to focus on a specific problem or domain. For example, the mini language we mentioned before can be defined as a Kotlin subcategory:

```kotlin
fun <T> identity(x: T): T = x

fun intToString(x: Int): String = x.toString()

fun boolToString(x: Boolean): String = x.toString()

fun isEven(x: Int): Boolean = x % 2 == 0

fun isOdd(x: Int): Boolean = !isEven(x)

fun reverse(s: String): String= s.reversed()
```

This way we can verify the associativity law:

```kotlin
fun `subcategory respects the associativity law`(){
    val f1 = (::isOdd andThen ::boolToString) andThen ::reverse
    val f2 = ::isOdd andThen (::boolToString andThen ::reverse)

    repeat(100) {
        val number = random.nextInt()
        expectThat(f1(number)).isEqualTo(f2(number))
    }
}
```

And, we can verify the identity law:

```
fun `subcategory respects the identity law`(){
    val idOdd = ::isOdd andThen ::identity

    repeat(100) {
        val number = random.nextInt()
        expectThat(idOdd(number)).isEqualTo(isOdd(number))
    }
}
```

In general, subcategories are useful for studying specific aspects or subsets of a larger category, and they can provide a more focused and specialized approach to understanding and analyzing the structure and relationships within a computer language.

While discussing events and representing entities as finite state machines, we stumbled upon an interesting subcategory example. We can establish a category in which every event serves as a morphism between two states of the entity. As you remember, each event represents a state change of the entity. This subcategory would be a part of the larger category PK.

Diagrams

Throughout this book, you've seen many diagrams with arrows that provide an intuitive idea of how to combine functions for a given task. While these diagrams draw inspiration from the formal diagrams used in category theory, they aren't defined with any accuracy.

In contrast, category diagrams are highly precise tools used for proving properties of categorical constructions.

A diagram *in* a category C is a collection of vertices and arrows corresponding to objects and morphisms existing in C. Note that these diagrams are different from diagrams *of* categories; they aren't representing a complete category; they only focus on some objects and morphisms.

A diagram is said to *commute* if, for any pair of vertices, all the paths from one to another are equal.

For example, saying that the diagram shown on page 400 commutes is exactly the same as saying f . g' = g . f'. In other words, the paths from A to B are the same.

Note that, generally speaking, functions don't commute. One exception is the add operation, so 5 + 6 is equal to 6 + 5, but reverse(intToStr(123)) isn't the same

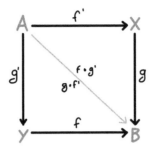

as intToStr(reverse(123)). It doesn't even compile! That's why in our diagram f is different from f' and g from g'; it's only their combination that commutes.

It's All About Morphisms

> If I haven't convinced you yet that category theory is all about morphisms then I haven't done my job properly.

—Bartosz Milewski

One crucial moment in my understanding of category was when I realized that what's important in a category isn't the objects/types that are inside but the morphisms/functions that connect them. To help you to better grasp what this means, let's look at some different types of morphisms.

Isomorphism

Equality is a very tricky concept. How can we determine if two objects are equal? It may be difficult to prove for complex types. However, in many cases, we don't require strict equality. Instead, we can consider two objects as equivalent if we can transform one into the other in both directions.

This is the concept of *isomorphism*, a mapping between two objects that preserves the structure and properties of the objects. The term comes from the Greek word *iso*, meaning "same." In other words, if two objects are isomorphic, then they have the same structure and properties, and even though they may not be identical in other respects, we can always go from one to the other. If f is a morphism from X to Y, and g is morphism from Y to X, then f . g == id means that f and g form an isomorphism. Then we can say that X and Y are isomorphic, which is almost like saying that they are equals but not quite.

Looking at it from another perspective, most functions are *lossy*. They lose information when they transform a value into another type. For example, isOdd returns a Boolean value from a number, but you can't get the original number from the Boolean.

When a function isn't lossy, in other words, it doesn't lose any information during the transformation, it must have a reverse function that returns the original input from its output. The union of the function and its reverse forms an isomorphism.

We can express it in code:

```
fun <T,U> isomorphism(f1: (T) -> U, f2: (U) -> T): (T) -> T = { f2( f1( it))}
```

If you think about a byte and 8-bit ASCII characters, they have a perfect match. They aren't identical—since 122 is different from z—but they are isomorphic. We can verify this with a few lines of code:

```
fun `verify isomorphism`(){
    val iso: (Byte) -> Byte = isomorphism(Byte::toChar, Char::toByte)

    repeat(100){
        val x = Random().nextInt(256).toByte()

        expectThat(iso(x)).isEqualTo(x)
    }
}
```

Note also that if we change the order of the two functions, we can create the isomorphism for the other type, Char in our example:

```
val iso2: (Char) -> Char = isomorphism(Char::toByte, Byte::toChar)
```

When studying categories, it's very common to define things as "equal up to an isomorphism." This expression denotes that two things can be transformed into each other by an isomorphism.

This means that even if the two things may have differences, they can be considered essentially equal from a structural point of view. In other words, any difference between the things can be "ignored," because it doesn't affect the essential properties that we're interested in.

Let's proceed with our exploration of categories by introducing a couple of additional definitions.

Initial and Terminal Object

In a category C, the *initial object* is an object with a single morphism to all the objects of C. The focus is about the uniqueness of the morphism, and when I say unique, of course, I mean unique up to an isomorphism.

It's important to note that in the context of programming, "object" in this sense refers to a type, rather than an instance of a class or object. Additionally, inheritance and subtyping aren't directly related to morphisms.

In our tiny language, and in Kotlin itself, there is no initial object. You may wonder if Unit is an initial object, but we can verify that by taking a type, say Boolean, as an example:

```
fun initial(): Boolean =...
```

This function has type (Unit) -> Boolean, so if it's unique, and if we can construct similar functions for any type, then we have demonstrated that Unit is the initial object.

But initial() has two possible implementations, one returning True and one returning False. So Unit can't be our initial object.

If we squint hard enough, we can consider Nothing in PK as the initial object, since we can write the initial object in this way, and it's unique:

```
fun <T> initial(x: Nothing): T = TODO("this will never be called")
```

But as far as I know, there isn't much use for such a function.

The terminal object is the opposite. If all the elements in C have a unique morphism to an object X, then X is the terminal object of C.

If we look at the previous example and reverse the types, this function is effectively unique up to an isomorphism:

```
fun terminal(x: Boolean): Unit = Unit
```

We can implement it in a different way if we want, but with the same result: whatever we pass as input, we get Unit.

This isn't specific to Boolean; we can make it generic:

```
fun <T> terminal(x: T): Unit = Unit
```

Here, no matter the argument type, there is only a unique function that returns Unit. So Unit is a terminal object of PK. This isn't specific to Unit; any singleton object in Kotlin is a terminal object in PK. This comes directly from the definition of singleton as a type with only one instance.

Opposite Category

If we draw the diagrams for the initial and final objects, as shown in the figure on page 403, we can see how they are the same with the arrows in the opposite direction.

Each category has its opposite, defined by reversing all the arrows. This means that in the original category C, two objects A and B are related by a morphism

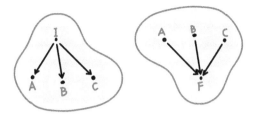

f: A -> B. In the opposite category, let's call it Cop, they are related by a morphism fop: B -> A.

This symmetry between a category and its opposite category is called *duality*. It's important, because it doubles the productivity of category theorists: for each theorem or construction, there is a corresponding theorem or construction in the opposite category that can be derived automatically.

The opposite constructions are traditionally prefixed with "co," so there are products and coproducts, monads and comonads, limits and colimits, and so on. We'll cover some of these later in this appendix. Just remember that if something starts with "co," it refers to something else with the arrows reversed.

Types over Types

We discussed algebraic data type Union Types, on page 123. Now, let's have another look at them in a more theoretical context.

Product and Coproduct Types

In computer languages, the product of two types is a tuple with those two types, like Pair in Kotlin. Data classes can be considered products of types as well. It's easy to see that, for example, a data class with a string and an integer is equal to a Pair<String, Int> up to an isomorphism.

```
data class User(val name: String, val id: Int){
    constructor(pair: Pair<String, Int>):
            this(pair.first, pair.second)

    fun toPair(): Pair<String, Int> = name to id
}
val userPairIso: (Pair<String, Int>) -> Pair<String, Int> =
    isomorphism(::User, User::toPair)
```

This perspective is putting all the attention on the types that constitute the product, but we know that it's all about morphisms. So, how can we define the product of two types in terms of morphisms?

From this perspective, a type C, which is a product of two types A and B, is a type that comes with two functions, one that returns A and one that returns B. In Kotlin, data classes have embedded functions to return each of the components.

For example, Pair has the functions first() and second(), and User has the functions name() and id(). These are sometimes called the projections of the type.

But, there could be any number of types with morphisms to the same object. To continue with our example, we can have a data class with many fields, one of which is a String and another of which is an Int.

So, to define a product we also need to make sure that it's the most basic type and that it can be factored out from more complex types. We can render this with a diagram:

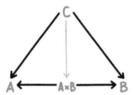

We can interpret this as saying that for any object C with two arrows f and g that go from C to A and B, there is exactly one mediating arrow h: C -> AxB, making the diagram commute. It goes without saying that the mediating arrow is unique up to an isomorphism.

I mentioned duality before, so what is the representation of the same diagram with the arrows reversed? By definition, we can call this the *coproduct* of A and B, but it may come as a surprise that what we're looking at here is the sum type A + B. In other words, it's a composite type that has a value that can be of either type A or B, the equivalent of a sealed class in Kotlin.

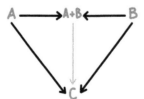

If you look at the diagrams long enough, you'll see how this is possible: both A and B can be extracted from the tuple A x B. The union type A + B can be generated from either A or B.

Exponential Types

Now let's pose a question: if functions are arrows and types are objects, how can we represent the type of a function in a category?

As an example, in PK, the type of the function intToStr is (Int) -> String, so is there an object in PK to represent that type? Of course there is!

But first, another definition: in a category, the set of all morphisms between two objects A and B is called the *hom-set*, and it's written Hom(A,B). So the elements of the hom-set are the elements of the function type. In other words, all the functions from A to B, and only those, have type (A) -> B.

As we saw, function types are called exponentials (see Calculate the Cardinality of Composite Types, on page 123), so we can write the type of f: A -> B as B^A, which we can read as "if A then B." Exponential types have a special function *eval*, such as B^A x A -> B. This is implicit in the definition of exponential types as function, but it may not be evident.

Remember that a function that has a product A x B as input is equivalent to a function taking two arguments A and B, so when we translate eval in code we can see that it is the invoking of the function.

```
fun <A,B> eval(fn: (A)->B, x: A): B = fn(x)
```

And now the interesting part: let's say there is a function f: (A x B) -> C, which means that it takes A and another parameter B to return C. A property of eval is that for any f, there is always a function from B to C^A. This function is the *curry* function we discussed (see Partial Application, on page 83). Let's visualize this with a diagram, showing when currying f we replaced B with C^A, which is a function A -> C:

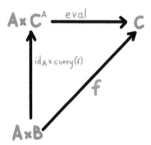

This is pretty neat! We just discovered that currying is a consequence of exponential types.

Translating this as code would be:

```
fun <A,B,C> f(a: A, b:B): C = //a pure function
fun <A,B> eval(a: A, f: (A) -> B): B = f(a)
fun <A,B,C> curryB(f: (A, B) -> C, b:B): (A) -> C = { a:A -> f(a,b) }

f(a,b) == eval(a, curryB(::f, b)) //always true
```

Note that not all categories allow for exponentiation. Categories with terminal objects, binary products, and exponentiation are called *Cartesian Closed Category*, CCC for short. Our PK is a CCC, and most static-typed computer languages form a CCC.

Finally, we may wonder if there is a relationship between products and exponential types, or to use our PK category, between Pair<Int,String> and (Int) -> String. As a matter of fact, there is! It involves a special pair of functors known as *Adjoint Functors*. But first, we need to talk about functors.

Functors Are Mappers

> In category theory, when we say one category is "like" another category, we usually mean that there is a mapping between the two. For this mapping to be meaningful, it should preserve the structure of the category. Such a mapping has a name: it's called a functor.
>
> —Bartosz Milewski

As we saw earlier (see Defining Functors in Code, on page 167), a functor is a bit like a function, but instead of mapping elements of a set to another set, it operates on categories. The functor should map not only all the objects in the initial category, but also all the morphisms present within it. Actually, what's really important is the mapping of morphisms, as the mapping of objects follows as a natural consequence.

Formally, a functor is a mapping F from one category C to another category D that assigns to each object X in C an object F(X) in D, and to each morphism f: X -> Y in C a morphism F(f): F(X) -> F(Y) in D, such that the following conditions are satisfied:

1. F(f) is a morphism in D whenever f is a morphism in C.

2. F(idX) = idF(X) for every object X in C, where idX is the identity morphism on X and idF(X) is the identity morphism on F(X).

3. F(g . f) = F(g) . F(f) for every pair of composable morphisms f: X -> Y and g: Y -> Z in C.

A useful image to help visualize this is imagining that a functor f projects an image of the category C into another category D. Note that the image of C into D doesn't have to cover all of D.

Adjoint Functors

Since I mentioned them before, let's have a little teaser of what *adjoint functors* are.

As we discussed, functors are required to preserve the structure of the category, but they can forget some information if we aren't interested in it. In this case they are called *forgetful functors*.

A forgetful functor often has a special relation with a *free functor* in the other direction. A free functor is the opposite of a forgetful functor, because it creates some information "for free."

So, if we have a free functor that maps from category C to category D, and a forgetful functor that goes back from category D to category C, they can form a special relationship called an *adjunction*. Adjoint functors are a pair of functors that allow us to "transpose" concepts from one category to another, while preserving their fundamental structure.

More precisely, two functors F: C -> D and G: D -> C are considered adjoint if there is a correspondence between the hom-sets C(X, G(Y)) and D(F(X), Y) for all objects X in C and Y in D. The functor F is referred to as the left adjoint, and the functor G is referred to as the right adjoint.

Now, I mentioned before that there is a relation between a product type—say, a tuple—and an exponential type—say, a function. This relation is expressed by the adjunction between the product functor, which plays the part of the free functor, and the exponential functor that works as forgetful functor.

Unfortunately, we don't have the space to properly cover adjoint functors in this appendix, but you can find more about them in the blogs and videos listed in the resources appendix.

Endofunctors

When we talk about functors in functional programming, we always mean endofunctors—that is, functors from a category, say PK, to the same category.

Now you may wonder, why bother? If we have to stay in the same category, we can save ourselves the effort of involving functors at all.

It's a fair question, so let's try to answer it. By definition, when we're doing functional programming, we're using types and functions in the CCC of our language, what we called PK for Kotlin. The reason we're interested only in endofunctions is that we're interested in functors that can operate on everything—objects and morphisms, types and functions—inside PK and they should give us a result also inside PK; otherwise, they would produce something that isn't valid Kotlin code.

Intuitively, an endofunctor projects PK inside PK itself, in a kind of smaller image of PK. For example, we saw that List is a functor (see Looking at Lists as Functors, on page 171). We can create a List for any type in Kotlin, including functions and other lists.

```
           Int ===endofunctor===> List<Int>
        String ===endofunctor===> List<String>
(Int) -> String ===endofunctor===> List<(Int) -> String>
   List<String> ===endofunctor===> List<List<String>>
```

In other words, we're mapping the whole PK into the smaller subcategory, let's call it L, that contains all kinds of lists. Since L is still inside PK, we can say that List is an endofunctor.

So, what can we obtain by using an endofunctor? We aren't mapping an external category, but we can use it to allow functional effects inside our type system. In other words, by putting a function (A) -> B inside an (endo)functor, we can operate on IO, for example, making it explicit and avoiding side effects. Functional effects don't have to be impure; Lists are functors with the effect of forming lists. Other effects can be related to concurrency.

What benefits do we gain from using an endofunctor? Although we aren't mapping an external category, we can use it to enable functional effects within our type system.

In other words, by encapsulating a function (A) -> B within an (endo)functor, we can manipulate IO operations, for instance, by making them explicit and avoiding side effects. Note that functional effects don't have to be impure; the effect of the functor List is to create ordered collections, while other effects can be tied to concurrency, handling state, and so on. More generally, an effect is a change in the status of the system that's outside the computation environment.

Natural Transformations

> I didn't invent categories to study functors; I invented them to study natural transformations.

—Saunders Mac Lane (the inventor of Category Theory)

If functors are mapping morphisms from one category to another, can we have morphisms operating on the functors themselves? Of course we can. They are called *natural transformations*. Why such a lame name? Why not call them "morphfunctors" or something like that?

The reason is that, chronologically, natural transformations preceded functors and categories. To determine what was considered "natural" in natural transformations, Saunders Mac Lane introduced the concepts of functors and categories. As with many other fundamental mathematical concepts, these ideas proved useful in their own right.

To visualize a natural transformation, let's draw a diagram where F and G are two functors from the category C to D, and f is a morphism in C from A to B. A transformation NT is said to be natural if this diagram commutes for all objects and morphisms in the category C.

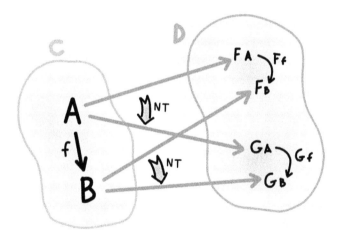

In other words, we can consider functors F and G as each projecting an image of C inside D. The two images are different but somehow related. NT transforms one image into the other.

When looking at natural transformations from a computing perspective, they are polymorphic functions operating on functors. As an example, let's consider a function that takes something Bar<T> (which is a functor) and returns something else Foo<T> but doesn't care at all about T.

Intuitively, this is the meaning of natural: there are no constraints on T; any type will do. So for example, converting a list to a set is a natural transformation:

```
fun <T> toSet(l: List<T>): Set<T> = HashSet(l)
```

A natural transformation can also return a functor of the same type, possibly modified in some way. For example, we can write a function that reverses any list, regardless of the type of the elements in the list. Also, this function is a natural transformation:

```
fun <T> reverseList(l: List<T>): List<T> = l.reversed()
```

The Mysterious Monad

Monads have a reputation for being difficult to understand from a programming perspective, but from the category theory perspective, they are a natural extension of functor, if you forgive the pun.

Technically, a monad is an endofunctor M with two natural transformations attached:

1. unit takes an object a and returns its monad M(a).
2. join transforms M(M(a)) into M(a).

The first natural transformation unit—nothing to do with the Unit in Kotlin—allows us to create a monad from any object; it's similar to a constructor in programming.

To better understand join, let's consider what we said about endofunctors—they create a smaller image M of the category C in C itself. Now in this smaller M, there must also be the image of M itself—let's call it M^2. This is what's called the square of the endofunctor. Applying join means to project M^2 back into M, reinflating it in a sense.

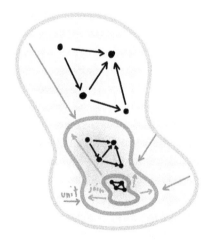

From a code perspective, unit is the monad type constructor, and join is the same join() function we defined for each monad—for example:

```
fun <T, E> Outcome<E, Outcome<E, T>>.join(): Outcome<E, T> =
    bind { it }
```

So far, when we've written monads, we focused on the many uses of the bind function and we implemented join in terms of bind. This makes sense, because in this way, we can avoid an additional memory allocation. But from a mathematical point of view, join is somehow more fundamental than bind, and it's more common in category theory to define monads in term of join rather than bind.

Now, another way to look at monads is that, by definition, they are also objects in the category of endofunctors. In this category, the monad's join and unit operators give birth to a monoid instance, with join acting as the composition operation and unit acting as the identity element. So we can say, as Philip Wadler allegedly did, that monads are monoids in the category of endofunctors.

Comonads

As the name says, comonads are the dual of monads—in other words, a monad with the arrows going in the opposite direction. For example, instead of a unit: Id -> M a, we have the natural transformation extract: W a -> Id. And instead of join: M^2 -> M we have duplicate: W -> W^2. By the way, have you noticed that W is an upside-down M? This is how comonads are usually referred to.

If monads are all about running some operation in a context, limiting the possibility of extracting the value, comonads are all about adding context and extracting the value any time we want.

An interesting use of comonads is to create a builder from an external context—for example, a configuration file. But since this appendix is already very long, this will be left as an exercise for the reader.

Kleisli Category

We saw that monads are functors that we can compose like monoids. An interesting idea to consider is: what would happen if we were to create a category composed only of monads? In other words, each object would be a monad and each morphism would be a function that takes a value and returns a monadic value. Well, we aren't the first to think about it, and it already has a name—the *Kleisli* category.

Those morphisms, from a value to a monad, are called Kleisli arrows. It's possible to use Kleisli arrows instead of bind to compose monads in programming. It creates quite a different style. Let's have a go.

First, we need to define a function to compose two arrows. This operation in Haskell uses the operator >=> which is nicknamed fish for obvious reasons. Unfortunately, we can't use it in Kotlin, so let's call it kleisli and let's make it infix:

```
typealias KArrow<A,B> = (A) -> ContextReader<SomeContext, B>

infix fun KArrow<A,B>.kleisli(other: KArrow<B,C>): KArrow<A,C> =
    {a -> this(a).bind {b ->other(b) } }
```

Now, let's write an example of using ContextReader to extract some information from a configuration file using the bind style:

```
typealias ConfReader<T> = ContextReader<Properties, T>

val myProperties = Properties().apply {
    setProperty("environment", "DEV")
    setProperty("DEV.url", "http://dev.example.com")
    setProperty("PROD.url", "http://example.com")
}

fun readProp(propName: String): ConfReader<String> =
        ContextReader { it[propName].toString() }

val envUrl = readProp("environment")
  .bind{ envName -> readProp("${envName}.url") }
  .runWith(myProperties)  //http://dev.example.com
```

We can now rewrite the last expression in a Kleisli way:

```
val readUrlFrom = ::readProp kleisli ::readUrl
val envUrl = readUrlFrom("environment").runWith(myProperties)
```

They are both valid styles and you can choose the one that better fits your needs.

It's now time to put it all together and look at one of the most amazing theorems of category theory.

Connecting Everything with Yoneda

> Yoneda lemma is the hardest trivial thing in mathematics.
>
> —Dan Piponi

The story goes that the Japanese mathematician Nobuo Yoneda, while visiting Paris, met the father of category theory, Saunders Mac Lane, at the Gare du

Nord. During their stroll, Mac Lane learned about Yoneda's amazing theorem, which Yoneda himself never bothered to write down.

To give you a taste of this theorem, what Yoneda lemma says is that every object in a category is determined by the morphisms pointing to it, or in other words, by the relationship with the other objects. It's a bit like saying that inside Twitter, who you follow determines who you are. And there is also the dual co-Yoneda that says that it's your followers who determine who you are.

But before looking at the actual definition, we need to consider two special functors.

Hom-Functors

We defined the hom-set as the set of morphisms between two objects in a category. So if we consider an object X in a category C, it will have a set of morphisms for any other object in the category, considering composition of morphisms.

Since each of these hom-sets is a set, by definition, it has to be represented in the category Set of all sets. So fixing an object in C, we can map every object in C to an element of Set; this means we have created a functor. This functor is called, somewhat lamely, hom-functor and it's written C(X, -), where the dash means any possible object. As programmers, we would probably have written C(X, *).

More generally, any arbitrary functor F from a category C to Set is called set-valued if it has an isomorphism with a hom-functor of an element of C. In other words, if there exists an object Y in C such that F and C(Y, -) have a one to one correspondence between them, then F is considered set-valued.

Contravariant Functors

To conclude the panorama of functors, let's look at their dual. We mentioned (see Contravariant Functor, on page 324) that there is a kind of functor that maps in the other direction, called contravariant.

If C(X, -) is the hom-functor that maps all the morphisms from X to Set, what is C(-, Y)? This is the hom-functor that maps all the morphisms from any object of C to Y, and this functor is contravariant, which makes sense, because it will always transform something in Y; we can only change the starting object.

But what happens to C(-, Y) if we consider the opposite category Cop? Remember that the Cop has the same objects and morphisms but going in the opposite direction, so C(-, Y) is equal to Cop(Y, -). More generally, any covariant functor from C to D is a contravariant functor from Cop to D, and vice versa, since the opposite category of Cop is just C.

Yoneda Lemma

We're now ready for the full definition of the Yoneda lemma: given a category C, there is an isomorphism between natural transformations from C(X, -) to any functor F from C to Set. Not only this, these natural transformations have a one-to-one correspondence with the elements of the set determined by F(X).

This is an astonishing result, especially considering that it's valid for all locally small categories. Let's try to visualize this with a diagram:

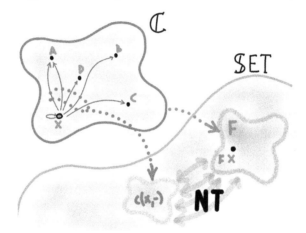

One important consequence is that a valid candidate for F(X) is C(Y, X). If you aren't convinced, look again at the definition of set-valued. In how many ways can you transform your hom-functor to an arbitrary set-valued functor? You may be tempted to say that's impossible to know, it could be any number, but Yoneda is telling us that they are the exact number as the number of morphisms between Y (that is the element on which F is based) and X.

Another consequence is that any two objects in C, X, and Y are isomorphic only if the functor C(X, -) is isomorphic with C(Y, -).

We don't have the space here for a full proof, but if your interest is high enough, you can dig into this by yourself with a good textbook.

> We have already encountered the hom-functor under the guise of the Reader functor. The Yoneda lemma tells us that the reader functor can be naturally mapped to any other functor.
>
> —Bartosz Milewski

What does this mean for a developer? This means we're used to considering data types the "real stuff," and functions are something that go from one type to another, but what Yoneda is telling us is that a type is identified by the set of functions that return it. The functions that return a type ultimately are the constructors, since all other functions that return a type have to call one of the constructors.

Personally, I'm convinced that the Reader functor (see The Context Reader, on page 222) is the most useful of all the functors to handle functional effects. Yoneda tells us that the Reader can be naturally mapped to any other functor.

With this consideration we end this appendix. However, there are still many fascinating concepts that have a connection to functional programming. While studying category theory may present some difficulties, it can ultimately sharpen your functional programming skills and provide a never-ending source of enjoyment.

Conclusion

Congratulations on making it this far in the book! You now possess a powerful set of tools to manipulate your code as a composition of mathematical transformations. But of course, the journey is far from over, and there is always more to discover. As they say in Japan, *gambare* (do your best)!

Additional Resources

Following are some of the best resources for further reading and studying.

Programming

Kotlin

- Venkat Subramaniam. *Programming Kotlin*. The Pragmatic Bookshelf, Raleigh, NC, 2019.

A nice, easy-to-read introduction to the Kotlin language. The concepts are presented in an engaging and humorous way.

- Nat Pryce, Duncan McGregor. *From Java To Kotlin: A Refactoring Guidebook*. O'Reilly & Associates, Inc., Sebastopol, CA, 2021.

An excellent book with a slightly misleading title, it provides much more than just help in converting Java code to Kotlin. The book focuses on increasing the readability and flexibility of your code. It introduces many functional concepts and refactoring techniques that aid in the transition from Java to Kotlin. It's not a guide to learning Kotlin; it's a great resource if you want to learn how to write idiomatic Kotlin code.

Functional Programming

- Eric Normand. *Grokking Simplicity: Taming Complex Software with Functional Thinking*. The Pragmatic Bookshelf, Raleigh, NC, 2019.

This book is an excellent starting point for those unfamiliar with functional programming concepts. It doesn't explore advanced topics, but the author's writing style is clear and illuminating, making it easy to grasp the fundamentals.

- Paul Chiusano, Rúnar Bjarnason. *Functional Programming in Scala*. Manning Publications Co., Greenwich, CT, 2014.

Probably this is the book that more than everything else converted me to functional programming. It's not a light read and requires both careful study and practical application, as the exercises are necessary for fully grasping the concepts presented in the text.

- Rebecca Skinner. *Effective Haskell*. The Pragmatic Bookshelf, Raleigh, NC, 2023.

A good book to learn Haskell, the most widely used pure functional language. In particular, this book is a great guide on how to build a full application in Haskell, rather than just learning the language.

- Scott Wlaschin. *Domain Modeling Made Functional*. The Pragmatic Bookshelf, Raleigh, NC, 2018.

A good book to better understand the core concepts of domain-driven design and how to apply them to functional programming. It uses the F# language for the examples.

TDD

- Kent Beck. *Test-Driven Development By Example*. Addison-Wesley, Boston, MA, 2002.

The first and probably still one of the best books about test-driven development.

Category Theory

Here are some of the resources I found helpful for learning about category theory.

Books

- Eugenia Cheng. *The Joy of Abstraction: An Exploration of Math, Category Theory, and Life*. Cambridge University Press, Cambridge, UK, 2022.

Probably the only book about category theory written for a general audience. It's a testament to the author's skill that she managed to make such a technical subject so engaging and easy to understand. I highly recommend it.

- Benjamin C. Pierce. *Basic Category Theory for Computer Scientists*. The MIT Press, Cambridge, MA, 1991.

Very slim book, quite dense, but full of diagrams to clarify concepts. It doesn't require any prior knowledge of mathematics, but it can be cryptic in some passages if you aren't already familiar with the concepts.

- Brendan Fong, David I. Spivak. *An Invitation to Applied Category Theory: Seven Sketches in Compositionality.* Cambridge University Press, Cambridge, UK, 2019.

It's quite an advanced book; it requires some familiarity with undergraduate level mathematics, but it's never dull or dry. The most interesting parts are the examples that give an indication of many application areas of category theory.

- Emily Riehl. *Category Theory in Context.* Dover Publications, Mineola, NY, 2016.

A very good textbook if you have graduate-level knowledge of mathematics and you want to fully understand how category theory can illuminate problems in algebra and number theory.

Blogs

- https://bartoszmilewski.com

  Bartosz Milewski's blog and free e-book are arguably the best source of material on functional programming and category theory.

- https://boris-marinov.github.io/category-theory-illustrated

  A nice and soft introduction to category theory that progresses to advanced concepts. The many colorful diagrams make concepts easy to grasp.

- https://www.math3ma.com/

  Interesting blog on mathematics and computer science.

Videos

- https://www.youtube.com/@DrBartosz

  The full course on category theory for programmers by Bartosz Milewski.

- https://www.youtube.com/user/thecatsters

  Video lessons on various category theory topics; not particularly aimed at programmers.

Bibliography

[DS09]   Rachel Davies and Liz Sedley. *Agile Coaching*. The Pragmatic Bookshelf, Dallas, TX, 2009.

[Eva03]   Eric Evans. *Domain-Driven Design: Tackling Complexity in the Heart of Software*. Addison-Wesley Longman, Boston, MA, 2003.

[FP09]   Steve Freeman and Nat Pryce. *Growing Object-Oriented Software, Guided by Tests*. Addison-Wesley Longman, Boston, MA, 2009.

[GHJV95]   Erich Gamma, Richard Helm, Ralph Johnson, and John Vlissides. *Design Patterns: Elements of Reusable Object-Oriented Software*. Addison-Wesley, Boston, MA, 1995.

[HF10]   Jez Humble and David Farley. *Continuous Delivery: Reliable Software Releases Through Build, Test, and Deployment Automation*. Addison-Wesley, Boston, MA, 2010.

[Nyg07]   Michael T. Nygard. *Release It! (out of print)*. The Pragmatic Bookshelf, Dallas, TX, 2007.

[PP06]   Mary Poppendieck and Tom Poppendieck. *Implementing Lean Software Development: From Concept to Cash*. Addison-Wesley, Boston, MA, 2006.

[Red18]   Luc Perkins, Jim Wilson, Eric Redmond. *Seven Databases in Seven Weeks, Second Edition*. The Pragmatic Bookshelf, Dallas, TX, 2018.

[Sub21]   Venkat Subramaniam. *Programming DSLs in Kotlin*. The Pragmatic Bookshelf, Dallas, TX, 2021.

Index

SYMBOLS

-> (arrow), declaring function type with, 376
:: function syntax, 375
= (equals sign), function syntax, 357, 375
? (question mark), nullable types with, 29, 387
_ (underscore) for mutable variables, 358
{} (curly brackets)
  function syntax, 357
  routes, 29

A

acceptance tests
  actors, 44–46
  continuous integration and, 345
  defined, 11, 21
  displaying lists, 30–39, 43–53, 55–68
  domain-driven, 57–68
  facades, 46–51
  hub interface, 55–68
  negative cases, 44
  principles, 43
  scenarios, 44–46
  steps as a function in, 49–51
  walking skeletons, 22, 28
accumulators
  byte counting example, 116–121
  folding, 120
ACID properties, database transactions, 206

actions
  domain-driven tests, 61–67
  extension functions and, 50
  modifying lists, 77–81
actions at a distance, see side effects
actors
  acceptance tests, 44–46
  advantages of in tests, 63
  creating, 65
  domain-driven tests, 62–67
  facades, 47–51
  higher-order functions, 51
  implementing methods after writing tests, 108
  purity, 46
  side effects, 45
Adapter design pattern, 27
adjoint functors, 406–407
aggregates, see entities
Agile Coaching, 3
also, 380
andApply, 290, 292
anemic objects antipattern, xxi
applications, starting, 28
applicative effects, 291
"Applicative Programming with Effects", 287
applicatives
  applicative effects, 291
  defined, 263
  diagrams, 290

  exercises, 299
  infix notation, 289, 292
  laws, 290
  vs. monads, 291
  sequential applicatives, 287–290
  swapWithList(), 285
  traverse, 283–286
  understanding, 283–293
  validating user input, 275–293
apply, 380
applyDelta, 253
architecture
  continuous integration, 345
  defined, 331
  deployment and, 346
  design approach, 331–339
  modularization, 332–347
  serverless, 338, 347
  simplicity and, 332, 338
Armstrong, Joe, xx
Arrange-Act-Assert template, 13
arrow (->), declaring function type with, 376
associativity law
  monads, 230
  morphisms, 395
asynchronous communication, modular approach to architecture, 338
atomicity and database transactions, 206
audit data, event sourcing, 113

B

Backus, John, 349, 352

Basic Category Theory for Computer Scientists, 419

Bauer, Friedrich L., 41

Beck, Kent, 8, 418

behaviors
  Behavior Driven Design, 60
  mapping to states, 258

beta reduction, 352

bind
  HTTP action calls, 80, 109, 134
  monads and, 228, 230–235, 237, 411

bindOutcome, 247

Bjarnason, Rúnar, 163, 177, 418

booleans
  cardinality, 93
  HTML template engine, 294

BooleanTag, 294

Bootstrap style sheets, 99

Bowling kata, 350, 355, 357, 359, 361–369

Brandolini, Alberto, 5

breakpoints, 343

Brown, Simon, 346

browsers
  headless, 132, 299
  simulating for testing, 132

business logic
  domain-driven tests, 59–68, 74
  event sourcing, 113
  functional programming focus on data transformations and, 92
  identifying, 53, 55
  modular approach to architecture, 334
  object-oriented programming focus on business processes, 92
  separating domain from infrastructure, 53–57
  separation with functors, 193

bytes
  byte counting example, 115–117
  cardinality, 93

C

"Can Programming Be Liberated from the von Neumann Style?", 349

cardinality
  calculating, 123
  defined, 93
  keeping low, 93, 123
  projections, 191, 198

Cartesian closed categories, 406

cash register exercises, 18, 69

category theory
  advantages of studying, 392
  basics, 353–354
  Cartesian closed categories, 406
  categories, defined, 163, 394
  defined, 391
  defining categories in code, 166
  diagrams, 164, 354, 399
  duality, 403
  empty categories, 395
  functors, 406–410
  identity and, 164, 166, 394–395
  locally small categories, 395
  monads, 227, 410–412
  monoids, 125, 396
  natural transformations, 409
  opposite categories, 402
  profunctors, 325
  resources on, 418
  sets and functions, 393, 395–396
  types and, 403–406
  understanding, 163–171, 391–415
  uses, 391
  Yoneda lemma, 412–415

Category Theory in Context, 419

checked exceptions, 162

Cheng, Eugenia, 418

Chiusano, Paul, 163, 177, 418

Christmas tree indentation, 36

Church, Alonzo, 351

classes, *see also* data classes; sealed classes
  avoiding mutable state, xxii
  avoiding unnecessary interfaces, xxii
  category theory and, 398
  class instances as objects, xxi
  declaring function type classes, 86
  functions as invokable classes, 86–87, 104
  Kotlin syntax, 32, 380
  open, xxii, 381

cloud-monitoring platforms, 302

Cockburn, Alistair, 22, 53

code
  for this book, xiv, 12
  conciseness and, 90–92
  declarative vs. imperative, 332, 361, 364–367
  printing for debugging, 91
  quality and test-driven development, 10
  re-use, xx, 102
  repository and modular approach to architecture, 343
  TODO() placeholder, 377
  writing one's own vs. using a library, 295
  writing requirements as, 8

codomain, 393

Collatz conjecture exercise, 127

collections
  folding, 117–121
  as functors, 170–171
  mutability and Kotlin collections, 358
  sequences, 387

colon (::) function syntax, 375

columns, creating, 217

combine, 140

command and query responsibility segregation (CQRS), 200, 258

commands
  concurrency and, 248
  vs. events, 137
  failing, 146
  generating events with, 136–156

handling with contexts, 245–258
listing all in design process, 258
managing state with, 135–155
names, 153, 258
renaming lists, 264
syntax, 137
communication, modular approach to architecture, 333, 338
comonads, 411
composability
Exposed and side effects, 217
morphism composition and functors, 169
mutability and, 116
composition law, applicatives, 291
computer language category, 396–399
conciseness, debugging and, 90–92
concurrency
commands and, 248
event sourcing and, 113
immutability and, 358
consistency and database transactions, 206
Console monad, 260
constructors
defining, 94
function type classes, 86
internal, 142
null and, 94
private, 94
type constructors as functional effects, 177
contexts
bounded contexts, 335
comonads and, 411
diagrams, 246
handling commands with, 245–258
logging messages and, 315, 317
querying projections from database, 250–258
read/write to databases with monads, 237–245
wrapping database transactions in, 221–224
Continuous Delivery, 345

continuous integration, 22, 345
contravariant functors, 324, 413
coproduct types, 403–404, see also union types
copy, 358, 382
coupling
classes, 381
shared data structures, 337
covariant functors, 324
CQRS (command and query responsibility segregation), 200, 258
crashes and logging, 310
credentials, PostgreSQL setup, 209
Crockford, Donald, 225
CRUD, example of routes with higher-order functions, 78–81
CSS, 297
Cucumber, 60
Cunningham, Ward, 25
curly brackets ({})
function syntax, 357
routes, 29
Curry, Haskell, 84
currying
category theory and, 405
defined, 84, 288
exercises, 104
sequential applicatives, 288–290

D
data
data class syntax in Kotlin, 32
fixture data, 31
higher-order functions, understanding, 51–53
logging and data structures, 304
shared data structures and modular approach to architecture, 337
treating functions as, 361–363
type definitions, 32
data classes
cardinality, 124
Kotlin syntax, 32, 381

product types, 403–404
wrapping strings with, 35
data transformations
chaining functions, 36
focus on in functional programming, xxi, 23, 92
functionality diagrams, 33
HTTP handler setup for Zettai app, 23–28
databases, see also PostgreSQL
ACID properties, 206
closing, 238
concurrency and event sourcing, 113
connecting to Kotlin with Exposed, 210–221
converting events to/from JSON, 212–214
creating tables, 216
custom methods and tables, 244
event streaming and, 240–250
handling commands with contexts, 245–258
isolation level, 248
logging database calls, 327
migrations, 113, 259
NoSQL, 208
opening sessions, 219
querying projections, 250–258
read/write with monads, 237–245
read/write from table, 218–221
relational vs. document-based databases, 206
rolling back, 238
starting, 209
stopping, 209
storing projections in, 185, 224, 250, 254, 259
storing state in, 153
versioning, 259
wrapping transactions in contexts, 221–224
Davies, Rachel, 3
@DDT annotation, 61
debugging
conciseness and, 90–92
laziness and, 367

logging and, 301, 304–305, 314

modular approach to architecture, 343

printing for, 91

pure functions and, 358

source of event and, 212

using domain-only version for, 271

declarative style, 332, 361, 364–367

DeepRecursiveFunction, 386

delegation

    Kotlin syntax, 382

    querying projections, 192

dependencies

    dependency injection, 82–90

    in Port and Adapter pattern, 54

deployment, 23, 294, 343

deserializing, JSON, 212, 215, 318–323

design, *see also* test-driven development

    Adapter design pattern, 27

    architecture and design approach, 331–339

    Behavior Driven Design, 60

    composing over smaller functions, 102

    deployment and, 346

    domain modeling for improvements, 92–102

    facades, 46–51

    finite state machine tips, 258

    Four Rules of Simple Design, 281

    functionality diagrams, 33

    functors and, 197

    modularization and, 332–347

    morphisms approach, 360–369

    patterns approach to in object-oriented design, 351

    Port and Adapter pattern, 53–57

    separating domain from infrastructure, 53–57

    splitting functionality with arrows, 33

Design Patterns, 351

diagrams

    category theory, 164, 354, 399

    commute in, 354, 399

Dijkstra, Edsger W., 41, 54, 95

dimap, 325

discardUnless, 276

disjoint union types, 123

doRun, 255

Docker, 208, 210

domain

    bounded contexts, 335

    converting to string, 320

    debugging in domain-only version, 271

    domain modeling for improvements, 92–102

    domain modeling with states and events, 136–144

    mathematical definition, 393

    modeling with event sourcing, 258

    modular approach to architecture, 332–335

    repository organization and, 343

    separation and dependency injection, 82–90

    separation from infrastructure, 53–57, 240

    switching domains in domain-driven testing, 75, 81, 90

Domain Modeling Made Functional, 418

Domain-Driven Design, 154

domain-driven tests

    acceptance testing with, 57–68

    advantages, 58

    continuous integration and, 345

    creating lists, 107

    creating lists, user interface for, 131–135, 151

    described, 57

    diagram, 75

    displaying lists, 57–68

    exercises, 69

    handling commands with contexts, 249

    marking tests as work-in-progress, 74

modifying lists, 73–90

pending items page, 198, 200

Pesticide, 60–69

protocols, 58, 61–63

renaming lists, 264, 268–273

speed of, 345

starting tips, 73

switching domains in, 75, 81, 90

use of specific examples vs. randomly generated values, 74

user lists page, 107–112

DomainOnly, switching domains in domain-driven testing, 75, 81, 90

doors, finite state machine understanding, 121–126

drop, 196

duality, 403

duplication, removing, 280

durability and database transactions, 206

E

Eclipse IDE, 372

Effective Haskell, 418

effects, *see* applicative effects; functional effects; side effects

Eisenhower, Dwight, 341

Either, error handling with, 176

elevator as state machine exercises, 156

ELK-stack, 302

Elvis operator (?:), nullable types with, 388

empty category, 395

end-to-end testing, *see* domain-driven tests

endofunctors, 170, 226, 407, 410

endomorphisms, 395

entities

    defined, 137

    domain modeling with states and events, 137–141

    event diagram, 139

    identifying transactional, 258

    identity, 138, 154, 211

locking events, 249
natural keys, 241
table schema for event
store, 211
transactional scope, 258
EntityId, 139
enum, 99
env field, 67
equals, 381
equals sign (=), function syntax, 357, 375
Eriksen, Marius, 24
errors, *see also* exceptions
break on failure, 174
checked exceptions, 162
combining, 276–283, 293
creating new lists, 146,
150
database integration, 217
defined, 157
error messages, 279
exercises, 182
flash attributes, 297–299
handling with functors,
162, 171–181
handling with non-local
return, 174, 226, 280
handling with null, 96,
146, 150, 157–160
handling with null and
functors, 177–178, 180
handling with precision,
174–177
HTTP response codes, 28
KondorJson and, 319
logging and, 305–313
read/write to databases
with monads, 239, 242
removing non-local re-
turn, 280
renaming lists, 269–273
storing projections in
databases, 254
totality referential transparency principle, 359
validating user input,
275–293, 297–299
Evans, Eric, 154, 335
event offset, 211
event sourcing
advantages, 113
command and query re-
sponsibility segregation
(CQRS) and, 200
vs. event driven pattern,
149

modeling domain with,
258
modifying state with,
112–126, 136–155
projections, 190
event store
event diagram, 144
handling commands with
contexts, 245–258
persistence and, 147
projections and, 241
read/write to databases
with monads, 240
table schema for, 211
versioning, 259
event storming
development with, 5,
339–342
exercises, 18
identifying transactional
entities, 258
event streams, *see* projections
events
combining, 140
vs. commands, 137
converting to/from JSON,
212–214
creating to translate into
PgEvent, 219
domain modeling with
states and events, 136–
144
event diagram, 139, 144
event driven pattern, 149
folding, 121–126, 140,
144–149
generating with com-
mands, 136–156
keeping internal, 153
locking, 249
modifying state with
event sourcing, 112–
126, 136–155
monoids, 125
names, 153, 258
notifying other systems,
149
progressive ID/event off-
set, 211
projecting, 185–197
projecting on a map, 189
public, 153
renaming lists, 266–273
resetting, 155
returning information,
150
reverting, 155

sequential identifiers for
projections, 187
source of, 212
streaming and databases,
240–250
syntax, 137
timestamps, 211–212
eventual consistence, 241
exceptions
catching, 161, 182
checked, 162
database integration, 217
read/write to databases
with monads, 239, 242
runtime, 162, 217
throwing, 160–162
throwing with functors,
174
totality referential transparency principle, 359
exercises
about, xiv
applicatives, 299
chaining functions, 40–
42
currying, 104
domain-driven tests, 69
errors, 182
finite state machines, 155
folding, 127
functors, 181
higher-order functions,
70, 103
laziness, 201
logging, 329
monads, 235, 259
monitoring, 329
monoids, 128
null, 103, 202
projections, 201
property testing, 18
recursion, 127
user stories, 18
exponential types, 405–406,
see also function types
Exposed
about, 210
connecting databases to
Kotlin with, 210–221
logging interface, 327
extension functions
actions and, 50
advantages, 143
code conciseness and, 91
scope function, 380
syntax, 378

F

facades, acceptance tests, 46–51

faiIIfNull, 276

Farley, Dave, 345

findAll, 256

finite state machine
design tips, 258
diagram, 122
exercises, 155
generating events with commands, 144–149, 153
understanding folding in, 121–126

first-feature paradox, 21

firstOrNull, 377

fixture data, 31

flash attributes, 297–299

flatten, 323

flexibility, 102, 347

fold, 119, 254

folding
collections, 117–121
event store and, 147
events, 121–126, 140, 144–149
exercises, 127
functors, 286
left vs. right, 120
order, 119
storing projections in databases, 254

Fong, Brendan, 419

forgetful functors, 407

FORTRAN, 349

Four Rules of Simple Design, 281

Fowler, Martin, 32, 135

free functors, 407

Freeman, Steve, 21

functional effects
applicatives and, 291
error handling with functors, 177
functors, 177, 197
vs. side effects, 53, 197

functional programming, *see also* category theory
advantages, xi, xvii
basics, 349–369
mathematical reasoning, 350–354

mixed paradigm languages and, xix, 25
origins, 349
principles, xxi–xxii
problem-solving with functions, 52
re-use of code and, xx
resources on, 417

Functional Programming in Scala, 163, 177, 418

functions, *see also* category theory; currying; higher-order functions; referential transparency
cardinality and function types, 124
chaining, 35–37, 40–42, 103
currying, 84, 104
displaying lists setup, 35–37
exercises, 40–42
functionality diagrams, 33
as invokable classes, 86–87, 104
isomorphism and, 400
lifting, 168, 176
logging pure functions, 306
mathematical definition, 393
with multiple parameters, 273
names, 91
partial application, 83, 359
private, 86
scope functions, 91, 379
splitting functionality with arrows, 33
stand-alone, 362, 373
steps as a function in acceptance testing, 49–51
syntax, 357, 375
transforming with functors, 168
treating as data, 361–363
type definitions, 32, 376
using smaller, 102, 275
web server routes with Http4k, 27

functors, *see also* applicatives
adjoint, 406–407
advantages, 193
category theory, 406–410
collections as, 170–171
combining, 181, 274

contravariant, 324, 413
covariant, 324
creating, 167
defined, 163, 165, 225
endofunctors, 170, 226, 407, 410
error handling with, 162, 171–181
exercises, 181
folding, 286
forgetful, 407
free, 407
vs. generics, 168
hom-functors, 413–414
identity and, 166, 169
laws of, 169, 182
lax monoidal, 287
lazy projections, 194
lazy resources, 195
lifting functions, 168, 176
lists as, 171
as mappers, 170, 406–410
natural transformations, 409
order, 164, 166
profunctors, 323–327
projecting events with, 185–197
querying on with projections, 193–197
separation of concerns with, 193, 197
type classes and, 233
as type constructors, 225
understanding, 163–171, 197
understanding monads and, 225–229, 234
wrapping database transactions in contexts, 221–224

G

gRPC, 338

generateSequence, 96

generics
advantages, xxii
creating, 167
folding with, 118
vs. functors, 168
generic programming, 167
as type builders, 167, 175

getLogger, 303

Given-When-Then template, 13

Gradle, 12, 344, 372

grain of the language, xix

greeting email examples of error handling, 158–163, 172–177

Grokking Simplicity, 417

Groovy, 372

groups, in set theory, 125

H

Haskell, 418

headless browsers, 132, 299

Hello World examples, 26, 372

Hexagonal Architecture, *see* Port and Adapter pattern

higher-order functions
   defined, 361
   defining routes with, 78–81
   exercises, 70, 103
   extracting example, 101
   lifting functions, 169
   morphism approach to design, 361–363
   purity, 51
   referential transparency, 51, 222
   reusing, 102
   understanding, 51–53

Hoare, Tony, 95, 367

Holder functor example, 167–173, 181, 284

hom-functors, 413–414

hom-set, 405, 413

homomorphism law, 290

hot-deploy, 343

HTML
   Bootstrap style sheets, 99
   CSS, 297
   forms and renaming lists, 266
   handler setup for Zettai app, 23–28
   parsing, 100–102, 111
   styling user interface, 293–297
   template engine, 294–297
   user interface buttons, adding, 132

HTTP
   defining routes with higher-order functions, 78–81

displaying lists, 66–68

domain-driven tests advantages, 58

domain-driven tests examples, 66–68, 75, 77–81

error handling with functors, 176

handler setup for Zettai app, 23–28

modifying lists, 75, 77–81

parsing responses, 38

renaming lists, 265, 272

response codes, 29

user interface routes, 134, 149–152

user lists page, 109–112

Http4k, 25–28, 30, 79

hub
   creating lists, user interface for, 149–152
   displaying lists, acceptance testing, 55–68
   domain-driven tests, 59–68
   error handling with functors, 177–181
   functional dependency injection, 82–90
   logging and, 306–311
   pending items page, 198
   purity, 56
   renaming lists, 264
   separating domain from infrastructure, 53–57
   storing lists outside of, 86–87

I

id field, 139

identity
   applicatives identity law, 290
   categories and, 164, 166, 394–395
   entities, 138, 154, 211
   functors and, 166, 169
   left identity law, 229
   monads, 229
   right identity law, 229
   sets, 396

IDEs
   Eclipse IDE, 372
   IntelliJ IDE, 372
   running tests, 14
   running tests in debug mode, 33

IDs
   entities, 139, 211

event identifiers for projections, 187

event progressive ID, 211

reading and writing from tables, 219

row identifiers for projections, 188, 215

immutability
   entity identity and, 154
   functional data structures and, 93
   performance and, 359
   referential transparency principle, 355, 357–359

imperative style, 332, 361, 364

Implementing Lean Software Development, 2

indentation, Christmas tree, 36

infix, 388

infix functions, 40, 388

infix notation, applicatives, 289, 292

infrastructure
   domain-driven tests, 59
   separating domain from, 53–57, 240

initial object, 401

InMemory, switching domains in domain-driven testing, 75, 81

inputs/outputs, *see also* higher-order functions
   chaining functions, 36
   focus on in functional programming, xxi, 23
   functionality diagrams, 33
   HTTP handler setup for Zettai app, 23–28
   modular approach to architecture, 338
   totality referential transparency principle, 355, 359, 364
   treating functions as data in morphism approach to design, 361–363

inside-out approach to test-driven development, 11

integers
   cardinality, 93
   conversion example of sequential applicatives, 288

integration tests, 11, 208
IntelliJ, 358
IntelliJ IDE, 372
interchange law, 291
interfaces
    Kotlin interfaces as read-
        only, 358
    type classes and, 233
internal, 194, 384
internal constructors, 142
*An Invitation to Applied Cate-
    gory Theory*, 395, 419
isolation and database trans-
    actions, 206, 248
isomorphism, 400, 413–414
it as implicit operator in
    lambdas, 377

J
Java
    converting to Kotlin, 374
    decompiling Kotlin to,
        374
    module, 333
From Java To Kotlin, 417
javap, 374
JetBrains, 372
Jetty, 25
join, 230–235, 410
The Joy of Abstraction, 418
JSON
    conversion with profunc-
        tors, 323–327
    converting events
        to/from, 212–214
    JSON format for logs,
        314–329
    KondorJson, 319–323
    parsing, 210, 214, 318–
        323
    querying projections from
        database, 256
    serializing/deserializing,
        212, 215, 318–323
    testing and parsing
        HTML, 101
Jsoup, 100, 111
JUnit, 12, 17

K
Kafka, 338
Kay, Alan, 360
keys, entities, 241
Klaxon, 214, 329

Kleisli category, 411
KondorJson, 319–323
Kotlin, *see also* lambda vari-
    ables; sealed classes; se-
    quences
    advantages, xviii
    basics, 371–389
    collections as mutable,
        358
    computer languages in
        category theory, 397
    data class syntax, 32,
        381
    Http4k library, 25–28
    lack of type classes in,
        233
    nullable types, 96, 98,
        387
    project setup, 12
    resources on, xiv, 358,
        371, 386, 389, 417
    scope functions, 91, 379
    setup, 371–374
    stand-alone functions,
        362, 373
    syntax, 374–387
    type system, 387–389
    version, 372
    viewing bytecode, 374

L
labels, JSON conversion and,
    322
lambda calculus, 351
lambda variables
    syntax, 352, 377, 379
    web server routes with
        Http4k, 27
languages
    advantages of mixed
        paradigm, xix
    Backus on nonfunctional
        languages, 349
    computer language cate-
        gory, 396–399
    grain of the language, xix
    ubiquitous language, 32
lax monoidal functors, 287
laziness
    defined, 367
    delegated properties, 383
    exercises, 201
    morphism approach to
        design, 361, 367
    performance, 202
    projections with functors,
        194

resources with functors,
    195
sequences, 387
lazy, 383
Lean, 3
left identity law, 229
let, 36, 380
libraries
    mutable types and, 27
    selecting, 25
    spikes and, 25
lift, 169, 176
lifting functions with func-
    tors, 168, 176
lists, *see also* collections
    adding items to, 151
    archiving, 4
    creating, 4, 107
    creating lists, user inter-
        face for, 131–152
    deleting exercise, 300
    displaying, acceptance
        testing, 30–39, 43–53,
        55–68
    displaying, first example,
        28–39
    displaying, user story, 4
    displaying, walking
        skeleton for, 28–30
    editing exercise, 300
    frozen state exercise, 330
    as functors, 171
    holding, 4
    HTML template engine,
        294
    infinite lists with se-
        quences, 387
    marking items, 4
    modifying, 4, 73–90
    names, 267
    pending items page, 198–
        203
    querying with projections,
        190–197
    reading, 151
    reading/writing to
        databases with mon-
        ads, 237–245
    renaming, 263–283, 292
    storing outside of hub,
        86–87
    user lists page, 107–112
ListTag, 294
LocalDate, parsing strings to,
    101
locking, events, 249

Logger monad, 260
logging
    configuring, 304
    database calls, 327
    debugging and, 301, 304–305, 314
    defined, 301
    diagram, 307
    exercises, 329
    in JSON format, 314–329
    log levels, 314
    metrics with, 302
    monads and, 313
    Pepperdine's law of, 305, 312
    with streams, 311, 316–329
    test-driven development of, 305–311
    traditional, 303
    uses of, 302
loops
    folding example, 117–121
    temporary mutability, 115

M

Mac Lane, Saunders, 409, 412
MacCready, Paul, 294
Manji, Asad, 297
map
    sequences and, 387
    vs. traverse, 284, 286
mapping
    displaying lists with, 37–39
    functors as mappers, 170, 406–410
    JSON converters, 320
    projecting events on a map, 189
    tags in HTML template engine, 296
Martin, Bob, 350
mathematical reasoning of functional programming, 350–354
McGregor, Duncan, 417
memory, storing projections in, 185, 190, 192, 250, 254, 259
methods
    category theory and, 398
    custom, 244
    names, 31, 43

metrics with logging, 302
microservices, 346
migrations, database, 113, 259
Milewski, Bartosz, 165, 287, 400, 406, 415, 419
mock-ups, developing with, 6–8
mocks, testing with, 16
modeling
    domain modeling for improvements, 92–102
    domain modeling with event sourcing, 258
    domain modeling with states and events, 136–144
modularization
    architecture and, 332–347
    continuous integration and, 345
    deployment, 346
    diagrams, 333–335, 342
    planning approach, 339–342
    rules, 333
modules
    aggregating during development phase, 342
    breaking, 335
    defined, 332
    fractal nature of, 335, 337
    internal visibility, 384
    rules, 333
    size of, 335
monads
    advantages, 234
    vs. applicatives, 291
    category theory, 410–412
    comonads, 411
    defined, 226
    diagrams, 228, 232
    exercises, 235, 259
    Kleisli category, 411
    laws, 229, 235, 260
    logging and, 313
    monad transformers, 247
    vs. monoids, 227
    Outcome example, 230–234
    read/write to databases with, 237–245
    Reader monad, 232, 245–258, 415
    type classes and, 233

understanding, 225–234
    when to use, 313
monitoring, see also logging
    cloud-monitoring platforms, 302
    defined, 302
    exercises, 329
    importance of, 301, 303
monoids
    category theory, 125, 396
    defined, 125
    exercises, 128
    finite state machine, 125
    vs. monads, 227
    sequential applicatives and, 287
    signs of, 140
monorepo, 343
morphisms
    defined, 164, 353, 394
    design approach, 360–369
    endomorphisms, 395
    functors and, 169, 406
    hom-set, 405, 413
    product types and, 403
    types of, 400–403
    understanding, 400–403
multiple receivers, 379
mutability, see also event sourcing
    avoiding, xxii, 358
    functional programming approaches to, 113–126
    managing with recursion, 116–121
    performance and, 359
    temporary, 115

N

names
    breaking modules and, 336
    commands, 153, 258
    converting to JSON and, 322
    events, 153, 258
    functions, 91
    lists, 267
    methods, 31, 43
    modular approach to architecture and, 336–337
    monadic composition and, 227
    precision in, 84, 93

renaming lists, 263–283, 292

replacing hashed names in domain-driven tests, 68, 76

states, 258

tests, 61, 74, 192

transforming with functors, 169

types, 32

natural transformations and category theory, 409

non-local return, 174, 226, 280

Normand, Eric, xviii, 356, 417

NoSQL databases, 208

Nothing type, 174, 376

notifications, flash attributes, 297–299

null
chaining nullable functions, 103

challenges of, 95

checking for, 101

constructors and, 94

error handling with, 96, 146, 150, 157–160

error handling with functors, 177–178, 180

exercises, 103, 202

nullable types in Kotlin, 96, 98

nullable types
in Kotlin, 96, 98, 387

question mark (?) for, 29, 387

NullPointerException, 95

Nygard, Michael, 23

O

object-oriented programming
approach to state, 154

declarative style in, 366

dependency injection, 82

design approach, 351, 360

focus on business processes, 92

re-use of code and, xx

unlearning, xxi

objects
anemic objects antipattern, xxi

category theory, 164

class instances as objects, xxi

creating without methods as common in functional programming, xxi

delegated properties, 383

initial object, 401

isomorphism, 400

Kotlin syntax, 381

representing state with, 122

terminal object, 401

onFailure, 232

open, 381

operators, overriding in Kotlin, 388

opposite categories, 402

order
chaining functions, 36

folding, 119

functors, 164, 166

stacks exercise, 41

Outcome
about, 176

combining, 276–283

error handling with functors, 172–181

exercises, 182

HTML template engine, 295

joining, 247

logging with, 305, 307, 312

monads example, 230–234

nested, 247

parsing JSON, 318

swapWithList(), 285

testing functions that return, 180

wrapping database transactions in contexts, 223

outputs, see inputs/outputs

outside-in approach to test-driven development, 11, 76, 81

P

Pair
category theory and product types, 403

error handling with, 159

parameterized tests, 17

parameters
chaining functions and, 36

currying, 84, 104

function type classes, 86

functions with multiple, 273

parsing
HTML, 100–102

HTTP responses, 38

JSON, 210, 214, 318–323

partial application, 83, 359

path(), 29

Pepperdine, Kirk, 305

Pepperdine's law of logging, 305, 312

performance
event sourcing and, 113

headless browsers, 132

immutability and, 359

JSON parsing with KondorJson, 320

laziness, 202

logging and, 304

monitoring and, 302

projections, 190, 250, 254

sequences, 202

tests and, 10

traversing Outcome and, 286

persistence
about, 205

event store, 147

projections, 185

Pesticide, 60–69

Pierce, Benjamin C., 419

Piponi, Dan, 412

Port and Adapter pattern, 53–57

ports
PostgreSQL setup, 209

URI, 48

PostgreSQL, see also databases
about, 207

concurrency and isolation level, 248

connecting to Kotlin with Exposed, 210–221

converting events to/from JSON, 212–214

creating tables, 216–217

dropping tables, 217

locking tables, 216

opening sessions, 219

reading/writing from table, 218–221

setup, 208–210

starting databases, 209

stopping databases, 209
storing projections in databases, 224
table schema for event store, 211
table schema for projections, 215–216
wrapping transactions in contexts, 221–224
prepare, 66
prime numbers exercises, 202
primitive types
  as immutable, 114
  primitive obsession antipattern, 363
printlt, 91
printing, debugging with, 91
private, 384
private constructors, 94
private functions, 86
product types, 403–404, *see also* data classes
productivity, xviii, 335
profunctors, 323–327
Programming DSLs in Kotlin, 389
Programming Kotlin, xiv, 417
progressive ID, 211
projections
  accessing databases with monads, 238
  advantages, 250
  cardinality, 191, 198
  declaring as internal, 194
  diagram, 197
  event id field and, 212
  event sourcing, 190
  event store and, 241
  events, 185–197
  eventual consistence, 241
  exercises, 201
  lazy, 194
  management of own transactions, 253
  migrations and, 259
  pending items page, 198
  performance, 190, 250, 254
  projecting events on a map, 189
  querying projections from database, 250–258
  renaming lists, 267–269
  running queries on functors, 193–197

storing in databases, 185, 224, 250, 254, 259
storing in memory, 185, 190, 192, 250, 254, 259
table schema for, 215–216
testing, 192, 196
updating, 251–254
using separate tables for, 216
properties, delegated, 383
property testing
  defined, 13
  exercises, 18
  parameterized tests and, 17
  randomly generated values, 96–98
protected, 384
protocols, domain-driven tests, 58, 61–63
Pryce, Nat, 21, 54, 58, 60, 387, 417
public, 384
purity
  actors, 46
  defined, 355–356
  functional dependency injection, 84
  higher-order functions, 51
  hub in Port and Adapter pattern, 56
  logging and, 304, 306
  modular approach to architecture, 336
  referential transparency principle, 355–357
  testing advantages, 87

Q

queries
  accessing databases with monads, 238
  command and query responsibility segregation (CQRS), 200
  diagrams, 257
  pending items page, 199
  PostgreSQL, 212
  projecting events, 185–197
  querying projections from database, 250–258
  renaming lists, 272

running queries on functors with projections, 193–197
steps that query status in domain-driven tests, 76
question mark (?), nullable types with, 29, 387
Quine, Willard Van Orman, 352

R

randomly generated values
  functors exercise, 182
  unit testing and, 74
readability
  chaining functions, 36, 40
  composing over smaller functions, 102
  domain-driven tests, 65
  functional code, 332
  lifting functions, 169
  non-local returns, 174
  onFailure and, 232
Reader monad, 232, 245–258, 415
reading
  databases with monads, 237–245
  read/write from table, 218–221
receivers, extension functions, 378
records (projections), *see* rows
recover, 176, 180
recursion
  DeepRecursiveFunction, 386
  defined, 116
  exercises, 127
  folding collections, 117–121
  managing state with, 116–121
  resources on, 386
  tailrec keyword, 117, 386
red-green-refactor cycle, 9
reducers, 117, 299
referential opacity, 352, 356
referential transparency
  CPU utilization and system effects, 353
  defined, xix, 356
  higher-order functions, 51, 222

immutability and, 355, 357–359
lambda calculus and, 353
mathematical principles of functional programming, 352
principles of, 355–360
purity and, 355–357
totality and, 355, 359, 364
writing extensions and, 219
Release It!, 23
repositories, organizing, 343
requirements, writing as code, 8
resources
access to in functionality diagrams, 35
handling static content, 294
hub and functional dependency injection, 82–90
lazy resources with functors, 195
resources for this book
category theory, 418
continuous integration, 345
deployment, 23
Docker, 210
extension functions, 379
functional programming, 417
Kondor, 323
Kotlin, xiv, 358, 371, 386, 389, 417
recursion, 386
scope functions, 380
sequences, 387
test-driven development, 418
versioning, 259
Response type, 27, 29
responsibility, command and query responsibility segregation (CQRS), 200, 258
RESTful approach, 109–112
return
error handling with null, 159
error messages, 279
non-local, 174, 226, 280
reverse Polish notation (RPN) calculator exercises, 41, 261

Riehl, Emily, 419
right identity law, 229
routes
{} (curly brackets) for, 29
defining with higher-order functions, 78–81
error notifications with flash attributes, 297
with Http4k, 79
logging, 306, 310
renaming lists, 265
static content, 294
user interface, 134, 149–152
web server routes with Http4k, 27
routes function, 79
rows
accessing databases with monads, 238
cardinality, 191, 198
combining for transactions, 253
creating, 188
deleting, 188
projections, 186–189
sequential identifiers for projections, 188
table schema for projections, 215
updating, 188, 224
run, 380
runWith, 239, 242, 255
runtime exceptions, 162, 217
Russell's paradox, 396

S
Saga pattern, 334
scenarios
acceptance tests, 44–46
domain-driven tests, 60, 65, 73
facades, 47–51
higher-order functions, 51
scope
modular approach to architecture, 334
scope functions, 91, 379
transactional, 258
SDKMAN!, 372
sealed classes
combining errors, 293
converting in JSON, 321–322
defined, 385

finite state machine example, 122
managing state with commands and events, 136
products and coproducts in category theory, 404
union types, 123
sealed interfaces
converting in JSON, 322
defined, 385
logging and, 315
security
logging and, 304
PostgreSQL setup, 209
selectWhere, 219
Self generic parameter, 194
semantics, coupling with state in nonfunctional languages, 349
semigroups, in set theory, 125
sequences (Kotlin)
exercises, 202
lazy projections with functors, 195, 202
random value generator, 96
syntax, 387
sequential applicatives, 287–290
Serializable isolation level, 248
serializing, JSON, 212, 215, 318–323
serverless architecture, 338, 347
services, *see* integration tests
sessions, opening PostgreSQL, 219
Set, 396
sets
category theory, 393, 395–396
set theory and monoids, 125
Seven Databases in Seven Weeks, 206
showList(), 29
side effects
actors, 45
Exposed and, 217
vs. functional effects, 53, 197
minimizing, 53, 356

purity and, 356
running scenarios in facades, 47
as term, 356
skeletons, *see* walking skeletons
Skinner, Rebecca, 418
SLF4j library, 303
smart-casting, 385
soft assertions, 12, 16
software architecture, *see* architecture
spaces, removing exercise, 128
spikes
    advantages, 28
    handler setup for Zettai app, 25–28
Spivak, David I., 419
Splunk, 302
SQL
    logging, 327
    queries and renaming lists, 272
SqlLogger, 327
StackOverflowException, 117, 386
stacks exercise, 41
stand-alone functions, 362, 373
state, *see also* finite state machine
    coupling with semantics in nonfunctional languages, 349
    diagrams and design process, 258
    domain modeling with states and events, 136–144
    event sourcing, 112–126, 136–155
    folding events, 121–126, 144–149
    functional vs. object-oriented programming, 154
    managing with commands, 135–155
    managing with recursion, 116–121
    mapping different behaviors to, 258
    modular approach to architecture, 336
    monoids, 125
    names, 258

reconstructing with event sourcing, 113
representing with objects, 122
storing in database, 153
storing in function type classes, 86
temporary mutability, 115
statistics, event sourcing, 113
steps
    domain-driven tests, 63, 65–66, 68, 74, 76
    steps as a function in acceptance testing, 49–51
stores, *see also* event store
    defining, 86
    projections, 185
    storing lists outside of hub, 86–87
    storing projections in databases, 224
streams, logging with, 311, 316–329, *see also* projections
Strikt, 13
strings
    cardinality, 93
    conversion example of sequential applicatives, 288
    converting domain to, 320
    HTML template engine, 294
    logs as, 304
    parsing to LocalDate, 101
    random string generator, 96–98
    wrapping in data classes, 35
StringTag, 294
stubs, testing with, 16
styling
    Bootstrap, 99
    user interface, 293–297
subcategories, 398
subdomains
    aggregating modules, 342
    modular approach to architecture, 332–335, 342
Subramaniam, Venkat, xiv, 417
sum types, *see* union types
swapWithList(), 285

synchronous communication, modular approach to architecture, 338
Sysout, 313

T
table schema
    event store, 211
    projections, 215–216
tables
    creating, 216
    creating columns, 217
    custom, 244
    dropping tables, 217
    locking, 216
    reading/writing from table, 218–221
tailrec, 117, 386
take, 196
takeIf, 276
TDD, *see* test-driven development
template engine
    exercise, 70
    HTML, 294–297
terminal object, 401
test fixtures, 38
test-driven development
    about, 31
    advantages, 8–10
    breaking deliberately, 266
    defined, 8
    first-feature paradox, 21
    inside-out vs. outside-in approach, 11, 76, 81
    listening to tests, 10
    logging, 305–311
    property testing and, 16
    red-green-refactor cycle, 9
    resources on, 418
    setup for Zettai app, 12–17
    understanding, 8–17
Test-Driven Development By Example, 418
testing, *see also* acceptance tests; domain-driven tests; integration tests; property tests; test-driven development; unit tests
    about, 1
    accessing databases with monads, 239
    by example, 13

composing over smaller functions and, 102
environment for, 67
functions that return Outcome, 180
handling commands with contexts, 249
logging and, 304
marking tests as work-in-progress, 74
method names in, 31
mocks and stubs for, 16
naming tests, 61, 74, 192
negative cases, 44, 87
Outcome monads example, 231
parameterized tests, 17
performance and, 10
projections, 192, 196, 251
purity and, 87
read/write from tables, 218
read/write with monads to databases, 242–245
reusing tests, 10
separating domain from infrastructure with Port and Adapter Pattern, 54
setup for Zettai app, 12–17
simulating browsers for testing, 132
soft assertions, 12, 16
test fixtures, 38
test libraries, 12
types of tests, 10
user interface, 100, 299
this, extension functions, 378
timestamps, 211–212, 215
TinyType pattern, 363
TODO(), 377
toString, 381
totality
    defining specific types and, 364
    referential transparency principle, 355, 359, 364
    Set category, 396
transactional entities, see entities
transactional scope, 258
transactions
    ACID properties, 206
    database, defined, 206

passing explicitly in Exposed, 218–221
wrapping in contexts, 221–224
transform
    applicatives and, 292
    error handling with functors, 172–181
    lazy projections with functors, 195
    lifting functions with, 168
    monads and, 228
transform2
    applicative laws, 290, 292
    combining errors, 277–283
    combining functors, 274
    with traversables, 284
traversables, 284
traverse, 283–286
Triple, 281
try...catch block, 161, 182, 239, 242
type aliases, 50, 145, 383
types, see also generics; union types
    building with generics, 167, 175
    cardinality, 93, 123
    category theory, 403–406
    declaring function type, 376
    defining precisely, 361, 363
    displaying lists setup, 35–37
    exponential types, 405–406
    extension functions, 378
    functors as type constructors, 225
    interfaces and type classes, 233
    JSON conversion and, 322
    Kotlin type system, 387–389
    lack of type classes in Kotlin, 233
    libraries and mutable types, 27
    names, 32
    nullable types, 96, 98, 387
    primitive types as immutable, 114

product and coproduct types, 403–404
TinyType pattern, 363
type constructors as functional effects, 177
type definitions, 32
wrapping mutable, 27

U
ubiquitous language, 32
UI
    creating lists, 131–152
    headless browsers and, 299
    simulating browsers for testing, 132
    styling, 293–297
    testing first, 100
unaryPlus, 255
underscore (_) for mutable variables, 358
union types
    category theory, 403–406
    error handling with functors, 172–181
    exercises, 128
    sealed classes and, 123
Unit
    initial and terminal object theory, 402
    Kotlin syntax, 376
    logging with, 307
    pure functions and, 355
unit (monads), 410
unit tests
    defined, 10
    first unit test for Zettai app, 14–17
    Given-When-Then template, 13
    libraries, 12
    randomly generated values, 74, 96–98
update, projections, 251–254
Uri, matching client and server, 48
use-cases, modular approach to architecture, 334, 340
user input, validation, 275–293, 297–299
user stories
    about, xii
    acceptance tests and design and, 43
    developing with, 3–6, 263

event storming and, 5
exercises, 18
UUID, 139

V

Vaccari, Matteo, xx
val, 375
validation, user input, 275–293, 297–299
values, randomly generated values in unit tests, 74, 96–98
var
  avoiding, xxii, 375
  Kotlin syntax, 375
variables
  avoiding mutable, xxii, 358, 375
  declaring temporary variables in Kotlin, 374
  lambda variables, 27, 352, 377, 379
versioning, databases, 259
Versioning in an Event Sourced System, 259
versions
  JUnit, 12–13
  Kotlin, 372
views, multiple views with event sourcing, 113
visibility, internal, 194, 384
Vitruvius, 331

W

Wadler, Philip, 227, 234, 411
walking skeletons
  acceptance tests, 22, 28
  advantages, 28
  displaying lists, 28–30
web servers
  setup for Zettai app, 23–28
  starting, 26
  URI, 48
when, 122, 146, 152, 384
wip, 74
Wlaschin, Scott, 418

words, replacing hashed words in domain-driven tests, 65, 68, 76
work-in-progress marker, 74
wrapping
  combining types in sealed classes, 123
  entity IDs, 139
  functors as more than wrappers, 198
  strings in data classes, 35
writing
  databases with monads, 237–245
  read/write from table, 218–221
  requirements as code, 8

Y

Yoneda lemma, 412–415
Yoneda, Nobuo, 412
Young, Greg, 259
"Your Server as a Function", 24

Z

ZeroMq, 338
Zettai app
  adding items to lists, 151
  changing orders exercise, 330
  conciseness of code, 90
  creating lists, 107
  creating lists, user interface for, 131–152
  defining app, 2–8
  displaying lists, acceptance testing, 43–53, 55–68
  displaying lists, first example, 28–39
  displaying lists, walking skeleton for, 28–30
  error handling with functors, 177–181
  functional state machines, 144–149

handling commands with contexts, 245–258
HTTP handler setup, 23–28
improvements with domain modeling, 92–102
limiting lists to owners, 44
logging, 305–329
logging in JSON format, 314–329
mock-ups, 6–8
modifying lists, 73–90
modular architecture example, 339–347
parsing HTML, 100–102, 111
PostgreSQL database, connecting to Kotlin with Exposed, 210–221
PostgreSQL database, setup, 208–210
project setup, 12
projecting events with functors, 185–197
querying lists with projections, 190–197
read/write to databases with monads, 237–245
renaming lists, 263–283, 292
separating domain from infrastructure with Port and Adapter Pattern, 55–57
storing lists outside of hub, 86–87
styling, 99, 293–297
test setup, 12–17
unit testing, first, 14–17
user feedback example, 339–347
user interface, 293–299
user lists page, 107–112
user stories, 3–6, 263
validation, 275–283, 297–299
What's Next page, 198–203

Thank you!

We hope you enjoyed this book and that you're already thinking about what you want to learn next. To help make that decision easier, we're offering you this gift.

Head on over to https://pragprog.com right now, and use the coupon code BUYANOTHER2023 to save 30% on your next ebook. Offer is void where prohibited or restricted. This offer does not apply to any edition of the *The Pragmatic Programmer* ebook.

And if you'd like to share your own expertise with the world, why not propose a writing idea to us? After all, many of our best authors started off as our readers, just like you. With up to a 50% royalty, world-class editorial services, and a name you trust, there's nothing to lose. Visit https://pragprog.com/become-an-author/ today to learn more and to get started.

We thank you for your continued support, and we hope to hear from you again soon!

The Pragmatic Bookshelf

Effective Haskell

Put the power of Haskell to work in your programs, learning from an engineer who uses Haskell daily to get practical work done efficiently. Leverage powerful features like Monad Transformers and Type Families to build useful applications. Realize the benefits of a pure functional language, like protecting your code from side effects. Manage concurrent processes fearlessly. Apply functional techniques to working with databases and building RESTful services. Don't get bogged down in theory, but learn to employ advanced programming concepts to solve real-world problems. Don't just learn the syntax, but dive deeply into Haskell as you build efficient, well-tested programs.

Rebecca Skinner
(668 pages) ISBN: 9781680509342. $57.95
https://pragprog.com/book/rshaskell

Creating Software with Modern Diagramming Techniques

Diagrams communicate relationships more directly and clearly than words ever can. Using only text-based markup, create meaningful and attractive diagrams to document your domain, visualize user flows, reveal system architecture at any desired level, or refactor your code. With the tools and techniques this book will give you, you'll create a wide variety of diagrams in minutes, share them with others, and revise and update them immediately on the basis of feedback. Adding diagrams to your professional vocabulary will enable you to work through your ideas quickly when working on your own code or discussing a proposal with colleagues.

Ashley Peacock
(156 pages) ISBN: 9781680509830. $29.95
https://pragprog.com/book/apdiag

Programming Kotlin

Programmers don't just use Kotlin, they love it. Even Google has adopted it as a first-class language for Android development. With Kotlin, you can intermix imperative, functional, and object-oriented styles of programming and benefit from the approach that's most suitable for the problem at hand. Learn to use the many features of this highly concise, fluent, elegant, and expressive statically typed language with easy-to-understand examples. Learn to write maintainable, high-performing JVM and Android applications, create DSLs, program asynchronously, and much more.

Venkat Subramaniam
(460 pages) ISBN: 9781680506358. $51.95
https://pragprog.com/book/vskotlin

Functional Programming in Java, Second Edition

Imagine writing Java code that reads like the problem statement, code that's highly expressive, concise, easy to read and modify, and has reduced complexity. With the functional programming capabilities in Java, that's not a fantasy. This book will guide you from the familiar imperative style through the practical aspects of functional programming, using plenty of examples. Apply the techniques you learn to turn highly complex imperative code into elegant and easy-to-understand functional-style code. Updated to the latest version of Java, this edition has four new chapters on error handling, refactoring to functional style, transforming data, and idioms of functional programming.

Venkat Subramaniam
(274 pages) ISBN: 9781680509793. $53.95
https://pragprog.com/book/vsjava2e

Designing Data Governance from the Ground Up

Businesses own more data than ever before, but it's of no value if you don't know how to use it. Data governance manages the people, processes, and strategy needed for deploying data projects to production. But doing it well is far from easy: Less than one fourth of business leaders say their organizations are data driven. In *Designing Data Governance from the Ground Up*, you'll build a cross-functional strategy to create roadmaps and stewardship for data-focused projects, embed data governance into your engineering practice, and put processes in place to monitor data after deployment.

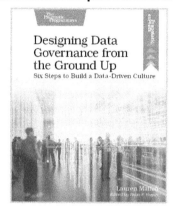

Lauren Maffeo
(100 pages) ISBN: 9781680509809. $29.95
https://pragprog.com/book/lmmlops

Domain Modeling Made Functional

You want increased customer satisfaction, faster development cycles, and less wasted work. Domain-driven design (DDD) combined with functional programming is the innovative combo that will get you there. In this pragmatic, down-to-earth guide, you'll see how applying the core principles of functional programming can result in software designs that model real-world requirements both elegantly and concisely—often more so than an object-oriented approach. Practical examples in the open-source F# functional language, and examples from familiar business domains, show you how to apply these techniques to build software that is business-focused, flexible, and high quality.

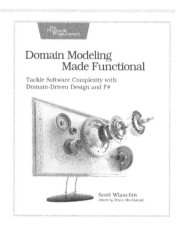

Scott Wlaschin
(310 pages) ISBN: 9781680502541. $47.95
https://pragprog.com/book/swdddf

Numerical Brain Teasers

Challenge your brain with math! Using nothing more than basic arithmetic and logic, you'll be thrilled as answers slot into place. Whether purely for fun or to test your knowledge, you'll sharpen your problem-solving skills and flex your mental muscles. All you need is logical thought, a little patience, and a clear mind. There are no gotchas here. These puzzles are the perfect introduction to or refresher for math concepts you may have only just learned or long since forgotten. Get ready to have more fun with numbers than you've ever had before.

Erica Sadun

(186 pages) ISBN: 9781680509748. $18.95

https://pragprog.com/book/esbrain

Program Management for Open Source Projects

Every organization develops a bureaucracy, and open source projects are no exception. When your structure is intentional and serves the project, it can lead to a successful and predictable conclusion. But project management alone won't get you there. Take the next step to full program management. Become an expert at facilitating communication between teams, managing schedules and project lifecycle, coordinating a process for changes, and keeping meetings productive. Make decisions that get buy-in from all concerned. Learn how to guide your community-driven open source project with just the right amount of structure.

Ben Cotton

(190 pages) ISBN: 9781680509243. $35.95

https://pragprog.com/book/bcosp

Exploring Graphs with Elixir

Data is everywhere—it's just not very well connected, which makes it super hard to relate dataset to dataset. Using graphs as the underlying glue, you can readily join data together and create navigation paths across diverse sets of data. Add Elixir, with its awesome power of concurrency, and you'll soon be mastering data networks. Learn how different graph models can be accessed and used from within Elixir and how you can build a robust semantics overlay on top of graph data structures. We'll start from the basics and examine the main graph paradigms. Get ready to embrace the world of connected data!

Tony Hammond
(294 pages) ISBN: 9781680508406. $47.95
https://pragprog.com/book/thgraphs

SQL Antipatterns, Volume 1

SQL is the ubiquitous language for software developers working with structured data. Most developers who rely on SQL are experts in their favorite language (such as Java, Python, or Go), but they're not experts in SQL. They often depend on antipatterns—solutions that look right but become increasingly painful to work with as you uncover their hidden costs. Learn to identify and avoid many of these common blunders. Refactor an inherited nightmare into a data model that really works. Updated for the current versions of MySQL and Python, this new edition adds a dozen brand new mini-antipatterns for quick wins.

Bill Karwin
(378 pages) ISBN: 9781680508987. $47.95
https://pragprog.com/book/bksap1

The Pragmatic Bookshelf

The Pragmatic Bookshelf features books written by professional developers for professional developers. The titles continue the well-known Pragmatic Programmer style and continue to garner awards and rave reviews. As development gets more and more difficult, the Pragmatic Programmers will be there with more titles and products to help you stay on top of your game.

Visit Us Online

This Book's Home Page
https://pragprog.com/book/uboop
Source code from this book, errata, and other resources. Come give us feedback, too!

Keep Up-to-Date
https://pragprog.com
Join our announcement mailing list (low volume) or follow us on Twitter @pragprog for new titles, sales, coupons, hot tips, and more.

New and Noteworthy
https://pragprog.com/news
Check out the latest Pragmatic developments, new titles, and other offerings.

Save on the ebook

Save on the ebook versions of this title. Owning the paper version of this book entitles you to purchase the electronic versions at a terrific discount.

PDFs are great for carrying around on your laptop—they are hyperlinked, have color, and are fully searchable. Most titles are also available for the iPhone and iPod touch, Amazon Kindle, and other popular e-book readers.

Send a copy of your receipt to support@pragprog.com and we'll provide you with a discount coupon.

Contact Us

Online Orders:	*https://pragprog.com/catalog*
Customer Service:	*support@pragprog.com*
International Rights:	*translations@pragprog.com*
Academic Use:	*academic@pragprog.com*
Write for Us:	*http://write-for-us.pragprog.com*
Or Call:	+1 800-699-7764

Milton Keynes UK
Ingram Content Group UK Ltd.
UKHW030725031123
431765UK00004B/4